IMAGES OF WOMEN IN ANTIQUITY

Images of Women in Antiquity

Edited by AVERIL CAMERON and AMÉLIE KUHRT

London

First published by Croom Helm in 1983

Revised edition published 1993
by Routledge
11 New Fetter Lane, London EC4P 4EE

Printed in Great Britain

British Library Cataloguing in Publication Data
Images of Women in Antiquity. – 2nd rev. edn
I. Cameron, Averil   II. Kuhrt, Amélie
305.42

ISBN 0-415-09095-4

CONTENTS

LIST OF FIGURES

LIST OF PLATES

INTRODUCTION

The papers in this volume were collected with an object in mind — that of bringing together comparative material on women from different ancient societies. They range chronologically and geographically over vast areas — from the second millennium BC to the early medieval period, and from Iran to Ireland — but although the societies under discussion vary greatly in the type and complexity of their development, the questions which suggest themselves are remarkably constant. For this reason we have not attempted to arrange the papers chronologically or by geographical area, but broadly according to the type of questions and answers that they propose, and the approach that they adopt. This is a risky procedure, in that it runs the risk of forcing the material into over-rigid categories. But we hope that the juxtaposition — never implying more than broad similarity — will suggest other questions, continuities or differences.

In so wide-ranging a collection there are naturally equally wide differences of approach, in part reflecting the very different degree to which women's studies have been developed in relation to individual periods and areas of the ancient world. In particular, women in classical Greece were an object of study long before the growth of modern feminism, and have shared fully in the recent growth of interest in anthropological and structuralist approaches. Scholars writing on Greek women, therefore, can assume a sophisticated body of existing work. By contrast, in some of the fields covered here (Sancisi-Weerdenburg, Davies) it is a matter of defining the problem almost for the first time, so that a survey that would be inappropriate for Greek women is here essential. In other cases (Archer, Harvey), a presentation of the state of the problem in relation to a specific group will, we hope, make detailed information available to non-specialists and suggest points of comparison and difference. In some instances the reading of the evidence itself is in point (Williams, Pomeroy); in others it is more a matter of conceptualisation, of drawing the right conclusions from the data (Padel, Van Bremen).

Basic, of course, to the understanding of attitudes to women in a given society is the question of their material life and economic condition, but this can be difficult to establish, through the ambiguity of the evidence (Williams), or suggestive of wrong conclusions (Van Bremen).

Nor have we always the kind of evidence that we would like; thus Greek historians are forced to work extensively with material drawn from literature and myth (Padel, Lefkowitz) and to face the question of its relation to 'real' life. Perceptions of the physical nature of women and the details of menstruation, sex and birth recur as determining factors of male attitudes to women in general (King, Pringle), and in these traditional societies with their strong religious bonds, women were often seen as dangerously borderline, to be controlled and tamed (Padel, Rollin), or as best kept wholly outside the male sphere of cult (Archer); their early freedom in Syriac Christianity was an exception not long permitted to survive (Harvey). Religion in these ancient societies saw women either as suspect or as potentially especially holy (Ackroyd); in either case, it tended to relegate them to a restricted and specialised sphere of influence (Jeyes), and this remained true also of Christianity, even though it opened up certain limited new avenues for them (Harvey, Davies, Herrin). The Christianisation of the Roman Empire (though it was far from uniform and its effects changed and developed over time and in relation to differing sets of circumstances) was undoubtedly one of the greatest transformations which took place in the situation of women in these societies; it was, however, complex and ambivalent (Davies). We should not forget, either, that the Roman Empire itself comprised in the first two centuries AD and later as many or more Greeks and Greek-speakers as Latin-speaking Romans (not to mention the native masses still speaking their local languages); far from being a single entity, it included much of the then civilised world, and needs to be studied by area (see Van Bremen on the well-to-do women of the Greek east).

This volume could not be expected to be comprehensive, and we are conscious, for instance, that there is good deal on Greek women and hardly anything on Roman. Most of the papers originated in the series, *Images of Women in Antiquity*, organised by Fergus Millar and the editors in the Ancient History Seminar of the University of London, which gave us the happy chance of combining classical with Near Eastern, Jewish and early medieval papers. We are grateful to the Institute of Classical Studies, London, and its Director, Eric Handley, for the support which has enabled this seminar to reach its present lively and established state, and which has also allowed this generous definition of 'antiquity'. As with the subject-matter of the papers in this volume, there is considerable variation in the degree of their commitment to feminist approaches; our primary aim has been to gather for comparative purposes the results of some of the research currently going on in these different fields. It offers much food for thought, both for feminists and for historians.

Averil Cameron
Amélie Kuhrt

INTRODUCTION TO THE REVISED EDITION

Since this book appeared, a decade ago, there has been an explosion of writing about women in antiquity, in the context of a much broader concern with feminism and women's history. Gender studies, in particular, have burgeoned in all periods of history, including antiquity. Many of the contributors to the original volume have themselves subsequently written more detailed studies in which they have taken the issues raised here much further. A number of useful general works and collections have appeared, and the subject of women in antiquity has become firmly established on the scholarly agenda. As several of the contributors make clear in the additions to their original articles, their particular subjects have moved on since the publication of the present book. Nevertheless, we know that it has been widely used, especially in teaching, and it continues to provide a coverage of the various periods and geographical areas of the ancient world that cannot easily be found anywhere else. Several of the articles which open up areas hitherto little studied or not studied at all from the point of view of women's studies have still not been superseded, and while distinguished work has appeared in certain other fields, especially perhaps on ancient Greek women, we believe that the comparative perspective provided here remains extremely valuable, and that the collection as a whole provides a useful, and indeed a unique, way of approaching the sheer variety of the material.

Contributors have been prevented by reasons of space and practicality from being able to revise the actual text of their articles, but the majority have provided a short addendum or further bibliography of works which they consider important. In addition, rather than burying them in the general bibliography, we wish to draw attention in this introduction to some of the more important general works that have appeared since 1983, and to significant recent works in areas such as the Roman Republic, early Christianity and late antiquity, which were not covered in the original volume.

A recent general bibliography is provided by A.-M. Vérilhac and C. Vial, with L. Darmezin, *La femme dans l'antiquité classique: bibliographie*, Travaux de la Maison de l'Orient (TMO) 19 (Lyon, 1990), and see also the bibliography by S.B. Pomeroy, with R. Kraemer and N. Kampen, in J. Peradotto and J.P. Sullivan (eds), *Women in the Ancient World: The Arethusa Papers* (New York, 1984). A useful brief survey of recent work on Graeco-Roman women is provided by S.B. Pomeroy, 'The study of women in antiquity: past, present and future', *AJP* 112 (1991), 263–8, and a fuller and very useful introduction, with bibliography, by Gillian Clark, *Women in the Ancient World*, Greece and Rome New Surveys in the Classics 21 (Oxford, 1989). J. Snyder, *The Woman and the Lyre: Women Writers in Classical Greece and Rome* (Bristol, 1989), returns to the quest for women's writing from classical antiquity. Among general histories and collective works we now have, for instance, *La femme dans le monde méditerranéen I. Antiquité*, Travaux de la Maison de l'Orient (TMO) 10 (Lyon, 1985); R. Uglione (ed.), *La donna nel mondo antico* (Turin, 1987); G. Duby and M. Perrot (eds), *A History of Women in the West* I: P. Schmitt-Pantel (ed.), *From Ancient Goddesses to Christian Saints*, Eng. trans. (Cambridge, Mass., 1992); there is also a useful general introduction to women in the Graeco-Roman world, as well as information on topics such as marriage, dress, housing, childbirth and birth-control, in M. Grant and R. Kitzinger (eds), *The Ancient Mediterranean World* I (New York, 1988), section I. Among collective volumes we would point to Helene P. Foley (ed.), *Reflections of Women in Antiquity* (New York, 1981); J. Peradotto and J.P. Sullivan, *Women in the Ancient World: The Arethusa Papers* (see above); J. Blok and P. Mason (eds), *Sexual Asymmetry: Studies in Ancient Society* (Amsterdam, 1987); Sarah B. Pomeroy (ed.), *Women's History and Ancient History* (Chapel Hill, NC, 1991); U. Mattaioli (ed.), *La donna nel pensiero cristiano antico* (Genoa, 1992); L. Archer, S. Fischler and M. Wyke (eds), *An Illusion of the Night: Women in Ancient Societies* (London, 1993), and, among teaching aids, to the revised and expanded edition of M. Lefkowitz and M. Fant, *Women's Life in Greece and Rome* (London, 1992). Several journal issues have been dedicated to the subject, including *La femme dans l'antiquité grecque*, *Pallas* 32 (1985); M. Skinner (ed.), *Rescuing Creusa*, *Helios* 13.2 (1987); A. Scafuro, (ed.), *Studies on Roman Women*, *Helios* 16.1 (1989).

In Near Eastern history (third to first millennium BC), perhaps the most generally useful book is that edited by B. Lesko, *Women's Earliest Records: From Ancient Egypt and Western Asia*, Brown Judaic Studies 166 (Atlanta, 1989); it contains the papers of a conference devoted to non-royal women in the periods of the third, second and first millennia BC. It is selective, in that the regions considered are limited to Mesopotamia, Egypt and pre-exilic Israel. Nevertheless, its coverage is wider than most, and it contains a useful bibliography of books and articles on women's studies, arranged by region. Almost as wide-ranging is J.-M. Durand (ed.), *La femme dans le proche-orient antique* (Paris, 1987), presenting the papers of the Rencontre Assyriologique held in Paris in 1986. Though there is no thematic organising principle beyond the unproblematised category 'woman', it includes some good papers, and, while Egypt is excluded, there is more on Syria and Assyria than in Lesko; neither volume discusses women in either Anatolia or Iran.

Study of women in Egyptian society is now made easier by B. Watterson, *Women in Ancient Egypt* (New York, 1991), a useful, up-to-date introduction (cf. also C. Desroches-Noblecourt, *La femme au temps des Pharaons* [Paris, 1986]). Women in hellenistic Egypt are studied by S.B. Pomeroy in *Women in Hellenistic Egypt: From Alexander to Cleopatra* (New York, 1984); Egyptian sexual attitudes and *mores* are the subject of a lively small book by L. Manniche, *Sexual Life in Ancient Egypt* (London, 1987). In the vast and complex field of Mesopotamian civilisation three studies should be particularly mentioned, including J. Asher-Grève, *Frauen in altsumischer Zeit*, Bibliotheca Mesopotamica 18 (Malibu, 1985) – a careful analysis using economic texts, archaeological remains, iconography and some literary material to try to penetrate Sumerian social structures. Immensely useful and a model of lucidity is M. Roth, *Babylonian Marriage Agreements: 7th to 3rd centuries BC*, AOAT 222 (Neukirchen-Vluyn, 1989), an analysis of Late Babylonian marriage practices (dowry, age at marriage, family and household structure) based on editions and translations of the documents with full commentary. Very wide-ranging, though unfortunately still available only in Dutch, is M. Stol, *Zwangerschap en Geboorte bij de Babyloniers en in de Bijbel* (Leiden, 1983), in which a wealth of evidence is presented relating to sex, conception, pregnancy, birth and naming. As is to be expected, feminist perspectives within the field of the ancient Near East find their fullest expression in the study of ancient Israel: a helpful introduction is provided by G. Emmerson, 'Women in ancient Israel', in R. Clements (ed.), *The World of Ancient Israel* (Cambridge, 1989), 371–94. One of the most stimulating books in this field in recent years is Carol Meyers, *Discovering Eve: Ancient Israelite Women in Context* (Oxford, 1988). Its focus rests on the reconstruction of Israelite life in the pre-monarchic period, exploiting house-plans, size and layout of settlements and comparative anthropological studies, and offering a new analysis of key Old Testament texts, as a result of which the author is able to present a picture of early Israel as a relatively egalitarian 'pioneer' society, in which women participated actively and positively.

Feminist insights are also now influencing the practice of archaeology, in particular in suggesting questions about gendered assumptions in the interpretation of archaeological remains; an introduction is provided by J. Gero and M. Conkey (eds), *Engendering Archaeology: Women and Prehistory* (Oxford, 1991). While most of the papers in Gero and Conkey are concerned with areas and periods that lack a written record, one, by S. Pollock ('Women in a man's world: images of Sumerian women', *ibid*., 366–87), considers the problems of understanding the rich remains of the Ur graves from the early historic period in Mesopotamia.

As for the Roman Republic, readers should note in particular Mary Beard, 'The sexual status of Vestal Virgins', *JRS* 70 (1980), 12–27; Judith P. Hallett, *Fathers and Daughters in Roman Society: Women and the Elite Family* (Princeton, 1984); Beryl Rawson, (ed.), *The Family in Ancient Rome, New Perspectives* (Ithaca, NY, 1986); Jane F. Gardner, *Women in Roman Law and Society* (London, 1986); Suzanne Dixon, *The Roman Mother* (London and Sydney, 1988), Susan Treggiari, *Roman Marriage* (Oxford, 1991) and S. Dixon, *The Roman Family* (Baltimore, 1992).

The subject of women in early Christianity has produced a very large secondary literature in recent years, partly under the influence of feminist theology; unfortunately this material is still often excluded from general works on ancient women, though this tendency is rightly now beginning to break down, perhaps because of the recognition that the field of early Christian attitudes to women offers to ancient historians a wealth of material relative to the body and to sexuality comparable to that from classical Greece. The latter has produced some important recent books, especially G. Sissa, *Greek Virginity*, Eng. trans. (Cambridge, Mass., 1990); D.M. Halperin, J.J. Winkler and F.I. Zeitlin (eds), *Before Sexuality: The Construction of Erotic Experience in the Ancient Greek World* (Princeton, 1990) and J.J. Winkler, *The Constraints of Desire: The Anthropology of Sex and Gender in Ancient Greece* (London, 1990). Similarly, the developing asceticism of late antiquity in both Christian and pagan contexts, itself expressive of a distinctive discourse surrounding the body, has, not surprisingly, captured a great deal of attention: see especially Aline Rousselle, *Porneia*, Eng. trans. (Oxford, 1987); Peter Brown, *The Body and Society: Men, Women and Sexual Renunciation in Early Christianity* (New York, 1988); Averil Cameron, 'Virginity as metaphor', in *ead*. (ed.), *History as Text* (London, 1989), 184–205 (with counter-arguments by G. Gould, 'Women in the writings of the

Fathers: language, belief and reality', in W.J. Shiels and D. Wood (eds), *Women and the Church*, Studies in Church History 27 (1990), 1–13). Ascetic literature itself demands close analysis: a recent source-book on asceticism is V. Wimbush (ed.), *Ascetic Behavior in Greco-Roman Antiquity: A Sourcebook* (Philadelphia, 1990); more generally on women's religious experience, see R.S. Kraemer, *Maenads, Martyrs, Matrons, Monastics: A Sourcebook on Women's Religions in the Greco-Roman World* (Philadelphia, 1988). Elaine Pagels, *Adam, Eve and the Serpent* (London, 1988) vividly brings out the textual plots of early Christianity and the politics of Christian writing on women.

In recent years, feminist theologians have themselves been much concerned with the attempt to recover a more positive attitude to women than seems to prevail in the early Christian texts: see notably E. Schussler Fiorenza, *In Memory of Her* (Philadelphia, 1983); R. Ruether, *Religion and Sexism* (New York, 1974); R. Ruether and E. MacLaughlin (eds), *Women of Spirit* (New York, 1979). Two scholarly and useful books on women in the earliest period of Christianity, lacking the overtly feminist agenda and dealing also with the contemporary historical context, are B. Witherington III, *Women in the Ministry of Jesus* (Cambridge, 1984) and id. *Women in the Earliest Churches* (Cambridge, 1988). For women in Christianity generally, there is a very useful sourcebook which covers the period from earliest Christianity to the patristic period (late antiquity) by Elizabeth A. Clark, *Women in the Early Church* (Wilmington, Del., 1983).

With the general burgeoning of interest in late antiquity has come also a focus on women in that period. Gillian Clark, *Women in Late Antiquity* (Oxford, 1993) addresses most aspects of the subject, and there is much that is relevant in Peter Brown, 'Late antiquity', in P. Ariès and G. Duby (eds), *A History of Private Life* I, ed. P. Veyne, Eng. trans. (Oxford, 1987), 235–311, while developments in the legal and social position of women from Constantine to Justinian are covered in detail by J. Beaucamp, *Le statut de la femme à Byzance (4e–7e siècle) I–II* (Paris, 1990, 1992). Elizabeth A. Clark's collection, *Ascetic Piety and Women's Faith* (Wilmington, Del., 1986) contains several fundamental essays on women and Christianity, and see the forthcoming book on women's religious communities by Susanna Elm (Oxford). For the Christian women of the senatorial class in the late fourth and early fifth centuries see J. Bremmer, 'Why did Christianity attract upper-class women?', in A.A.R. Bastiaensen, A. Hilhorst and C.H. Kneepkens, *Festschrift G.J.M. Bartelink* (Dordrecht, 1989), 37–47 and M. Salzman, 'Aristocratic women: conductors of Christianity in the fourth century?', *Helios* 16 (1989), 207–20. S. Ashbrook Harvey and Sebastian P. Brock, *Holy Women of the Syrian Orient* (Berkeley and Los Angeles, 1987) and Benedicta Ward, *Harlots of the Desert* (Oxford, 1987) are both illuminating on the popularity of the repentant prostitute theme in Christian asceticism. The Christian family has also been receiving attention; see D. Herlihy, *Medieval Households* (Cambridge, Mass., 1985); Brent Shaw, 'The family in late antiquity: the experience of Augustine', *Past and Present* 115 (1987), 5–51; David I. Kertzer and Richard P. Saller (eds), *The Family in Italy from Late Antiquity to the Present* (New Haven, 1991) and see also (much more broadly) J. Goody, *The Oriental, the Ancient and the Primitive* (Cambridge, 1990).

This collection is high on women's history but generally low on theory, feminism and gender, all of which occupy a large amount of space in current work. A new collection would probably look rather different, for instance in foregrounding the contributions of French feminist writers such as Julia Kristeva, Hélène Cixous and Luce Irigaray, and in drawing attention to those scholars of classical antiquity who have used a more theoretical approach, such as Nicole Loraux (especially *Tragic Ways of Killing a Woman*, Eng. trans. [Cambridge, Mass., 1987]) and Christiane Sourvinou-Inwood (especially *Reading Greek Culture* [Oxford, 1991]). Among other notable contributions in the classical Greek field are S. Humphreys, *Women, the Family and Death* (London, 1983) and Page du Bois, *Sowing the Body: Psychoanalysis and Ancient Representations of Women* (Chicago, 1988); on the latter, see Ruth Padel, 'Between theory and fiction: reflections on feminism and classical scholarship', *Gender and History* 2 (1990), 198–211. In particular, 'feminist reading' can now be seen to have gone beyond the disciplines both of anthropology, which informed much 'women's history', and of psychoanalysis itself, which has been fundamental to the French feminist school in particular. It now involves the entire realm of representations of women, from the textual to the visual and the imaginative; quite how persistently these cluster round the theme of the female body itself is suggested in Marina Warner's book, *Monuments and Maidens: The Allegory of the Female Form* (London, 1985), and see also Susanne Kappeler, *The Pornography of Representation* (Cambridge, 1986). Feminist reading, which is, not surprisingly, especially at home among literary scholars such as Froma Zeitlin and Ruth Padel, is equally deeply involved in all historical reconstruction, including the construction of women's

history. Not least, the issue is political. Its politics have changed somewhat since the first edition of this book, which indeed did not aim to
locate itself in the political sphere of feminism and gender; if anything,
they have become both more sophisticated and more urgent.
Meanwhile, women's studies courses proliferate. We hope that this
revised edition will fulfil at least some of their needs.

Averil Cameron
Amélie Kuhrt

London, July 1992

PART ONE: PERCEIVING WOMEN

The conditioning of a society's thinking and writing about women by unchallenged preconceptions about their nature and function

1   WOMEN: MODEL FOR POSSESSION BY GREEK DAEMONS[1]

Ruth Padel, London

My starting-point is such patterns of male fantasies about women, and of male strategies for controlling women in social life and cult, as we can conceivably attribute to fifth-century BC Athenians. Behind these patterns, I shall suggest, is a sense that women contain an inner space and inner darkness, which together interact with, and provide one model for, traditional popular thinking about that inner space belonging to all normal, i.e. male, human beings, in which the Greeks located the organs of what we call the mind. That relationship of metaphorical interaction is part of the background to Greek notions of daemonic possession, especially to the image of possession as erotic entry.

Evidence for male systems of controlling women in real life is thin and ambiguous; evidence for male patterns of thinking or fantasising about women is more plentiful but far more ambiguous (Gould, 1980, pp. 38-42), being mainly literary, and so liable to the distortion by convention and literary tradition which such evidence always creates. Statements about Greek societies, especially about what a genre reflects of its immediate environment, should always be prefaced with an enormous 'perhaps'.

My evidence and my interests, nonetheless, are chiefly literary, and they centre on fifth-century Athenian tragedy. I end by speculating that fifth-century patterns of fantasy about women may have been a significant element in the formation of male Athenian literary structures such as tragedy. In these patterns of fantasy, the feeling that women are especially open to daemonic possession has an important part.

Society and Cult: Male Control and Enclosure

Greek systems of fantasy and family generally reflect, amid the usual ambivalence in male perceptions of women, a view that women can threaten male order, male life and sanity. Most Greek daemons, especially two classes, those which hunt human victims in groups (like

3

Erinyes, 'Furies') and those which persecute the mind (again the Erinyes, or single daemons such as Lyssa, 'Madness'), are female. They are also chthonic (born from *chthon*, 'earth') and are sometimes described in phrases like 'daughters of Night'. Their femaleness is linked with their earth-born status, their attack on the mind and their habitation in darkness. Fears of the carnivorousness in female sexuality, underlying some of this material, are reflected in popular names for prostitutes like 'The Lioness', 'The Panther'.[2]

Patterns of economic and social control presumably express the male sense that the threat posed by what is female should be contained. Such patterns varied across Greek societies, and there is little dense evidence for any society except Athens, where control seems to have been especially energetic (Schaps, 1979, p. 198). Women had no control over their own marriages, either as daughters or as widows. They were central to the social system as transmitters of property but had no control over that property themselves (Lefkowitz and Fant, 1982, pp. 33-40). Legal protection of their inheritance-rights depended effectively on defining them as incapable of a self-determining act (Gould, 1980, pp. 43-56). 'A sympathetic wife is the greatest *ktema*' ('possession', a neuter word).[3]

At Athens, therefore, women were themselves possessions. Athenian speculation about women's activity at Sparta, furthermore, is the filter through which the Spartan material reaches us. Athenians are shocked to think that Spartan women live more publicly than at Athens, where even the names of respectable women are concealed in public discourse.[4]

A high degree of enclosure for their women, therefore, underpinned the prevailing self-image for fifth-century Athenian males. So did other forms of rule over people. The period during which Athenian tragedy flourished was the period of Athens' imperial control over other Greek states. Thucydides, the fifth-century Athenian historian, attributes a critique of the Athenian character to a Corinthian, who is encouraging the Spartans to stand up to Athenian imperialism: Athenians, he says, are energetic, reckless, 'most adventurous abroad, while you stay at home'. They have a lust to possess: the verb *ktasthai*, 'to gain possession of', figures largely in these paragraphs. Athenians never allow themselves to 'have' peace of mind, nor allow other people to do so: repose is the one possession, he implies, they do not want. These attributes make them extremely dangerous to other people. Thucydides fabricates an Athenian reply: the Athenians accepted 'rule' when it was offered; moreover, it is an eternal law that the stronger should rule the weaker.[5] He suggests a picture of an Athenian (male) self-image orientated round the need to control what is *allotrion*, the word for 'foreign', 'abroad', which is also often used for 'other' as opposed to 'self'. The application of such activity to male-female relationships is simple; and helps, perhaps, to explain Athenian attitudes to Spartan women. Men who do not 'go out to control' other people, as the Athenians do, are naturally perceived as weaker, and less controlling, than their women.

The Greek city-state, developing from the archaic into the classical age, was defined imaginatively by the character of its tutelary deity (Snodgrass, 1977) and also, I suggest, by the kinds of relationship which that deity traditionally made with human beings. The Athene of classical Athens was essentially kourotrophic: her prime function, in her central state cult, was to guard the mythical Athenian princeling Erichthonios (Hooker, 1963) as, in Homeric narratives, Athene protects central male figures like Diomedes, Achilles or Odysseus.[6] As Aeschylus makes her say (*Eumenides*, 736), she has no mother. Her identity turns on her exclusive relation to the male. A male Athenian, identifying with his city's role as a controller of others, might well feel supported in this activity by a sense of his relation with the city's armed and kourotrophic guardian.

Greek societies, male-ordered, generally assigned to women ritual presidency over the transitional experiences, dying and birth, which are perceived as passages into and out of darkness. Dying is 'going into the dark', being born is 'coming into the light',[7] an image often doing double service for the body's emergence from the womb and passage into the grave, and for the soul's passage into whatever obscurity is imagined to precede life, and into Hades. In the archaic age death was perceived and feared with increasing sharpness (Sourvinou-Inwood, 1981) and a sharper sense of death's contaminating power collected around the very rites of burial and mourning which were traditionally assigned to women. In male perception, a supposed female aptitude for monitoring passage out of or into darkness is linked with a supposed female aptitude for making contact with what is polluting. In Greek as in some other cultures, concepts of the sacred are interwoven with concepts of pollution: *hagnos* or *hagios*, 'sacred', is cognate with *agos*, 'pollution'. In Greek as in some other cultures, aspects of female biology are also perceived as polluting to men. There are taboos on touching women during menstruation or after childbirth, or on entering a temple after intercourse with a woman; as, in the society for which ancient Tamil poetry was written, any female excreta, the touch of nursing milk on a masculine chest, for example, pollutes the male, though at the same time women function as a focus of sanctity (Hart, 1973), or as in some periods of medieval European culture women's supposed aptness for handling the more polluting and 'darker' aspects of divinity is interdependent on their biological and cultural associations with what comes into and what comes out of darkness, whether the darkness be that of the underworld or of the female body.[8]

Some of the roles assigned to women in Greek cult likewise reflect feelings about their biological functions. Women are usually confined in the cult buildings or cult procedure, as they are confined in domestic homes (Walker, this volume). They sometimes guard sacred objects, which are normally hidden or secret and are only revealed under strict ritual conditions, like the *arrheta*, 'unspeakable things', in the Panathenaic festival at Athens. They can reveal and bring forth, but only under male control; as the male priests at Delphi patterned into hexameters the sounds that came from the mouth of the priestess, the Pythia (according to one Delphic tradition, Parke and Wormell, 1965, vol. i, p. 34).

One can interpret female involvement with darker, 'black' cults, in Greece or in medieval Europe,[9] in two ways: as chosen by the women themselves, or as assigned to them by men. It has been argued that women, disqualified from political participation, turn to ritual and cult activity in some ways 'alternative' to state-controlled, which often in Greek contexts means Olympian, cult (Vernant, 1980, p. 108). However, against this interpretation is the fact that in Greek societies women were given central functions in some state cults, as the guardianship of the *arrheta* in the central Athenian festival (Gould, 1980, p. 51). Since it was men who controlled women's role in state cults, and who avoided direct contact with what was polluting and threatening by women's involvement in chthonic cults, it seems more likely that in Greece, at least, where men perceived women's physical functions as polluting to themselves, and also regarded contact with chthonic divinities as dangerous, women's role in chthonic and state cult alike was assigned to them by men. Women's propensity for being perceived as having an affinity with darkness may be used differently, and have a different relation to the imagination, in different cultures. In Greece, I suggest, men used, and carefully controlled, the kinship they felt women had with the darker, polluting side of divinity, and assigned them guardianship and activity by which the women would make contact, on their behalf, with potentially contaminating objects and forces.

Maenadism, part of the Bacchic cult, supposedly allowed women escape from the confinement which characterised male control of them in domestic or ritual life. However, evidence for the nature, status and even existence of maenadism in classical (as opposed to post-classical) Athens, is disablingly thin (Heinrichs, 1978). Euripides' *Bacchae*, which inspires our ideas of it, may well be only a literary construct made from elements of myth and imagination, and no true reflection of any contemporary cult known to the Athenians. As such, however, the *Bacchae* provides magnificent if ambiguous evidence for the ways in which male Athenian fantasies might respond to women escaping from confinement into the wilds. The play combines a picture of women who are 'out of their minds' with a picture of women out of their proper place within the home and city; and it links both to the tearing apart of an individual king (Dodds, 1951, pp. 271-6), the collapse of a royal palace, and the exile and fragmentation of the founding royal family (*Bacchae*, 633, 1350-63). It establishes women's potentially peaceful physical relation with savage nature through their reproductive functions — the maenads suckle the young of wild animals — but shows male order, and an individual male, destroyed through this relationship, and through the women's relationship with a god who 'drives them out of the house in madness' (*Bacchae*, 33). Other, earlier, poems and plays had brought these motifs together already. Aeschylus showed the maenads tearing apart Orpheus, who is, in a sense, the archetypal author of order (in that music, in the Greek tradition, was an image of balance and order) and wielder of the human power to tame animal nature: women here tear to pieces a man who makes, as Pentheus attempts to maintain, an image of order. Several earlier poets had used the story of the daughters of Proteus, who were maddened by a goddess, and ran wild on the mountains, desiring men but disgusting them by their own physical condition.[10] The ritual parallel, perhaps, to some of these elements in such myths, might be the Athenian festival known as the Thesmophoria, in which women were allowed out of the house, and sexual relations were upset (Gould, 1980, p. 51).

However male society may confine women, and control male contact with what comes out of them, it does crudely depend on their function of bringing things to light, of letting something emerge from themselves. Assigning women the ritual revelation of hidden sacred things, organising a festival in which women themselves 'come out', and elaborating in myth and poetry narratives in which women do escape from the city into the mountains, is a way of expressing, I suggest, and also of containing, women's closer connection with animal nature, through their capacity for childbirth, which Greek medical writers also express in describing the womb's mobile and aggressive nature (Lefkowitz, 1982, p. 225; King, this volume). As it is men who control the Pythia's ravings, so it is men who create and use the myths depicting women 'out of their mind', whose mental and physical displacement from the norm destroys society; and a male-ordered calendar contains the Thesmophoria. Male society controls, monitors, and also, one might say, exploits, the animal nature in women (as men perceive them), which requires emergence, but which is perceived as destructive to society if not controlled by it.

Inner Space and Inner Darkness: Metaphors for the Interior

The interior space, sacred or domestic, which encloses women in cult or home, is emblematic of the female interior itself, as perceived by men. The *muchos*, the 'women's quarter', was the inmost part of the inward-looking Athenian home (Walker, this volume). In a sense, fifth-century Athenian life, for the social classes for which we have evidence, must have been functionally divided between two roles, defined by the spaces inhabited (Gould, 1980, p. 48, n. 72), as if between two races: one at ease among marble buildings and public spaces like the agora, gymnasium and assembly, free of the city and of the lands beyond, the other confined to the inmost part of the mudbrick domestic house, with only limited exit even from the private home. As in H.G. Wells's fantasy *The Time Machine*, the race living in the light feared that which inhabited comparative darkness.

Most Greek buildings had a sacred centre which, in the domestic house was the hearth, whose presiding deity was Hestia: the divine embodiment of the sanctity at the centre of the home was female (Vernant, 1965). Inside a temple there was the inner shrine, called *abaton* or *adyton*, 'untreadable', 'unenterable'. Greek structuring of space, both domestic and sacred, made the centre dark (like the *muchos* in a house, and like the *abaton* in a temple, which had to be lit by torches), unenterable except to those properly consecrated, and, in a domestic context, female. Perhaps there was an unconscious parallel in male consciousness between a sacred centre or sacred precinct and the female interior.

Such a parallel, I suggest, underlies the response of the chorus to Oedipus in Sophocles' *Oedipus at Colonus*. At the start of the play Oedipus walks into a grove which Antigone at once recognises as sacred (16). The Stranger, not knowing Oedipus's identity, says he has walked on to 'a place not holy to tread . . . untouchable, not to be inhabited' (37-9). The chorus call him *ektopios*, 'out of place'. When they find him in the grove they exclaim 'terrible to see, terrible to hear' (118-41). Sophocles balances their horrified responses here with their response when they learn who he is (since all the Greek world knows that 'Oedipus' has killed his father and lain with his mother). They are terrified when he tells them that he is Oedipus (222-3) even though he characterises himself as one who did not act knowingly (539, 548), just as he 'ignorantly came where I came' (273). His unwitting entry into the goddesses' sacred grove has become, Sophocles lightly suggests, also a symbolic echo of his equally unwitting sexual entry. In neither case did he know 'where' he was going. The scene in which Oedipus asks, and the chorus explains, how he can purify himself from having entered the grove (461-509) is mirrored in the sung lyrical exchange of the following scene in which they ask, and he tells, how he came to murder his father and marry his mother (510-48). In the first part of this play, therefore, Sophocles establishes Oedipus as one who has gone where no man ought to go. He rounds out this role for Oedipus at the play's end. Oedipus enters the earth, walks 'viewless fields' (1681). He disappears somehow, with a god calling him, into the earth. The parallel between the unenterable place he penetrates at the beginning and the unapproachable, unseeable place which receives him at the end, suggests that other place which he forbiddenly and self-definingly entered earlier in his history, his mother's womb.

A sacred place, whether grove, temple-*abaton* or Hades itself, is entered only after careful rites, for fear of the pollution sanctity carries. Equally, the female interior and what comes from it pollutes. In Ceylon, where contact with lower castes pollutes, intercourse with a lower-caste woman pollutes a man 'externally'; intercourse with lower-caste men gives a woman 'internal pollution' far harder to purify (Yalman, 1967, pp. 177-8). The fear of some polluting and pollutable power within semen may play a different role in the imagination of different societies; in Greek culture it resembled fears of pollution incurred by entering the unenterable part of a shrine. The second-century AD satirist Lucian mentions someone whose wife is *akathartos*, 'unpurified', 'unpurifiable', 'unpurged'. She is ill; 'she no longer flows', so her husband 'no longer mounts her; she is *abatos* and uncultivated' (*Lexiphanes*, 19). She is impure largely because she is not menstruating; and hence 'untreadable', the word used of the forbidden inner shrine. Moreover, darkness characterises many places where the Greeks arranged to meet divinity: such as the shadowy oak-grove at Zeus' oracle of Dodona, the subterranean cave at Trophonios's oracle in Levadia, the night and sleep of 'incubation', consultation of the god through dreams.[11] *Muchos*, 'women's quarter', is a word which can also refer both to Hades and to a prophet's shrine: essentially a hidden recess. If in its hiddenness it was emblematic of the space enclosed within women, as well as being the space which enclosed them, then also in its darkness it was emblematic of darkness ascribed by men to the female interior. The concept of inner space as the psycho-sexual determinant (in a male-ordered society, at least) of women's social roles (Erikson, 1964; 1968, pp. 261-94) should be augmented in a Greek context by that of inner darkness. Fantasies about the female interior are interdependent with fantasies both about sacred precincts, especially prophetic sites, and about Hades itself.

One might support this suggestion etymologically, by looking at the popular Greek derivation of Hades from *a-idein*, 'not to see', and associations of both with *aidoia*, 'genitals'. But one should give it a context: the framework of metaphor characterising the inner space inside human beings, in which Greek tradition sited the organs of thinking and feeling. Classical Greeks popularly located emotion and intellect in the breast and stomach, rather than the head: a fact which marks the enormous difference between our and their understanding of how human beings function (cf. McCulloch, 1951). The generic word for the relevant organs — heart, liver, lungs and so on — is *splanchna*, 'entrails'. Poets' images indicate an indigenous belief that in emotion the *splanchna* swelled with dark liquid. Passion is often depicted as an inner liquid darkening the *splanchna*, or as breath filling and moving them. 'A wave of bile stands before my heart', sing the chorus of Aeschylus' *Choephoroe* (183), and again, 'my *splanchna* darken as I hear his speech' (413). This appears to us like poetic metaphor, but it probably reminded the audience of a picture of anatomical reality shared with the poet.[12] The notion of madness as *melancholia*, excess of black bile, surfaces in popular references in classical literature; it was crystallised in various Hippocratic versions of humoural pathology, and fostered medieval speculation about melancholy as a physical and emotional condition;[13] it derived, however, from a larger general framework of traditional Greek belief, expressed in what we receive as metaphor, about black liquid darkening the *splanchna* in passion.

The *splanchna* 'speak'. The Homeric picture of dialogue with one's heart or mind seems to have encouraged Aeschylean images of *splanchna* 'foreboding'. The *splanchna* 'do not speak in vain' (*Agamemnon*, 995) when they are indignant or afraid. An important local association to images like these is the practice of extispication, entrail-divination (Blecher, 1905), an ancient and enduring feature within the range of Greek methods for divination (Bouché-Leclerq, 1879). *Splanchna* markings tell diviners 'what pleases the gods' (Aeschylus, *Prometheus*, 493). To use an anachronistic image, the *splanchna* function as an internal receptor and transmitter for divinity.

The *splanchna* are also vulnerable to emotion pictured as a divine missile, aggressive animal, or personified aggressive daemon: emotions 'besiege', 'capture', 'bite', 'pierce', 'wound', 'graze', 'mangle' the *splanchna*. This network of imagery is interdependent with the ready personification of any forces and experiences which face humanity, from sexual passion to modesty, terror, old age, and which were depicted as winged or aerial aggressors in Greek poetry, painting and cult.[14] The *splanchna*, therefore, are a dark inward area which daemonic forces enter and inhabit.

The biology and demonology of emotion overlap in Greek belief. The *splanchna* are both receptacles filling with black liquid or with breath, and the site of daemonic invasion. We can explain this partly by realising that *splanchna* could also mean 'womb'.[15] This usage colours, I suggest, Greek use of the word to mean 'mind'. Female *splanchna* obviously fill with dark liquid (blood, in Greek, is usually characterised by the word we translate 'black'); and women are commonly perceived as more easily enterable by daemonic passion. Hence images of nourishment and fertility qualify organs of 'mind'. Thoughts grow and flower in the mind; inspiration for song is 'planted' in the mind by god.[16] The image underlies Plato's ascription to Socrates of a 'midwife' role, as one who delivered other people's thoughts (Burnyeat, 1977). The mind, like the womb, is dark, open to external impregnation and occupation. Its issue may be human, but it is often imagined that what originally entered was somehow divine, as in myths of human female's rape by male gods. Divine entry into the mind is fertilising. As the breath of the North Wind supposedly fertilised Thracian mares (Pliny, *Natural History*, XVIII.34), divine 'inspiration' — breathing in — fertilises the *splanchna*.

Women, body and mind, are regarded generally in classical literature as more open to passion and daemonic infiltration: a piece of male perception which is part of the more general notion that women endanger men by being enterable. Aristotle expresses this idea when he says women's flesh is more porous than men's (*De Generatione Animalium*, 747 A). The late Hippocratic *Oath* links the physician's entry into his patient's house with surgical entry into his body and sexual entry into his wife: he swears not to use the knife, rob the house, or violate its women. Literary allusion and legal arguments (e.g. Lefkowitz and Fant, 1982, p. 44) conflate a male stranger's entry into the house, with easy sexual access to the wife (see Gould, 1980, p. 47). Euripides in the *Hippolytus* shows women's openness to passion endangering the men of her house. Phaedra is ashamed of female desire as she suffers it: it makes women rightly despised, and untrustworthy; sex and the longing for it are shameful (406 f.): commonplaces,[17] with an active function in this play. Hippolytus, rejecting Phaedra's desire, voiced to him secretly in the house by Phaedra's Nurse, states that women plot evil inside the house, abetted by their maidservants, and their maidservants carry the evil outside (642-50). The whole play endorses the idea that women destroy men by their openness to Aphrodite, i.e. their sexuality.

Possession

Women are perceived as open to other deities than Aphrodite, however. A possessing deity may be male or female, but when a possessing deity is male there is often a sense of divine rape; as in most Greek myths, male gods have sexual relations with human women[18] rather than the other way round, as the goddess Calypso complains (Homer, *Odyssey*, V.119). Male controlling activity is projected on to divine society. In other cultures in the Western tradition, women have been regarded as the more successful mediums (Dodds, 1965, p. 65); in extant Athenian tragedy it is mainly women who are called possessed.[19]

Understanding of daemonic possession in classical Greece is complicated by three factors, however. Our reactions to it are naturally influenced by Christian appropriation of the Greek vocabulary, which has distorted the resonance of that vocabulary: Christian demonology is foreign to pagan Greek in dividing the spirit world into good and bad, so that daemonic possession is *ex hypothesi* malign (Eitrem, 1950). Around the second century AD the word *daimon* ceased to refer to a being which could also be called a *theos*, 'god', and became more like our word 'demon', something unalterably evil (Dodds, 1965, pp. 37-8). We must drain away the Christian associations to understand possession in a classical context.

Secondly, most explicit evidence for pagan Greek possession is post-classical. Are we justified in referring apparent references to possession in fifth-century texts to belief-patterns of a later age? It has been argued that we are not (Smith, 1965). This argument as it stands seems superficial: it is based on isolated metaphors, without reference to a whole framework of metaphor and belief, and it gives no good reason why the Delphic oracle, for instance, should begin to be explained in a new way, if the preceding ages had not accounted for its procedure by believing in possession. However, the fact that the case has been argued at all suggests that there is a high degree of ambivalence about possession in the fifth century. The later Greek evidence is far more explicit, but it is probably being explicit about beliefs that were held earlier, despite classical ambivalence about them.

Thirdly, in our own language the word 'possession' has resonances from our own interlocking systems of social, economic and sexual 'ownership'. Do these distort our responses and interpretation of possession in Greek material? Luckily, some Greek words from the vocabulary of daemonic possession have some similar associations.[20] Their range suggests that Greek consciousness accepted underlying analogies between a tutelary god's occupation of human territory, the invasion of a human conqueror, male 'self-possession' or mental control, and male economic and sexual possession of women. So, in spite of potentially distorting factors due to the differences between our own assumptions and the Greek thoughtworld, we can allow ourselves to speculate to some extent on the role of daemonic possession in classical imagination.

The key word is *entheos* (see Dodds, 1951, p. 87). *Entheos* means, most probably, 'with god inside'. It distinguishes 'possessed' from *ekphron*, 'mad': if you are *entheos* you are also *ekphron*, but if you are *ekphron* you are not necessarily *entheos*. Greek interest in possession, like that of the Dinka (Lienhardt, 1961, pp. 151-3), 'begins where ours might end', in what the daemon, rather than the human psyche, is up to. The chorus of the *Hippolytus*, faced with Phaedra's delirium, ask 'Are you possessed by Pan or Hecate or the holy Corybants or the Sacred Mother . . .?' (141-2). The Nurse, however, finds the right piece of the external world to which Phaedra responds, when she utters Hippolytus's name. Dinka diviners 'make a division in the experience' of the possessed person, a division which corresponds to the agreed division of experience between different divinities, and find the appropriate image for each, to test the nature of the possessing force. The Greeks felt that a specific external image or sound could reveal which divinity was in possession (or whether the possession was genuine, as the flute-test in Menander's *Theophoroumene*, '*The Girl Possessed*').[21] Once identified, the divinity could be expelled in forms of exorcism. A fragment of a fifth-century mime[22] shows a prelude to an exorcism: a room with closed doors, women with laurel blocking their ears, and a sorceress making ritual preparations. It ends with her invocation to the goddess, and presumably included the unstopping of both door and ears, and the exit of the goddess from house and women. Comic literature, certainly, but it presumably satirises actual fifth-century attitudes, if not rites. Divinity can be an unwelcome guest in a house and a female body. But it may be a welcome guest (see Horton, 1960) in a female body and mind when it is useful to society, i.e. in prophetic possession. Greek culture knew prophetic possession at various levels. 'Belly-talkers' were known in society (Eurycles is one named from classical Athens, Dodds, 1951, pp. 71f.); but Apolline possession of a woman, as in contemporary Delphic practice, was the literary norm. Cassandra appeared in a state of possession in Aeschylus's *Agamemnon* and at least twice in Euripides (*Troades* and *Alexandros*, a play surviving only in fragments). In these scenes she swings between frenzied prophecy and rational explanation. Apollo makes her *ekphron* (*Troades*, 408-9), breathes 'grace' into her (*Agamemnon*, 1207); the frenzy comes at her like fire, whirling her round (*Agamemnon*, 1216). Her prophetic gift was given because she promised that he could make love to her (though she later broke her word); it peeps shyly at the world like a new bride (*Agamemnon*, 1179). The implications of physical pain and erotic penetration here helped to establish in the tradition the idea that prophetic possession by a male god involved pain, which the priestess naturally resisted.[23] Cassandra feels 'god-bearing pangs' (*Agamemnon*, 1150, 1214). The entry of god into woman is painful: as, in medieval fantasies about the Black Mass, women's copulation with the devil was painful, since he was very cold (Trevor-Roper, 1967, p. 125). Erotic penetration becomes one of the main images for any possessing deity in relation to the human soul.[24] Greek associations to female openness to the daemonic, working with Greek associations to the mind as in some way functioning like female *splanchna*, contributed to later imagery by which philosophical and religious writers might characterise divinity's invasion of the self.

Women: Entrances and Inwardness in Male Literary Structures

Fifth-century perceptions of the female interior and of women's relation to men, also contributed to contemporary dramatic and narrative structures. Early tragic story-patterns began with rights of entry into a woman. The *Iliad* begins with the quarrel over possession over Briseis, and its heart is possession of Helen. Both issues give the poet opportunity to confirm but also question the values on which his fictional society, and his poem, repose. ('His', for, to my knowledge, nobody has argued yet for an authoress of the *Iliad*, and what we know of the societies which transmitted the poem make her existence unlikely.) In the nineteenth-century tragic novel adultery is often the shaping event for a narrative which may eventually destroy the woman, and threaten the structures and systems on which the society it depicts, and thereby the novel itself, depends (Tanner, 1979). From the *Iliad* onwards, a suitable starting-point for tragic structure (as for later lyric narrative like the *Roman de la Rose*, see also Aske, 1981), has been secret, forbidden entry into, and 'possession' of, a woman.

Athenian tragedy in particular, however, as developed in the fifth century, depended on some 'dialectic of inside and outside' in the conditions of its performance as well as the conflicts of its narrative. A powerful new approach to tragedy has come through the study of the use of entrance and exit (Taplin, 1977). It is sometimes helpful to see a tragic text as an emotional analogue to the space in which the play was produced. Its dialectic, if that is the right word, between inside and outside, public and private, seen and unseen (Dale, 1956) was emotional as well as physical. There was a physical tension between a fictive inside, the palace behind the scene-front, the character behind the mask, and an apparent outside, the real space surrounded and perceived by the audience. But the texts also offer an answering tension between imagined inward experience and its public expression. Racinian tragedy likewise gestures towards some inner chamber, always invisible, where the important things happen (Barthes, 1960, pp. 9-26), and the important things ultimately consist in the emotional experience expressed in the text.

In tragic opposition between inside and outside, the female stage-figures have a special role. In that culture, as in most, women stand for the inside and the unseen, the *muchos*, the *abaton*. When they emerge, they often indicate a sense of something wrong within; within not only themselves, but society. The maenads in the *Bacchae* indicate something wrong in the state of Thebes. In Aeschylus's *Seven against Thebes* Eteocles complains that the female chorus has come outside, panicked the city, and so helped the besiegers: 'we ourselves are plundered from within' (194). Women are sometimes told, 'be within' (e.g. Aeschylus, *Choephoroe*, 233); it is interestingly unclear whether the comment means 'go inside the house' or 'get back in your mind'. A scene or a play may centre on the threat posed to male life by what a woman brings from her *muchos*. Hippolytus's tirade elaborates on this threat, but we find it in smaller details too: the poison which kills Heracles has been kept for years by his wife in her *muchos* (Sophocles, *Trachiniae*, 686). Aristophanes' comments on Euripides suggest that contemporary society really felt threatened by explicit female 'ex-pression'.

How far, however, are female tragic figures really women? They are oddly masculine (Gould, 1980, p. 57) and perhaps a tragedian searching for images to express the tragic situation, in which divinity may fatally invade human life (Loraux, 1973), found women's easily invaded nature a useful vehicle to explore the susceptibility of all humanity to divinity. Women, being particularly dark and unpredictably vulnerable within, are the perfect paradigm for any tragic figure and his mind, which tragedians often represent as perilously, self-destructively vulnerable to daemonic passion. Women are the possessed; natural victims in the human system, as humanity is the natural victim in the divine world. A fictive female voice can most sharply express the pain and resentment against the apparently unjust system productive of such pain.

Female suffering, within the male system, is a useful tragic instrument. Aeschylus uses Clytemnestra's anger about Iphigenia as a motivating force, as Euripides uses Medea's fury:

> We women must buy a husband . . . Coming to new custom, we have to prophesy, with no background experience, what sort of bed-partner he will be . . . The man, when tired of life within, relieves his heart by going out; but we . . . Men say we live a danger-free life in the house, while they fight . . . They are wrong. I would rather stand three times in battle, than give birth once . . . (*Medea*, 232 f.)

This instrument is used by a male dramatist aiming exclusively at male sensibilities,[25] meaning to write a good play and gain the prize. His aim is not to emancipate contemporary women, but to find a useful image of suffering: not so much imaginative sympathy with, as literary exploitation of, women's victimised position.[26] Female figures in tragedy are there partly as a natural site for inner pain,[27] a social and sexual emblem of private parts (Blair, 1981) suffering invasion, human and daemonic, by the outer world.

Poetic structures offer society ways of seeing its own perceptions (see e.g. Kavolis, 1964). Athenian tragedy expresses a local version of traditional Greek projection: inner states, individuated as gods, invade human life and mind. The mind pictured is a womb-like receptacle for divine intrusion and inner pain. Tragic poets, perhaps, offered their society an equation: as female *splanchna*, womb and sensibility, is to the external world, human and divine, so men's *splanchna*, mind, is to the gods and to daemonic passion. The relation of women to men — their possessions — is one possible image for men's relation to the gods: controlled, limited, manipulated. Western tradition owes the enduring form of tragedy partly to male feelings in fifth-century Athens about what was in women, how it got there, and the danger of its emergence from inner darkness. But particular local patterns of feeling created texts of universal power. Ambivalence about women's openness to intrusion, being based on biological as well as cultural fact, has universal resonance in other societies than fifth-century Athens; even our own.

Notes

1. This paper is based on Padel (forthcoming). I am grateful for the chance of presenting it here in an expanded form.
2. Greek religion reflecting fear of female sexuality: e.g. Slater (1971), chs. 1 and 2; Pomeroy (1975), *passim*; Gould (1980), p. 57. Prostitutes' names in Aristophanes: Taillardat (1965), p. 107.
3. Euripides, fr. 164 N; Gould (1980), pp. 43-6.
4. Cartledge (1981); Gould (1980), p. 45.
5. Thucydides, *Histories*, I.68-70, 76.2. Athenian methods of imperial control, Meiggs (1972), pp. 205-72.
6. E.g. *Iliad*, 5.793; 22.276; *Odyssey*, 7.14; 22.205 *et passim*.
7. Lattimore (1942), pp. 161-4; Alexiou (1974), pp. 187-9.
8. Compare the 'bride of Hades' motif, Rose (1926); Winnington-Ingram (1980), p. 96 n. 15; the motif underlies much of Antigone's language, or language used about her, in the *Antigone*. She defends the claim of the 'lower' gods against Creon's defence of human laws. Creon suggests she marry in Hades since she is so keen on the dead; *Antigone*, 654. On Persephone, cult and myth, Sourvinou-Inwood (1978).
9. Braudel (1975), i, p. 37; but cf. Thomas (1971), pp. 678-9.
10. Euripides, presumably, is drawing directly on Aeschylus's *Bassarids*, see Aeschylus, Loeb Classical Library, ii (1976), pp. 385-8, in connecting the motif of women's strong bond with wild nature, their tendency to be driven mad by divinity, and their destructiveness towards men. Proetides: Loeffler (1963).
11. Pausanias, III.10.6; IX.39.5; Deubner (1903); Dodds (1951), pp. 110-16, 123 n. 83.
12. Onians (1951), pp. 37-48; Sideras (1971), p. 196; Sansone (1975), p. 76; Padel (forthcoming), chs. 2, 3; cf. Rozaldo (1980), pp. 31-52.
13. Flashar (1966); Klibansky, Panofsky and Saxl (1964); Hill (1965); Pagel (1981).
14. Poetry (Reinhardt), 1960, pp. 7f.; vases, Körte (1874), Ellinger (1953), pp. 1180f. See particularly the concept of *phthonos*, 'envy' felt by the gods, whose embodiment was the evil eye, Eitrem (1953). Metaphors of emotion:

Sansone (1975), pp. 6-13; Padel (forthcoming), ch. 5. Cults of personified forces, Farnell (1909), vol. v.

15. E.g. Pindar, *Olympians*, VI.43, Aeschylus, *Seven against Thebes*, 1036.

16. Homer, *Odyssey*, 22.348, cf. Sophocles, *Trachiniae*, 998, Aeschylus, *Agamemnon*, 754; thought as 'fruit of the mind', Pindar, frag. 211 (*pradidōn karpos*). The heart 'feeds on laments', Aeschylus, *Choephoroe*, 26, God 'plants the seed' of disaster in a life or family, Aeschylus, frag. 156 N.

17. Aphrodite destroys women's *phrenes*, 'wits', like a disease, Euripides, frag. 164 N, cf. Gould (1980), p. 55.

18. The chief account of such a rape in extant tragedy, of Creousa by Apollo, happens in a cave, Euripides, *Ion*, 176f.

19. E.g. Cassandra, Aeschylus, *Agamemnon*, 1209; Phaedra, Euripides, *Hippolytus*, 141; references to maenads such as Sophocles, *Antigone*, 964. But Oedipus's sons are *entheoi* with Ares, Aeschylus, *Seven against Thebes*, 497, and cf. *Eumenides*, 17.

20. *Katochos* is commonly used in fourth-century Greek for a 'possessing' deity and 'possessed' person; and *katecho* for 'I possess', of a deity, with passive participle 'possessed', of a person. *Katoche* or *katokoche* are 'possession', 'delirium'. The word-stem is used in contexts of land-occupation, whether by human invader or tutelary deity. In late Greek it has sexual connotations too; the passive participle can mean 'covered', of a female animal. It is also often used in contexts of self-'control'. One controls oneself from doing something; one is in possession of one's senses. Other verbs too can 'take' women, geographical territory, or the mind, as objects; *synoikizo*, 'I colonise with' can mean 'establish a settlement', but it can also mean 'I give a woman in marriage' (e.g. Euripides, *The Madness of Heracles*, 68); *katoikizo*, 'I colonise', is used of a deity 'establishing' hope in human minds, Aeschylus, *Prometheus*, 252. The common concept is of some alien force intruding on a place, and remaining in occupation of it.

21. Handley (1969). At Plato, *Ion*, 536, the poetry-citer's relation to Homer is compared to that of the Corybantes, an enthusiastic sect (with a firm hold, by the fifth century at least, in Athenian imagination) who danced wildly to the particular tune of the deity possessing them.

22. Sophron, see *Greek Select Papyri (Literary)*, ed. Page, Loeb Classical Library, vol. 3, pp. 278f.

23. Virgil's Sibyl tries 'to see if she can shake the great god from her breast', *Aeneid*, VI.77; Lucan's priestess feigns possession twice, in order to escape the real thing, until sent back to do it properly, *Civil War*, V.169.

24. It is endemic in Neoplatonic and Christian writing about the soul, as well as biblical and Christian liturgical writing. See also Jones (1923).

25. Pickard-Cambridge (1968), pp. 264-9.

26. The male novelist, from *Moll Flanders* on, and male authors of such quasi-pornographic fictional female autobiography as Defoe there inaugurated, penetrates inside the female interior, mental or physical, subjecting this to the destruction his story embodies. For the novel form was created partly to invade the female psyche (as its offshoot, pornography, enables a male author to present sexual invasion through the 'I' in a female body), see Padel (1980).

27. As the pain of childbirth is a male literary topos in tragedy, so tragedy, to my knowledge, confines an individual suffering on behalf of another person to the female characters. Tecmessa would rather bear the pain of her knowledge of Ajax's madness alone, and spare him that pain, Sophocles, *Ajax*, 265 f.; the Nurse suffers through her love for Phaedra, Euripides, *Hippolytus*, 260; Jocasta, when she realises the truth, begs Oedipus not to ask further: 'it is enough that I am suffering', Sophocles, *Oedipus Rex*, 1061. Female stage-figures specialise in inner pain on other people's behalf: an emotional analogue to childbirth.

Further Reading

Gould, J.P. (1980), 'Law, custom and myth: aspects of the social position of women in Classical Athens', *JHS* 100, 38-59 (basic)

Beard, M. (1980), 'The sexual status of Vestal Virgins', *JRS* 120, 12-27

Cartledge, P. (1981), 'Spartan wives: liberation or licence?', *CQ* 31, 84-105

Dodds, E.R. (1951), *The Greeks and the Irrational*, Berkeley

Douglas, M. (1970), *Witchcraft Confessions and Accusations*, London

Graham, H. (1976), 'The social image of pregnancy: pregnancy as spirit-possession', *The Sociological Review* 24, 291-308

Hertz, R. (1979), 'The pre-eminence of the right hand', *Right and Left: Essays in Applied Symbolic Classification*, ed. Needham, Chicago

James, W. (repr. 1962), *The Varieties of Religious Experience*, London

Jones, E. (1923), 'The Madonna's conception through the ear', *Essays in Applied Psychoanalysis*, London, vol. II, ch. 13

Lefkowitz, M. (1982), *Heroines and Hysterics*, London

Lewis, I. (1971), *Ecstatic Religions*, Harmondsworth

Lloyd, G.E.R. (1979), *Magic, Reason and Experience*, Cambridge

Osterreich, J.K. (1960), *Possession, Demoniacal and Other*, Eng. trans., New York

2 EXIT ATOSSA: IMAGES OF WOMEN IN GREEK HISTORIOGRAPHY ON PERSIA[1]

Heleen Sancisi-Weerdenburg, Utrecht

The majority of women in the ancient Orient have left no trace in the historical records. They remained nameless and unnamed. Exceptions that escaped anonymity are mostly of a notorious kind. To the qualities that guaranteed a number of these women a place in history belong love of intrigue, artful and treacherous seductiveness, cruelty and even murderousness. These qualities are closely associated with the 'unwholesome atmosphere of the harem', supposedly typical for oriental societies. From this secluded place in life these women apparently managed to obtain control over the men in power and to influence decisions that in turn affected the well-being of entire nations or empires.

I do not intend to diminish the influence women can exercise even when cut off from official sources of power, but I think there is good reason to question the traditional image of at least some of these women. In this paper I will discuss the reputation of the queens and princesses in the first Persian Empire, also called the Achaemenid Empire after its ruling dynasty. Their behaviour and influence at court, at least as we know it from the Greek sources on this period, would, moreover, have contributed to the decadence that marked the Persian Empire in the second half of the fifth and the fourth century BC. I believe that this whole concept of decadence, in its application to the second century of Persian rule over Asia, needs some re-examination. That, however, falls necessarily outside the scope of this study. In this paper I will be discussing in particular the queens and princesses of Xerxes' reign. I shall argue that most of the facts about their lives and actions in the Greek sources are not facts at all and that consequently generalisations based on the influence and the role of the women around the king lack any real historical foundation. Their historical reputation seems to be a product partly of a condescending Western attitude towards the Orient, usually regarded as effeminate, and partly of the use of sources that are unfit to supply historical evidence about the life of these women.

The Achaemenid Empire, founded by Cyrus the Great around 550 BC, came to its end in 330 BC when it was conquered by Alexander the

Great. The two centuries of its existence are usually described in terms of 'rise and fall' or 'flourishing and decadence'. Under Cyrus (550-530) and Darius (522-486) the empire was young and vigorous; under Xerxes, ruling from 486 till 465, the first signs of decay appeared. In the reigns of his successors the enormous empire gradually weakened and fell into inertia, to become an easy prey for the devouring Macedonian armies in 333. Such is the traditional view of the Achaemenid Empire, as it can be found in most handbooks.

Greek historiography (as well as most of its modern interpreters) have provided us with a picture of the Achaemenid Empire in which 480, the year of Xerxes' defeat at Salamis, is a crucial turning-point. Before, especially in the times of Cyrus, the Persians were vigorous, lived soberly and were capable of great conquests. They also had some other pleasant characteristics: they were remarkably tolerant and respected the national traditions and cultures of conquered territories. They had high educational ideals: their children were taught to shoot the bow, to ride a horse and to speak the truth. Cyrus's successor Cambyses added Egypt to his father's conquests, just in time before going mad. Next came a temporary usurpation by a Magus, a priest from a Median tribe. Darius, a young man from the younger line of the Achaemenids, put an end to this usurpation. After re-establishing peace in the empire, he set out to reorganise the enormous conglomerate of nations, tribes and cities. With a firm hand he created a bureaucratic structure and instituted regular taxes.

Darius is generally regarded as one of the best kings of the dynasty. Under his son Xerxes everything took a turn for the worse. As is well known, Xerxes tried in vain to conquer Greece. After the 'fatal' defeats at Salamis, Plataea and Mycale the empire went downhill. The central government was no longer strong and firm. Luxury, wealth, the harem and female intrigues heavily corrupted the highest regions of the government. In Xerxes' reign women started playing all-important roles. Queens decided and kings complied with their wishes. Amestris, and later on Parysatis and Stateira, were extremely powerful and their relative husbands and sons were no match for them.

This view, largely dependent on Greek sources for ancient Persia, is still very common in modern literature. Usually some allowance is made for the hostile bias of the Greeks versus their traditional enemies. But the way in which in modern syntheses high-quality Greek historiography (such as Herodotus, whose Persians are far less stereotyped than those of later generations of Greek writers) is used indiscriminately along with poor historical material (as e.g. Ktesias) to provide the basic 'facts' of Persian history, seriously blurs the picture.

Greek fifth- and fourth-century historiography furthermore had serious shortcomings: 'there was no effort to see what kept the empire together behind the administrative facade' says Momigliano in a beautiful analysis of Greek historiography on Persia (Momigliano, 1979, p. 150). Sadly enough the same could be said of much modern literature on the subject.

As often in Achaemenid history it is impossible to confront the Greek sources with Persian evidence. Iranian sources for this period are already scarce, and about women we have hardly any information at all. The royal inscriptions never mention mortal women, even in those instances where it might be expected on the basis of the Greek reports, as in Xerxes' accession record, the so-called Harem-inscription (Kent, 1953, p. 149 f). According to Herodotus (VII, 2-3) Atossa played a prominent role in the selection of Xerxes as heir to the throne. But neither she, nor her father Cyrus the Great, are mentioned in the official Persian document. The goddess Anahita figures as the only female in the texts. Her antecedents and functions, however, are so enigmatic that she certainly cannot be used as a clue to the position of women in Iranian society. In the palace-administration of Persepolis some women are mentioned. Some princesses and queens — their relation to the king usually has to be inferred from the Greek sources — are given travel-provisions (Hallock, 1969). Notably absent from these records is Atossa, who in the period covered by the tablets (509-493), figured prominently at the Achaemenid court, again according to our Greek information. An interesting series of these tablets deals with extra rations for female workers at Persepolis after childbirth. These rations are premiums and not a form of wages, as can be deduced from the fact that the portions are not the same in all cases: mothers with male babies get twice the amount given to women who have delivered a daughter (Hallock, 1969, p. 37f.).

Most striking is the absence of women on the most elaborate representation of the Persian Empire: the palace-reliefs of Persepolis. King, courtiers, guards and nobles, representatives of all the peoples, united in stone, show the empire as, no doubt, the kings wanted it to be seen. Among the many figures in Persepolis women are completely absent. The hidden force in history is particularly hidden in this first Iranian Empire. Even the animals carried as gifts for the king by various delegations are, with one exception, male. And the presence of the only female creature, a lioness, brought by the Elamites, can easily be explained by the age of the two cubs she accompanies: they still need suckling (Walser, 1980, p. 27).

In the minor arts we do get a few glimpses of women. In a three-page article Agnes Spycket exhaustively sums up the sculptural representations of women, including some supposedly pre-Achaemenian statuettes and some portraits that have been regarded usually as beardless male heads (Spycket, 1980). From a carpet, one of the earliest Persian specimens still extant, found in the frozen tombs of Siberia, we can at least see what Persian women looked like (Wiesner, 1976). The scene on the carpet shows some kind of cultic act in which two, probably royal, women are involved. A similar enigmatic scene can be seen on a seal found in Persepolis. More interesting than worrying about the meaning of the ritual on carpet and seal is speculating about the way in which this unmistakably Persian item reached far distant Siberia. Could it have been brought in the luggage of a princess, married off to a Scythian prince for diplomatic reasons as e.g. to obtain peace and quiet on the northern borders of the empire?

In Asia Minor, too, women are depicted, on gems belonging to the so-called group of Graeco-Persian gems, and on funeral stelae from Dascylium. None of these remarkable hybrid objects provides sufficient congruency with the Greek sources to be helpful for a comparison. For the Persian women mentioned in Greek literature no counterpart can be found in the extant Persian evidence. This may be explained partly by the hazards of time. One would not expect a golden statue of his favourite wife commissioned by Darius according to Herodotus (VII 69), to have survived 25 centuries. But the reliefs of Persepolis are extremely well preserved.

Apparently it is no accident that Persepolis in stone, as we know it, is an all male gathering. One should be careful, however, to rush to conclusions based on the absence of women and to assume that women did not play an important role in Iranian society. The Persian sources merely do not allow any conclusion whatsoever.

So we must turn to the Greek sources and see what room for conclusions they leave us as to the activities and roles of women. Do we have any real evidence for a growing influence of women at the Achaemenid court? Since the presumed decadence would have set in during Xerxes' reign, it is most useful to have a closer look at the queens and princesses of this period. That, incidentally, gives us the advantage of having mainly the honest guidance of Herodotus, whose 'brilliance and intellectual generosity' was unequalled by any of his successors (Momigliano, 1979, p. 142).

The first to catch our attention is Atossa, Xerxes' mother. Besides encountering her on the pages of the *Histories*, she is also the leading character in Aeschylus' tragedy, the *Persae*, staged for the first time in Athens eight years after the battle of Salamis. Although the *Persae* is frequently used as a source for Atossa's position, it is doubtful whether this is justified. In the tragedy Atossa is portrayed as a model of motherly care for her son Xerxes, who has undertaken a foolish and ill-fated expedition against Greece: Xerxes is every bit the young daring rascal and Atossa is consistently pictured as his counterpart, the wise old lady, comporting herself in a queenly dignified way. There is, however, nothing really Persian in her behaviour. Nothing which suggests that explicit information about Persian queens was available to the poet (Vogt, 1972, p. 136). In the text itself, her name is not even mentioned. She is addressed as 'queen', but never by name. In his comment on Atossa's role Broadhead says that for an Athenian public Atossa must have been 'hardly more than a name' (Broadhead, 1960, p. XXVI). It may be doubted whether she was even that. Von Wilamowitz has suggested that her name, undoubtedly known from Herodotus, was transferred from the scholia into the list of characters (see Broadhead, 1960, p. XXVI, n. 1). She may well have been less than a name to the Athenian public and consequently her conduct in the tragedy more dependent on dramatic necessities than on real historical data.

Better evidence is to be found in Herodotus, though not all of Herodotus' information on Atossa is equally useful for historical purposes. There is no reason to doubt the main data about Atossa's life as they appear in the *Histories*. Atossa, daughter of Cyrus the Great, was married to her brother Cambyses (Hdt. III 31). After his death the false Smerdis who had seized the throne took her as wife (Hdt. III 68). The failure of this usurpation resulted in a new marriage for Atossa (Hdt. III 88). She became the spouse of king Darius, prince of a younger line of the Achaemenid family. Along with Atossa all the wives of his predecessor entered Darius' harem. So Atossa was again in the company of a daughter of the noble Otanes, Phaidymiè, who had assisted her father in unmasking the usurper. Darius also took Artystone, the still virgin daughter of Cyrus, and Parmys, daughter of the real Smerdis, as wives. It looks as if he wanted to leave no loose ends.

There are two other stories in the *Histories* in which Atossa figures prominently. The first relates Atossa's successful attempt to persuade Darius to prepare an expedition against Greece (Hdt. III 134). Atossa acts at the instigation of the Greek physician Democedes, held against his will at the Persian court. Democedes hopes to profit from an intelligence mission in order to escape from his captivity. And in fact does so.

Relatives of Democedes may have reported this story to Herodotus. That does not make it true. The tale is 'in part patently fictitious' (Snodgrass, 1980, p. 168). It certainly does not prove anything about Atossa's position or influence. One wonders whether Greek doctors, even if highly honoured at court for their unequalled abilities, were really in a position to obtain secure knowledge about the bedroom secrets of the king and queen. The results produced by a later Greek doctor on the Persian scene, Ktesias of Knidos, physician to Artaxerxes II, leave some doubt as to the access Greeks could have to the inner circle of Achaemenid kingship, surrounded as it was by all kinds of tabus and encumbered by a heavy ceremonial ritualism.

The next episode about Atossa in the *Histories* again concerns a Greek protagonist, this time the banished Spartan king Demaratus (Hdt. VII 2-3). He volunteers his good advice on the difficult problem of which son should succeed Darius, Xerxes, Atossa's son, born during the kingship of his father, or the eldest son, born before 522, whose mother is a daughter of the noble Gobryas, one of Darius' fellow conspirators against the Magus. The candidacy of Xerxes prevails. Not so much because of Demaratus' good advice, says Herodotus, but 'while Atossa was all powerful'.

Why was Atossa so powerful? Herodotus' story is confirmed in its outline by Xerxes' own words in his Harem-inscription 'Other sons of Darius there were, [but] – thus unto Ahuramazda was the desire – Darius my father made me the greatest after himself. When my father Darius went away from the throne, by the will of Ahuramazda I became king on my father's throne' (Kent, 1953, p. 150, Il. 27-36). From 'the other sons of Darius', mentioned by Xerxes, we may conclude that the succession was by no means automatic and that a struggle took place between the possible candidates, involving also their respective mothers. Quite probably, though, Xerxes' designation as crown prince took place somewhat earlier than shortly before Darius' death, as Herodotus has it.[2] Xerxes' own inscription is absolutely silent about his maternal lineage. His mother and, more surprisingly, his maternal grandfather are passed over in complete silence. It is usually assumed that Atossa's powerful position was due to her birth as the daughter of the founder of the empire. In that case shouldn't we expect a reference to Cyrus in Xerxes' inscription? Or did Atossa become so important as a *result* of her son's designation to the throne? Her powerful position would then be due not to her status as a daughter, but to her position as the mother of the king to be. This would tie in with the evidence of the Persepolis tablets that unequivocally prove how much value was attached to the production of male children and with Herodotus's remark (I, 136) that annually the fathers of the largest number of children were rewarded by the king. There may have been one other reason for bypassing the other candidate, the grandson of Gobryas. In the fifth century we see an increasing number of marriages within the Achaemenid dynasty. Before his accession Darius had agreed that future queens should not be chosen outside the families of the prominent men who had helped him to put an end to the usurpation of the Magus (Hdt. III, 84). A marriage with the king meant more power for the family that provided the bride and therefore the possible interference by those groups whose influence the Achaemenids sought to cut down. After Darius the royal family was so prolific that, without breaking the agreement, sufficient candidates for marriage within their own family were available. Later on we often find the king married to his sister or half-sister. Thus the danger was avoided of having a wife affiliated to an already mighty family. Darius's marriage to all the female descendants of Cyrus alive at his accession can be explained in this way. These women, the last heiresses of the older royal line, if married to other nobles, might have given considerable support to any attempt of rebellion against the king.

Altogether the hardcore information about Atossa does not amount to much. It is certainly not sufficient to justify a lifesketch like the one by Kornemann (1942) in his *'Grosse Frauen des Altertums'*. In the chapter dedicated to Atossa, Kornemann states that the queen, during her marriage with the Magus, must have become deeply religious. In Darius's reign she actively helped to build up the administrative structure of the Empire. At the end of her life, and thus the beginning of Xerxes' reign, Atossa, religious as she was, according to Kornemann, inspired her son to fanatical religious behaviour. It was really her work that in Xerxes' reign the first union between church and state in history was brought about.

This Kornemann romance is not so much based on sources as on a Kinder, Kirche, Küche ideology. In his footnotes Kornemann says that he made use of an (at that moment) still unpublished doctoral thesis of P.J. Junge on Darius I. Junge's book is probably one of the most striking examples of Nazi-historiography, based on the newest results of the new science 'Rassenforschung' that, in Junge's words, 'Seele, Charakter und innere Beweggründe einzelner Menschen wie ganzer Völker neu und viel tiefer als bisher erfassen lassen wird' (Junge, 1944/3). Kornemann wrote a popular book and Junge has disappeared in the battle around Stalingrad. Do their writings have any relevance?

It would be nice if we were able to answer this question in the negative. But there are still examples, and quite easy to find, of opinions similar to those of Kornemann and Junge in very recent literature. There is some similarity between a remark made by Junge about Parysatis: 'die berüchtigte Halbsemitin ... die den unglücklichen babylonischen Fraueneinfluss am stärksten zum Ausdruck bringt ...', and a statement by Bengtson in the latest edition of his *Handbuch* (1977) where he ascribes the downfall of the Persian Empire to 'der narkotisierende Einfluss der altorientalischen Hochkulturen'. These generalisations, however, are not confined to national-socialist historiography, nor to Germany; they can be found in many twentieth-century studies on the Persian Empire. But in national-socialist terms the Persians presented a particularly difficult problem. For Junge and Kornemann the Persians were the real Aryans – which in fact they were – and they had to solve the problem of how this first Aryan empire had not managed to survive. Corrupting influences were easily found in the oriental cultures or in the women around the king or in a combination of both. In this interpretation they could follow closely *some* of their Greek predecessors for whom Persian, barbarian, oriental was equal to feminine. Greek culture was male, oriental culture was female. Greeks were brave, orientals were drowned in luxury, they slept on soft beds, ate dainty spices and wore jewellery (e.g. Xenophon, *Cyropaedia*, VIII, viii). Whereas Greece was governed by men, all the slave-like subjects of the kings of Persia were ruled either by effeminate kings or, indirectly, by women. This dualistic thinking is not confined to Greek descriptions of Persia. To quote one modern example: in 1954 Nyberg wrote on Xerxes: 'es ist bezeichnend dass sein stattlichstes Gebäude in Persepolis gerade der Harem ist'. Nyberg and most modern writers on the subject observe the first signs of decline in Xerxes' reign. The reasons are clear: he is highly influenced by women and therefore weak. Yet Atossa' influence on Xerxes is based, in fact, solely on the passages we have just discussed. So it is more important to recognise what our main sources for Atossa really are: in part fictitious stories which, more than anything else, reflect an attitude which regarded the history of a complete empire in terms of personalities. Since the Greeks had mostly no real knowledge of the general social and cultural background of the Persians, they reported or interpreted at face value the tales and stories that reached their ears.

This is also the case with the famous story of Artaynte, another notorious woman of Xerxes' court, whose adventure is frequently used to demonstrate the weakness of Xerxes' character. The story (Hdt. IX, 108-13) is loosely connected with its surroundings and stands rather on its own (Wolff, 1965).

On his way back from Greece, Xerxes falls in love with the wife of his brother Masistes. As this lady, who remains nameless throughout the story, does not give in to royal temptation, Xerxes seeks to achieve his end in another way. He marries his son, the crown prince Darius, to the daughter of Masistes, Artaynte. Herodotus thinks that in this way the king might have more success with the mother of the young royal bride. But, in fact, once back in Susa, Xerxes falls in love with the daughter, this time with more success. One day he visits the young lady, wearing a beautiful robe, woven by queen Amestris herself. Xerxes is very pleased with this outfit. Equally pleased with Artaynte he tells her to ask him whatever she wants. He will fulfil any wish. Artaynte, not very surprisingly, demands the robe. Xerxes foresees serious trouble and tries to dissuade her. Artaynte persists in her original request. Xerxes can do nothing but give her what she wants. Real drama becomes unavoidable when Artaynte shows off her new possession at court. Amestris is, not surprisingly, furious and plans revenge. Her chance comes at the annual banquet on the occasion of the king's birthday. On this occasion the king is obliged to fulfil any wish addressed to him. Amestris asks, strangely enough, for the wife of Masistes (and not for the daughter whom we would consider the true offender). Again the king is greatly embarrassed. In vain he tries to convince Masistes to marry his own (Xerxes') daughter. Masistes flatly refuses. When he comes home he finds his wife tortured by Amestris: her breasts, nose, ears, lips and tongue are cut off.

Masistes does not lose much time and together with his sons he sets out for his satrapy of Bactria to raise a revolt against his brother. Xerxes manages only just in time to catch up with Masistes and company and Masistes, his children and his army are all killed. 'Thus far about the death of Masistes and the love of Xerxes', says Herodotus.

This dramatic tale forms a closed unit within the *Histories*. The story, like several others in Herodotus' work, originates from Persian oral tradition. Its relation to historical reality therefore is different from that of a written source. Recent research in the Homeric oral tradition, in the Yugoslav guslar tradition and in Near Eastern traditions, have made us more familiar with the workings of oral literature. An example of the Sargon-legend, studied by Drews (1974), presents a useful comparison with our story. Drews shows that the Sargon-myth, orally transmitted for ages, only a couple of times surfacing in the written records, contains themes that are also to be found in the legends concerning Cyrus's birth and youth. He concludes that older legends have simply attached themselves to the figure of the new king. Similar instances are also found in the Yugoslav tradition. To quote A.B. Lord: 'the story mold came first and the attachment to the historical figures second' (Lord, 1970, p. 27).

It is quite likely that the Artaynte story, too, is older than the named personalities. The themes from which the narrative is built up occur in other Persian stories as well (Sancisi-Weerdenburg, 1980, p. 59ff.). Briefly, in this drama the theme of the robe plays a conspicuous role and is crucial for the dénouement of the plot. It is extremely beautiful and therefore wanted by Artaynte, it is woven by Amestris and the queen's fury is quite justified. But there is more to it than just that. From other similar stories we know more about the king's robe. There is a taboo on wearing the royal robe by anyone else but the king (cf. Plut. *Artaxerxes*, V 2). On the level of literature the person wearing the royal robe is the king: the first act of any usurper of the throne is to put on the royal robe. It is part of the regalia with which the king is invested on his accession. What Artaynte asks for in the tale is not only a beautiful garment but the kingship with it. This element was easily overlooked by Greeks who were not familiar with the workings and connotations of sacral kingship. In the Greek version, therefore, the robe is surrounded by emotional feelings that completely hide its original meaning.

If the robe equals the kingship, our next question must be for whose sake Artaynte tries to get hold of the kingship? Not for herself, obviously. Her husband, Darius, was already sharing the kingship of his father as can be seen on the famous Treasury reliefs, where he stands behind the king's throne and wears the same crown as his father (Calmeyer, 1974). But Masistes, as a candidate supported by Artaynte, fits in well with the end of the story, the death of Masistes and his entire family. It also makes the revenge of queen Amestris slightly more understandable. The form of this revenge, moreover, recalls exactly the usual punishment for rebels.[3] Under the surface of this romantic tale might be hidden an attempt to rebel by a brother of the king.

But why is it Artaynte that asks for the robe; why is a woman the protagonist in a story about a conflict between two men? This brings us to the crux of the matter. In this kind of conflict women do indeed play crucial roles, since they are bound to two families that may have opposed interests (Gluckman, 1970; Fishburne Collier, 1974). Often their marriages are arranged to tighten the relationship between two families. The marriage between Artaynte and the crown prince Darius, provided with such an improbable motive in the story, may have had exactly this function: to reconcile the two royal brothers. In marriages of this kind, however, if original hostilities develop further, the women concerned are torn in two different directions, towards the family that has raised them and with which there are strong emotional ties and towards the family they have married into and whose procreative future they should ensure.

It is, of course, impossible to extract *historical* evidence from this story, though we do have a few indications that a rebellion by a younger brother of Xerxes actually took place (Sancisi-Weerdenburg, 1980, p. 67 f.). Furthermore the satrapy of Bactria is known to have shown regular inclinations to revolt. A real rebellion may well have been the origin of the story we find in Herodotus. The few generally known data may have served as the backbone for a tale which was elaborated in the oral tradition using age-old motifs. No proof of this can be found in the story itself. The five chapters in the *Histories* should be treated as literature and not as historiography. They certainly do not contain reliable information about either Xerxes or his entourage.

Literature can disclose information about the society that created it. Not about chronologies and events, but about values. Artaynte who, if my interpretation of the tale is correct, chooses the side of her own family even against the interests of the family of her husband, is a recurrent type in stories with a Persian background (Momigliano, 1977, p. 26). To the same category belong Otanes' daughter Phaidymiè, who accepts the risky task of unmasking pseudo-Smerdis (Hdt. III, 68-9) and Esther whose mission obviously is not without danger (Esther, 4, 17). Closer to Artaynte, however, is the wife of Intaphernes (Hdt. III, 119). After a real or imaginary attempt at rebellion against Darius, the king has Intaphernes and his entire family taken prisoner. When Darius sees how Intaphernes' wife weeps and laments at the gates of the royal palace, he takes pity on her and promises that one member of her family will be saved; all the others will perish. The choice is hers. To the king's great surprise the lady chooses her brother. Her reason is that since her parents are dead, she can never have another brother, whereas she is still young enough to have another husband and children.

The unexpected choice of Intaphernes' wife has been interpreted as the vestiges of a matriarchal or matrilineal society. This is unnecessary. The dilemma of the choice between cognates and agnates occurs in all kinds of societies, both patrilineal and matrilineal (Gluckman, 1970, pp. 54-80), though in different forms. In a patriarchal society such as the Persian, the first duty of a married woman is to provide her new family with offspring and to take motherly care of the children that guarantee the future of the husband's family. This is what Darius seems to say when he grants Intaphernes' wife not only her brother but her eldest son as well. Both obligations may lead to a conflict of loyalties. In the Iranian society of the sixth and fifth century BC there still existed strong tribal tendencies. The centralised kingship was by no means safe and secure. Marriages were used by the kings, as well as by the tribal chiefs, to strengthen their relative positions. Pressure on the women from both sides in this uneasy situation must have been very strong, and the outcome of this conflict of loyalties never entirely predictable. It is important to see in these queens and princesses not the life and blood personages their historical names or, when they are nameless, their kinship relations seem to suggest. They are literary prototypes that will have served primarily as models for female behaviour within the context of Iranian society.

It is quite clear that these stories do not say anything about a decline setting in during Xerxes' reign. (And I must add again that nothing similar to this is said or hinted at by Herodotus.) There are no connections between the defeats in Greece and these partly romantic, partly tragic, tales. So any conclusion linking Xerxes' military failure with a flight into love-affairs and making Salamis in some sense the cause of the downfall of the mighty Empire, is unjustified. The real downfall did not take place until 150 years after Salamis and that is a rather retarded effect. In the meantime Persian gold managed to bring Greece virtually under complete Persian control. The Great King's cumbersome armies had failed; his subtly and carefully distributed *darics* were very successful.

But what about the period after Xerxes? In the reigns of Artaxerxes I, Darius II and Artaxerxes II we 'witness' an uninterrupted series of intriguing queens and princesses, to name only the most famous, Parysatis and Stateira. Most information on this period comes from Ktesias, court physician to Artaxerxes II. His histories are for the largest part only preserved in an excerpt by the Byzantine patriarch Photius. Even Photius's summary proves beyond doubt that as an historian Ktesias is far inferior to Herodotus. He is predominantly interested in personalities and then mainly in their plotting and intriguing against each other and against the king. We never find the excursions about the more structural aspects of the Persian Empire that make Herodotus such a precious source for Achaemenid history. This is not due to the summarised form in which we have Ktesias's book. In Photius's concluding remarks at the end of the summary we read: 'no digressions in his book [Ktesias's] as in the other's [scil. Herodotus's] which deviate from the main story'. Photius is obviously pleased with the narrative structure rich in emotions and full of unexpected turns (Photius, *Bibl.* 45a). According to Diodorus Ktesias would have consulted the so-called 'royal books', the *basilikai diphtherai* (Diodorus II, 32 4). This remark has generated much discussion, since Ktesias' results hardly give the impression of being based on an official source. Photius, however, introduces his excerpt of Ktesias by stating that he had been in Persia, and had seen or *heard* from the Persians themselves about their history: he has been *autekoos* (Photius, *Bibl.* 36a). He must have heard more than he read. Nearly all the numbers of years he gives for the duration of the reign of kings are wrong. Such a detail might have been right if he had consulted written sources. Once we recognise that his sources were oral, it becomes understandable why we again and again find the same story-mould filled each time with different actors. Some themes are particularly recurrent: the jealous vindictive mother occurs under different names, Parysatis, mother of Artaxerxes II and Cyrus the Younger being the most famous of them.

One of the acts which has secured her the reputation of the most cruel lady in Achaemenid history is an incident fully preserved by Plutarch (*Artaxerxes* XVII) where Parysatis plays dice with her son the king. At stake is the life of an eunuch who after the battle of Cunaxa had cut off the head and right hand of Cyrus. The queen wins, of course, and the poor eunuch is flayed alive. Gruesome behaviour indeed. But here again there may be something under the surface of the story. From Indian epic we know of the custom of playing dice in order to select a human sacrificial victim. We may suspect a ritual significance behind a story which in its Greek elaboration looks like a vendetta. Careful analysis of Ktesias, Plutarch and fragments of other fourth-century historians and careful comparison of their stories with Indian epic literature may reveal more about the contents of the Iranian oral tradition. Our knowledge about the actual events of Persian history will be considerably reduced by such a procedure. But that, to borrow an appropriate statement, is 'a pity, not an argument' (M.I. Finley).

It is time, I think, to liberate ourselves from the Greek view on Persian history. The notorious women in this history should be confined to their real place, that is in literature. They should not be used as a basis for superficial and condescending judgements of the decline and fall type. Such judgements do not further our understanding of the functioning of the Achaemenid Empire. They merely reinforce the tendency already existent in Antiquity, to see the Orient as female, weak and worthless and Western civilisation as male, valiant and valuable: a dichotomy offensive to both women and the East, understandable in its original Greek surroundings, but no longer justified in twentieth-century historiography.

In their true context, literature and, provided they are cautiously used, the tales about queens and princesses may give us a clue to one of the important problems that had to be faced by the Persian kings: the tendencies of tribal chieftains and heads of satrapies to turn their back on the central government. In these attempts to get away from an increasingly centralised power, women occupied a crucial position, torn as they were in two directions. Their choice must have been unforeseeable and therefore feared.

Notes

1. Acknowledgement: I wish to thank Josine Blok (Groningen) for suggestions and critical remarks on both this paper and an earlier (slightly different) version that appeared in Dutch in *Tweede Jaarboek voor Vrouwengeschiedenis*, Nijmegen, 1981, 14-45.

2. This seems to be indicated by a relief in the Taçara, the earliest construction in Persepolis, where Xerxes is shown as crown prince behind the throne of his father Darius. Such a monument could not have been produced in the few weeks Herodotus allows between Xerxes' designation and Darius's death. For further indications see Calmeyer (1976).

3. The best known instance is to be found in the Behistun-inscription (Kent, 1953, p. 124) where Darius recounts how he treated two rebels: he had cut off their noses and ears and put out one eye.

3 WOMEN AND WITCHCRAFT IN ANCIENT ASSYRIA (c. 900-600 BC)

Sue Rollin, London

The land of Assyria lay in the north of ancient Mesopotamia, corresponding roughly with the northern part of present-day Iraq. South of Assyria was Babylonia, with its centre in the region of modern Baghdad. The Neo-Assyrian period, with which this paper is primarily concerned, covers approximately the three centuries between 900 and 600 BC. It is the period which saw the growth and decline of the great Assyrian empire. As well as the Neo-Assyrian period, reference is also made to the preceding Middle Assyrian period, which began in the mid-fourteenth century BC, and to certain periods of Babylonian history, in particular the Old Babylonian period, which dates between c. 1894 BC and 1595 BC.

Many cuneiform documents, dating to various historical periods and written in the ancient Semitic language known as Akkadian, contain evidence to show that throughout ancient Mesopotamian history the belief existed that human beings could harm others illicitly by supernatural means. The term 'witchcraft' is here used to describe the range of such activities. In much anthropological literature, witchcraft is distinguished from sorcery, following the work of Evans-Pritchard on the Azande, who make a distinction between an inborn power to injure people without material means and the manipulation of material objects for evil purposes (Evans-Pritchard, 1937). Evans-Pritchard used the word witchcraft to describe the former and sorcery to describe the latter. Most societies, however, including that of ancient Mesopotamia, do not make this precise distinction, and therefore the English words 'witch' and 'sorcerer', when used to translate Akkadian terms, should be viewed as roughly synonymous, and not seen as expressing a dichotomy made explicit in the Mesopotamian texts. Several different Akkadian words for 'witch' occur in these texts, but any clear differences in concept which may originally have underlain the various terms are no longer evident.

In Mesopotamia witchcraft was regarded as just one of many possible causes of sickness and misfortune. It was clearly considered to be evil and belonged to the field of unjustified, non-legitimate action. However,

34

the types of power used by witches for evil ends could also be used by other human beings for legitimate purposes. The curse, for example, was often thought of as evil, but when wielded by the king it was considered to be a legitimate way of asserting power and authority. Mystical power was believed to inhere not only in words but also in looks, and again kings were thought to wield this power. The non-legitimate equivalent of this was the idea of the Evil Eye. Magic was used for legitimate purposes by a priest called the *āšipu*, who performed rituals aimed at controlling the forces held responsible for the succession of events, using both material substances and verbal formulae. Many forms of magic, however, were available not only to these expert magicians, but also to ordinary members of society, and could be used both with and without social approval. In this context it can be seen that the methods employed by the *āšipu* to rid a patient of the supposed effects of witchcraft were often similar to those presumed to have been used by witches to harm their victims. The distinction between the social and antisocial uses of magic was therefore a matter of public opinion regarding the person carrying out the activity rather than an essential difference in the power and magic themselves.

One of the main sources of evidence for a study of witchcraft in Mesopotamia in general and in Assyria in particular is the incantation series *Maqlû* ('burning'), which consists of nine tablets, of which the first eight are made up of incantations, and the ninth gives directions for performing the magical actions required to render the incantations efficacious (see Meier, 1937). The series as a whole is concerned with the evil of witchcraft. Unfortunately the period of the original compilation of most of the incantations in *Maqlû* has not been determined with any certainty, and it is therefore impossible to connect the ideas contained in the text with any particular time in Mesopotamian history. However, although some of the specific details may relate to earlier periods, all the general concepts were definitely still current in the Neo-Assyrian period, when *Maqlû* was a royal ceremony, probably performed in the month of *Abu* (July/August), perhaps during the period of the disappearance of the moon at the end of that month (Abusch, 1974). A letter to the Assyrian king in which the writer shows concern about 'many sorceresses' mentions the performance of a different Assyrian royal ritual, the *bît rimki* ('house of ritual bathing'). Within this series are several incantations also found in *Maqlû* and others addressed to the sun god Šamaš designed to ward off witchcraft and sorcery (Laessøe, 1955). There is also a letter to the Neo-Assyrian king Esarhaddon (680-669 BC) which refers to the performance of another ritual, designed to counteract the evil of sorcery. A piece of ritual and two connected incantations addressed to Šamaš, almost every phrase from which can be paralleled in *Maqlû*, are likewise concerned with combating the evil caused by witches (Lambert, 1957/8). On stylistic grounds the composition of the longer incantation can probably be dated to 1000 BC or later. One of the tablets on which this incantation appears was written for Šamaš-šumu-ukin, king of Babylon (668-648 BC) and brother of the Neo-Assyrian king Assurbanipal (668-627 BC), providing further evidence that witchcraft ideas and fear of witches were particularly prevalent in the Neo-Assyrian period.

As well as the difficulty of relating the material contained in the above-mentioned texts to the historical background, there is a second important problem concerning the type of evidence available. The rituals and incantations provide a stereotyped, ideal-typical picture of the witch, a picture which presumably reflects in a generalised way the concepts and ideas of the population as a whole, but in specific details may perhaps be seen as more particularly representative of certain sectors of Mesopotamian society. These would be either the people concerned with the compilation or professional usage of the texts or those likely to be involved in rituals or other situations where the extant anti-witchcraft literature would have been used. Most such people were presumably men, and the anti-witchcraft literature may therefore represent to some extent concepts and beliefs which were initially male rather than female in origin. All this, however, is necessarily speculative. What we *can* say is that rituals involving the *āšipu*-priest, for example, were probably far above the means of the poorer sectors of the community. Certainly the *āšipu*s of whom we know in the Neo-Assyrian period were members of a learned and probably wealthy profession held in great esteem by the royal family, but the evidence is not extensive enough to determine whether or not there were others of that profession in Assyria who were of a lower status and did not enjoy the royal favour. Furthermore, although the texts give a clear and in many respects very informative stereotyped view of witches, there is virtually no evidence from the Neo-Assyrian period of the direction which actual witchcraft accusations might have taken. This is unfortunate, because anthropological studies of witchcraft in many areas of the world have shown that one cannot usually find a connection between general ideas about witches and the direction of accusation in particular cases (Mair, 1969, p. 102). The former belong to the overall belief system of a society, whereas the latter are indications of specific social tensions and conflicts.

Considering first the stereotyped picture of witchcraft as presented both by the rituals and incantations which we know were in current use in Assyria, and by other Mesopotamian texts which illustrate the same concepts, the Assyrians clearly believed that a wide range of persons could seek to harm others by supernatural means, and it has proved useful for purposes of analysis to group witches into five categories. At one end of the scale witches were seen as non-human or semi-human figures who were associated with demons and ghosts. Although witches of this type could be of either sex, the female witch is several times mentioned independently of her male counterpart, but the reverse is not attested. Like demons, these witches may be seen as the antithesis of the Mesopotamian idea of civilised, and were associated with the steppe, the mountains and the underworld, all of which lay beyond the area where the Mesopotamians imposed their social control.

Close in some respects to this concept was the idea that foreigners and foreign countries in general were potential sources of witchcraft and evil. Some incantations are concerned explicitly with keeping foreign witches outside Mesopotamia, with preventing them from crossing the Tigris and Euphrates. Such ideas are illustrative of the Mesopotamian fear of foreigners, who not only encroached upon and sporadically invaded the settled lands of Assyria and Babylonia throughout Mesopotamian history, but also lay socially and culturally, as well as politically, outside Mesopotamian civilisation. In *Maqlû*, although references to foreign men as sorcerers occur, the emphasis is on foreign women from various neighbouring lands.

The third group of witches distinguished are internal enemies, in marginal social categories, and more incantations in *Maqlû* are concerned with this type of witch than with any other. Among the people in ancient Mesopotamia who were clearly considered as marginal were the actor, the male and female snake charmer and the pedlar. The actor is known from both Assyria and Babylonia, whereas the snake charmer and pedlar occur only in Babylonian texts. Little is known about the activities of these professions, but it is not unlikely that at least some of them travelled around the country like many of their modern counterparts and had no settled or permanent home. Several actors and actresses were, however, employed by the palace in the Neo-Assyrian period. The livelihood of snake charmers was of course snakes, which were considered in many situations to be ominous, and their stare was also thought to carry the Evil Eye as in the Middle East today.

Although both men and women in certain marginal social categories were conceived of as potential witches, women in general were considered to have a far greater propensity towards witchcraft than men. There are many incantations in *Maqlû* and also many other texts in which only female witches are mentioned. The unknown sorceress is a common theme, and several incantations begin with the words 'Who are you, sorceress . . .?' It is no accident that women were particularly liable to suspicion of witchcraft in Mesopotamia. They were involved less deeply than men in the central institutions of their society, and may therefore be regarded as 'peripheral' in the sense that most positions of authority and status within the central social structure were denied to them and any power which they held usually had to be achieved and wielded indirectly. What the witchcraft ideas therefore illustrate is the general social disadvantage of women both in Assyria and in Mesopotamia as a whole. Their social role was more strictly defined than that of men, and therefore any unusual behaviour, or any traits or actions which prevented them from fulfilling their women's functions, could have made them suspect. The Mesopotamian anti-witchcraft literature highlights a wide range of female occupations and life styles which must have been common in the society, but which nevertheless deviated from the norm and were therefore regarded with suspicion. When women not only behaved in an unusual fashion but also belonged to marginal social categories, they must have been viewed as particularly prone to practising witchcraft and sorcery.

An incantation in *Maqlû* which lists various types of sorceress includes the *qadištu*, *nadītu*, *ištarītu* and *kulmašītu*, all of whom were in some way connected with the cult. The date of the compilation of this incantation is unknown, so it is not apparent which historical period its contents reflect, and the role of these women and ideas concerning them may have changed over the course of time. The *nadītu*, *ištarītu* and *kulmašītu* are only attested in Babylonian texts, whereas the *qadištu* occurs in fragmentary context in one of the Middle Assyrian harem edicts from the reign of Assur-uballit I (1365-1330 BC) (Weidner, 1954-6, p. 228). The status of these women is in any case unclear, but there are suggestions in the texts which may explain, at least in part, why they could be regarded as potential witches. One of the obvious aspects of the *nadītu* of the Old Babylonian period which was contrary to the normal role of women and which therefore may have made her suspect was the fact that she did not bear children, and usually, though not always, remained unmarried, often spending most of her life in a type of temple cloister (Harris, 1964). The *qadištu*, *ištarītu* and *kulmašītu* could have children, but nevertheless the *ištarītu* and *kulmašītu* at least were apparently regarded as far from ideal wives. A collection of moral exhortations has the following to say about them:

> Do not marry a prostitute whose husbands are legion,
> An *ištarītu* who is dedicated to a god,
> A *kulmašītu* whose favours are many.
> In your trouble she will not support you,
> In your dispute she will be a mocker,
> There is no reverence or submissiveness with her.
> Even if she dominate your house, get her out,
> For she has directed her attention elsewhere.

> (Lambert, 1960, pp. 102-3)

A *qadištu* could be a wet nurse, although not necessarily married, and her behaviour may therefore also have been contrary to that which was generally acceptable (Renger, 1967, pp. 181-2).

At least one incantation in *Maqlû* appears to be describing a prostitute and her activities, and it is not difficult to imagine why her behaviour should have been considered deviant, and why she should therefore have been regarded with suspicion and mistrust. Other incantations may be describing beggarwomen. Beggars do not belong to the closely knit community, and are therefore generally suspect, and owe much of their income to fear and suspicion. Many foreign women in Mesopotamia may have been beggarwomen, prostitutes or had other low status positions, perhaps having arrived there originally as a result of military campaigns and expeditions.

The fourth category of witches are also internal enemies, who may be described as belonging to a rival faction of the sufferer. There are just two incantations in *Maqlû* which include various terms for adversary and adversary in court in a list of people likely to have practised sorcery. Several other texts also link witchcraft with adversaries. Such witches, however, do not figure prominently in the Mesopotamian anti-witchcraft literature, and it is probable that this category belongs less to the stereotyped view of the witch than to the field of hostility as it must have existed between full members of the community in reality. The concept of right and wrong when dealing with two opposing factions always depends very much, of course, on what faction one belongs to or supports. Several incantations against adversaries or adversaries in court suggest very similar procedures to those presumed to have been used by witches in order to incapacitate or triumph over one's opponent, and such actions could well have been interpreted by the opposing side as witchcraft. It is interesting that in these texts the adversaries are conceived of as predominantly male.

Finally, other people who had a close relationship with the victim of supposed witchcraft could also be viewed as witches, and such people can be described as representing the antithesis of the good kinsman or neighbour. There are few references to such witches, although that does not mean that friction in close relationships did not exist in reality and that witchcraft ideas and accusations were not involved on such occasions. The function of Mesopotamian anti-witchcraft literature in general, however, was not the specific illustration of such tensions between colleagues and members of the family.

The extant rituals referring to witchcraft may be divided into those which were apotropaic in character and those which were designed to combat the effects of harm which had already occurred. Considering first the former, anthropological studies have shown that it is sometimes the duty of persons in authority to rid the country of witches and to protect the community against their attack (Mair, 1969, p. 58). The performance of *Maqlû* as a royal ceremony in the Neo-Assyrian period is a case which illustrates this principle. Protection against witches in general may also be regarded as one of the underlying themes of the *bīt rimki* ritual which, as already mentioned, contained many incantations to ward off witchcraft and sorcery. As far as the individual was concerned, an apotropaic ritual designed to protect a pregnant woman from sorcery suggests that pregnant women in Mesopotamia, as in many other cultures, were thought to be particularly susceptible to witchcraft (Reiner, 1966, p. 93). A prototype of an amulet from the city of Assur is inscribed with an incantation against witchcraft and evil, and such amulets and other charms, not necessarily inscribed, were perhaps worn for protection by many people (Schroeder, 1917).

Most rituals and incantations, however, appear to be designed for use in cases where a person believed himself to have been already bewitched, and wished to dispel the witchcraft and its effects. It is not clear exactly when and how a particular illness or misfortune was attributed to witchcraft as opposed to any other agent, but the texts provide certain ideas relating to this question. Harm thought to be caused by witches ranged from insomnia to death, but certain maladies and misfortunes were especially characteristic. In many incantations they take the form of stereotyped lists, one of which seems to be describing mental disorders and speech problems, which may be seen as an inversion or degeneration of the normal faculties. A second list of ills ascribed to witchcraft can be put under the general heading of weakness and paralysis. The personal god of a witchcraft victim deserted him, he was subject to the anger of gods and kings, people in general were hostile to him and he was surrounded by evil signs and portents.

Divinatory techniques for the detection of witches in the Neo-Assyrian period are not attested, although there are a few earlier omen texts which diagnose sorcery. Sometimes the *āšipu*, when called upon to diagnose an illness, may have attributed it to witchcraft. The diagnosis would doubtless be followed by the required procedure to cure the victim. There are many so-called medical prescriptions for combating the effects of witchcraft, but there is no indication of how a particular one was selected for a particular victim. Several rituals for individual sufferers aimed at dispelling an evil caused by sorcery are also known (see e.g. Caplice, 1970, no. 40, pp. 134-40). One of these is apparently concerned with sorcery caused by unknown agents, and is the ritual referred to in the letter to king Esarhaddon previously mentioned, showing that it was in current use in the Neo-Assyrian period. The incantation and ritual known to have been used for King Šamaš-šumu-ukin also appear to have been intended to combat the harm caused by witches in general rather than by specific persons. Another ritual, however, may be to dispel the evil of known witches, as it necessitates the writing of the names of the sorcerer and sorceress on the left hips of figurines. Interestingly, this ritual is concerned with the victim's adversaries, suggesting an area where specific witchcraft accusations or at least the attribution of suffering to particular people may have been made. Special procedures and materials were needed for the performance of these and other rituals concerned with dispelling witchcraft, including *Maqlû*.

Several forms of attack were imputed to witches. A common one was to acquire certain types of material, which were part of or closely connected with the person they wished to afflict, for use in sorcery. Such material included spittle, hair, nail parings, dirty washwater, a garment fringe and dust from where the victim's feet had trodden. This may be classed as dangerous, marginal material, following the analysis of Mary Douglas in her discussion of pollution and taboo (Douglas, 1966).

Another common form of attack ascribed to witches was to make figurines of their victim and use them in various ways which caused him to suffer. Witches were believed to bury these figurines in various places, obviously with a particular significance, which is sometimes, but not always, clear. They could be put together with a corpse and buried with it in a grave, enclosed in a wall or buried in a dark house. The fear of death and darkness is evident. They could be immured in a drain through the wall or buried in the reed mats of the fuller, both situations where they would be covered with dirty, polluting water. Several places suggest areas where they would be constantly trodden upon, including a threshold, the entrance to the city gate, river banks, a causeway and a crossroads. Figurines were also burnt in various places. Making figurines and burning them was one of the most common forms of defence against witches, and *Maqlû, bit rimki* and other rituals also prescribe washing hands over the figurines.

Witches were also thought to tie magic knots which made their victims suffer, and the same idea occurs in the Koran, where this evil activity is attributed to women (Koran, cxiii). The *Maqlû* ritual prescribes the burning of knots to release the magic. They could also bewitch food and water and thereby cause illness. Many forms of attack, however, involved less the use of material substances than the ability to harm with evil words or thoughts. The power of words is, of course, a central concept in ritual, and the anti-witchcraft incantations were an essential part of the defence against witches. Evil curses and incantations, pointing of fingers at and spitting at a victim were all common methods of bewitching and causing harm. Some witches were thought to cast the Evil Eye, and references to the Evil Eye also occur outside the anti-witchcraft literature. It is undoubtedly of the same order of phenomena as witchcraft and seems to be an institutional recognition of envy (Maloney, 1976; Spooner, 1970).

The Mesopotamian texts only provide the barest suggestion concerning the direction of suspicion and accusation in particular witchcraft cases. Anthropological studies have shown that witchcraft accusations are indices of social tension, and by studying the relative frequency of accusations in various social relationships it is possible to show where some of the tensions and conflicts in a particular society lie (see e.g. Marwick, 1970, p. 17; Mair, 1969). Individual accusations must have existed in Mesopotamia, because they are provided for in both the Babylonian and Assyrian law codes, but there is no clue as to their frequency or the relationships of the accusers to the supposed witches. The available information does suggest, however, that those accused were full members of the society, rather than outsiders or on the periphery. In the Middle Assyrian laws either an *awilum* or a *sinništum* was envisaged as practising sorcery.[1] These are the Akkadian words for a man and a woman of normal status within society. Interestingly, this clause is included in a tablet predominantly concerned with women, reflecting perhaps the idea that women practised sorcery more than

men, rather than the frequency of actual direct accusations. The Old
Babylonian laws of King Hammurapi (1792-1750 BC) provide for the
case of an *awīlum* accusing another *awīlum* of sorcery.[2] No other laws
mention witchcraft specifically, but there are references to cursing
which may be connected with it, and here the emphasis is strongly on
women as the offenders. The laws of King Ur-Nammu (2112-2095 BC),
for example, allow for the case where a slavewoman has presumed herself the equal of her mistress and sworn at her (Finkelstein, 1969, no.
22). A presumably common situation of domestic conflict is self-
evident. Two of the Middle Assyrian harem edicts are concerned with
the cursing of palace women, which was obviously stringently forbidden, perhaps because of its supposed undesirable consequences. It is
worth noting that as neither slave women nor harem women were main
wives, a certain amount of envy of the main wife and discord among
the secondary wives vying with each other for position and prestige
would be expected.

No legal documents are known from either Assyria or Babylonia
showing actual cases of direct witchcraft accusations, but there are two
Old Babylonian letters which are illuminating in this respect (Walters,
1970). Although the information contained in these letters has no
direct relevance to Assyria, situations of a similar nature, which are not
preserved to us, may have occurred also in the Neo-Assyrian period.
The letters deal with a court case between father and son concerning
the alleged misuse of a quantity of barley and a field belonging to the
father. Although sorcery is not the direct charge put before the court,
indirect accusations are made on both sides. The father suspects his
daughter-in-law and her mother of witchcraft and the son also accuses
his father of having a 'sorceress', whose identity cannot be ascertained.
The anthropological literature indicates that accusations and suspicion
of witchcraft are common among affines, as in this case, which may be
illustrative of an area of tension in Old Babylonian society, which had a
patrilineal descent system, and where the wife was presumably generally
brought in to join her husband's household from an outside group.
Such a wife could be suspected of having divided loyalties, a concept
which might help to explain why witches in patrilineal societies are so
often women (Mayer, 1954, p. 62). The women in this case seem to
have been scapegoats in the hostility between father and son.

One of the most important points arising from this case is that
although sorcery was suspected, no direct accusation was made. Whether
this reflects a common occurrence it is impossible from a single example
to say, but the lack of evidence for witchcraft cases might suggest that

actual accusations were infrequent. To accuse a witch in public was certainly dangerous in the Old Babylonian period. If the charge could not be proved the accused man had to undergo the river ordeal. If the ordeal showed him to be innocent, the case turned against the accuser, who was himself put to death and had to forfeit his estate to the innocent man. Sorcery was also a capital offence in the Middle Assyrian laws. Suspicion of witchcraft in Mesopotamia may therefore have taken more the form of slandering and backbiting, and certain hatreds, anxieties and social tensions may often have been expressed in this manner. Gossip and slander nevertheless incurred social disapproval in Mesopotamia, and could in themselves cause harm. Heavy punishments for cursing were laid down in the Middle Assyrian harem edicts. The penalty for the slave woman who swore at her mistress in the Ur-Nammu law code was to have her mouth scoured out with salt. Salt was known to displace the Evil Tongue in Mesopotamia, and is generally regarded as inimical to the Evil Eye in the Middle East today.

Due to the nature of the sources, this analysis has necessarily been concerned in the main with Mesopotamian witchcraft in general, rather than with witchcraft in the Neo-Assyrian period in particular. However, it has been shown that much of the anti-witchcraft literature was used in Neo-Assyrian rituals, and the assumption is therefore made that the general ideas and concepts contained in the texts were current in the Neo-Assyrian period. The symbolism of witchcraft beliefs shows a concern to protect the norms and values of Mesopotamian civilisation against forms of deviance and anomaly which were regarded as an attack on those norms. Women hold a particularly prominent place in the witchcraft myth, a fact which can only be fully explained by reference to the position of women within the society itself. This has not yet been adequately analysed, but women generally were clearly at a disadvantage in the sense that their social and political options were fewer than those of men. This combined with the fact that after marriage they presumably entered their husband's household, where they were outsiders and therefore easily suspect, accounts in general terms for their position in the witchcraft beliefs. Therefore, although both men and women, particularly those in peripheral social groups, could be suspected of witchcraft, women could be said to hold a doubly anomalous position.

Notes

1. Middle Assyrian Laws Tablet A § 47 (ANET, p. 184)
2. Laws of Hammurapi § 2 (ANET, p. 166)

PART TWO: WOMEN AND POWER

Limitations on women's access to power in ancient societies

4 INFLUENTIAL WOMEN

Mary R. Lefkowitz, Wellesley, Mass.

When Greek colonists set up new cities in the then unknown frontier of Italy, they were quick to compose myths that connected them to their ancestors, and that gave their customs and their shrines legitimacy. So I suppose it is no surprise that people who initiate new styles of government or patterns of living — political colonists, we might call them — also seek precedents in the prestigious civilisations of the past. Proponents of slavery in the United States discovered Greek and Roman writings that supported their views; so, of course, did the Abolitionists.[1] Karl Marx found that the notion of free (rather than enforced) sale of labour first occurred in the Roman army.[2] Most recently, and in some ways most absurdly, feminists have come up with supposed evidence for matriarchal societies, such as the Amazons, and have called attention to extraordinary achievements of a few women, as if they set a pattern that twentieth-century women could emulate and revive, and finally bring into full realisation.[3]

But as Simon Pembroke has shown, there is no evidence whatever for the existence of matriarchal societies in the ancient world, and the myths about Amazon societies that have come down to us were originally designed only to indicate how bad things could be when women got the upper hand.[4] Similarly, at first sight, the ancient world may seem to offer some encouraging examples of women who played important roles in political life. When I observe that women neither had nor sought political power, but worked through their husbands or fathers or sons, people often object: what about Antigone or Clytemnestra or Artemisia or Agrippina? But I believe that it is possible to show in all these cases, as well as in many others, that women take political action only under certain closely defined conditions, and that unless they do so at least ostensibly on behalf of a male relative, they and others around them come to a bad end. I will begin by talking about women in myth, as represented in specific works of literature, because myths illustrate common attitudes more clearly and simply than history; but history too can be shown to follow the patterns of myth, in part because those were the only terms in which most writers could interpret human experience, and in part because ancient societies

49

for practical reasons offered women little opportunity to act as individuals outside the context of their families.

Ancient women could certainly be courageous, but they could not be truly independent. Antigone herself is an example. In Sophocles' drama, she contrives to bury her brother in defiance of an order by her uncle Creon, the king of Thebes, that her brother Polynices, who had attacked his homeland, should remain unburied. Denial of burial was a traditional penalty for treason;[5] but Antigone has the moral sensibility to see that Creon's order runs counter to another established custom, the obligation of the family or *genos* to bury and to worship the remains of their deceased members.[6]

Recently feminist critics have suggested that Antigone, in taking action against her sister's advice and Creon's edict, assumes an essentially masculine role;[7] that in defending her blood relationship to Polynices, she 'must undercut the form and potential of the family';[8] that Antigone has adopted the aggressive stance of an Orestes, 'a younger son revenging or redeeming the death of an unburied brother'.[9] In the process of interpretation these critics assume that Creon, or the city elders in the chorus, represent not themselves but the state, a government supported and accepted by the majority of Theban citizens, whose laws and customs Antigone is threatening;[10] therefore, the drama *Antigone* calls into question the traditional structure of society.

But I do not believe that Sophocles or his audience would have seen Antigone's action as unconventional, or have recognised in the play an attempt to define or promote new family structures or modes of behaviour. In the first place, it is not established custom that Antigone opposes, but the orders of one particular individual, Creon; Creon himself may equate his own opinions with the city's (e.g., 736), but the outcome of the drama makes it clear that he is mistaken. The analogy of Antigone to Orestes is misleading, because Antigone is not trying to avenge or redeem her brother's death, but is seeking only to bury him with appropriate rites for the dead. The difference may seem trivial to us, but to the Greeks it was (and in remote villages still is) essential; men avenge murders of kin, women prepare bodies for burial and sing laments over the body.[11]

If Sophocles from time to time in the play states explicitly that Antigone and her sister Ismene are women, it is to emphasise to his audience that Creon's edict violates established custom, and that by demanding obedience to it he is misusing his power as a ruler, that is, he is behaving like a tyrant.[12] 'Consider', says Ismene to Antigone at the beginning of the drama, 'that we two are left alone [i.e., without father or brothers to protect them], and how cruelly we will perish, if we oppose the edict of the king [*tyrannon*] or his power. You must remember that the two of us are born women and as such do not fight with men; since we are in the power of those who are stronger, we must obey these orders, and orders even more painful than these' (61-4).[13] When he has Creon complain that he would be weaker than a woman if he allowed her to get away with disobeying his order (525, 579), or insist that 'she and her sister must now be women and not allowed outside the house' (579), Sophocles is not describing normal male-female relations; he is portraying a man desperately trying to justify a decision that only he in the whole city (690ff.) considers to be correct.

In fact, far from being unconventional or independent, Antigone is only doing what her family might have expected of her, as she herself says: 'but I have great hope that when I come [to the lower world] I shall come welcome to my father, and welcome to you, mother, and welcome to you, dear brother, since when each of you died I washed and dressed you and poured libations on your tombs' (897-902). In the fifth and fourth centuries (that is, in Sophocles' lifetime and for a century afterwards), it was common belief that families were reunited in death.[14] Special care was taken to bury family members in the same plot, even if bones had to be exhumed from other localities and re-buried. I do not think an ancient audience would have considered it unusual or excessive when Sophocles' Electra laments over what she supposes to be the urn that holds her brother's ashes: 'so now you receive me into this house of yours, I who am nothing to your nothing, so that for the rest of time I can live with you below; for when we were above ground I shared the same things with you, and now I wish to die and not be left outside your tomb' (*El.*, 1165-69). When Antigone is captured, even Ismene asks to die with her and to give the rites to their dead brother (544-5). The guard who catches Antigone says that when she saw the corpse of Polynices unburied, 'she wailed out the sharp cry of an anguished bird, as when in its empty nest it sees its bed stripped of its nestlings' (424-5). To us Antigone's or Electra's failure to distinguish between living and dead may seem strange; but to Antigone the important link was not life but blood-kinship: 'my life died long ago, so that I might serve my dead [family]' (559-60). Antigone says explicitly that she would not have risked her life for a husband, or if she had had children of her own; but without any other family, her first duty was to her brother — whether dead or alive does not seem to matter.[15] Nor does Ismene count as a reason for her to stay alive, because she is female, and so not able to inherit or continue the family line. When

Antigone replies to Creon's accusations that she could disobey his edict, but not the 'unwritten customs' (*agrapta nomima*) of the gods, she is simply claiming that family loyalty must take precedent over rulings that have not existed since time immemorial; she is not questioning Creon's right to power or the structure of government, but his own intelligence and judgment: 'if I had put up with [?] my mother's son having died an unburied corpse, that would have caused me pain; but I am not pained by what I have done. If I seem to you to have acted foolishly, then I have been accused of folly by a fool' (466-70).

To put it another way, Antigone must be female for the dramatic action to occur in the first place, because only a mother or sister would have felt so strongly the obligation to bury the dead.[16] As Ismene suggests, it would have been possible for her instead to ask the gods of the lower world for forgiveness, if she had failed to bury her brother, on the grounds that she was forcibly prevented by the rulers of Thebes (66-7). It would also have been possible for her to have tried first to work through a man, like Haemon; as Aethra persuaded her son Theseus to allow the mothers of the Argive heroes who fell at Thebes to bury their sons, 'it's natural for women, if they are clever, to do everything through men' (Eur., *Suppl.* 40-41). We might choose to call her courageous or generous, but the chorus state that she is foolish: 'unhappy child of an unhappy father Oedipus; what has happened? It isn't true that they have caught you in folly and bring you in disobedient to the king's laws?' (379-82). They regard her, as she does herself, as a victim of the family curse that destroyed her parents and her brother: 'your respect [for your brother] is one kind of right respect, but one also ought not to transgress in any way the power of him to whom power belongs. Your self-willed anger has destroyed you' (872-5). This anger and folly (*aphrosyne*, 'un-thinking') are aspects of the family curse, and the action of the curse, far from being disapproved of by the gods, is part of their system: 'evil seems good to the person whose mind the god is leading toward delusion' (622-3).

I would not have been able to see several years ago, and in a way regret that I must now admit, that Sophocles' audience would have seen Antigone's action as courageous, laudable, but risky (she does end up dead, after all), and certainly within the bounds of acceptable female behaviour. Antigone's conduct does not set a new revolutionary standard any more than it can be said to serve as a prototype of female Christian martyrdom — an interpretation that profoundly impressed the composer Mendelssohn, even though he knew Greek.[17] Like other women in epic and drama, Antigone wins praise for acting on behalf of her family: Penelope deceives the suitors (and so holds out for her husband Odysseus) for three years before she is discovered unravelling her weaving at night; Andromache defies Hermione and Menelaus in order to protect her young son; Iphigenia tricks the wicked king in order to save her brother Orestes; Helen tells lies to rescue Menelaus. It is important to note that in all these cases the women offer only passive resistance. Apparently acts of treachery are acceptable in a woman only if they are non-violent and are undertaken on behalf of a male relative.

But a woman is not permitted, even with justification, to take the law into her own hands.[18] After the fall of Troy, when all the Trojan men are dead, Hecabe herself avenges the murder of her youngest son Polydorus. He had been sent to Polymestor in Thrace for safekeeping, but Hecabe discovers that Polymestor has murdered him, and when Polymestor arrives in Troy with his young sons in the hope of collecting more money, Hecabe and her servant women use their brooches to put out Polymestor's eyes and to stab his sons to death. Polymestor asks Agamemnon to punish Hecabe, but Agamemnon lets her get away with her revenge. 'Alas,' Polymestor complains, 'it seems that I have been defeated by a woman and a slave, and suffer vengeance from my inferiors' (Euripides, *Hecabe*, 1252-3). But Hecabe's triumph is short-lived: Polymestor predicts that Hecabe will throw herself from the ship that takes her from Troy and be turned into a dog, and that her grave will be known as the 'poor dog's tomb', a landmark for sailors (1273). Her death, in other words, will be sordid (the Greeks did not like dogs), and more significantly, anonymous. On the other hand, for Penelope, who could leave the execution of the suitors to her husband and son, 'for her the fame of her virtue [*arete*] will never perish; the immortals will fashion a lovely song for mortal men about good Penelope; she did not devise evil deeds, like Tyndareus' daughter [Clytemnestra], killing her wedded husband; but for Clytemnestra there will be a hateful song among men, and she will give women a bad reputation, even to the woman who does good deeds' (*Od.* 24, 196-202).

It may seem unfair that the speaker of these lines, the dead Agamemnon, believes that no woman can be trusted after what Clytemnestra did. Polymestor, too, after he has described to Agamemnon how the Trojan women stabbed his children and put his own eyes out, concludes by condemning women in general: 'neither sea nor land sustains a race like them' (1181-2), in other words, they are monsters (cf. Aeschylus, *Choephoroe*, 585ff.). Semonides of Amorgos, in his satire on women (fr. 7 West), identifies nine types of bad women, but only one good type. Perhaps the low proportion of good women could be taken as evidence of enduring misogyny on the part of (male) Greek poets; but it is important to remember that these statements about bad women all occur in the context of invective, and so are likely to be exaggerated. Compare how an angry woman who feels she has been wronged, like Medea in Euripides' drama, contrasts the unfortunate lot of (all) women with the enviable life led — without exception — by men (230ff).

I think that it is also possible to argue that the limitations that apply to women in epic and in drama apply as well to the 'political' women in Aristophanes' comedies. Lysistrata in particular is often cited as the first liberated woman; but consider what she actually accomplishes. In order to bring about peace, she summons all Greek women to a meeting (they of course arrive late), and gets them to swear not to have sexual intercourse with their husbands until the men agree to end the war between Athens and Sparta. Her plan works, and then her organisation of women disbands and the women go back to their husbands. So even in the fantasy world of comedy, women only take action to preserve and to return to their families. Women have intelligence and understanding, but speak out only in emergencies, and even then their models are men. Lysistrata says, as she concludes the peace, ' "although I am a woman, I have intelligence" [quoting from a lost play of Euripides] ;[19] for my own part, I do not have bad judgment. I have listened to many speeches by my father and older men and so am not badly educated' (*Lysistrata*, 1125-7). When in the *Thesmophoriazusae* the women meet to attack Euripides, their proceedings are a burlesque of the Athenian men's assembly. Aristophanes realises that his audience would find the very notion of women meeting together, making speeches and voting, hilariously funny.[20]

In the comedy *Ecclesiazusae* (or 'Women Meeting in the Assembly') women in male disguise manage to infiltrate the assembly and vote to let women run the city, on the grounds that 'we [the assembly] ought to turn the city over to women, for we use them also as guardians and stewards in our households' (210-12). The infiltrated assembly passes two new laws: (1) that all possessions (including wives and children) shall be held in common; (2) that the ugliest and oldest women will have first chance at getting men. The first law is a parody of what Athenians understood to be the constitution of Sparta; after Athens lost the war to Sparta, the Spartan system of government appeared to have special merit. In 392, when the *Ecclesiazusae* was performed, Aristophanes could still make fun of the notion that women might have equal rights with men. A generation later Plato realised that people might still ridicule the idea that women should be educated (*Resp.*, 452b), but nonetheless he incorporated into the model government of his *Republic* equal education for men and women and common marriages and children, so that women might be able to be companions of men and co-guardians of his ideal state (456b). But even in his utopia Plato included the proviso that women, because their natures were weaker, should be assigned lighter duties in wartime (he doesn't specify what they would be).

Of course such socialistic theories, however much they were debated in intellectual circles, were never practised, at least in Athens.[21] In fact, Aristotle claimed that the liberty permitted to Spartan women in the days of Sparta's great military successes had by the middle of the fourth century led directly to her defeat by the Thebans. Women, he observed, had not been subject to the same restrictions as men under the Spartan constitution, and so lived intemperate and luxurious lives, while the men remained in military training. As a result, the Spartan women at the time of the Theban invasion of 369 were 'utterly useless and caused more confusion than the enemy' (*Politics*, 1269b5). 'The disorder of women,' he observed, 'not only of itself gives an air of indecorum to the state, but tends to foster avarice' (1207a9). In his view, one particularly unfortunate consequence was that two-fifths of Sparta was owned by women (1270a10-11), who unlike their Athenian counterparts could inherit and bequeath property.[22]

Here, as in his theories of human physiology, Aristotle appears to regard as normative what was acceptable in Athenian life and to consider all other practices deviations. But he and not Plato had the last word. If Greek women – in history or in literature – ever had an opportunity to govern, it was only for a brief period, in order to cope with a particular problem or emergency, or in the case of monarchies and tyrannies, if they happened (like Artemisia or Cynna) to be related to the man in charge.[23]

I will now consider briefly the role played by women in history, as opposed to women in literature, to the extent that the two can be separated. References to women by biographers and historians tend to be anecdotal, and so not necessarily pinned down to particular times or events; rather, they are illustrative of character in general and timeless ways. For example, Cornelia is praised by several ancient writers for having educated her sons the Gracchi, but how and when and what she taught them is not specified.[24] But whatever the source of the information, the same rules seem to apply in history as well as in myth: women can affect the course of political events only if they act through or on behalf of the men in their families. They can take independent action, like Lysistrata, in an emergency, but then must retire when the problem is solved. The earliest instance of such an event in history is recorded by Plutarch in his treatise on the bravery of women. Early in the fifth century, according to Plutarch, Telesilla of Argos, an aristocrat who because of her weak constitution had been encouraged to compose poetry,[25] when the Argive army had suffered a severe setback, organised the women of Argos to arm themselves and successfully defend their city's fortifications against the Spartans (*Mor.*, 245c-f). But as soon as the crisis was over the women resumed their conventional roles; according to Herodotus (who doesn't mention Telesilla) the Argive women were married to slaves (6.83.1), or as Plutarch insists, because they deserved better, to the aristocratic citizens of the neighbouring cities.[26]

Plutarch also preserves another dramatic instance of a woman's political effectiveness in a crisis, this time as he says, from a period much closer to his own time, the first century BC.[27] Aretaphila of Cyrene was compelled to marry the tyrant who had murdered her husband; first she tried to poison him, then survived torture when her plot failed, and finally succeeded in getting rid of her tyrant husband by marrying her daughter to his brother and persuading him to murder his brother, and then contrived to have the ruler of a neighbouring state capture her son-in-law and turn him and his mother over to the citizens of Cyrene to be murdered. The people of Cyrene treated her like a hero, and asked her to share in the government and management of the city with the aristocrats, but she 'as if she had played in a sort of drama or competed in a contest up to the point of winning the prize' returned home to the women's quarters and spent the rest of her life working at her loom in the company of her family (*Mor.*, 257d-e).

Even if the original story of Aretaphila has been embellished by Plutarch or his sources to the point where it conforms with the standard pattern of women's behaviour in myth, it does indicate how implausible it seemed even in the Hellenistic age that women should share in the actual process of government (*synarchein, syndioikein*, 257d). It seems clear from papyri and inscriptions — the most authentic contemporary evidence preserved about the role of women in public life — that even when women were legally entitled to own property and to make wills, they were welcomed as benefactors of cities and given honorific titles, but never a real place on the town council or an actual vote in the assembly. The traditional female virtues were listed along with their benefactions, and even though their own names are now conspicuously mentioned (unlike proper aristocratic women in the fifth and fourth centuries, who remained incognito),[28] due credit was always given to the *men* in their families: 'Phile, daughter of Apollonius, wife of Thessalus son of Polydeuces; as the first woman *stephanephorus*, she dedicated at her own expense a receptacle for water and the water pipes in the city [Priene]' (Pleket 5, 1st cent. BC); 'the council and the people, to Flavia Publicia Nicomachis, daughter of Dinomachis and Procle ... their benefactor, and benefactor through her ancestors, founder of our city, president for life, in recognition of her complete virtue' (Pleket 19, Asia Minor, 2nd cent. AD); Aurelia Leite, 'daughter of Theodotus, wife of the foremost man in the city, Marcus Aurelius Faustus ... she was gymnasiarch of the gymnasium which she repaired and renewed when it had been dilapidated for many years ... She loved wisdom, her husband, her children, her native city [Paros]' (Pleket 31, AD 300).[29] (See further Van Bremen, this volume).

Philosophical theory, as so often, was based on and reinforced social practice. Aristotle believed that women were capable of virtue and of understanding, though he could not accept what Plato proposed, that self-control, courage and justice were the same for women and for men. Aristotle stated that 'man's courage is shown in commanding [or ruling, *archein*] and women's in obeying' (*Pol.*, 1260a8). A treatise on women written in the third or second century BC by Neopythagorean philosophers in Italy, in the form of a letter from one woman to another, also assumes that women's capacity to govern was considerably less than a man's: 'some people think that it is not appropriate for a woman to be a philosopher, just as a woman should not be a cavalry officer or a politician ... I agree that men should be generals and city officials and politicians, and women should keep house and stay inside and receive and take care of their husbands. But I believe that courage, justice and intelligence are qualities that men and women have in common ... Courage and intelligence are more appropriately male qualities because of the strength of men's bodies and the power of their minds. Chastity is more appropriately female.'[30]

The apparent exceptions only prove the rule that women could not be accepted as governors unless they acted in conjunction with a man. Hellenistic queens have been regarded as the first examples of truly independent women. They organised court intrigues (including murders); they directed strategy of naval and land battles; they made decisions affecting governmental policy. But it is important to remember that even the most capable of these women worked through or at least with the titular presence of a male consort.[31] Arsinoe, queen of Egypt from 274-70, enjoyed power as the consort of her brother; Berenice, wife and cousin of Arsinoe's adopted son Ptolemy III Euergetes, was praised by Callimachus for the courage she showed as a young girl, which won her her husband.[32] The unwritten law appears to be that the co-ruling (*synarchein*) and co-management (*syndioikein*) unthinkable for Aretaphila in conjunction with unrelated males (above, p. 56), is available to women with husbands, fathers or brothers. Cleopatra VII came to the throne with her brother. Then she enlisted the aid first of Julius Caesar, who became at least for a short time her consort, to remain on the throne by defeating her brother and installing a younger brother as co-ruler. Then she used Mark Antony to stay in power, though even when she sat with Antony on twin thrones she was addressed as 'co-ruler with Caesarion', her son (allegedly) by Caesar (Plut., *Ant.* 54).[33] For ordinary women also civil law ensured that men had at least nominal control. Women in the Hellenistic age could draw up contracts and make wills, but only with the consent of a male guardian or *kyrios*, usually a close relative.[34]

Upper-class Romans in Cicero's day could claim that their wives enjoyed greater social freedom than (certainly) women in Greek cities (Nepos, *Praef.*, 6); the aristocratic Aretaphila of (Greek) Cyrene returned to the women's quarters and saw only other women and members of her family. Inscriptions and letters explain how women assisted the men in their families in their political careers. A husband records in a long eulogy of his wife (neither of their names is preserved) how she managed to have him brought back from exile in 43BC: 'you lay prostrate at the feet [of the triumvir Lepidus] and you were not only not raised up, but were dragged along and carried off brutally like a slave. But although your body was full of bruises, your spirit was unbroken and you kept reminding him of [Augustus] Caesar's edict with its expression of pleasure at my reinstatement, and although you had to listen to insulting words and suffer cruel wounds, you pronounced the words of the edict in a loud voice, so that it should be known who was the cause of my deadly perils' — the husband even claims that his wife's accusations helped contribute to Lepidus' downfall.[35] The proscriptions of the triumvirs apparently elicited similarly heroic behaviour on the part of other aristocrats' wives: Acilius' wife (like a proper Athenian woman, her own name is not given) bribed soldiers with her jewellery not to turn her husband over to be executed; Lentulus' wife donned male disguise in order to join her husband in exile;[36] Reginus' wife hid her husband in a sewer; Coponius' wife slept with Antony in order to purchase her husband's safety, 'thus curing one evil with another', as the historian Appian remarks (*Bel. Civ.* 4.39-40).

Brutus, the murderer of Caesar, appears to have been aided at every step in his career by his mother Servilia.[37] Certainly one reason that Caesar pardoned Brutus after he had fought against him in 48 was that Servilia had been his mistress. After the conspiracy that led to Caesar's death, she received and transmitted messages for her son (*ad Att.* 416.4). Cicero in a letter describes how she took charge of a family conference at Antium at which she contrived to silence even Cicero with the comment that she had 'never heard anything like' what he was proposing; she herself proposed to have legislation changed on her son's behalf, and apparently was successful (389.2). But for all her initiative, Cicero himself clearly thinks of her as her son's agent, rather than as an independent operator. He remarks to his friend Atticus (whom he teased about having Servilia as a 'pal,' *familiaris*, 389.2): 'it's just like you not to fault Servilia, which is to say, Brutus' (394).

Women in Pompeii joined with men in supporting candidates for local political offices, as graffiti on painted walls reveal: 'Amadio along with his wife asks you to vote for Gnaeus Sabinus for aedile' (*CIL* iv. 913). Some of the men and women appear to have been co-workers in shops: 'Appuleia and Narcissus along with their neighbour Mustius, ask you to vote for Pupius' (*ILS*, 6408a). One woman, Statia, asks on her own for support of her candidate (*CIL* iv. 3684) — she of course couldn't vote for him herself.

But generally women who spoke out on their own behalf, rather than that of a close male relative, were criticised for being selfish, licentious and avaricious. The speech attributed by Livy to the formidable moralist Cato the Elder provides an example of the kind of thing that was said about ambitious women; the issue is whether to repeal the Oppian law limiting women's rights to own property (195 BC): 'our ancestors did not want women to conduct any — not even private — business without a guardian; they wanted them to be under the authority of parents, brothers or husbands; we (the Gods help us!) even now let them snatch at the government and meddle in the Forum and our assemblies... Give rein to their unbridled natures and these unmastered creatures, and hope that they will put limits on their own freedom! They want freedom, nay licence (if we are to speak the truth) in all things ... If they are victorious now, what will they not attempt? As soon as they begin to be your equals, they will have become your superiors ...' (xxxiv, 2.11-3.2). Of Sempronia, who supported the conspiracy of Catiline (who was not a relative of hers), it was said, 'there was nothing she set a smaller value on than seemliness and chastity, and she was as careless of her reputation as she was of her money' (Sallust, *Catiline*, 24-5).[38] We are told that one could use the name of Gaia Afrania (a contemporary of Caesar's) who brought lawsuits herself, without using (male) lawyers, to designate *any* woman with low morals (Val. Max. 8.3).

In popular belief, not only was self-assertion on a woman's part regarded as self-indulgence and licentiousness; crowds of women were considered a public menace. Livy has Cato complain of the women seeking repeal of the Oppian law 'running around in public, blocking streets, and speaking to other women's husbands'. In practice, women were permitted to organise themselves into formal groups only for some social or religious purpose, rather on the lines of a modern ladies' auxiliary; for example, in the third century BC the matrons 'purely and chastely' dedicated a golden bowl to Juno out of contributions from their dowries (Livy, xxvii. 37. 8-9).[39] Inscriptions from the Empire record grants of money donated to women's organisations for public services; and women apparently could meet to set rules of social conduct and to discipline one another (Suetonius, *Galba* 5. 1; *Historia Augusta, Life of Elagabalus*, 4. 3-4).

On the other hand, Hortensia, herself daughter of a famous orator, was praised for pleading in 42 BC to the triumvirs that rich women be relieved of a special tax: 'Quintus Hortensius lived again in the female line and breathed in his daughter's words' (Val. Max. 8.3). Her speech — unlike that of any other woman — was said to have been preserved verbatim, probably because what she said would have won male approval. In the one version of the speech that has come down to us, she claims that women had never supported despotic governments in the past; she recalls to the triumvirs what women have done to serve the state, and also reminds them that in the present crisis the women have lost fathers, husbands and sons. Significantly she does not dwell on issues like taxation without representation or women's rights, or the pleasures and luxuries that their money might buy (Appian, *Bellum Civile*, 4. 32-3). If such arguments had had any appeal, Livy would have put them into the mouth of Valerius, the opponent of Cato the Elder in the senatorial debate about the repeal of the Oppian law. But instead Livy makes Valerius concentrate on the services that Roman women in the past performed on behalf of their country. He allows Valerius only one 'equal opportunity' argument, and this with great condescension: men can wear the purple in civil magistracies not available to women; depriving men of such honours 'could wound the spirits of men; what do you think it could do to the spirits of our little women [*mulierculae*], whom even small problems disturb?' Livy's Valerius concludes by arguing that women prefer that their adornment be subject to their husband's or father's judgement rather than to a law: 'a woman's slavery is never put off while her male relatives are safe and sound, and they hate the liberty that widowhood or orphanage allows them . . . It is for the weaker sex to submit to whatever you advise. The more power you possess, all the more moderately you should exercise your authority' (xxxiv. 6-7).

Given this background, I do not find it at all surprising that during the Empire, when the principal liberty guaranteed to male citizens was the right to petition, that women's initiative was restricted to helping male relatives.[40] Arria killed herself before her husband, who was about to be taken away to be executed, while uttering the famous words, 'look, it doesn't hurt' (Pliny, *Ep*. 3.16). Agrippina, Nero's mother, was even more aggressive than Servilia, Brutus' mother, in promoting her son's career. She married her uncle, the emperor Claudius, and got him to appoint her son as his heir.

Wives and mothers of emperors appeared on coins for propaganda purposes, for example, Antony with Cleopatra.[41] Clearly the rulers of these vast and constantly threatened realms needed the participation of wives and mothers for political as well as for personal reasons.[42] Again mythology (that is, literature) gives us the best indication of the response the emperors were seeking to elicit from their subjects. A man who had the support of a wife or mother was more easily approachable and more capable of clemency. In Euripides' drama the *Suppliant Women*, the mothers of the Argive captains who helped Polynices attack Thebes first ask Aethra, Theseus' mother, not Theseus himself, to help them get military protection so that they can bury their sons (Polynices' burial was not the only problem created by that war). The mothers appeal to Aethra: 'you have borne a son yourself, O queen' (55-6). When the king of Argos, Adrastus, fails to convince Theseus to help, Aethra intercedes. Theseus listens to her, because 'even women can provide much intelligent advice' (294). Aethra is successful where Antigone fails, because she is able to persuade Theseus to help; he is of course a much more reasonable man than Creon: 'for what will my detractors say, when you, my mother, who are anxious on my behalf, are the first to tell me to undertake this task [of allowing the Argive women to bury their dead]' (342-5).

In Rome, emperors' wives and even mistresses could save the lives (or fortunes) of individuals who were able to approach them directly and so get the emperor's ear.[43] That, as we have seen, was only a traditional pattern of behaviour. But the pattern survived through the

Middle Ages and well into our own time. By the fifth century AD the characterisation of Christian divinities had undergone subtle but important changes. In iconography Jesus, once kindly and approachable, becomes more closely identified with and sometimes even indistinguishable from his Father. To receive his mercy, appeal must be made to his Mother, who in the synoptic gospels is not at all an important or influential figure.[44] Thus the model of the 'power behind the throne' was incorporated into religion from the world of politics, and survives not only in modern Christianity, but in notions of approved behaviour for women in the twentieth century.[45]

Notes

1. Wiesen (1976), pp. 199-212.
2. de Ste. Croix (1981), pp. 24-5.
3. Lefkowitz (1981), pp. 1399-401; Cantarella (1981), pp. 19-34. That graves of armed women from the fourth century BC have been found in the Ukraine does not prove that the Sauromatians were matriarchal (Herodotus, iv. 114-17); only that some women in that society were warriors, as in nineteenth-century Russia; cf. David (1977), pp. 130, 148, 151.
4. Pembroke (1967, 1965); cf. Cartledge (1981), pp. 104 n. 126.
5. Lacey (1968), pp. 80-81.
6. Lacey (1968), pp. 54-5.
7. E.g., esp. Foley (1975), p. 36; Sorum (1982), p. 206; cf. O'Brien (1977), pp. xiii-xxx.
8. Sorum (1982), p. 207.
9. Heilbrun (1973), p. 9.
10. Foley (1975), pp. 33-6. Heilbrun (1973), p. 10, cites an unidentified verse translation: 'but to defy the State – I have no strength for that.' The Greek says only 'do you intend to bury him, when it is forbidden [by Creon] to the city?'
11. Campbell (1964), pp. 193-4, 168-9; Alexiou (1974), p. 22; Daube (1972), pp. 5-10. Alcmena refuses to sleep with Amphitryon until he has avenged her brothers' deaths (Hesiod, *Scut.*, 15-17).
12. Cf. the behaviour of Mithridates (first century BC). He decreed that the corpse of his enemy Poredorix be left unburied, but when the guards arrested a woman burying the body, Mithridates permitted her to complete the burial and gave her clothes for the corpse, 'probably because he realised that the reason behind it was love' (Plutarch, *Moralia*, 259d).
13. Translations, unless otherwise noted, are my own.
14. Humphreys (1980), pp. 112-13; Lacey (1968), pp. 148-9.
15. Cf. the behaviour of Intaphernes' wife, who chooses to have her brother spared rather than her husband (Herodotus, iii. 119.6), and of Althaea who brings about the death of her son because he killed her brothers (Bacchylides, 5. 136-44). The 'illogicality' (in modern terms) of Antigone's argument and its similarity to the Herodotean passage have caused scholars to question its authenticity, e.g., most recently, Winnington-Ingram (1980), p. 145 n. 80; but cf. Lefkowitz (1981a), p. 5, n. 8.
16. Daube (1972), pp. 6-7.

17. See Jacob (1963), p. 290; Jebb (1900), p. xlii.

18. Cf. also Althaea (n. 15), listed first in a catalogue of evil women by the (female) chorus of Aeschylus, *Choephoroe*, pp. 603ff.

19. *Melanippe the Wise*, according to the Aristophanes scholia; the play provided later writers with many quotations both for and against women (e.g., 497-9, 502, 503 N).

20. Cf. Pomeroy (1975), pp. 112-14.

21. See esp. Annas (1981), pp. 181-5. Cf. Adam (1963), I 345.

22. See esp. Cartledge (1981), pp. 86-9. Redfield (1978), by analysing the condition of Spartan women in terms of the artificial polarities of *oikos* and *polis*, suggests that 'we can see the Spartan policy as a somewhat extreme enactment of general Greek ideas' (p. 160); but surely Aristotle regarded it as anomalous, and ultimately self-destructive. On women's status in the *polis*, see Gould (1980), p. 46.

23. Lefkowitz (1983).

24. E.g., Plutarch, *Gracchi*, 2, 19; Cicero, *Brutus*, 58. 211; Seneca, *de Consolatione*, 16; Tacitus, *Dialogus* 28, Valerius Maximus, 4.4 praef. Cf. Lefkowitz-Fant (1982), p. 138.

25. Pausanias saw a statue of her in Argos (ii., 20. 8-10). Cf. the male poets Solon of Athens and Tyrtaeus of Sparta, both of whom were assumed to have been generals, perhaps because of the hortatory stance they adopt in their poems; Lefkowitz (1981b), pp. 38, 42.

26. In part, the story appears to be an aetiology for the annual Argive festival of Impudence (*Hybristika*), one of several Greek rituals involving transvestism and role-change; Burkert (1977), p. 388 n. 53. Cf. how an Argive woman was celebrated for killing king Pyrrhus when he attacked the city in 271; Stadter (1965), p. 52.

27. See esp. Stadter (1965), pp. 101-3.

28. Cf. Schaps (1977), pp. 323-30.

29. Cf. also Pleket (1969), no. 15, and *CIL* viii. 23888, and see Van Bremen in this volume for discussion of women's dedications in the Hellenistic period.

30. Thesleff (1965), p. 151.

31. See esp. Cantarella (1981), pp. 113-4.

32. Callimachus (in Catullus' translation, 66. 25-6) may have been alluding to how Berenice helped assassins dispose of her first husband Demetrius (her mother's lover, whose presence kept her mother in power) so that she could marry Ptolemy (Justin 26.3); Macurdy (1932), pp. 130-6.

33. Cf. Pomeroy (1975), p. 124; Macurdy (1932), pp. 202-5. Her daughter Cleopatra Selene issued coins in her own name, but with her husband Juba on the reverse; Macurdy (1932), p. 225.

34. Cf. Pomeroy (1975), pp. 126-7.

35. Tr. Wistrand (1976), p. 25; cf. also Balsdon (1962), pp. 204-5.

36. Probably Sulpicia, wife of Cornelius Lentulus Cruscello, Valerius Maximus, 6.6.3; *RE* IV (1901) 1384.

37. Balsdon (1962), p. 51.

38. Balsdon (1962), pp. 47-8.

39. Cf. Lefkowitz-Fant (1982), pp. 244-6.

40 Millar (1977), pp. 546-8.

41. Macurdy (1932), p. 205.

42. E.g., the titles awarded to and coins issued by the women in Elagabalus' family, Balsdon (1962), p. 160; cf. p. 142.

43. E.g., Antonina is alleged to have got her husband Belisarius's life spared through Theodora's intervention: Procopius, *Secret History*, 4.

44. Warner (1976), pp. 285-6.

45. Perhaps one reason Theodora's contemporaries (like Cleopatra's) disliked her is that she often seemed to function literally as well as figuratively as co-ruler, oaths, for example, being sworn to Justinian and Theodora jointly — though not too much should be made of this either: see Bury (1923), II, pp. 30f.

Further Reading

Balsdon, J.P.V.D. (1962), *Roman Women: Their History and Habits*, London

Cantarella, E. (1981), *L'Ambiguo Malanno: Condizione e immagine della donna nell' antichità greca e romana*, Rome

Daube, D. (1972), *Civil Disobedience in Antiquity*, Edinburgh, pp. 1-40

Lacey, W.K. (1968), *The Family in Classical Greece*, London, repr. Auckland, 1980

Lefkowitz, M.R., Fant, M.B., eds. (1982), *Women's Life in Greece and Rome*, London, pp. 63-79, 205-14

Macurdy, G.H. (1932), *Hellenistic Queens*, Baltimore

Pomeroy, S.B. (1975), *Goddesses, Whores, Wives and Slaves*, New York

5 THE GOD'S WIFE OF AMUN IN THE 18TH DYNASTY IN EGYPT

Gay Robins, Atlanta, Georgia

My aim in this paper is to outline what we know of the office of god's wife and its function during the 18th dynasty, and then to look briefly at the careers of three of its holders.

First, I shall sketch in the historical background. The 18th dynasty royal family with which we shall be dealing was no more than a continuation of the 17th dynasty, which may be given the rough dates of 1650-1565 BC. Although the rulers of the 17th dynasty used the titles of king, they only controlled the south of Egypt with their capital at Thebes. The north was in the hands of the Hyksos, who had moved into Lower Egypt from Syria-Palestine. While it seems that north and south existed fairly peaceably for some time, the rulers in Thebes became increasingly restive at the situation, probably for mainly economic reasons, though national pride may have played its part.

The last king of the 17th dynasty, Kamose, has left a record of his offensive thrust against the Hyksos, in which he had some successes, but it was left to the next king, Ahmose, to complete the expulsion of the foreigners, some time in the second half of his 25-year reign. The absolute date cannot be precisely calculated, but we can put it very roughly around 1550 BC.

In retrospect, Ahmose was considered the founder of the New Kingdom and of a new dynasty, the 18th. Although his family was from Thebes, he moved the administrative capital north to Memphis for geographical reasons, since that city lay at the meeting point of Upper and Lower Egypt, and was close both to the Delta, by now the economic centre of the country, and to the land and sea routes to the Near East. Thebes, however, remained the provincial administrative centre for Upper Egypt, but, more than this, it became the religious capital for the whole of Egypt. The god Amun of Thebes had first come to prominence as a national god under the earlier Theban ruling families of the 11th and 12th dynasties at the beginning of the 2nd millennium, and was already then associated with the sun god Re, the national god of the Old Kingdom, in the form Amon-Re. With the victory of another line of Theban princes, the paramount position of Amun was reinforced.

65

The successes of the 17th and 18th dynasties were attributed to him, first those against the Hyksos, and then every victory that the warrior kings of the New Kingdom achieved, as they directed their aggressive energies towards building up Egyptian control in Syria-Palestine. The temples of Amun were made rich with booty and endowments, and eventually became the wealthiest in the land and the priesthood the most powerful.

It is against this background of expansion of the wealth and power of Amun and his priesthood that we must set the god's wife of Amun, for the title immediately links the holder with the god Amun and his city, Thebes.

Before we ask what the title meant to the Egyptians of the 18th dynasty, it will be useful to look briefly at the material which we must use in our enquiry, and the sort of information we may hope to get from it. First, it must be stressed that we have to rely on chance finds, so that we must assume that there are gaps, possibly large ones, in the evidence, and that much vital information has simply not survived. Stone monuments, such as temples, stelae, tombs and statues, have a good chance of coming down to us, but they often suffer from weathering or deliberate attack, so that important details may be missing. Further, buildings were often subject to dismantling, and many have only been recovered in fragmentary form. Smaller objects, both royal and private, such as vases, scarabs, cosmetic items and jewellery, survive haphazardly, often with no provenance, and the information they give is fairly limited. Some of the material may provide us with long texts, such as the biographies of officials, and building or triumphal inscriptions of kings, with short inscriptions, such as captions to scenes and titularies, and possibly with representations. What we do not have are texts, official or unofficial, which explain the position of the god's wife, or any documents, such as letters or diaries written by the women themselves, which would give us a glimpse of their individual characters. It is doubtful whether these types of document would have ever existed.

This material, royal and private, comes, therefore, from an official milieu and reflects the official view of things, but rarely explains it. So the kind of information which we can glean about the god's wife of Amun will be concerned with her official position rather than with the individual woman, although it is possible that the amount of material surviving for each god's wife suggests roughly the importance of these women, relative to each other.

Since it is vain to ask questions which the material cannot answer, we must be content to examine the official position of the god's wife of

Amun in the 18th dynasty. First, the title is held by women of the royal family. Taken at face value, it suggests a woman dedicated to the service of Amun, with a sexual role to play towards the god. While this may conjure up the vision of a virgin consecrated to the god alone, it is quite clear that in the 18th dynasty this was not the meaning, for the title could be used by women who were kings' wives and kings' mothers. This has given rise to a misconception about the role of the god's wife, which has its origin in ideas that became current at the end of the last century concerning the role of royal women in the transmission of the right to the throne. These gave rise to the belief that the right to the throne of ancient Egypt passed through the female line, so that the king, even if the son of his predecessor and his predecessor's wife, had to legitimise his claim to the throne by marriage with the royal 'heiress', who would be the daughter of the previous king and his principal wife, and so normally the sister or half-sister of the reigning king. Thus the right to the throne would have descended through the female line, but the office of king would be exercised by the man the 'heiress' married.

Two kings of the 18th dynasty, Hatshepsut and Amenhotpe III, have left reliefs depicting the myth of their divine birth. In them, it is related how the god Amun came to their mothers and fathered the future kings. The idea that the king was the bodily child of a god, by the 18th dynasty Amun, but earlier the sun god Re, was a well-established tradition, and probably applied to all the kings of the 18th dynasty. Here, it was thought, was a sense in which the king's wife was literally the god's wife of Amun, and so the title was linked with the 'heiress' theory, and the legitimisation of kingship. Not all bearers of the title were mothers of kings, nor even wives of kings, so it was assumed that the title marked the designated 'heiress', that is, the king's daughter destined to become king's principal wife, and, hopefully, the mother of the heir.

If this ingenious theory is correct, each king must be shown to have married a woman of royal birth, who together should form a line in direct descent from one another. Egyptian kings were polygynous, and Egyptologists normally consider that the 'heiress' must be the principal wife of the king. If this were not so, the idea would become impossible to examine. Secondary wives are rarely mentioned, and if the king could make any woman his principal wife, provided he had the 'heiress' safely in his 'harim', it would be impossible to discover evidence for or against her existence. However, if the king could only claim the throne through marriage to the 'heiress', one might expect that this would be part of the official myth of kingship, and that there would be evidence of the existence of the 'heiress' on the monuments. That this is not so

Figure 5.1: Genealogy of the Kings of the 18th dynasty, Ahmose to Tutankhamun (c. 1565 B.C.– c. 1350 B.C.), showing god's wives of Amun (underlined) king's principal wives (kpw), king's wives (kw) and king's mothers (km)
The table is to be read from top to bottom, with lines running from parent (mother or father) to child. A broken line means filiation is not certain.

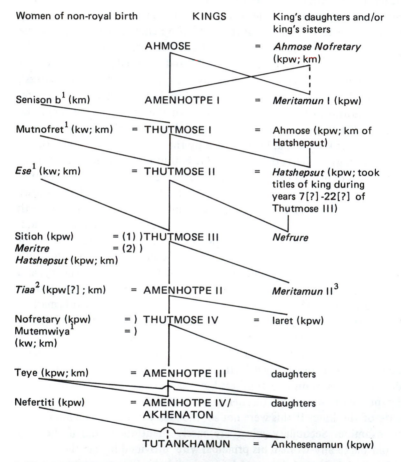

1. First attested in the reign of her son.
2. Last attested god's wife in the 18th dynasty, the title only being found on monuments dating to the reign of her son. The title god's wife is revived in the 19th dynasty for Sitre, the wife of the founder, Ramesses I, after an interval of 80-100 years.
3. Only attested from the end of the reign of her father.

makes the theory suspect to start with, and a simple examination of the genealogy of the dynasty (Fig. 5.1) shows that there is no such line of 'heiress' queens. Although brother-sister marriages occur in the royal family of the 18th dynasty, they are not consistently practised, as the theory would demand. In fact, the whole 'heiress' theory is founded on very shaky grounds, and is an example of an idea which has become generally accepted without being subjected to a critical examination.

In one direction, the roots go back to Fraser and *The Golden Bough*. Fraser said that all Egyptian men married their sisters, and although inheritance appeared to pass from father to son, it did so really in the son's dual role of his father's sister's son and his father's daughter's husband; that is, inheritance went through the women. Around that time, texts from the tomb of a man called Paheri became known, in which he traced his descent through the female line. Further, in giving filiation, many Egyptians named only their mothers. All this suggested to scholars that Egyptian society had once been a 'matriarchy' with descent going through the women, that it had then been overlaid by a system of 'patriarchy', but that strong 'matriarchal' tendencies remained, most notably in the royal family, where the women continued to carry the right to the throne.

Today, the work of Fraser and his followers cannot be accepted uncritically, and thus the very origins of the 'heiress' theory makes its reappraisal necessary. Fraser's original statement that all Egyptian men married their sisters is clearly untrue. Not only is such a model unrealistic and unworkable, but it has now been demonstrated that full brother-sister marriage among ordinary people was rare, if it existed at all, in Pharaonic Egypt. Although it is unknown why some Egyptians gave filiation only to their mothers, there are clearly other possible explanations besides 'matriarchal' tendencies within the society. The reason for Paheri's interest in his descent in the female line was probably because his only important ancestor, a hero of the Hyksos wars, lay in this line.

Neither the way the term 'matriarchy' has been used, nor the idea that primitive societies were originally matriarchal and that many patriarchal societies contain memories of the earlier system is acceptable to anthropologists today.

If we return to brother-sister marriage within the royal family, and look at the genealogy of the dynasty (Fig. 5.1), it is clear that while this type of marriage is practised, it is not obligatory. The existence of such marriages has been one of the main supports of the 'heiress' theory, but they can be explained in another way. These unions are not found with non-royal people, but they occur among the gods. This is a result of the type of creation myth in which a creator god produces a pair of offspring, who in their turn produce offspring, and so on; in creation, but not necessarily thereafter, choice of partner is limited to brother or sister. Therefore, by practising brother-sister marriage, the king removed himself from his subjects and approached the divine circle. Thus his sister would be a desirable marriage partner for the king.

Since there is no evidence for an 'heiress' either on the monuments nor in the pattern of royal marriages, the idea of transmission of the right to the throne through the female line should be discarded. This obviously affects our understanding of the title god's wife, which has been so firmly linked to the 'heiress' theory. Although it cannot mark the non-existent 'heiress', it might still belong to the woman picked out to be the mother of the next king. An examination of the two surviving birth cycles, however, shows that neither of the two king's mothers involved is called god's wife. We must, therefore, accept that the title god's wife had nothing to do with the myth of the king's divine birth. Looked at from a practical point of view, we can say that a queen's involvement in the birth cycle must be retrospective; that is, only once a particular prince has obtained the throne can the myth be applied to him and his divine origin known, together with his mother's part in it. Of course, the title god's wife might have been bestowed retrospectively, but these two cases show that it was not.

Therefore, we must discard not only the 'heiress' theory, but also any attempt to link the title god's wife with the myth of the divine birth of the king, and we must look for the significance of the title elsewhere. The earliest attestations date from the Middle Kingdom, over 200 years before the 18th dynasty. They occur with the names of non-royal women, but, since there is no accompanying god's name, it is uncertain whether Amun is meant. In the First Intermediate Period, earlier still, a wife of Min is known, and from the Old Kingdom onwards, a related title, that of divine adoratrice of the god, appears in the cults of other gods. In the 18th dynasty, the title god's wife as used by the women of the royal family is shown to refer to Amun by the full version god's wife of Amun, but it more often appears simply as god's wife.

The first royal god's wife of whom we know anything is Ahmose Nofretary, the wife of king Ahmose, founder of the 18th dynasty. During her tenure of the office, a legal act formally established the office of god's wife on Ahmose Nofretary and her heirs. This is known from a document called the 'Donation' stela, which was set up in the temple of Amun at Karnak. Although there is not full agreement on its interpretation, it is basically a legal document providing an endowment of goods and land which was to be linked with the office of god's wife and handed on with it in perpetuity.

The nature of the office is made clear by several scenes from the 18th dynasty showing a priestess who is called god's wife functioning within the context of temple ritual alongside male priests. So she appears as part of a procession of priests; she is shown being purified in the sacred lake before entering the temple; she takes part in the rite calling the god to his repast; she plays a role in execration rites, burning the image of the enemy; she is present when boxes of clothes are offered to the goddess Wadjit. The earliest of these scenes is from the reign of Amenhotpe I, and the priestess is clearly called Ahmose Nofretary; in the other examples, from the reigns of Hatshepsut and Amenhotpe III, she is unnamed. In all of them, she wears a short, close-fitting wig with a thin fillet tied at the back of the head with the ends falling down, which derives from the costume of priestesses in the Middle Kingdom, and is totally unrelated to the costume and insignia worn by king's mothers, king's wives and occasionally king's daughters. Clearly, the god's wife was a priestess.

At first, the title was held by women who were members of the royal family by birth, so that the holders before the sole rule of Thutmose III were all also king's daughters. During the sole rule of Thutmose III to the reign of Thutmose IV, three of the holders were not members of the royal family by birth, but only by 'marriage', suggesting a possible shift of emphasis from royal birth to simple membership of the royal family (Fig. 5.1). After this, the title disappears from the royal family until the beginning of the 19th dynasty.

The god's wives Ahmose Nofretary, Hatshepsut and Nefrure have left a large number of attestations, in which they make frequent use of the title god's wife, often as their only title. Between the end of the reign of Hatshepsut and the end of the reign of Thutmose IV, the evidence from the monuments suggests that there were no royal women of similar influence or calibre. While the mothers of Amenhotpe II and Thutmose IV should probably not be considered negligible, they are attested fewer times, rarely make prominent use of the title god's wife, and are seldom referred to by it alone. Undoubtedly, the wives of Amenhotpe III and Akhenaton, Teye and Nefertiti, should be considered on a par with Ahmose Nofretary and Hatshepsut, but, by this time, royal women no longer used the title god's wife. Thus the heyday of the title in the 18th dynasty was during the reigns of Ahmose to Hatshepsut, a period of roughly 80 years. I shall now look at the three royal women, who according to the evidence were the most important holders of the title at this time.

The 'Donation' stela of king Ahmose's reign (above) is the first surviving official document concerning Ahmose Nofretary, and it at once introduces her as a person of importance. Later evidence, from the last years of Ahmose's reign, suggests that Ahmose Nofretary took an interest in the building projects of her husband. Two rock stelae carved at the limestone quarries of Ma'sara, across the river from Memphis, record the reopening of the quarry in year 22. Above the text of each stela is carved the cartouche of Ahmose in the centre, flanked on either side by the cartouche and very full titulary of Ahmose Nofretary, thus showing her involvement. Her name also appears in the alabaster quarries at Bosra near Assiut. A royal stela found at Abydos is concerned with the cult of the mother of the king's mother and the mother of the king's father, Tetisheri. Although this lady was already buried at Thebes, the stela records Ahmose's decision to erect a cenotaph for her at Abydos, and how he sought the approval of Ahmose Nofretary for his plans. Possibly, she stood in the same relationship to Tetisheri as Ahmose, explaining her interest in the matter, but it may also reflect a more general concern with the religious building projects of the reign. Such a participation is not recorded for any other queen of the period, and could relate to her position as god's wife. (I use the term 'queen' to refer both to king's mothers and to king's principal wives, since these women used the same insignia and titles, and were shown in similar types of scene.)

In the reign of her son Amenhotpe I, Ahmose Nofretary contributed bricks to his mortuary temple at Thebes, showing that she was continuing her interest in cult buildings. Amenhotpe also built a mortuary temple in honour of his mother, to house her funerary cult. There is some evidence that most members of the royal family had a place for their cult in the mortuary temple of the king with whom they were most closely connected. This separate building for Ahmose Nofretary stresses her special position.

Ahmose Nofretary survived into the reign of Thutmose I, still highly honoured, although Thutmose was most likely not related to her (Fig. 5.1). She appears on a stela of that king dated to year 1 of his reign, and a statue of her was set up by him in the temple of Karnak. A private stela actually mentions her death 'when the god's wife Ahmose Nofretary justified with the great god, lord of the west, flew to heaven', but no date or king's name is given.

A number of ritual objects dedicated by Ahmose Nofretary have been found in temples at Karnak north, Deir el-Bahri, Abydos and the temple of Hathor at Serabit el-Khadim in Sinai. Other queens and kings also dedicated such objects, but chronologically and numerically she heads the list and perhaps set the trend. Ahmose Nofretary's involvement in cult, both in the buildings to house it and in its performance through participation and dedication of objects used in it, comes across clearly, and one may guess that it was partly related to her office of god's wife.

In the scene where Ahmose Nofretary functions as god's wife, she has none of the titles of a queen, but in the majority of her titularies as queen, the title god's wife is included. A study of queens' usage of titles shows that when only one title is selected to appear before the name, it is an important one, most frequently king's wife, king's principal wife or king's mother. Ahmose Nofretary had the right to these three titles, but used them rarely as sole titles, preferring god's wife. No other queen, except Hatshepsut (below), used god's wife alone like this, and it is clear that Ahmose Nofretary regarded her position as god's wife as very important, perhaps equal to her position as queen. The large number of scarabs with the title presumably relate to the estate of the god's wife, suggesting that it had a sizeable administration, which probably meant considerable economic power, at least, for the woman who headed it.

The mantle of Ahmose Nofretary seems to have fallen, not on her daughter Meritamun, who is poorly attested, but on Hatshepsut, the daughter of Thutmose I. While Thutmose was clearly the chosen and legitimate successor of Amenhotpe I, it is unlikely that he was either his son or his brother, and it is probable that he was of totally non-royal origin, in which case, Hatshepsut was no blood relation of Ahmose Nofretary.

Little is known of Hatshepsut during the reigns of her father, Thutmose I, or her brother and husband, Thutmose II. An undated stela from the reign of the latter shows her with the titles king's principal wife and god's wife, but she seems to have had little prominence until the death of Thutmose II. The biography of an official of this time explicitly states that Thutmose II 'went up to heaven and was united with the gods. His son arose on his throne as king of the Two Lands and ruled on the seat of the one who begot him. His relative, the god's wife, Hatshepsut, controlled the affairs of the land.' (In our terms, Hatshepsut was the aunt and stepmother of Thutmose III. The Egyptian term used here, normally translated 'sister', means a female collateral.) Since Thutmose III had a long reign of nearly 54 years, it may be deduced that he came to the throne as a boy, and that Hatshepsut was regent for him. It is now that she comes into prominence on our material. She was still shown on the monuments as a woman, wearing the insignia and using the titles of a king's principal wife, although, like Ahmose Nofretary, almost the only title used alone before her name was god's wife. In addition, however, she appeared in scenes drawn from the iconography of kings, and used titles modelled on those used by kings, which described her position as ruler. Officials used titles and phrases which would normally contain a title or phrase referring to the king, but now contained the title god's wife or lady of the Two Lands. This last title is the feminine counterpart of the king's title lord of the Two Lands, and is used in titularies by other 18th dynasty queens, but its use as a sole title seems to be another example of adoption of a kingly usage. While Hatshepsut was still regent, she had a pair of obelisks quarried and set up at Karnak, and by doing so, took over an act which was the prerogative of the king. She thus reinforced her position as *de facto* ruler of Egypt by drawing on kingly iconography, titulature and actions.

On a practical governmental level, we can image that she carefully chose the officials who were to serve her, and with whom she had to work. Some had previously held office under her husband or even her father, and some were new, but presumably they were all men who were congenial to her and whose fortunes were to some extent linked to hers, since at any change-over of rulers, officials always faced the possibility of being unacceptable to the new ruler. One wonders whether these officials were worried about what might happen to them when the young Thutmose III took control for himself.

At some point in Thutmose's reign, not later than year 7, Hatshepsut ceased to appear with the titles and insignia of a queen, and instead used the five-fold titulary of a king and, iconographically at least, appeared in the male costume of a king.

It was once supposed that Hatshepsut took the throne, because she regarded herself as the last representative of the pure royal line descended through the 'heiresses' from the beginning of the dynasty, while Thutmose II and III were only sons of so-called concubines. In addition, her claim to have been appointed king by her father was taken at face value. Now we know both that there was no line of 'heiress' queens, and that the account of Hatshepsut's coronation during her father's reign must be fictitious, since Thutmose I's successor was Thutmose II, and during his reign, Hatshepsut appeared only as his principal wife, being shown no differently from other queen consorts.

Her position changed only with the accession of Thutmose III.

Presumably Hatshepsut was meant to hand over control to the young king when he was considered old enough to rule for himself. But, like many regents, she probably found the prospect of giving up power unpleasant. Yet she could hardly prolong the regency indefinitely, nor would murdering her nephew help, since he was her means to power. There was, however, in ancient Egypt, a system whereby two kings might rule at the same time. Originally, it was instituted so that an ageing king might associate his heir with him on the throne, in order to accomplish a smooth transfer of power from one ruler to the next. Hatshepsut now made use of this system, and was crowned king with the full royal titulary, without having to oust Thutmose from the kingship. He remained king throughout her period of rule, and the regnal dates used during their joint reign are his. Although at this time he appeared less often on monuments than Hatshepsut, he was shown alongside her in temple scenes, even in her mortuary temple, and the names of the two kings were used together by a number of officials to head their own monuments. Hatshepsut, however, was clearly the dominant partner.

A careful examination of the monuments where Hatshepsut and her daughter Nefrure are named together shows that in most cases where Hatshepsut is god's wife, Nefrure is not, and that when Nefrure is god's wife, Hatshepsut is king. So it seems that Hatshepsut handed on the office of god's wife to her daughter, when she took the title of king.

Of all the king's daughters in the 18th dynasty, Nefrure stands out through her large number of attestations and occasional use of items of queenly insignia, and above all, by her almost consistent use of the uraeus, the royal cobra worn on the forehead, which at this time is attested on the contemporary monuments of no other princess.

Nefrure is not certainly mentioned in the reign of her father, Thutmose II, but she is in evidence by the time of her mother's regency. The majority of her attestations, however, date from the reign of her mother. At this time, Nefrure was shown in temple scenes following her mother who, as king, offered to a god. It is rare, but not unknown, for royal women other than queens to appear in this type of scene. In one such scene, Nefrure is called god's wife, and wears the short wig and fillet of this priestess (above). She also supplied bricks for her mother's valley temple at Thebes, which is reminiscent of Ahmose Nofretary's provision of bricks for her son's mortuary temple.

The large number of Nefrure's scarabs far exceeds those of other king's daughters and many queens. A few of the scarabs have only the titles of king's daughter or king's daughter and king's sister, but the majority use the title god's wife, and must relate to this office and its estate.

The most extraordinary monument of Nefrure is a stela from Serabit el-Khadim at Sinai, now in the Cairo Museum, which shows Nefrure, followed by her steward Senenmut, offering to Hathor; the text below is almost totally illegible. Nefrure wears the double feathered crown on the vulture headdress which were the insignia of a queen. The stela is dated to year 11 under the person of the god's wife Nefrure. This date really belongs to the regnal years of Thutmose III, but even so, it is unknown elsewhere for either a queen or princess to have such a date attributed to her.

What should we make of this princess? Her appearance in offering scenes with her mother is not unknown for a king's daughter, but it is rare. I would suggest, however, that this function of Nefrure was vital to Hatshepsut. As a female king, Hatshepsut could not have a principal wife, but in certain rituals it was necessary for a king's mother or king's principal wife to be present, or, much less commonly, a king's daughter. Since Hatshepsut's mother was dead by this time, she needed her daughter Nefrure to fill this role. (This may explain why Nefrure never married her brother Thutmose III.) The interpretation of the Sinai stela with its queenly insignia and regnal year attributed to Nefrure is more difficult. The monument was probably set up on the orders of Senenmut, Nefrure's steward, who appears on it. The large number of his monuments which link him with the princess suggests that he attached great importance to his connection with her. Perhaps he was simply trying to enhance her prestige, and thereby his own. It is unlikely that the stela represented the official status of the princess, for it was set up outside Egypt, and there is no hint of a comparable position for the princess on monuments from within Egypt itself.

When Nefrure died is uncertain. A stela of Thutmose III dating to the beginning of his sole reign may originally have depicted the princess. The name has been changed to that of Sitioh, first principal wife of Thutmose III, but the sole title given is god's wife, Nefrure's most important title, but one which is never attested for Sitioh.

After Nefrure, the god's wife never achieved such prominence again in the 18th dynasty, and the title finally died out in the royal family. The office had clearly been developed into a position of religious and economic importance by Ahmose Nofretary. It is possible that while she had worked in consort with the king, her successor, Hatshepsut, may have used the office as a base from which to achieve her own ambitions to the detriment of the king. In this case, we might speculate that with the disappearance of Hatshepsut and Nefrure, Thutmose III took steps to reduce the office to its cultic function and to make sure that it could not again serve as a rival power base to the king.

I would like to finish by looking briefly at the society which produced the institution of god's wife, and by considering a few points arising from what we have established about this office.

The institution of god's wife developed within a society where women were respected both socially and legally. There is no obvious segregation of women. Tomb scenes show men and women mixing together from the peasants working in the fields to the official classes at their feasts. For want of a better word, Egyptologists often speak of the king's harim, but there is no evidence for eunuchs and all that goes with them. Legally, women could own property, carry on business, conduct law suits and make a will in their own right. Despite Herodotus's statement that 'no woman holds priestly office', women had a definite part in ritual as sistrum players, chantresses and priestesses.

The road to official success and power lay, however, in knowing how to read and write, and becoming a scribe. It is doubtful whether education was generally available to women, and they had no place in the bureaucracy as a whole. There is no reason to believe one way or the other that an exception was made for royal women, though it is hard to accept that the women we have been discussing did not acquire the skills of reading and writing at some point in their careers, even if they were not taught as children.

Given the favourable position of women in ancient Egypt, socially, legally and ritually, if not politically, we need not be surprised to find an important religious office vested in a woman. But we must be clear that the generally high regard that women were held in was not due to surviving matriarchal tendencies. Egyptian tradition makes it plain that the ideal was to hand on office, including the kingship, from father to son, and there is no hint that women played any part in this.

If we deny that royal women and the god's wife in particular have a role in passing on the throne and legitimising the rule of the king, then we must ask how this was done. First, we must rid ourselves of the habit of making subjective judgements by using terms like 'usurper', 'illegitimate' or 'of non-royal blood', based on Western usage; we must start from scratch and work from the Egyptian evidence. A full answer is unlikely ever to be possible, as the Egyptians naturally took the system for granted, and never wrote it down.

However, it is only when we have removed this question of

legitimisation of the succession from any enquiry into the roles of royal women and of the god's wife that we begin to get acceptable answers to our questions about their nature. We can then see that the office of god's wife, although vested in the women of the royal family, is a priestly office distinct from the role of the king's principal wife.

The institution of god's wife shows that through ritual roles women in ancient Egypt could obtain a certain amount of power. However, lack of education prevented their entry into the bureaucracy, while the ultimate office of king was barred to them by the official myth of kingship which did not allow for a woman to be king. Hatshepsut and a few other women in the course of Egyptian history managed to occupy this office, but only by adopting the masculine role of the king. Thus while the position of women in ancient Egyptian society was a favourable one, they could not achieve political equality with men.

Further Reading

Background to 18th dynasty

Cambridge Ancient History,[3] 2 part 1, Cambridge, 1973, chs. 8 and 9

Women in ancient Egypt

Baines, J. and Málek, J. (1980), *Atlas of Ancient Egypt*, Oxford, pp. 204-8.
Černý, J. (1954), 'Consanguineous marriages in pharaonic Egypt', *JEA* 40, pp. 23-9
Wenig, S. (1969), *The woman in Egyptian art*, New York, translation of *id. Die Frau im alten Ägypten*, Leipzig, 1967

God's wife of Amun

Gitton, M. (1975), *L'épouse du dieu Ahmes Nefertary: Documents sur la vie et son culte posthume*, Paris
Gitton, M. (1976), 'Le rôle des femmes dans le clergé d'Amon à la 18e dynastie', *BSFE* 75, pp. 31-46
Gitton, M. and Leclant, J. (1976), 'Gottesgemahlin', in *LÄ* 2, Wiesbaden, pp. 792-812

PART THREE: WOMEN AT HOME

Non-literary evidence — and its problems — for the study of women in their domestic context

6 WOMEN AND HOUSING IN CLASSICAL GREECE: THE ARCHAEOLOGICAL EVIDENCE

Susan Walker, London

Many houses of classical date have now been excavated in Athens and Attica. The finds have been meticulously examined (Jones, 1975), but the evidence from archaeological sites has not yet been incorporated into that body of knowledge from written sources made familiar in recent work on Athenian women and family life (e.g. Lacey, 1980; Gould, 1980). Despite the poor state of preservation of most excavated houses, it is possible to interpret certain features of their remains and associated finds as responses on the part of the occupants to contemporary customs and social aspirations. It is the purpose of this paper to suggest ways of assimilating the archaeological evidence about women and housing in classical Greece to that acquired from other sources. It has been argued recently (not for the first time) that women of 'respectable' families were deliberately secluded from public life (Gould, 1980). Evidence of this is particularly apparent at Athens, though impressions may be distorted by the large body of surviving evidence from varied sources, not matched in any other Greek city. Here as in other societies practising purdah it appears that 'keeping women in seclusion may be something that most people in a given area desire, but it may entail expenses which the very poor cannot meet' (Jeffrey, 1979, p. 24).

The seclusion of women may thus become a status symbol, indulged in by those who can afford it, and emulated by others striving for respectability. Lacey (p. 170) sees an example of the latter in Euphiletos, charged with the murder of his wife's lover, whose description of the division of his humble household is recorded in Lysias I,9: 'My dwelling is on two floors, the upper equal in area to the lower, comprising the women's apartments and the men's apartments.' The trierarch involved in a fracas over security for missing ship's gear (Demosthenes, xlvii, 35-42), a story well used by Gould (p. 47) to illustrate the reluctance of respectable men to intrude upon women secluded at home, is a member of a class whose wealth has been extensively documented (Davies, 1971). Indeed, many of the individuals who provide us with evidence of the dependent and secluded status of women in classical Athens are known to us through their quarrels over the inheritance of family property, quarrels so serious that they had to be brought to court. It was perhaps the maintenance of family wealth, sometimes quite substantial, and the transfer of that wealth with the right to citizenship from one generation of men to the next, that led the Athenians to place such a high value on legitimate childbirth, and thus to seclude women of the wealthy families who played so prominent a part in Athenian public life.

We may learn much from a discourse of Xenophon (*Oeconomicus*, 7-10), in which the Athenian gentleman Ischomachos recounts to his friend Socrates the guided tour he offered to his unnamed wife on her arrival in her new home. The house was portrayed as a shelter for moveable property, arranged in orderly fashion. The home was considered a miniature centre of production in which clothes and food were made from wool and crops. It was a nursery for the children who would care for their parents in their old age, and who would (in their own right, if they were male) inherit both the family property and the coveted right to Athenian citizenship (Schaps, 1979). The home, a sanctuary protected by household gods, was managed by the Athenian gentleman's wife, brought up to this task but preferably otherwise uneducated (*Oec.*, 7). She was expected to guard against the dangers of indolence, ill-health and self-indulgence by participating with the servants in household jobs such as shaking out blankets and clothes and moistening and kneading bread (*Oec.*, 10), an interesting instance of ancient awareness of problems encountered in other societies in which wealthy women are secluded (Jeffrey, 1979, p. 130).

Condemning the luxury of his own time, Demosthenes commended the poverty of private houses in fifth-century Athens and praised the consequent lack of distinction between the homes of its most illustrious citizens and those of the poor (*Ol.* 3 iii, 25-6; *On Organisation* xiii, 29; *Against Aristocrates* xxiii, 207). Even in the Roman Empire the old and illustrious city was considered synonymous with twisted streets and cramped quarters (Philostratos, *Life of Apollonius of Tyana*, II, 23). No disparagement of Athenian architects was intended; domestic poverty seems to have been a matter of deliberate choice. According to Xenophon (*Oec.*, 8) 'it is more shameful for the man [of a married couple] to stay indoors than to busy himself with outdoor affairs.' Many Athenians passed their time among those public buildings whose remains still astound and delight us, while their wives were confined to cramped and dreary quarters, unless they were of families sufficiently wealthy to own property in the suburbs or in the countryside. Even that was not accessible in wartime, and for much of the later fifth-century Athens was at war (see below).

The apparent reluctance to spend money on comfortable housing is confirmed by archaeological evidence. It has been observed in reports of excavations of fifth-century Athenian houses that the finds of pottery and metalware indicated a greater wealth than their architectural context might suggest (Thompson, 1959, p. 103). Failure to invest in good housing may well have been a result of attempts to move towards egalitarianism, but the divided nature of Athenian society in the fifth century is obvious from the unequal distribution of land and property (Davies, 1971). Poor housing may have been an expression of the modesty that surrounded an Athenian family, modesty required of the wives and daughters of Athenian citizens in their behaviour and in their dress, on which legal controls were occasionally imposed (Plutarch, *Solon* 21,4; Humphreys, 1980, p. 100).

Modesty in scale and appointments may be easily assessed in excavated houses. Other characteristics revealing social customs and contemporary attitudes towards women may also be observed in the archaeological record and evaluated in the course of excavation. The known functions of an Athenian house — seclusion, shelter and the production of goods for consumption by the household — demand a measure of self-sufficiency, traces of which may be sought in the surviving remains.

Is there access between the house and neighbouring properties? Does the house have its own water supply, at least for washing? — Euphiletos' wife moved downstairs to wash her baby, presumably in water drawn from a well in the courtyard (Isaeus, I,9). Does the house have cooking and storage facilities? Is there a place for a loom? If in the country, is the house surrounded by productive land?

How are the least secure parts of the house treated, areas such as the entrance from the street and the *andron* (men's dining-room) where it was considered essential to prevent unsupervised meetings between women and men who were not their kinsmen (Demosthenes, *Against Euergos*, xlvii, 38, 60)? Does the *andron* have a separate entrance from the street? Or is it located so close to the street that it is possible to reach it without crossing the rest of the house? Is it further isolated from the other apartments by an anteroom? How many rooms of the house are visible from a point just inside the entrance, through which a man would have to pass in order to reach the *andron*? Is the entrance itself controlled by a porter's lodge?

If we accept the view suggested in the case of Euphiletos, that the women's apartments were located upstairs, then we must accept the fact that none has survived in houses excavated in Athens and Attica, where the form of the upper storey is a matter for conjecture. However, storerooms, rooms with hearths and 'workrooms' where loom-weights have been found are known at a number of sites, and the association of women with such rooms is well-documented in contemporary and earlier Greek literature (Homer, *Iliad*, 22, 440; Hesiod, *Works and Days*, 520ff; Aeschylus, *Agamemnon*, 95; see also Gould, 1980, p. 48). How are these rooms located in relation to the entrance of the house and to the *andron*? Is there evidence of direct access from them to the upper storey?

Many of these features may be observed in surviving remains. I shall consider here four houses, one of which was excavated in Athens, and one in Attica. For comparison I have included a well-preserved stone-built house in Euboea and a modern house in an Islamic tribal community in northern Nigeria. Each house is illustrated in two plans. The first, prepared by the excavator or architect for publication, shows the surviving remains as interpreted at the time of excavation or survey. The second plan distinguishes areas of the house frequented by men and those designated as working or sleeping quarters for women. Evidence for self-sufficiency is also noted. The first house was excavated in the 1950s by Dorothy Thompson. It lies at the foot of the northern slope of the Areopagus Hill, just above the Athenian Agora. In the plan drawn by John Travlos (tidier, I fear, than the occupational history might suggest), the relationship of this block of houses to the public dining-rooms of the South Stoa is clear (Fig. 6.1).

The block of houses was built in the fifth century after the Persian Wars. Like all houses so far known from Athens and Attica, these were built of mud-brick laid on a stone socle. In the south-west house, it is possible that the *andron* was set totally apart from the domestic units and was approached from a separate entrance. When the house was subdivided to form two discrete dwellings some time after 300 BC, the division was made along the wall that had formerly separated public from private areas (Fig. 6.2a and b).

This is an unusual solution to the problem of isolating the *andron* from the household; the more conventional arrangement, in which the *andron* is located next to the street entrance to the house, may be seen in the block of houses of fourth-century date excavated at Olynthus in northern Greece.

The second house illustrates the point made earlier in this paper that seclusion was largely the prerogative of the rich. The so-called Dema House at Ano Liossia to the north of Athens is apparently a non-

functional country house. No evidence of farming or of any other productive activity was found in or near it. The household equipment was
found to include a *lebes gamikos*, a vessel used in marriage ritual, and a
krater (wine bowl) decorated with scenes suggestive of festivities in the
andron, along with standard household utensils. The finds suggest that
the house was occupied by a well-to-do family. Here the *andron* was
apparently located at the back of the courtyard, far from the entrance
(Fig. 6.3a). However, the room with a hearth and the area identified as
the workroom were located as far as possible from the *andron*, and
traces of a staircase to an upper storey were found in the workroom,
suggesting that the women of the household could move freely from
storey to storey without leaving their designated area (Fig. 6.3b).
Moreover the entrance to this house was controlled by a porter's lodge.
Water was probably brought by conduit, traces of which were found
nearby. The house seems to have been occupied after the Archidamian
War (probably after the Peace of Nikias in 421) and was abandoned
before the attack on Dekeleia in 413. This may represent a short-lived
attempt to reoccupy family land after enforced evacuation to Athens in
wartime.

Built of stone, the house at Dystos in Euboea is better preserved
than the Attic examples, some walls of the upper storey standing to a
considerable height. It was surveyed in the late nineteenth century
(Wiegand, 1899) and was recently re-examined by J.V. Luce (Luce,
1971; see also Lawrence, 1967). The house has yet to be excavated and
few of the rooms are securely identified. Large and well-built, it is
located close to the fort and is thought to have belonged to a senior
officer. The style of the masonry suggests a date in the fifth century
BC.

The very strictly controlled narrow entrance is striking (Fig. 6.4a).
The room identified as the *andron* is well separated from the working
area by an open court. The entrances to rooms are staggered, making it
difficult to see into more than one room at a time. As in the Dema
House, there may have been a stair from the workrooms to the upper
storey (Fig. 6.4b).

For comparison I include a house of the Hausa tribe, an Islamic
community living in northern Nigeria. The published plan (Fig. 6.5a)
was made about 1950 (reproduced in Denyer, 1978). Here the wives
of the householder have extensive quarters at the back of the house,
well supplied with water, sunlight, shade and access to latrines and
storerooms. The street frontage of this house is in contrast narrow. As
in many Athenian houses, there is only one entrance and a separate

shop. The courtyards in the men's part of the house are much smaller than those used by the women; one served as a stable. No visitors were admitted beyond the 'vestibule', and there was no access from this room to the women's quarters, which could not be seen from the public part of the house (Fig. 6.5b).

Figure 6.1: Block of Houses Excavated on the North Slope of the Areopagus, Athens (after Travlos, 1971)

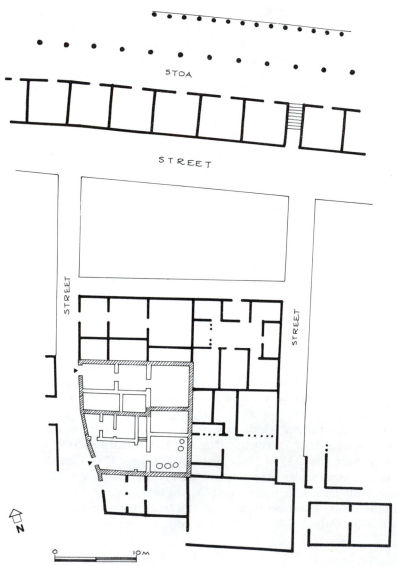

Figure 6.2a: House on the North Slope of the Areopagus: probable functions of rooms

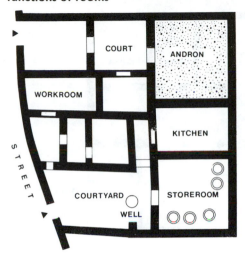

Figure 6.2b: House on the North Slope of the Areopagus: use of rooms by men and by women

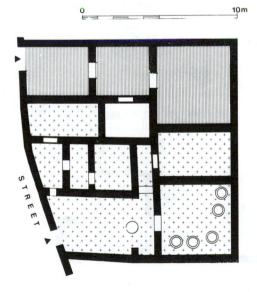

Areas used by women are marked +; those used by men are shaded. Entrances to houses from the street are marked with arrows.

Figure 6.3a: The Dema House at Ano Liossia: probable functions of rooms (after Jones, 1962)

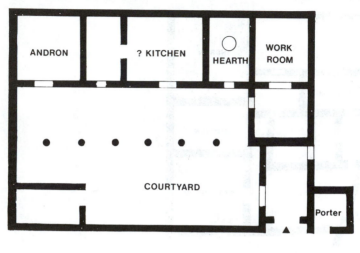

Figure 6.3b: The Dema House at Ano Liossia: use of rooms by men and by women

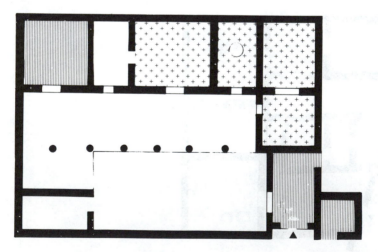

Areas used by women are marked +; those used by men are shaded. Entrances to houses from the street are marked with arrows.

Figure 6.4a: House at Dystos, Euboea: probable functions of rooms (after Lawrence, 1967)

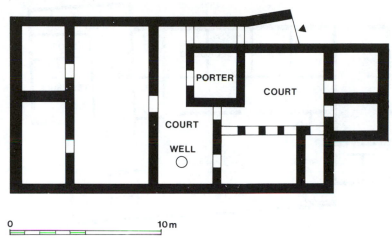

Figure 6.4b: House at Dystos, Euboea: use of rooms by men and by women

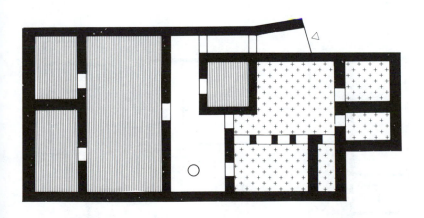

Areas used by women are marked +; those used by men are shaded. Entrances to houses from the street are marked with arrows.

Figure 6.5a: House of the Hausa Tribe at Kano, Nigeria: probable functions of rooms (after Denyer, 1978)

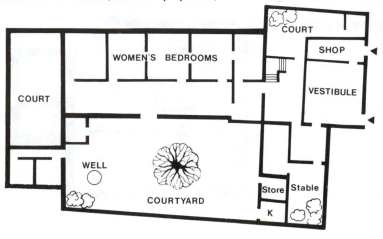

Figure 6.5b: House at Kano, Nigeria: use of rooms by men and by women

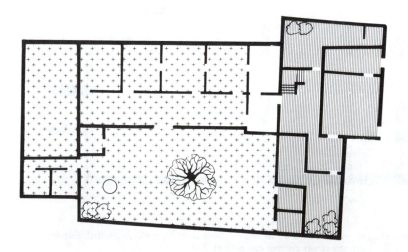

Areas used by women are marked +; those used by men are shaded. Entrances to houses from the street are marked with arrows.

For archaeologists there are many problems in interpreting such evidence. Much depends on the secure identification of rooms. The *andron* was usually the largest room in the house and in many cases has been recognised from its superior flooring (such as pebble mosaic in place of beaten earth), sometimes surrounded by the foundations of the platforms on which wooden dining-couches were set. The doorway was usually built off-centre to accommodate the requisite number of couches. Entrances to houses normally present no problem of identification. The same may be said of courtyards, water supplies and storerooms. Other areas are difficult to interpret, especially in houses occupied for centuries, where drastic modifications may have obscured the elements of the original design. The difficulty of establishing the existence, let alone the form, of an upper storey of an ancient mudbrick house has already been noted. But though the women's quarters themselves are lost, many vestiges of the history of their inhabitants may be recovered.

Further Reading

Denyer, S. (1978), *African Tribal Architecture*, London
Jones, J.E. (1975), 'Town and country houses of Attica in classical times', *Thorikos and the Laurion in Archaic and Classical Times*, *Miscellanea Graeca* 1, Ghent
Lawrence, A.W. (1967), *Greek Architecture*, Pelican History of Art, Harmondsworth, p. 241 and fig. 135
Luce, J.V. (1971), 'The large house at Dystos in Euboea', *Greece and Rome*, 2nd ser., 18, 143-9
Wiegand, T. (1899), 'Dystos', *Athenische Mitteilungen* 24, 465-6, pl. 6.

Acknowledgements

This paper was generated by work undertaken with Ian Jenkins on 'Women and Space in Classical Greece'. I have learned much from discussions with 'Matrix', a group of women architects developing a feminist analysis of the environment in contemporary Britain and in other societies. I should also like to thank John Wilkes and Ian Jenkins for their helpful comments, and John Camp for providing information on the houses excavated on the north slope of the Areopagus.
The drawings were prepared for publication by Susan Bird.

7 WOMEN ON ATHENIAN VASES: PROBLEMS OF INTERPRETATION

Dyfri Williams, London

The purpose of this paper is to take a brief look at some of the evidence for the lives of ancient Greek women as supplied by the scenes on Athenian vases, and to bring out some of the problems that surround the interpretation of such scenes.[1]

Figure 7.1: A Warrior's Departure. White-ground funerary Lekythos, c. 440 BC

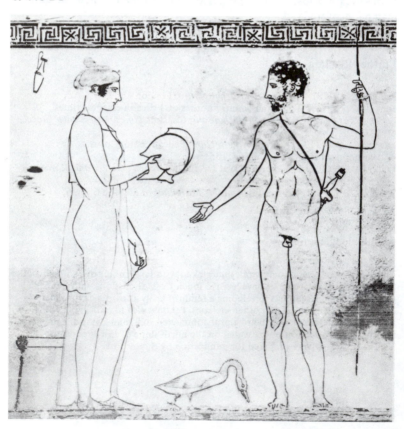

Figure 7.2: Domestic Scene. Red-figured Hydria, 440-430 BC

Let us begin with a delicately painted white-ground lekythos in the British Museum, which dates from around 440 BC and was made specifically for funerary use (Fig. 7.1).[2] The scene is the departure of a warrior to battle. He wears a sword on a belt and rests one hand on the shaft of his spear, while his wife holds out his helmet for him. Between them a goose pecks at the ground. In Greece geese were not only domesticated, but they also seem to have been kept as pets and were regarded pre-eminently as symbols of love. It is, therefore, perhaps more than just a coincidence that this particular vase was found in a tomb at Marion on Cyprus, Aphrodite's island — one of the very rare exports of a classical white-ground lekythos. The scene is a moving one, evoking the solemn sadness of departure to war, a departure that was so often final, and something perhaps of the tranquillity and tenderness one might like to find in ancient Greek domestic life.

A vase of similar date in the Harvard University collection shows us what such an Athenian citizen might have hoped was a typical moment in the life of his wife while he was away (Fig. 7.2).[3] On this red-figured hydria we see a well-to-do woman seated in the centre, handing her baby to a maid-servant on the left. On the right is a young man, probably the eldest son — vase-painters were never very precise in their depiction of age — and on the extreme left we see a loom. This scene seems to celebrate the primary functions of a woman as they are set out by ancient Greek writers: to produce and rear children and to contribute to the self-sufficiency of the household by weaving textiles for use in the home.[4] Furthermore, like the previous vase, this hydria was probably intended as a gift for the tomb either of a woman or of her husband who left such a family behind. Indeed the vase is said to come from a tomb near Vari in the countryside south-east of Athens.

Another characteristic occupation of women was spinning. In fact the distaff became a literary symbol for the dedicated housewife.[5] A similar symbolism seems to have occurred to the vase-painters, for on an unpublished red-figured lekythos in Paris a woman is seen spinning, while nearby we read the word *philergos*, she is 'industrious'.[6] There are a good number of representations of women spinning on Greek vases, but one of the finest is on a perfectly preserved white-ground jug in the British Museum, which dates from about 490 BC (Fig. 7.3).[7] Here a stately woman stands on her own, holding a distaff up in her left hand. The upper part of the distaff has been wound with dyed roves of wool which appear as a solid red ball. The thumb and index finger of the right hand hold the thread, while the spindle whirls below. The thread has been attached to a hook at the top of the spindle which is clearly visible on the vase, as is the conical weight at the bottom that helps to hold the thread in tension. Our lady's spindle has almost reached the ground and she will soon have to stop and wind up the thread, adding to the already visible lump in the middle of the spindle. Her head is slightly bent as she carefully watches the thread, a model of serious concentration.

The use of the white-ground technique on a jug is unusual and makes it very likely that this vase was intended to be sold as a dedication or a special gift. The subject makes it a very suitable gift for a woman, either on the occasion of her marriage as an example to follow in her new life or on her death in remembrance of her industry. The shape of the vase is also suitable for a woman, for in the important ceremony of libation it was the woman who poured the wine from a jug into a bowl, held by the man, who then poured it on the ground or altar.

Figure 7.3: Woman Spinning. White-ground Jug, c. 490 BC

From these few examples it is clear how one could use vases to add form and colour to the account of women presented by our ancient literary sources. But this approach must be used with caution, for it can lead one to overinterpret what may seem to be archetypal images. One might, for example, assume that all women represented on vases in the act of spinning wool must be respectable, or that any woman who sits on a *klismos* — the high-backed chair on which the mother sat in the scene on the Harvard hydria — must also be a *mater familias*. That this is clearly untrue is neatly illustrated by a late fifth-century red-figured hydria in Copenhagen (Fig. 7.4).[8] Here we see a *madam* seated on a *klismos* teaching a young hetaira, naked but for an amulet round her thigh, to spin wool. Similarly, on the outside of a cup in a German private collection from the end of the sixth century we see wool-working going on in a brothel.[9] On the far right of one side a girl is spinning as a man tries to opportune a companion who is playing the

Figure 7.4: A Madam Instructing a Hetaira. Red-figure Hydria, c. 440-430 BC

pipes. On the left a more patient customer watches two hetairai packing away full spindles of wool into a basket. That these women are hetairai is made very clear by the names the painter has given them — Aphrodisia and Obole.

Prostitution, proverbially the oldest profession, played a very important role in ancient Greece, where women were all too often excluded and secluded.[10] We hear of and find archaeological evidence for rich and successful hetairai from the beginning of the sixth century.[11] Indeed at Athens we learn that the lawgiver Solon tried to regularise prostitution by establishing state-run brothels, staffed by slaves.[12] On a fine vase in an American private collection which dates from around 480 BC we see a hetaira seated in the porch of what is surely a brothel, a familiar scene in any modern 'red light district' (Fig. 7.5).[13] This woman, however, is warmly dressed and is preening herself with the aid of a mirror as a boy leads forward her customers. The boy may well be one of the children of the house — we even hear stories of famous men who were accused of being the sons of hetairai.[14] Before the porch of the brothel is a man leaning on his stick as he holds out a heavy purse; behind him stands a young customer waiting his turn — unless, of course, the scene is that of a father paying for his shy son's first adventure.

The Kerameikos, where Athenian vase-painters and potters worked, was a byword for prostitution and it would not be surprising if excavations there were to reveal a brothel.[15] This reputation for prostitutes and the fact that many of the vase-painters were probably also slaves or foreigners, just like the hetairai, must inevitably have had an effect on the viewpoint of female life that such vase-painters presented. Furthermore, although some vases were no doubt designed as gifts for respectable women, as we have seen, by far the greatest market was the rich, wine-loving male population. Cups, mugs, mixing-bowls for wine and water jars were all necessary furniture of the drinking-party, and the subjects painted on them might well be expected to reflect the activities of the symposium and its 'after-glow'.

Once this natural bias of the vase-painters is fully recognised — status, neighbourhood and market — we quickly realise just why it is that there are so many more scenes involving hetairai than respectable women. Indeed by contrast to the relatively limited extracts from a family woman's day, we not only find many glimpses of hetairai at work — attending symposia with the young men of Athens, accompanying them on the drunken processions afterwards and, of course, making love — but we also see them learning their profession or even just relaxing.

On a small hydria of the latter part of the fifth century in the British

Figure 7.5: Entrance to a Brothel. Red-figured Hydria, c. 480 BC

Museum we see a 'madam' teaching two naked hetairai to dance (Fig. 7.6).[16] There are many other scenes of dancing lessons, but, although one presumes that respectable girls also learnt dancing to an extent, there are very few examples on vases where it is not absolutely clear that the scene involves hetairai. Similarly, on another small hydria in the

Figure 7.6: Madam Teaching Hetairai to Dance. Red-figured Hydria, c. 440-430 BC

British Museum very like the last, we find two hetairai preparing to wash (Fig. 7.7).[17] We look in vain for scenes of respectable women washing: respectable women, like goddesses, should not be seen naked nor shown naked. Stories like that of Teiresias are the models for normal attitudes.

There are, however, a number of scenes on vases involving women in which the identity of the participants is not so easy to determine. Some show groups of women on their own, as on the outside of a cup in Florence, which dates from around 470 BC (Fig. 7.8).[18] There are ten women in all, five on each side, some standing, some seated. Most hold fillets or garlands. Since no men intrude upon the scene, one might imagine that the setting was the women's quarters of a very rich and indolent household. Surely, however, given the bias we have now come to recognise and the general air of vanity, it is much more likely that we have here a group of hetairai preparing for their evening's business.

A rather more difficult group of scenes may be represented by a hydria in the British Museum of the third quarter of the fifth century

Figure 7.7: Hetairai Washing. Red-figured Hydria, c. 440-430 BC

(Figs. 9-10).[19] There are seven women set around the shoulder of this vase. On the left hovers an *eros*; to the right sits a woman playing the lyre and further on is another pet bird. Beyond another seated lyre-player stand two more women; the one on the right holds an open book-roll. Such groups of women involved in music and reading are most often Muses, and may be identified either because they are named, or because Apollo is present or because there are nine of them. There are also some in which the painter no doubt had the legendary poetess, Sappho, and her pupils in mind. Indeed, on a hydria in Athens a woman who sits reading from a book-roll is actually given the name Sappho.[20] Other examples may show professional musicians, or even some of the highly educated courtesans of the mid and later fifth century. It is unlikely, however, that many show ordinary housewives, whose education can, at best, have risen little above the ability to make lists or keep accounts, for their education was chiefly in the hands of their husbands.[21]

The interpretation of scenes like these is complicated, therefore, not only by the difficulty in recognising whether the women involved are professionals or family women, but also by the fact that they could well be legendary or even mythical. Indeed, in vase-painting myth and daily life often fuse, the iconography of the one invading and embellishing the other. Thus, for example, mortal marriages often seem to admit

Figure 7.8: Group of Women: Hetairai?. Red-figured Cup, c. 480 BC

Figure 7.9: Educated Hetairai Relax. Red-figured Hydria, c. 440 BC

immortal guests, while representations of heroic weddings assume the scheme of mortal ones.

A final group of vases, however, adds still further levels of complication to the interpretation of some scenes involving women. The setting is out of doors, which, because it is in itself unusual, tends to reinforce the literary picture of the seclusion of well-to-do women in cities. Here women have come to a fountain-house to fill their hydriai. The fountain-house is usually decked with fillets and branches indicating that the occasion is probably some festival in which water played an important role. This could, of course, be almost any festival in the Athenian calendar, but on a vase in the British Museum from late in the sixth century we find that Dionysos and Hermes are also represented, drawn on a larger scale than the mortal women busy within the fountain-house (Fig. 7.11).[22] The presence of these two deities seems to point directly to the festival known as the Anthesteria.[23] On the first day of the Anthesteria the new wine, the gift of Dionysos, was sampled, the second day was the key day and ended in an elaborate feast, while the third day was given over to Hermes of the Underworld. All three

Figure 7.10: Educated Hetairai Relax. Other side of hydria shown in Fig. 7.9

ceremonies needed water, but all were largely the concern of individual families. The state, however, seems to have had a special ritual, on the central day, in which water was poured into a chasm near the Olympeion. This was probably known as the Hydrophoria.[24] Our vase might, therefore, celebrate the role of water during the festival of the Anthesteria, or more precisely the ceremony of the state Hydrophoria which fell between the days of Dionysos and Hermes.

One problem remains, however, the identity of the women at the fountain-house. Respectable, well-to-do women did not go out of doors a great deal[25] and certainly not to the fountain-house, which seems to have been a busy and rather unsavoury place, unless, of course, a religious occasion like the Hydrophoria was an acceptable exception.[26] Furthermore, if we examine the names which are occasionally given by the vase-painters to the women involved in these scenes, we find that they are all too often slave names, and ones particularly suitable for

Figure 7.11: Women at a Fountain House. The Hydrophoria?. Black-figured Hydria c. 520-510 BC

hetairai, such as Rhodopis (the name of a very famous sixth-century hetaira[27]), Iope (probably the Lydian word for 'hither' — a very good name for a foreign enchantress!), or other names with meanings like 'Little Snub-nose' and 'Yielding'.

Should we, therefore, think of these women as the slaves of rich households? Or are they the wives of the vase-painters themselves? Or might they be hetairai, who must have done such good business during the festival of the Anthesteria with all its feasting and revelling? Or is it really just that the names of the favourite hetairai of the day are intruding on scenes of ritual?

The picture of women that we find on vases, therefore, is often indistinct, but in the social attitudes that we can observe there is much that echoes the bias preserved in other historical sources. After all, Athenian vase-painting was essentially a man's view of a man's point of view.

Notes

1. A useful list of women on vases and some brief comments: Webster (1972), pp. 226ff. I am grateful to my two colleagues, Dr Susan Walker and Ian Jenkins, for help and encouragement in the tripartite performance of which this paper formed a part. Ian Jenkins's work on marriage and death will be published elsewhere.
2. London D.51; Beazley (1963), 1000, 201.
3. Fogg Art Museum, Harvard University: *CVA Robinson*, ii, pl. 43 with text.
4. Cf. Xenophon, *Oeconomicus*, IV.7ff.
5. E.g. Theocritus, XXVIII.1ff.
6. Paris, Cabinet des Médailles: Beazley (1963), 624, 81.
7. London D.13: Beazley (1963), 403, 38; Williams (1982).
8. Copenhagen, Nat. Mus. 153: Beazley (1963), 1131, 161.
9. Munich, Zanker: Münzen und Medaillen AG, *Auktion* 51 (Basel, 1975), pl. 33, no. 148 with text.
10. See most recently Gould (1980), pp. 38ff.
11. E.g. at Naukratis, see Boardman (1980), p. 132.
12. Athenaeus, *Deipnosophistae* XIII.569 d-e.
13. Maplewood, Noble: Beazley (1963), 276, 70.
14. E.g. Themistocles, Athenaeus, *Deipn.*, XIII.576c.
15. Literary sources collected in Wycherley (1957), pp. 222f. It has been suggested that the recently discovered Building Z in the Kerameikos was a state brothel; we eagerly await its publication.
16. London E.203: Beazley (1963), 1131, 164.
17. London E.202: Beazley (1963), 1131, 155.
18. Florence 75770: Beazley (1963), 861, 15.
19. London 1921.7-10.2: Beazley (1963), 1060, 138.
20. Athens 1260: Beazley (1963), 1060, 145.
21. Cf. Note 4.
22. London B.332: Beazley (1956), 333, 27.

23. On the Anthesteria, see Parke (1977), pp. 107ff.

24. Hydrophoria: Diehl (1964), pp. 130ff.

25. The women seen shopping on vases (e.g. Etienne and Etienne-Germau (1975), nos. 35 and 36) may be slaves, for men usually did the shopping (Aristophanes, *Vespae*, 493ff. and *Ecclesiazusae*, 817ff.), but there were no doubt exceptions (cf. Aristophanes, frag. 318 Kock).

26. Cf. Aristophanes, *Lysistrata*, 327ff. We see men accosting women at fountain-houses on vases (e.g. Beazley, 1956, 387, 18 or 397, 31).

27. Herodotus II.134f.

PART FOUR: THE BIOLOGY OF WOMEN

The physical constraints of the female reproductive cycle and the social strategies by which it is managed

8 BOUND TO BLEED: ARTEMIS AND GREEK WOMEN

Helen King, Liverpool

In Edwin Ardener's influential paper 'Belief and the problem of women' (1972), the 'problem', that of finding out how women see the world of which they are a part when our only informants are men, is shown to be twofold. There is a 'technical' problem: women are less likely to 'speak', to act as our sources. There is also an 'analytical', or conceptual, dimension for, even when our informants are women, the model of the world and of their place in it which they give may be less acceptable to the observer than the neat, bounded categories given by the male informant (1972, pp. 1-3).

A particular form of technical/conceptual division can be applied to ancient Greek source material. The problem of Greek women is usually presented as a technical problem; that is, as something originating in the sources. In the words of Vatin: 'It is in the deeds, the words and the laws of men that we must look for the traces [of Greek women]' (1970, pp. 2-3: my translation). The evidence available to us was mostly written by Greek men; although this statement itself tells us something about Greek women it also acts as a screen to distance us from them. In addition, the sources are preselected so that, where comparative material raises interesting questions, the type of evidence required to answer them may simply be unavailable.

The often conflicting images of women which emerge from the evidence similarly tend to be seen in terms of the technical problems of the sources. Shaw's article on women in fifth-century Athenian drama (1975) criticises a very simple example of this approach, the division of the evidence into two main classes; firstly legal and historical material, in which women are 'defined as near slaves, or as perpetual minors' (p. 255), and secondly literature and the visual arts, in which women seem to have a prominent role. Either category of evidence can be discarded by those working on the period; law as only theory, drama as mere fantasy. A more sophisticated and inclusive division of the source material, as concerned with 'social organisation', 'popular morality' or 'myth', appears in Just's article (1975).

The 'problem' of Greek women, then, is firstly that we have no direct means of access to them; we only have sources written by men. Secondly, however, even these sources give us the contrast between the strong, dominant women of tragedy and the almost invisible women of the Funeral Speech of Thucydides, in which Pericles says that 'the greatest glory of a woman is to be least talked about by men' (2. 46). Both Shaw and Just claim that there is a coherent model of Greek women beneath these different images given in the evidence, but I would suggest that they are mistaken in giving so much weight to the problems of the sources. The discovery that different types of evidence give different, even contradictory, presentations of women is not a problem, but a solution, and it should be acknowledged rather than being concealed by the division of that evidence into categories such as 'law', 'custom' and 'myth' (as in Gould, 1980) based on our own society's criteria of rationality.

It is important to realise here that, even outside the Greek context, the concept of 'woman' has inherent potential for ambiguity. 'Woman' can be opposed to 'man', as female to male, or subsumed under the category 'man' so that humanity is set up against 'gods' or 'beasts' (cf. Hastrup, 1978, p. 54): 'woman' is thus both excluded and included, alien and familiar. For the Greeks woman is a necessary evil, a *kalon kakon* (Hesiod, *Theogony* 585); an evil because she is undisciplined and licentious, lacking the self-control of which men are capable, yet necessary to society as constructed by men, in order to reproduce it.[1]

In social terms, women can be put under the control of men, being assigned a specific space within male culture and society where they can give birth, weave and cook, while being excluded from economic and political spheres. The Greek word for woman, *gynē*, is also the word for 'wife', and it was as a wife and mother that woman was most fully brought into male culture. Her domestication could be so complete that she would express and enforce the male model of society, including the reasons for her own entry into it (Redfield, 1977, p. 149); yet even here the risk that she would run wild remained.

In the words of Sarah B. Pomeroy's title, women were 'Goddesses, Whores, Wives and Slaves' (1975): in conceptual terms these four identities are all strands which can be taken out of the basic, ambiguous term 'woman', but such a separation can never be complete because the sub-categories have a tendency to drift back towards their original unity.[2] The goddesses of the Greek pantheon include Hera the wife, Demeter the mother, and Artemis as the woman who rejects both marriage and motherhood; all women are potential whores, if they are allowed to surrender to their uncontrolled desires; all women are slaves to their emotions, of which only man can be a master.

In this paper I intend to look at another way in which the range of meanings of 'woman' was separated out in Greek thought. As the positive values of 'woman' tended to be centred on the concept of the reproducer, the *gynē*, so the negative values shifted to the unmarried girl. The focus of this paper is therefore not on the technical problems of the sources, but on the conceptual framework within which they were produced, the ideas about 'woman' which governed the perception of the female life-cycle; in particular, on the entry into what was culturally established as the category of the mature woman, the *gynē*.

From Parthenos to Gynē

All women start their lives conceptually 'outside' male society, but most are taken 'inside' through the process of maturation. Children, for the Greeks, are by nature wild (Plato, *Timaeus*, 44a-b; *Laws* II, 653d-e, 666a-e); in particular, the *parthenos*, 'childless, unmarried, yet of the age for marriage',[3] is untamed (*admēs*) and must be domesticated before it is even possible for a man to carry on a conversation with her (Xenophon, *Oeconomicus*, 7. 10: use of *tithaseuein*). A girl's upbringing is represented as the 'taming' or 'breaking in' of a filly, and marriage is the end of this process: marriage also opens the process of submission to the yoke of Aphrodite.[4]

There are a number of biologically and socially defined points at which the transition from *parthenos* to *gynē* can be situated, the most obvious being menarche, defloration, marriage and the first parturition. In connection with the choice[5] of one or more of these as involving a significant change of status the factor of control is particularly relevant. Menarche is a transition which neither men nor women can control (although Soranus, *Gynaecology* 1. 25, gives exercises to encourage it). Marriage, in Greek society, is under male control, being arranged between *oikos* heads. Defloration is more ambiguous, covering a spectrum ranging from male control (rape) to female control (seduction). The first parturition may appear as an entirely female event, but there is scope for male control;[6] men are necessary not only for conception (although see Detienne, 1976) but also to bring on labour by having intercourse with their wives (Aristotle, *Historia Animalium*, 584a 30-1) and as doctors to speed up labour with appropriate drugs (e.g. PG, 1. 34).[7] There is in addition the possibility that a registration or initiation procedure linked to age may be used, although this does not seem to have been the case with Greek women.[8]

In a society in which women are valued above all for their reproductive capacities, it is to be expected that a biological event or series of events will be used to form the entry to the category 'mature woman': in a society in which woman can also be seen as the 'Other' (Arthur, 1976, p. 390; Padel, this volume) to be brought under male control, it is to be expected that the cultural ideal will be one of a close connection between the male-controlled social event, marriage, and the less controllable physical changes in a woman's life. Ideally, therefore, menarche confirmed that a girl was 'ripe' for marriage (on ripeness see for example Pausanias 2. 33. 2 and *Greek Anthology* (hereafter *Anth. Pal.*), VII.600) and defloration (Soranus, *Gyn*, I.33.4, 33.6): she would be deflowered by her husband on her wedding night (the 'first yoke of Aphrodite' in *Anth. Pal.*, IX.245): she would begin bearing children as soon as possible. The temporal gap between *parthenos* and *gynē* would be short; the Greek process of becoming married, extending from betrothal to the birth of the first child, would cover it (Vernant, 1973) and the term *nymphē* would be applied to those in the 'latent period' stretching from marriageable to married (Schmitt, 1977, p. 1068; see also Chantraine, 1946-7, pp. 228-9 on *nymphē/gynē* overlap).

In practice, however, there are many reasons why a girl may be trapped between categories so that she becomes anomalous, not really a *parthenos* but not fully a *gynē*. Social and biological status may not coincide: menarche may not have occurred, although in all other respects (age, vocal changes, breast development — see Aristotle, *Hist. Anim.*, 581a 31-b 24) she is ripe for marriage (Soranus, *Gyn*. 1.29.6); she may be pregnant but unmarried (Coronis in Pindar, *Third Pythian* 34, is a *parthenos* although she carries Apollo's child); she may have difficulty conceiving; or she may not want to marry.

In view of Greek ideas about the two sides of 'woman' — the outsider, product of a separate act of creation (see Loraux, 1978), who must nevertheless be brought into society to reproduce it — gynaecological texts are a particularly appropriate field of study. Their concern is with woman as reproducer, yet the very autonomy of the study of female diseases reflects the separation of woman from the superior, complete[9] human form, man.

In the Hippocratic medical texts female functions such as menstruation and childbirth are regarded as pathological (cf. Ehrenreich and English, 1979, p. 99 on nineteenth-century medical theory) and hence require treatment: yet they are also natural, for it is wrong for a woman to develop masculine characteristics (as in Ep. VI, 8.32) and they can, as *katharsis*, have a healing effect (Burkert, 1977, p. 133, n. 31; Manuli, 1980, pp. 401-2). To circumvent this problem of women's physical processes as both negative and positive — itself a result of wider views of 'woman' — the texts establish physical 'norms'. Thus the normal blood loss during menstruation is set at about a pint over two or three days; any more or less is pathological and needs therapy (PG 1. 6; Aphorisms 5. 57 (*L* IV 552)). A further distinction is drawn between the 'womb-woman' and those 'outside the logic of generation' (*ek tōn tokōn*, PG 2. 127; see Manuli, 1980, pp. 398-9). The female object of the text is split, and the non-reproductive are exhorted to reproduce. Young girls are advised to marry, widows that 'it is best to become pregnant' (e.g. NW 3: PG 2. 127, 131, 135, 162).

The Peri Partheniōn

Text

The *Peri Partheniōn* is one of a series of gynaecological treatises in the Hippocratic corpus; it probably dates to the fifth or fourth century BC and, as a practical handbook for doctors, it may have been modified many times before reaching the form in which it survives (Lloyd, 1975, pp. 180ff.). The title is usually translated 'On the diseases of young girls' or 'On the diseases of virgins'; here the Greek term will be retained because, although virginity and youth were aspects of the ideal *parthenos*, there is no current English equivalent. The main focus of the semantic field covered by *parthenos* is not 'virgin' but 'unmarried' (see Loraux, 1981, p. 241, n. 183); the idea of youth is present but, if suitably qualified, the term can be applied to older unmarried women (e.g. 'older *parthenoi*' in PG 2. 127). Soranus clearly applies it to girls before menarche (*Gyn* 1.29.6).

This short fragment, on one set of problems preventing the *parthenos* to *gynē* transition, opens with a statement on the origins and nature of the *tekhnē* (profession, trade) of medicine and a reference to the symptoms of the 'sacred disease', epilepsy. Such symptoms, the writer explains, may result in suicide by hanging. This is more common in women than in men, and most common among *parthenoi* who, despite being 'ripe for marriage', remain unmarried.

Such *parthenoi* risk illness at menarche[10] when blood flows to the womb as if it were going to pass out of the body. In the *parthenos* who does not marry at the proper time the blood cannot flow out because 'the orifice of exit' is not open. The blood instead moves to the heart and diaphragm, where its effect is described as producing similar sensations to those felt in the feet after sitting still for a long time. However, when the heart and diaphragm are involved there is great danger, since the veins which return the blood are not straight, so that the return is delayed, and the area itself is a vital one. The *parthenos* therefore exhibits a number of symptoms; for instance, she is delirious, she fears the darkness, and she has visions which seem to compel her to jump, to throw herself down wells and to strangle herself. In the absence of visions she shows an erotic fascination with death (*eraō*: she welcomes death as a lover). The text ends:

> When her[11] senses return, the *gynaikes* dedicate many objects to Artemis, above all, the most splendid of their garments. They are ordered to do this by diviners (*manteis*) who thoroughly deceive them. But she is relieved of this complaint when nothing prevents the flow of menstrual blood. I order (*keleuō*) *parthenoi* to marry as quickly as possible if they suffer like this. For if they become pregnant, they become healthy. If not, then at puberty or a little later she will suffer from this or from some other disease. Among married *gynaikes*, the sterile suffer most from these conditions. (My translation).

The interpretation of this text is made more difficult by the apparently indiscriminate shifts between singular and plural. I would suggest that the plural forms should always be taken as '*gynaikes*'; thus we have, 'For if *gynaikes* become pregnant, they become healthy', another example of the common idea that the role of the *gynē* is to reproduce. Where the singular appears, we can read '*parthenos*'; for example, 'at puberty or a little later' covers the ideal age range for this term. This leaves as problematic only the first line of this section. Who are the *gynaikes* who are told by the diviners to dedicate their garments to Artemis? Are they perhaps close female kin of the afflicted *parthenos* offering their garments for her recovery?

There is, however, another possibility. No change of subject may be intended in this sentence (see, e.g. Fasbender, 1897, p. 229): the *parthenoi*, through their recovery, have become *gynaikes*. Menarche, the 'flow of menstrual blood' mentioned here, is thus the cause of the 'return of the senses' which is otherwise unexplained either by the ritual actions which precede it or by the social cure which follows it. In this text the *parthenos* to *gynē* transition would therefore seem to be centred on menarche, while still extending across marriage and into childbirth. It is with this interpretation that the remainder of the present paper is concerned. The doctor sees menarche in physiological terms, as due to the removal of something preventing the flow. Hence the recommendation of marriage, which may be related to the theory that childbirth widens the veins and so eases menstruation (PG 1. 1; Fasbender, 1897, p. 224) or to the idea that the menstrual flow is blocked by the hymen (Fasbender, 1897, p. 79). The diviners, in ordering dedications to Artemis after menarche,[12] make reference to the role played by this goddess at other stages of female maturation.

Context: Medicine

Many features mentioned in the *Peri Partheniōn* find parallels in other gynaecological texts. These include delayed menarche causing mental disturbances (SF 34), the close of the 'orifice of exit' preventing normal menstruation (PG 3. 213, 228), terror (PG 2. 182), the desire for death (*thanein eratai*, PG 2. 177), the use of *keleuō* by the doctor (PG 3. 220), the sudden and unexplained return of reason (SF 34) and the advice to *parthenoi* to marry (PG 2. 127).

Other aspects of the text can be located within wider themes. The condemnation of 'deceit' in others who claim they can treat the disease is part of the attempt to establish medicine as a specific *tekhnē*, and it is found in *On the Sacred Disease* as well as in *Articulations*, 42-44, where the writer condemns those who use the spectacular therapy of succussion on a ladder (illustrated in *L* IV 187) merely to impress the crowds, but does not reject the technique altogether. Direct competition seems to have been the norm in Greek medicine, sometimes between doctors and *manteis* but often between those claiming to be of the same *tekhnē* (Lloyd, 1979, p. 39 and n. 152). Each individual had to persuade his patient that, of all the available therapies, his was the best (Lloyd, 1979, pp. 89 ff.), and to this is related the emphatic use of the first person in these texts: 'But *I* say . . .' (e.g. SacDis 1, PP, PG 1. 1, 43). This suggests that the condemnation of dedications to Artemis should be taken not as a simple opposition between 'scientific' and 'religious' healers but as the product of a period in which competition for the existing clientele was intense, and in which it was necessary not only to offer a convincing explanation of one's own therapy but also to denigrate the work of all others working in the same field.

Another theme to which the *Peri Partheniōn* relates is that of abnormal blood loss in menstruation, mentioned briefly above. Excessive loss is always bad: if it is due to the nature of the woman (*physis*) then she must be sterile, but if it is the result of disease (*pathēma*) it may respond to treatment (PG 3. 213). Total absence of menstruation, a common symptom in the gynaecological texts, is always bad and often fatal (as in PG 2. 133 and Ep. VI 8.32). Its origin is usually either movement of the womb to another part of the body (e.g. PG 2. 128, 129, 133) or, as in the *Peri Partheniōn*, closure of 'the orifice' (*to stoma* — cervix? vaginal orifice? — in PG 2. 156, 157, 162-4; 3. 213, 228).

Movement of the womb is one component of the complex of symptoms which Littré (see Note 7) takes as constituting 'hysteria'; others include sudden loss of voice, coldness, grinding the teeth and *pnix*, or suffocation. The attempt to impose the category of 'hysteria' on these texts may be misguided: the concomitant symptoms vary in different cases, so that while the womb may move but a characteristic symptom be absent (no *pnix* in PG 2. 127), many of the symptoms may be present but the cause is something other than uterine movement (red flux, a visible cause, in PG 2. 110). An analysis of the sections which Littré describes as 'hysteria' shows that he is classifying together groups of symptoms which the Hippocratic writers separate in terms of cause and remedy (Bourgey, 1953, pp. 149-52; Littré's section headings are also criticised by Rousselle, 1980, p. 1090).

Littré also distinguishes between 'hysteria' and 'displacement' (e.g. VIII 275, 327, 389), an opposition not found in the texts. When Littré was writing, the cause of 'hysteria' was disputed: some doctors believed that there was an organic cause, others that there was none (Merskey, 1979, p. 12ff.). Since Freud, psychological explanations have been favoured. Littré's position in this debate is clear: the hysteria/displacement opposition corresponds not to psychological/physiological but rather to imaginary/real. In this it recalls the current usage of 'hysterical' as a pejorative term: 'She's just hysterical' is used to mean, 'There's nothing really wrong with her'. For Littré, too, the 'hysterical' woman is ill for no organic reason, and this judgement is repeated in more recent work on these texts (e.g. Simon, 1978, p. 242); yet in *Peri Gynaikeiōn*, *hysterikē pnix* has no such derogatory sense, for there *is* a physical cause, namely the tendency of the womb to run wild within the body if it is not allowed to conceive (e.g. Plato, *Timaeus* 91; the most detailed ancient description of 'hysteria' is Soranus, *Gyn* 3.26-9).

This judgement of the ancient sources occurs also in the labels 'psychic' and 'psychosomatic' which can imply 'imaginary'. Summarising the section in which he discusses the texts on women's diseases, Laín Entralgo says: 'In all these clinical and therapeutic descriptions the predominantly psychic state of the symptomatic picture is quite obvious.' Earlier in the same section he describes the *parthenoi* as 'certain ill — perhaps hysterical, to judge by what is said of them — women' (1970, 168; 158).

Such a 'diagnostic approach', which attempts to diagnose disease across two and a half millennia and through a text of this kind, is deeply unconvincing and takes us away from the text and the cultural values which it carries. Perhaps there were real girls, seen by the author, who exhibited symptoms for which there was no organic cause; perhaps these were the result of mental stress or perhaps the girls sought attention by a convincing deception:[13] perhaps there were real girls suffering from hormonal or glandular disturbances which could cause the same symptoms: or perhaps the text embodies a 'terrorismo igienico' (Manuli, 1980, p. 404) in order to scare women into acting as society dictated, marrying and giving birth at the age seen as appropriate. We simply cannot say. I intend here to concentrate instead on the internal logic of the representation and on other texts which show similar operations of thought, believing that at this level the question of the referent behind the text is of only secondary importance and also that a reading which emphasises what is specific to the text contributes more than one dominated by the principle of generalisation.

Two aspects of the *Peri Partheniōn* appear to be unique in the gynaecological corpus: firstly the outline of an alternative approach to difficulties at menarche, through the cult of Artemis, and secondly the use of the verb *(ap)ankhō* for the symptom of feeling strangled and for the girls' desire to strangle themselves. This may seem to link the text to the symptom of *pnix*, suffocation, found in many sections of the *Peri Gynaikeiōn* (e.g. 1. 7, 32, 55: 2. 116, 123-8, etc.), often in connection with menstrual retention. Later lexicographers and medical writers equate the two verbs (e.g. *ankhomenos = pnigomenos*, Galen 19.69 (ed. Kuhn): the Suda s.v. *apankhonisai : pnixai*), thus strengthening this suggestion, but a glance at their cognates shows that whereas *ankhō* suggests the pressure on the throat of strangulation or hanging, *pnigō* evokes suffocation through stifling heat (e.g. *pnigeus*, oven; *pnigos*, heat). *Pnix* is particularly common when the womb moves; remembering the womb/oven analogy (Aristophanes, *Peace* 891: cf. Herodotus 5. 92 on Periander), *pnix* is a very appropriate symptom in such cases.

Context: Myth

I would suggest that the use of *(ap)ankhō* in the *Peri Partheniōn*, which leads the writer into the subject of *parthenoi*, should be understood not as a sub-category of *pnix* but as an expression of the role of Artemis at transitions in a woman's life which involve bloodshed. While the doctor and the *manteis* disagree about the treatment which is best, they not only agree about the end in sight – the transformation of the *parthenos* into a reproductive *gynē* – but make reference to the same cultural tradition concerning *parthenoi*, strangulation and bleeding.

Plutarch describes a condition which is supposed to have afflicted the *parthenoi* of Miletus: it was manifested in a desire for death (*epithymia thanatou*) which made them hang themselves. As in the *Peri Parthenion* the verb used is (*ap*)*ankhō* and the text contains both 'medical' and 'divine' explanations of the condition (*Moralia* 249 B-D).[14]

To discover why *parthenoi* have what almost amounts to an 'elective affinity' with hanging and strangulation (cf. the myths listed by Brelich, 1969, pp. 443-4, n. 2), it is necessary to glance at other stories which involve this form of death, and in particular to look at a tradition associated with the goddess Artemis who has been granted eternal *partheneia* by her father Zeus (Callimachus, *Hymn to Artemis*, 5 ff.).

Artemis Strangled. Pausanias (8.23.6-7) tells a curious story about the origin of the epithet Apankhomene, the Strangled Lady, held by Artemis at Kaphyae in Arkadia. Once some children tied a rope around her image during a game, and playfully said that Artemis was being strangled. For this apparent sacrilege their elders stoned them to death. The *gynaikes* of Kaphyae were then struck with a disease, and as a result their babies were still-born. The priestess of Apollo was consulted and ordered that the children should be buried and should receive annual sacrifices, because they had been put to death wrongly. From then on, Artemis was called Apankhomene.

The *aition* reflects the role of the goddess in children's lives. As Kourotrophos she protects their upbringing and leads them to adulthood, receiving dedications of childhood toys (references in Van Straten, 1981, p. 90, n. 126). Another aspect of the story is the pattern by which an error is made, the guilty are struck by disease, and equilibrium restored after the Pythia gives advice. This is very common in myths of Artemis (see Calame, 1977, p. 281). Here, however, one other point should be drawn out of the text; that it is correct to call Artemis 'Strangled'. The children were right to give her this title, and their innocent game revealed the truth.

Assuming that the origin of such legends is the misunderstanding of ritual, scholars have suggested that Apankhomene arises from the practice of hanging images of vegetation deities on trees (e.g. Farnell, 1896, p. 428; Nilsson, 1967, p. 487). This misses the pertinence of the epithet to Artemis. It should be noted that the punishment in this text is not merely a disease, but is an interruption of the normal reproduction of the city through its *gynaikes*. Artemis, who herself never gives birth, can give or withhold a successful labour;[15] here she chooses to prevent birth because the Kaphyan women will not call her 'Strangled'.

Why should Artemis be 'Strangled'? Strangulation, for the Greeks, meant shedding no blood. In the field of sacrifice, for example, the Scythians were supposed to strangle their beasts; 'normal' Greek sacrifice of animals shed blood and so ensured communication between men and gods (Herodotus 4. 60; see Hartog, 1980, pp. 191-4). As a form of human death, strangulation or hanging evoked horror (see for example Phaedra in Euripides, *Hippolytus* 778, 802 and Hartog, 1980, pp. 195, n. 4) but as a means of suicide it can again be related to shedding no blood. To avoid the bloodshed of rape or unwanted defloration a bloodless suicide is appropriate. The Chorus in Aeschylus's *Suppliants* threaten to hang themselves (465) rather than sleeping with men whom they hate (788) and the Caryatides actually use this mode of suicide because they fear rape (see Calame, 1977, p. 270). The action of Phaedra is not merely a negative gesture performed from fear that Hippolytus will tell Theseus the truth (as in Diodorus Siculus 4.62); it is a positive action, for by choosing this death she inserts herself into an established tradition and thus strengthens her false claim that Hippolytus has raped her.

Strangulation can therefore be culturally opposed to unwanted sex; the avoidance of the latter may be appropriately achieved through the former, although it may be carried out after the event. In the *Peri Partheniōn* the afflicted *parthenoi* avoid not only the bloodshed of defloration but also that of menarche which ideally precedes it.[16] Defloration may be feared if the *parthenos* is not 'ripe':[17] these *parthenoi*, despite being 'ripe for marriage', are represented as fearing both menarche and marriage, preferring death.

Herodotus (4. 180) tells of a Libyan festival of Athena in which the most beautiful *parthenos* is dressed in a Corinthian helmet and Greek panoply and driven along the shores of a lake in a chariot. After this, the other *parthenoi* are divided into two groups and fight with stones and sticks. Those who die of their wounds are called '*pseudoparthenoi*'; that is, 'they distinguish the true from the false by metaphor: the true virgin is inviolate or unwounded, hence the survivors are true virgins' (Benardete, 1969, p. 125). The real *parthenos* does not bleed; the eternal *parthenos* Artemis does not shed her own blood in the hunt, in sex or in childbirth. Artemis Apankhomene can therefore be seen as expressing her *partheneia*, and the strangulation symptoms and chosen mode of death in the *Peri Partheniōn* as an identification with her as 'Strangled'.

Artemis does not bleed, but she does shed the blood of others, both as huntress and as director of the process by which a *parthenos* becomes a *gynē*. The 'true' *parthenoi* in Herodotus's story similarly shed the blood of others.[18] Those in the *Peri Partheniōn* are on the contrary 'ripe for marriage', ready to bleed and thus to enter the gradual transition which will make them *gynaikes*. The *gynē* is the opposite pole to the *parthenos*; she should bleed, in menstruation, defloration and childbirth, as part of her role of reproducing society — and the Hippocratic writers supply theories to support this idea — but she should not shed blood. Only a man may shed blood in war and sacrifice (see for examples Detienne, 1979, pp. 187-9); the *gynē* is explicitly compared to the sacrificed beast which bleeds (Aristotle, *Hist. Anim.* 581b 1-2; *PG* 1. 6, 72).

Becoming a *gynē* involves a series of bleedings, each of which must take place at the proper time. Artemis, associated with the correct time for delivery (contrast Hera in *Iliad* 19. 114-7) and death (Callimachus *H. Art.* 131-2, 126: cf. *Anth. Pal.* VII 228), is naturally also associated with this process.

Pausanias's story reflects Artemis as both the goddess who sheds no blood and the goddess who makes others bleed. The Kaphyan *gynaikes* only accept the second aspect: by denying that Artemis is strangled they claim her as a *gynē* like themselves. The children instead recognise the first aspect. The references to strangulation in the *Peri Partheniōn* show *parthenoi* clinging to the first when it is time for them to accept the second: in dedicating garments to Artemis they finally acknowledge her role in initiating the transition which takes them further towards being full *gynaikes*.

Parallel to the bleeding/strangulation opposition in stories of *parthenoi* and Artemis is the releasing/binding relationship. Artemis is Lysizōnos, releaser of the girdle: she is also Lygodesma, bound with the *agnos castus*.

Artemis Releaser. The use of the *zōnē* or girdle in female clothing reflects the stages of a Greek woman's life. The first girdle is put on at puberty and later dedicated to Artemis as part of the marriage process; a special girdle, tied with a ritual knot, is worn on the wedding night and untied by the spouse; a married woman unties her girdle in labour. There is evidence to suggest that loosening the hair and garments is a necessary precaution in dangerous situations and when performing magical acts (listed in Heckenbach, 1911, pp. 78ff.), but I believe that the association between Artemis and the *zōnē*, worn throughout the *parthenos* to *gynē* transition, deserves to be seen not as one of many examples of the release of all knots at times of transition but as a far more specific reference to the powers of Artemis.

As protector of childbirth, Eileithyia, Artemis is invoked by women calling on her, often as Lysizōnos, in labour (e.g. Theocritus 17.60-1, Euripides, *Hipp*. 166-9) and after childbirth the girdle may be dedicated to her (e.g. *Anth. Pal.* VI 200, 202, 272).

Birth is not, however, the only time when Artemis releases. The phrase *luein tēn zōnēn*, to release the girdle, is used not only in labour (Soranus, *Gyn*. 2.6.1) but also for defloration (*Anth. Pal.* VII 164, 324; Euripides, *Alcestis* 177; Kaibel, 319.3, 684.3: see Daremberg, 1887, p. 142, and Farnell, 1896, p. 444) and the epithet Lysizōnos evokes the presence of Artemis on both occasions. She releases the blood from those who are 'strangled' in the *Peri Parthenion*, and she performs a similar action at the transitions of defloration and parturition, where she 'releases' the *parthenos* to cross the threshold of bleeding into a fuller expression of the status of *gynē*.

The girdle is released at these times of bloodshed: it can also be tied as a noose when *parthenoi* commit suicide. Kylon's daughter Myro, 'loosing her girdle and making a noose of it', should be seen in this context: she is 'a *parthenos* ripe for marriage' but instead of her spouse releasing her girdle before defloration she must release it herself so that it may be tied as the instrument of her death (Plutarch, *Moralia*, 253Cff.). Marriage and death — more specifically, sexual bloodshed and hanging — are inverted, and from this the story derives its pathos.

There remains one other transitional bleeding which should be considered here. The birth of the first child is particularly important in making the woman into a true *gynē* (Schmitt, 1977, p. 1064, cf. Lysias 1.6: on the ancient Near East see Cassin 1982, pp. 252-5) and this is completed by the first lochia, the discharge from the uterus after childbirth. Among the epithets referring to her role in childbirth, Artemis is called Lochia (e.g. Euripides, *Suppliants* 958; *Iphigenia in Tauris* 1097: *SEG* III 400.9). When a woman dies in or just after childbirth she remains 'not fully a *gynē*' (Kaibel, 505.4), perhaps because she has not experienced the lochia. Medical texts regard their absence as a threat to future fertility or to life itself (PG 1. 29, 40, 41): in either case the woman would not reach the full status of *gynē*.

In the Hippocratic texts the lochia are analogous to menarche; both are normally 'like the flow of blood from a sacrificed beast' (PG 1.6/

1. 72 and 2. 113, NC 18 (*L* VII 502): Fasbender, 1897, p. 181 and n. 2, p. 225 n. 4) and the symptoms of lochial displacement are explicitly (PG 1. 41) compared to those caused by displacement of menstrual blood in the *Peri Parthenion*. The lochial bleeding is most difficult after the first parturition (PG 1. 72, NC 18). Menarche and first lochia thus seem to complement each other, forming the opening and the completion of the transformation of *parthenos* to *gynē*. At each of them Artemis is involved. As Apankhomene she expresses the ideal of the *parthenos* who does not bleed; but she is the goddess of transition, and assists other women to cross the boundaries which she rejects. Thus as Lochia and Eileithyia she assists in childbirth, although she has not given birth; as Lysizōnos she 'releases the girdle' both in defloration and in labour.

Chaste Herb, Virgin Goddess. Another epithet of Artemis acts to combine the 'strangled' *parthenos* who sheds none of her own blood with the goddess who makes other women cross boundaries of bleeding. This is Lygodesma, meaning bound with the plant called lygos or agnos castus, the use of which in the ancient world ranged from wickerwork and perfume-making to medicinal and ritual purposes. Pausanias (3.16.11), who gives the epithet as an alternative title of Artemis Orthia, explains it by a story that the cult image was found in a thicket of this plant which made it stand upright (*orthos*).

The most important work to date on this epithet is that of Meuli (summary 1975, 1043-7) which places it in the context of other 'gefesselte Götter', thus grouping deities by a shared feature. Here I prefer to focus instead on the links between different attributes of one deity, an approach which I believe is equally valid and which, by showing the axes on which epithets intersect, shows how it can 'make sense' that Lygodesma, Apankhomene and Lysizōnos 'are' all Artemis.[19]

No detailed study of the connection between Artemis and the agnos exists.[20] Recent work by Detienne concerns its use in a festival of Demeter, the Thesmophoria, where its apparently opposed associations with fertility and with chastity seem to be related to the image of the ideal *gynē*, fruitful but faithful (Detienne, 1972, pp. 153-4; 1976, pp. 79-80; 1977, p. 130, n. 197; 1979, pp. 213-4).

Calame has nevertheless isolated three possible connections between agnos and Artemis (1977, pp. 285-9). Firstly, Artemis is associated with the plant world; not just with wild trees, as Farnell supposed (1896, p. 429), but also with cultivated trees. Near the sanctuary of Artemis Kalliste in Arkadia were many trees, *akarpa* and *hēmera* (Pausanias

8.35.8): in human terms, both *parthenoi* who bear no fruit, and tamed *gynaikes*, are protected by Artemis. Secondly, plant and goddess are associated with wet and marshy areas (Daremberg, 1892, p. 135; Farnell, 1896, pp. 427-8; Motte, 1973, p. 93ff; Calame, 1977, p. 262). This in turn links both to women, usually seen as 'wetter' than men (e.g. NC 15).

Finally, and most importantly, Calame looks at the medical qualities of the agnos. It reduces sexual desire but encourages menstruation and lactation;[21] in the Hippocratic texts, which Calame does not use, these opposite qualities are brought out clearly. The final section of *Peri Gynaikeiōn* 1 (74-109) is devoted to recipes considered therapeutic in various gynaecological disorders; the wide range of ingredients includes the agnos, used as an astringent in a severe flux (2. 192), to encourage conception (1. 75), to bring on birth in an unusually long labour (1. 77) and to expel the afterbirth (1. 78). The last two uses, where the agnos expels, are supported by other texts which say that it drives away snakes and acts as an abortive; the first two show that it may cause retention.

Calame (p. 289) goes on to suggest that when young boys were beaten at the altar of Orthia the intention was to stimulate the forces of growth; he suggests that girls were consecrated to Artemis at menarche, hence for them Lygodesma implied the stimulation of the menses. Such a conjecture, while consonant with the suggestions I have made above, concentrates on only one side of the agnos, thus detracting from the dual mode of operation of plant and goddess. The agnos as repressive astringent corresponds to the strangled *parthenos* Artemis and to the *parthenos* whose *stoma* is closed so that her menses cannot flow out: the agnos which promotes menstruation to the Artemis of the *Peri Partheniōn* and to Artemis who releases. The epithet Lygodesma makes explicit the parallel between the agnos in the plant code and Artemis in the schema of deities concerned with women.

The analogy can be taken further. The strength and flexibility of the agnos/lygos make it ideal for use in bonds, thongs and ropes, but these uses also recall the role of the girdle in a woman's life. Artemis is both bound with the lygos and releaser of the girdle, spanning the two temporal aspects of 'woman': strangled, non-bleeding *parthenos* and released, bleeding *gynē*. Yet although she is concerned with the transition between them, she herself stays firmly on one side. She who sheds the blood of others is 'strangled': she who releases others is 'bound'.

Conclusion

The Greeks saw 'woman' as a contrast between the undisciplined threat to social order and the controlled, reproductive *gynē*. The presentation of female maturation as a movement from the first form to the second expresses the hope that women can safely be incorporated into society in order to reproduce it. The Hippocratic texts try to define what is normal for a woman, but their focus on the reproductive woman is achieved through the creation of categories which fall short of this ideal and through admitting that a supposedly 'tamed' woman may suddenly be afflicted by a disease which prevents normal childbirth. By presenting cures for such disorders they make the non-reproductive groups temporary phenomena; just as the *parthenos* will in time become a *gynē*.

The *Peri Partheniōn* expresses the fear that some *parthenoi* may not enter the category of *gynē*, identifying instead with an image of Artemis found in a number of stories concerning binding and releasing, strangling and bleeding. The doctor recommends marriage, accusing of deceit those who recommend dedications to Artemis after menarche; he emphasises the difference between the two sets of advice because he wants to prove the superiority of his own cure. The *parthenos* who chooses not to be a *gynē* and the man who can never be a *gynē* are however united in their wish to initiate the sequence of bleedings which will bring the *parthenos* to full maturity. The male doctor, even while trying to show that his cure is different, uses vocabulary which inserts the text into a tradition of stories about *parthenoi*: if the *parthenos* followed his advice and married, she would merely substitute another form of bloodshed and other dedications to Artemis at various stages of the process.

This overlap between cures reflects the wider problem of overlap between the two forms of woman. The *parthenos*, supposedly ignorant of 'the works of golden Aphrodite' (Hesiod, *Works and Days*, 521), whispers about love (Hesiod, *Theogony*, 205) and is highly attractive to men (Aeschylus, *Suppliants*, 1003-5; Aristotle, *Hist. Anim.*, 581b 11-21; Loraux, 1978, p. 50; Calame, 1977, pp. 189 and 256). It is logically difficult to make the *parthenos* wholly asexual, because every *parthenos* is a potential *gynē*. Similarly, every *gynē* was once a *parthenos* and even as a *gynē* may be struck by a disease which will prevent her from giving birth. The two terms thus drift back towards their original fusion in the ambiguous concept 'woman'. Artemis is the exception to the rule that all *parthenoi* are potential *gynaikes*; the true *parthenos*, she throws into greater relief the nature of her opposite pole, the true *gynē*, yet it is nevertheless the eternal *parthenos* who presides over the creation of new *gynaikes*.

Notes

1. Undisciplined and licentious: Detienne (1972), p. 128; Redfield (1977), pp. 148-9 on Spartan women. Self-control: Just (1975), pp. 164-5 and see Manuli (1980), p. 402. On the *kalon kakon*, Loraux (1978), pp. 43ff.

2. The model which I am using, of a separation followed by a process of 'drift' back towards the original fusion of the terms, owes much to the work of Pucci (1977); see for example p. 132 and pp. 32-3 on the re-merging of polarised terms in Hesiod. See below, pp. 124-5; an absolute dichotomy between two temporal aspects of 'woman' cannot be maintained because each pole of the precariously-established opposition in fact evokes and depends for its meaning on the other. Compare Pucci pp. 32-3: 'underneath these polarisations the *logos* undoes that fabric'.

3. Epitaph of Philostrata, Kaibel (1878), p. 463.

4. *Parthenos* as filly: Aristophanes, *Lysistrata* 1308; Euripides, *Hippolytus* 546-7; Merkelbach and West (1967), p. 59.4; Vernant (1979-80), p. 456. Taming/yoking metaphors: Calame (1977), pp. 411-20, pp. 330-33.

5. On choices in locating age-sex category transitions, Linton (1942), p. 591.

6. Grave monuments show both; only women on the *lekythos* of Pheidestrate (Conze, 1893, p. 308), some men on that of Theophante (*op. cit.* 309) and on the 'Stele of Plangon' (Johansen, 1951, p. 51).

7. In citing Hippocratic texts I am using the edition of E. Littré (Paris, 1839-61, 10 vols: reprinted Hakkert, Amsterdam). *L* followed by a Roman numeral refers to that volume of Littré. I also use the following abbreviations: PP = *Peri Partheniōn*, *L* VIII 466-471; PG = *Peri Gynaikeiōn*, *L* VIII 10-463; SF = Superfetation, *L* VIII 476-509; NW = On the nature of the woman, *L* VII 312-431; NC = On the nature of the child, *L* VII 486-538; Ep VI = Epidemics VI, *L* V 266-357; Sac Dis = On the Sacred Disease, *L* VI 352-397; *Articulations* can be found in *L* IV 78-327. Other ancient sources are given in full at their first citation and thereafter abbreviated.

8. The Attic Apatouria was related to marriage, not to age; a girl was admitted through her relationship to her spouse, not in her own right (Schmitt, 1977, pp. 1059-60). The stages in a girl's life given in Aristophanes, *Lysistrata* 641-7 have been much discussed since Brelich's attempt to extract from them a series of fixed age-grades (1969, pp. 229ff.); for a pertinent reminder that these lines can best be understood in the context of the play rather than as 'information' intended to instruct posterity on age categories, see Loraux (1981), pp. 174ff.

9. On woman as the incomplete form, see Aristotle, *de generatione animalium* 737a, and Clark (1975), p. 210; also Manuli (1980), p. 393, and Carlier (1980-1), p. 28. Greek medicine, like our own, did not have a branch to study 'the diseases of men'; maleness was the norm, and women were the deviant forms.

10. While *ta epiphainomena prota* (PG 1. 41; also in Soranus, *Gyn.* 1.17.2, 1.33.6) clearly means menarche, *hama te kathodō tōn epimēniōn*, used here, may mean 'at the descent of [every] menstrual flow'. Two considerations point towards the reading adopted here. Firstly, the phrase is followed by 'suffering disorders to which she was previously [*proteron*] not exposed'; as Geoffrey Lloyd has pointed out to me, *proteron* suggests that this is the first menstruation.

Secondly, PG 1.41, which specifies menarche, appears to be paraphrasing PP. I see no grounds for Lefkowitz's translation, '*After* the first menstrual period' (1981, 14).

11. Cf. the use of *anthrópos* for 'woman patient' in PG 2. 230 (*L* VIII 444).

12. Dedication of garments to Artemis is particularly associated with Artemis Brauronia in Attika: Van Straten (1981), p. 99, n. 170-1, for references.

13. Cf. Ehrenreich & English (1979), pp. 124-6. Hysteria as a strategy for gaining attention, Lewis (1971), especially Ch. 3.

14. Diepgen (1937), p. 194, notes the similarity between PP and *Mor* 249B-D.

15. Artemis preventing childbirth as a punishment: Callimachus, *H. Art.* 122 ff. and Cahen (1930), p. 123.

16. Defloration *before* menarche: Rousselle (1980), pp. 1104-5.

17. *Anth. Pal.* IX 245 claims that fear of the wedding night is 'a common fear among *parthenoi*'.

18. Cf. the analysis of the Herodotus story in Vernant (1968), pp. 15-16, where *parthenos* = true warrior.

19. Cf. Burkert (1977), p. 192: 'The great goddess of Ephesos, the cruel Laphria and the goddess for whom girls dance at Brauron are obviously different but are nevertheless called "Artemis" ' (my translation). I am interested here in the links between epithets which meant that the Greeks could regard supposedly 'different' deities as 'being' Artemis in some way.

20. Farnell (1896), p. 429 and Daremberg (1892), p. 136, make only brief mention of the epithet. Nilsson (1967), p. 487, links it to Apankhomene; scholars from Fehrle (1910), pp. 142-8, to Meuli (1975), p. 1043, have tried to privilege one of the poles with which the plant is associated above the other.

21. The main sources for this section are Pliny, *Natural History* 13.14 and 24.59-62; Dioscorides, *Materia Medica* 1.103 (ed. Wellmann); Galen 9 p. 810 (ed. Kuhn); Eustathius, *in Od*. 9. 453, *ad Il*. 11.106; Aelian, *de natura animalium* 9.26; Etymologicon Magnum *sv agnos, moskoisi lygoisin*.

Further Reading

Calame, C. (1977), *Les choeurs de jeunes filles en Grèce archaique*, Part 1, Rome

Gould, J.P. (1980), 'Law, custom and myth: aspects of the social position of women in classical Athens', *JHS*, 100, 38-59

Just, R. (1975), 'Conceptions of women in classical Athens', *Journal of the Anthropological Society of Oxford*, 6.3, 153-170

Lefkowitz, M.R. (1981), *Heroines and Hysterics*, London.

Loraux, N. (1978), 'Sur la race des femmes et quelques-unes de ses tribus', *Arethusa*, 11, 43-87

Manuli, P. (1980), 'Fisiologia e Patologia del Femminile negli Scritti Ippocratici dell' Antica Ginecologia Greca', in *Hippocratica* (ed. M.D. Grmek), *Actes du Colloque hippocratique de Paris*, 4-9 September 1978, Paris, pp. 393-408

Acknowledgements

I would like to thank Geoffrey Lloyd, Vivian Nutton and Jan Bremmer for their comments on the version of this paper, 'Approaching Greek women', which was delivered at the Institute of Classical Studies on 5 November 1981. The responsibility for this revised version is, however, entirely my own. I also wish to acknowledge the stimulation given to my work on Artemis by J.-P. Vernant's lectures at the Collège de France in spring 1981.

9 HITTITE BIRTH RITUALS

Jackie Pringle, London

By Hittites we mean the people who dominate the history of Asia Minor in the 2nd millennium BC, according to their documentary evidence, clay tablets with cuneiform characters, discovered in many thousands near the modern Turkish village of Boğhazköy. There, German excavations began in 1906 and are in progress even today. The documents testify that the site was once the great capital city Hattusas, from King Hattusilis I in the seventeenth century, until its destruction at the end of the thirteenth century BC. The overwhelming majority of these texts are concerned with religious belief and observance, reflecting the predominance of interest of the Hittite scribes under royal direction, rather than the chances of archaeological discovery.

Although referring to the people of their own Anatolian kingdom as 'men of the Hatti land', i.e. Hittites, they described their language as Nesili or Nesumnili, meaning 'of [the men of] Nesa', or Kanesh, the site of the Old Assyrian trading station of the early 2nd millennium, and the modern Kültepe. Nesite (Hittite), had a close affinity with another dialect of the Anatolian Indo-European languages, Luwian, which was spoken by peoples in western Anatolia and later, the south-east, in Kizzuwatna, which approximated to classical Cilicia. Other languages recorded in Hattusas included Akkadian, the diplomatic language of the Near East; Hattic, of the pre-Hittite and possibly indigenous inhabitants of the northern Halys region; and Hurrian, of the people whose presence may be detected historically in northern Mesopotamia for the 3rd and 2nd millennia. There are a few Hittite bilinguals, but usually Hattic, Hurrian and Luwian occur as passages inserted in otherwise Hittite texts, all of a religious nature. Hattic cannot be surely related to any known language, while Hurrian might be related to certain Caucasian languages. We understand Luwian better by virtue of its relationship to Hittite.

Luwian and Luwian-speaking scribes had an increasingly strong influence on Hittite-language texts during the late Empire period. Luwians spreading to the south-east, and Hurrians from Mesopotamia, meeting in Kizzuwatna, gave rise to a Hurro-Luwian culture. Evidence for the penetration of Hurrian culture to the Hittite kingdom, presumably from Kizzuwatna, may be seen in the royal names from the Middle Hittite period, i.e. the fifteenth and early fourteenth centuries BC. The queens had Hurrian names, and from this time on, Hittite kings bore Hurrian personal names, although assuming traditional Throne names on accession. In the thirteenth century Hurro-Luwian cultural influence was intensified with the marriage of Hattusilis III with Puduhepa, daughter of the Kizzuwatnian priest of IŠTAR, Bentipsarri, a Hurrian name. Under Hattusilis III came also a politically motivated renaissance of Hattic religion, myth and cult (Haas and Wilhelm, 1974).

Remembering also that Mesopotamian cultural influence penetrated to Hatti mainly via the Hurrians who had assimilated and remoulded ancient myths and religious traditions of Sumer and Akkad, and that the scribal tradition of Hattusas itself emanated from some, possibly North Syrian, centre, having its strongest links with a pre-Old Babylonian script and syllabary, one may ask, is there evidence for distinctively Hittite cultural traits and religious beliefs? This difficult question does have relevance to our subject of the birth rituals. This comparatively small collection of texts reflects the cross-cultural mixing of ideologies and practices evident in the mythological and cultic response to belief recorded in the Hattusan archives. Moreover, the rituals were written from the practitioners' point of view and concentrate on the ritual processes and mythological incantations with only occasional reference to the principal actor in giving birth, the mother. Consequently, it is mainly through the ritual and its expressed beliefs that one can gain some understanding of the woman's role in the family, and in this ancient society as a whole. We do find, I believe, essentially Hittite-Luwian divinised concepts, which lead to an understanding of the Hittite response, as Jacobsen (1973) expressed it for the Sumerian, to their perception of divinity in the power of procreation and birth.

The recent compilation and study of Hittite birth rituals by G. Beckman (1977) is a very welcome aid, and the texts I consider are referred to here according to Beckman's lettering. Occasionally my translation and interpretation have differed from Beckman's.

The birth rituals stem from Hittite, Luwian, Hurro-Luwian and Hattic milieux, judging from the language in which they have been recorded and the linguistic source of the technical terms. These are imperfect criteria but the best available. Separation of the texts according to archives is not feasible. While the majority of the Hittite-Luwian group were located in the archive area of the royal citadel, so also was Text K of the Hurro-Luwian group. A few fragments of the latter group were found in the Great Temple area in the lower city, but many of the texts, mainly of the Hurro-Luwian group, come from earlier excavations when findspots were not recorded. Dating according to internal criteria suggests that a few of the Hittite-Luwian rituals were inscribed earlier than the Hurro-Luwian, but that both groups, and the Hattic rituals, have copies datable to the late Empire period.

What clay tablets we possess must have been inscribed at the orders of a king or queen. We know that Queen Puduhepa commissioned the Chief Scribe to collect in Hattusas all the New Year Festival tablets from Kizzuwatna (Otten, 1975). Incantations for some birth rituals could be recorded on separate tablets, as we are told in Text B, while in the Hurro-Luwian Text K, scribal glosses remark that the procedure for the Festival of Birth was on a wooden *Kurta* tablet in Kizzuwatna, and since the scribe had not learnt it by heart, he would bring the tablet from there. Wooden tablets by other names were used to record cult and Festival procedure in Hatti itself, and may have served as mnemonics for birth ritual practitioners. There were certainly variations in the incantations at the time of delivery and the specific ritual procedures for the cleansing of mother and child.

The introductory formulae were consistent in type with those of other magic rituals, 'Thus (the words)' of a personal name and/or a professional title and/or city of origin, followed by the statement of occasion. For antenatal or parturition rituals this would be, 'If a woman is pregnant', or 'If a woman is giving birth'. Text I, in the Hurro-Luwian group, has 'If a woman is sitting on the birth-stool'. The naming of the practitioner was a peculiarly Anatolian practice in rituals, not paralleled in Mesopotamia (Gurney, 1977).

With the word 'to be/become pregnant', we find a singularly Hittite-Luwian usage and concept. The root *arma-* is identical in form to the name for the Anatolian Moongod, *Armas* and 'month'. The derivation of 'be pregnant' from *arma-* 'moon, month', is contested on logical, not philological, grounds, according to the Latin derivation of *menstruare* from *mens* (Kammenhuber, 1980). However, Laroche is decisive in his acceptance (1955, 1962), which I follow. Mythological texts as well as birth rituals count the months of a woman's pregnancy, and delivery was expected in the 10th month. It seems possible that the Hittites, Luwians and Kizzuwatnians counted the months as appearances of the moon from the last rising before the cessation of the menses.

Text L, written in Hittite but with many Luwian words preceded by the diacritical cuneiform wedges used by Hattusan scribes to distinguish such words from the end of the fourteenth century, illustrates the Hittite-Luwian connection of their Moongod with pregnancy and birth.

Albeit this is in a mythological introduction to the ritual which takes its theme from an ancient Mesopotamian source. The 'Slave of the Moongod' finds its earliest written expression in Sumerian texts and was continued through Babylonian to Neo-Assyrian times (cf. van Dijk, 1972; Finkel, 1980; Lambert, 1969). Basically, the story went that the Moongod, from Heaven, was seized with irrepressible desire for the cow grazing in the meadow and mated with her, causing her to conceive. When the time of her delivery came, she cried out in pain. The Moongod saw her, took pity, and dispatched the Mothergoddesses as Midwives to anoint her with soothing oil and waters. The success of their ministrations served henceforth as justification for the midwifery practice for all descendants of that offspring, whose birth represented all birth, and consequently that of humankind. A fragmentary version of the main theme in Akkadian, was discovered in Boğhazköy.

In Text L however, it is the Stormgod who took pity on mother and newborn child and dispatched the Mothergoddesses, reflecting his premier position in the Anatolian pantheon. The Moongod strides to battle, not love, having assumed the awesome aspect of a warrior with garments and weapons of blood-red, a literary topos for a terrifying deity, but untypical for the Moongod. This might signify, as Beckman suggests, a recognition of his role in the mother's distress, the weapons symbolising masculinity. But there is no mention of his fatherhood. According to Laroche, the Moongod in Hatti, unlike numerous other deities, had no established cult or personnel, being a magical and mysterious entity. I suggest that *Armas*, the warrior, plays a symbolic role which signifies the stress and pain of birth-giving, the blood of battle symbolising the blood of parturition. That last metaphor is actually found in the Middle-Assyrian birth ritual of the genre, published by Lambert (1969), which describes the mother, 'Like a warrior in the fray, she is cast down in her blood'. If this concept were derived from a Mesopotamian source, the Hittite composition presents it in a strikingly vivid and original manner, in keeping with the Anatolian association of the moon, *Armas*, with the fact and phases of pregnancy.

Another Mesopotamian version presents the sun as the amorous god, and may be of equal antiquity to that of the Moongod. It is found in Hittite-language texts as the Hurrian-derived myth of the Sungod and the Cow (Friedrich, 1950). The Sungod finds the cow in the meadow quite irresistible. The inevitable occurred. When she had given birth, the cow looked up at the blazing sun and said, 'That calf of mine has four legs; why have I borne this one with only two legs?', an uncomfortable question, reflecting possibly a substratum of derived tales.

The presence of specific practitioners indicates the cultural milieu of the rituals. In the Text group A to F and N, Hittite, as opposed to H to K, Hurro-Luwian, the principal practitioners are women, the *Hasnupallas* and the *Hasauwas*. The title of the former was usually written logographically *MÍ.ŠÀ.ZU*, meaning literally 'woman who knows the internal organs' (von Soden, 1957-8). In Text A, where the preparation of woman for imminent delivery is virtually identical to that in Text B, where the *MÍ.ŠÀ.ZU* officiates, the term *Hasnupallas* occurs instead. A derivative of the verb *has-* 'give birth', it means 'one who is skilled in causing to give birth'. In Text C, the *Hasnupallas* hands the child to the *Hasauwas* saying 'I, the *Hasnupallas*, have given birth to the child.' The Midwife's practice included antenatal rituals and preparations for the mother, and establishing the date of birth, possibly by oracular means, e.g. in Text B. During labour, she incanted mythological recitations and supervised rituals to avert and absorb evils. After the birth she incanted magical formulae to assure health for mother and child. If a boy were born, the Midwife in B gave him the 'goods of a male child', saying, 'Let a female child be born in a year forth'. If a girl were born, there was the same procedure, in reverse, 'the goods of a female child', saying 'Let a male child be born in a year forth'. It would seem that female children were as welcome to the Hittite family as the male. Van Dijk (1972) quotes Sumerian birth texts where the Midwife supervises the typical attributes for the male child, a mace and axe, and the spindle for the female. In Hittite texts the attributes of masculinity and femininity are well attested, e.g. in the Soldiers' Oath of Loyalty (Oettinger, 1976), with weapons, chiefly the bow and arrow, for the male, and distaff and spindle for the female.

In Texts A and B are preserved details of the delivery furniture associated with the *Hasnupallas'* practice. In A, one Midwife was present. She set out two wooden stools, *kupissar*, with cushions, which appear to have been in everyday use. The mother sat on one with the Midwife facing her on the other, and a cushion was laid on the ground between them to catch the child as it 'fell'. In B, there were two Midwives, who sat before and behind the woman. The *Hasnupallas* held a cloth, perhaps a receiving blanket as Beckman suggests, or to protect the mother during the delivery, which took place in the Inner Chamber. There is nothing in this group of texts to indicate that birth occurred elsewhere than in the woman's own home, which appears to be confirmed for the milieu represented by the Luwian-language birth ritual where the expectant mother and her husband ritually purify the confines of their house-territory preparatory to the birth (Starke, 1980).

The only possible, preserved, mention of surgical aids in the Midwife's equipment, such as a knife to cut the umbilical cord, is in the mythological passage of Text L, where the translation is not surely confirmed. In the damaged context of §2, Text C, where it seems that ritual objects were being prepared by the *Hasauwas* for the cleansing of a newborn child, a bronze knife and four bronze pegs are mentioned, but their purpose is not clear.

The title *Hasauwas* derives also from *has-*, meaning 'the one of birthgiving'. The evidence from ritual and mythology suggests that she was the 'Wise Woman' of the family complex, whose specialisations could include one or more of the following: family midwife, experienced from her own birthgiving and that of other relatives; nurse or wetnurse for other females of the family, or community; magico-medical attendant with an interesting line in divinatory techniques. At the historical period when we meet the *Hasauwas*, the specialist Midwife, the *Hasnupallas*, had appeared, to officiate at births. In Text C, the *Hasauwas*, as Beckman notes, acts as child's Nurse, and her employment was to be expected as such only when the child of a royal or exceptionally rich family was born. In §4 she says, 'If they hand over the child to me', in which event she performed ritual cleansing, the child being placed in wooden tubs, and then further rituals to achieve its health by substitution magic. Hoffner (1968) quoted in a footnote the two relevant last lines of §6 of this, then unpublished, text, while discussing the child's Nurse, e.g. in the Hurrian-derived epic 'The Song of Ullikummi'. There, the Midwives aided the delivery of the monster Ullikummi and the Nurses, the Fate and Mothergoddesses, lifted him and placed him on the knees of his father. The father expressed his joy and named the child. The same child-lifting occurred in the Appu story, also of Hurrian derivation, but only the Nurse, written logographically *UMMEDA*, is mentioned. In §6 of Text C the *Hasauwas* says, 'I, [the *Has*]*auwas*, wash his head. Then the Queen dresses him, and I take away from her, her own (child), [and] I place the child on his knees.' The damaged area at the beginning of the last line could contain the word for King. But we are certainly dealing with a royal occasion, since it is said earlier that a Palace official supervised the ritual cleansing of the child's mouth by the *Hasauwas*. There is some difference in this 'placing on the knees' ceremony and that of the Hurrian mythological scenes. The child is not set on the father's knees immediately after birth; in fact, the Luwian-language ritual prescribes that 'they lift the baby, turn it upside down, and then place it at the mother's breast'. In C, some time had obviously elapsed. As the Hittite royal family experienced generations of Hurrian influence, the presentation of the child to the father, with possibly, the 'name-giving', may have been borrowed but adapted to local custom.

A well-known ritual practitioner in Hittite texts is the 'Old Woman', a literal translation of the logographic writing *MÍ.ŠU.GI*. She performed a wide variety of purificatory and healing rituals, and operated under the aegis of the royal court a divinatory technique which cannot apparently be derived from any Mesopotamian source. One record dates from the Old Hittite period (Archi, 1974). Relevant to the birth rituals, is the alternance of *MÍ.ŠU.GI* with *Hasauwas* in the colophon and descriptive catalogue entry of an Empire-dated ritual text, recording the performance of ritual for a child. It is one of five, preserved on a composite tablet, edited by Kronasser (1961), intended principally for the alleviation of children's illness, and showing Kizzuwatnian influence in the mythological passages of the 3rd and 4th rituals. Otten assumed (1952) that *Hasauwas* must be the Hittite phonetic rendering of *MÍ.ŠU.GI*, and Kammenhuber, another eminent Hittite scholar, has since agreed to the identification (1977, p. 90).

The aetiological myths concerning the *Hasauwas* in Rituals 3 and 4 of the composite tablet provide an insight to the range of her practice and are relevant to my argument concerning Hittite beliefs. Both rituals are subsumed in the colophon and catalogue entries as, 'If Tongues come to anyone, Incantation of the Binding' and 'the Old Woman performs (the ritual) as follows'. In magical contexts, 'Tongues' and 'Binding' refer to sorcery. Ritual 4, the better preserved, is introduced by an account of the 'binding' by the Great River of its flood, the fish, the mountains, roads and valleys, and by the Stormgod, of the clouds, the cord, the eagle's wing and the bearded snake in its coil; the wild-sheep, the panther, the wolf, the lion, the antelope, the milk of the antelope and the Throne of the Protector god. 'Binding' recalls also the 'drying' and 'suffocating' themes which recurr in Anatolian mythology as the result of a deity's anger and disappearance (see Laroche, 1965, and our Text F). Here, the goddess IŠTAR speaks to the goddess Malliya, who speaks to the goddess Pirwa, and she in turn to Kamrusepa, who 'yoked her horses and drove to the Great River, whom she conjured by incantation'. Then all that had been bound was loosed, through the ritual agency of Kamrusepa.

This goddess is found frequently in the circle of IŠTAR (i.e. the Hurrian Shaushga), Malliya (a River goddess), Pirwa and Askasepa, the 'genius' of the Gateway. Pirwa, both god and goddess, honoured by songs in Nesite and Luwian, is described as the god upon a Silver Horse and depicted in the iconography of Kültepe/Kanesh with chariot and team of horses (Özgüç, 1965). In Empire-dated lists of gods protecting the Treaty oaths, IŠTAR, Pirwa and Askasepa appear in that order sufficiently often for Otten (1953) to have suggested that when Pirwa is omitted from the trio, an assimilation of the Horsegod's identity with IŠTAR may be assumed. The logographic writing IŠTAR represented a deity, at once male and female, of War and Love. Ritual 4 continued with the mythological case of the young child who was bewitched in every part of his body. They are listed, 14 in all, from hair to knees, 'And upon him his clothes are bound . . .' And the message went to the Birthgoddess, 'How shall we act when we perform the Incantation?' 'Go! Fetch the *Hasa(u)was* woman, and let her incant for him, over the skull, . . .' and so on. As a result of the *Hasauwas'* magical incantation all the afflicted organs were 'freed'. The final lines decree, 'Now, this important Word; Let [the *Hasauwas*] go, and speak the Good Incantation against "Bin[ding"]'.

Thus the *Hasauwas* received divine orders from the Birthgoddess, to heal the body organs, a ritual which she did indeed perform in Text C, for the newborn child. A fertility incantation precedes the substitution magic whereby the *Hasauwas* took a 'goat from the fold of Immarni', an Anatolian Pan-like figure, and pressed its separate parts to those of the child. The goat was then dismembered and burnt. The body parts, stipulated as '9', actually number 12. The Mesopotamian origin of healing rituals by animal substitution which name separate organs of the body, cannot be disputed (Haas, 1971), but there is a vague approach in Hittite rituals to precise numbers, which seldom concur with that stated in the purpose. An interesting suggestion of Benedetti's (1980) may be noted, that the female physicians, the Iatrinai, found in Anatolian (Greek) inscriptions of the Roman period, may record the persistence into more recent antiquity of the Anatolian Old Woman, the healer. It is she whom we recognise as the *Hasauwas*.

The Hittite Birthgoddess was usually designated by the logographic *DINGIR.MAH*, meaning 'August goddess', and ^{D}*NIN.TU*, 'Lady of Birth', corresponding to the Mesopotamian practice for the description of the Mothergoddess. As mother of all procreation and birth, the power that moulded the child in the womb, ^{D}*NIN.TU* was also the skilful Midwife who brought him to birth. The Sumerian Mistress and Mother of wild creatures, *NINHURSAG*, 'Lady of the Mountain Slopes', became associated and identified even, as an epithet, with *NIN.TU* (Jacobsen, 1973). One will recall the motif in our Ritual 4 of all the wild things that were bound and then freed through the agency of

Kamrusepa.

But Kamrusepa herself appears in a fragmentary Luwian birth ritual (Starke, 1980). In a mythological passage after the child's birth, taking '9' combs, she healed the body parts, and may thus be identified here as the divine *Hasauwas*. In other mythological contexts Kamrusepa is found subduing the thunderous anger of the Hattic god Telepinus. With a sheep from the fold of the Sungod, she removed the 'evils from the body parts of Telepinus', which were burnt away in the sacrifice. The combs motif reappears in another version, where the Sungod and Kamrusepa comb his sheep and then fall to quarrelling. They combed a pure young goat, and 'For mankind to perform she handled it and she treated the 12 parts of the human body'. If Kamrusepa's name, with its typical *-sepa* suffix indicating a 'genius', may be correctly derived with Laroche (1947) from the Hittite word *kammara-* 'smoke, haze', we may see her originally as the divinised concept of the sacrificial and cleansing smoke that rose to the sky from burnt offerings, and by extension, of the ritual itself and representative of its human performers.

Kamrusepa and the *Hasauwas* were mythological *alter egos* of the Hittite Birthgoddess, whose Hittite name, *Hannahannas* is considered to be a reduplication of the Hittite kinship term *hannas*, 'grandmother'. In the introduction to the Delivery incantation of Text A, the aetiological placing of a number of deities in their cities is related, but, last in the list, 'For *Hannahannas* there was no place remaining, so she took her seat with humankind'. Does this myth contain an ancient memory of the human nature of the divinised concept, the 'grandmother', who epitomised the skills of the Wise Woman in her elevated position as leading female of the Hittite family?

A semantic parallel to *Hasauwas* is found in the milieu of the Hurro-Luwian birth rituals, *MÍ harnauwas*, 'woman of the birthstool'. Both terms may be understood as referring to women who had given birth themselves, as well as assisting at another's delivery. Queen Puduhepa, mother of sons and daughters, called herself a '*Harnauwas* woman'. Beckman notes that a *MÍ harnauwas* received I mina of silver from the Palace stores from a *Patili* priest, which places her in a category of Palace functionaries, possibly as a 'wet nurse'. A detailed consideration of the cryptographic and philological problems that underlie the logograms for Old Woman and Nurse, which might provide a clue and link between the *MÍ.ŠU.GI* and *Hasauwas*, is not appropriate here. It may be noted that at least two Hittite, or Luwian, words are concealed by the logogram *UMMEDA*, which signifies 'Nurse' in Hittite texts (cf. Laroche, 1956; Hoffner, 1968).

Before we turn to the Hurro-Luwian group of birth rituals, a comment is due on the gynaecological aspect of the rituals. The term for a woman in labour, 'the one who keeps on wailing' (*wiwiskitallas*), implies that stoic silence was not expected in Anatolia, as it is in some contemporary primitive, or even modern, societies. Alleviation of obstetrical problems seems to have been mainly magical, showing little or no indication of real medical competence, as Beckman also concluded. The two short Hattic incantations with no stated practitioner, Text G, were intended respectively for the induction of the amniotic flow − if the translation of the verb is correct − and to relieve colic, when a woman was in labour, as stated in the brief Hittite introductions. In Text E, the last fragmentary ritual conjures the turning of the child in the womb by analogy to the twisted form of a plant, possibly to prevent breech-birth. Text P, in Luwian, includes a pre-parturition passage when the Physician (*LÚ A.ZU*) administered 'medicines' to the woman in labour. The two parallel Luwian rituals give no indication of the presence of the Physician, while the fragment cited above contains the incantation of Kamrusepa. The *Hasauwas* of Texts C and N applied 'medicines' to a newborn child, but not enough is preserved to tell what these were. In Ritual 1 of the composite tablet, a female (possibly a Nurse) − the slave of another woman − prepared a potion of garden plants, active yeast, beer and water, to cure a bewitched child when 'his internal organs are eaten'. She washed his mouth with the mixture, then administered a little orally. The rest was poured over his head and body and served as an enema, to the accompaniment of chants and sacrifices, with a final treatment of the body parts by a salve containing sheep's fat.

Although physicians, who applied medicine as well as magic to the sick, did exist in Hattusas, and medical texts in both Akkadian and Hittite have been discovered (Burde, 1974; Köcher, 1952), gynaecological competence was clearly limited. Beckman quotes a letter to Hattusilis III from the Egyptian Pharaoh Ramses II, who expressed amazement that the former should have written asking for an Egyptian doctor with medicines to help his 60-year-old sister conceive a child. This appears to speak against the presence of any genuine science in Hatti.

The Hurro-Luwian group, Texts H to K, are easily distinguishable by their use of Hurrian words as sacred ritual terms, the sacrificial burning of birds, a recurrent combination of cedar, olive and tamarisk woods for purifications, the presence of the *Patili* priest, a non-Hittite word, the *Katra* women, the *shinapshi*, a Hurrian term for a temple, and the use of the *harnau*, a form of birthstool. This was also a non-Hittite word. The premier gods were the Hurrian Stormgod, Teshub, and his consort, Hepat, Queen of Heaven, described by Puduhepa as the Kizzuwatnian counterpart of the Hittite Sungoddess of Arinna, the state goddess.

Text K, an unusual compilation of specifications for a woman's ante- and postnatal ritual and taboo observance, records two similar regimens, one on each side of the tablet. There are some variations and omissions. The taboos, according to verso and reverse of the tablet were:

1) Cessation in the 7th month of pregnancy of intercourse between husband and wife.

2) verso only: Restriction of the woman's entry, possibly, to a communal building (my translation). The context is damaged, and I feel Beckman may have over-interpreted in his restorations by reading a directive also for the woman to leave and not re-enter her own home. The reverse said that, after a sacrifice in the *shinapshi*, the woman might go with her husband, if he wished; she might go wherever she pleased. The following section describes purifications in 'the house of the birthstool', where the woman must stay until after the birth. Text H suggests that this was her own home, but K may present variations and relaxations in taboos and custom.

3) verso only: Prohibition of certain foods for the woman, but not for her husband. The foods were a kind of cress, and *ashtauwar*, the meaning of which is not known.

4) verso only: Wife and husband must sit at separate tables for meals, and use separate utensils. The wife must not eat at the same time as her husband.

5) reverse only: The woman must not leave the 'house of the birthstool' after the final purification of the premises.

An earlier section of the reverse probably describes the preparation of the birthroom with plastering and sprinkling. According to both regimens all the wooden and pottery vessels, the bed and *hassalli* stool, had to be new, while bronze utensils were to be 'fired'. The *harnau* received special purification. There is no description of the procedure during the birth itself. Throughout the antenatal regimen the Seer (*LÚ AZU*) dominated the proceedings, performing the majority of the rituals, including the Washing of the Woman's Mouth, the incantation for which was in Hurrian and on a separate tablet. They officiated also in the Festival of the Month for the Mothergoddesses of the Body, the statues of whom were installed in the 'house of the birthstool' after a ritual journey. The Old Women performed rituals against *marshya*, possibly 'Malevolence', and offerings for *mala*, possibly 'Abundance', to the goddess Apritta. The *Patili* priests, *Katra* women and Torchbearers were associated with the *shinapshi* rituals.

At the time of birth the Festival of Birth was to be celebrated. The verso details separately that on the day of birth the Festival of the Mothergoddesses and Hepat should be celebrated. If the offerings were performed for Hepat, the Seer ritually received the mother as a 'Slavewoman of Hepat', adjuring her to 'Keep the rule of the Temple and the Custom'. Seven days after the birth an offering for the *mala* of the birth was made. Three moons from the nearest rising to a male child's birth he was ritually cleansed by the Seers, while a girl received the same cleansing four moons after birth.

Remarkable mystique surrounded the *harnau*. In H, and as we will see, Text I also, the *Patili* acted as priestly warden of the birthstool. He purified the woman's chair, table, bed, wooden potstand, the *harnau* and the woman herself. Only after sacrifices and ritual washing could she approach the *harnau* in the Inner Chamber, which was sealed by the *Patili* after each visit. The series of purifications involved washing the woman's mouth, anointing her head and the binding of her hands with red wool. On one occasion, led by the *Patili*, she approached and sat on the *harnau*. Whereupon her husband, the *Patili*, the *Katra* women, all bowed low to her. Before her final entry of the Inner Room it was necessary for the *Patili* to sacrifice at night, at the Crossroads, a kid to the male gods of the *shinapshi* and another to the male gods of the city. The woman had previously libated wine, handed to her by the *Patili*, over the sacrificial goats before they were led away. However, she was still required to wake after that night 'pure from a dream'. If not, the sacrificial process was repeated.

The ritual of Text I was performed by Papanikri, a *Patili* of Kizzuwatna, when damage occurred to either the 'large pottery bowl' of the birthstool or one of the two wooden pegs which were bound to it, when the woman was sitting on the stool, but had not yet given birth, with the wooden tablets opened — hence, all was 'impure'. The *Patili* removed the *harnau* with utensils to the *shinapshi*, pausing to sacrifice birds at the city gate. He left the damaged furnishings outside, but the woman was to give birth within the temple (not outside, as Beckman interpreted), after which she consulted the oracle as to the cause of the damage. Some god may have been angry with her, or her parents may have sinned in the past. No mention is made of the delivery, nor yet of the child. Offerings were made in the temple with two birthstool bowls and four pegs to compensate the god, Teshub. The *harnau* and the pegs were smeared with birds' blood and the *Patili* sacrificed before the birthstool twice in *uzziya*, 'flesh', which recurs with *zurki* 'blood' and *keldi* 'good health', all Hurrian terms, frequently used in this group of rituals (cf. Laroche, 1976-7). After further sacrifices and invocation of Teshub and Hepat, the *Patili* confirmed that the woman had regained purity through double compensation.

One can scarcely doubt that the taboos and extraordinary, male-controlled, reverence for the birthstool, signified the intense response of a male-controlled society to the power of reproduction. The contrast with the previous group of texts is striking. It seems justified to connect this response with the Hurrians, but what of the Luwian influence which should be detectable? When the recent study and re-edition of Luwian texts by Dr Starke is published and when Hurrian-language texts are better understood, it may be possible to gauge more accurately the differences in culture of these people and their interaction.

In view of the dressing of the newborn child in Text C, the dressing of a substitute lamb in 'Papanikri' may be significant. After a feast in the woman's house presided over by *Patili* priests, a lamb was prepared. Its mouth and feet were washed, its head anointed and feet bound with red wool, a 'rite de passage', recalling the same procedure for the woman in Text H. The lamb was placed on the knees of a *Katra* woman and dressed in small red garments with silver wreath, rings and bracelets and carried by the mother as a substitute for her child to the *shinapshi*, where the *Patili* removed it to a 'pure place'. Beckman drew attention to the anointing of the bride's head in the marriage ceremony of Queen Puduhepa's daughter to Ramses II. He also cites a ritual for the dead, recorded on a tablet from Boğhazköy, but not belonging to the main corpus of royal funerary rites (Otten, 1958), where the *Patili* called the name of the deceased from the roof of his house, 'Where has he gone?' Finally the answer came: 'The mother came to him and took him by the hand, and she led him away.' One may interpret death metaphorically as a re-enactment of birth, thereby explaining the presence of the *Patili*.

According to the Hurrian-derived myths, midwives assisted the actual birth of a child, but no mention is made of midwives in the above rituals. The *Katra* women appear to have been merely temple assistants with a mainly musical function, while there is no more information available concerning the *MÍ harnauwas*, 'woman of the birthstool', apart from that already cited. One would hesitate to see the

Patili priest officiating at the birth itself, but the possibility cannot be excluded. Altogether, the presence of these Hurrian-derived rituals and the *Patili* and *Mí harnauwas* as Palace employees in Hattusas, may be ascribed to the royal connection with Kizzuwatna. Anthropological studies of primitive, semi-literate and even Westernised technological societies underline the resistance to change in the highly traditional and conservative field of birth practices and beliefs (Kay, 1982; Pedersen, 1968). In view of this we may appreciate the desire of Hattusan royal ladies of Kizzuwatnian extraction to have at hand rituals and priests from their native milieu.

The contrast between the practice, practitioners and ideologies of the two main groups of rituals suggests that one should expect, if not totally opposed forms of family and social structure, certainly ones where the control of women was markedly different. Tentatively, one might see women in the Hittite family increasing their power and status with seniority within the family, and not apparently subject to that social and religious control which dominated the Kizzuwatnian woman, even within her family, and in that most female of functions, giving birth.

Further Reading

Douglas, M. (1966), *Purity and Danger. An analysis of the Concepts of Pollution and Taboo*, London
—— (1970), *Natural Symbols. Explorations in Cosmology*, London
Engelhard, D.H. (1970), *Hittite Magical Practice*, Ann Arbor
La Fontaine, J.S. (1972), 'Ritualisation of Women's Life-crises in Bugisu', in *The Interpretation of Ritual*, London
Forbes, T.R. (1966), *The Midwife and the Witch*, New Haven
Goody, J. (1961), 'Religion and Ritual: The Definitional Problem', *British Journal of Sociology* 12, pp. 143-64
Landy, D. (1977), *Culture, Disease and Healing. Studies in Medical Anthropology*, London

PART FIVE: DISCOVERING WOMEN

The process of disinterring evidence about women in poorly
documented societies

10 CELTIC WOMEN IN THE EARLY MIDDLE AGES

Wendy Davies, London

Women in Celtic areas in the early Middle Ages enjoyed a status which varied from area to area and may well have changed over time. Indeed, since there was no uniformity of social structure in Celtic cultures one can scarcely expect the position of women to have been identical in all of them. There are, however, some similarities as well as contrasts and the combinations of both are interesting and of more than Celtic significance. As might be expected, the available source material is fragmentary and uneven in its distribution and can be difficult to interpret. It is therefore impossible to offer a comprehensive picture of structures and relationships, but there is sufficient material to comment on several aspects of the problem of women in Celtic areas; to comment, that is, on woman and/or groups of women and not merely on isolated individuals and events. It is therefore the intention of this paper to survey the status and role of women in Celtic areas in the early Middle Ages; to make clear those aspects of the subject that will bear immediate investigation and thereby highlight the lacunae; at the same time indicating some directions for future study.[1]

Some preliminary comment on Celtic social structures and on sources is essential in order to provide a context and to define the limitations of the survey. What, firstly, is indicated by the term 'Celtic'? Although its primary reference is to language, it is a useful shorthand term for referring to cultures in which Celtic languages predominated, that is, to the populations of Brittany, Cornwall and west Devon, Ireland, the Isle of Man, Scotland and northern Britain, and Wales, in the early Middle Ages. While the vernacular languages of all were Celtic, some Latin was written in all, and sometimes spoken. Welsh, Cornish and Breton were extremely closely related and must have been mutually intelligible at this period; the language of lowland Scotland and northern Britain (Cumbrian) was not much further distant. Irish was considerably different, and used in western Scotland as well as Ireland.[2] All areas were subject to the influence of the Christian clergy who, sooner or later, effected conversion; this had clearly begun before the fifth century in southern parts and was extended to Scotland and Ireland during the fifth and sixth centuries, if not before, although the change took centuries to complete. Wales, Cornwall and Brittany were also formerly part of the Roman Empire. In terms of language and background, then, these three had close similarities; Ireland was more distinctive, and Scotland shared some characteristics with each group.

There is considerable geographical diversity between the regions, but in the early Middle Ages all were strikingly rural, and also agrarian; urban background in the Roman-influenced cases was negligible (except for east Brittany) and there was hardly any new trend towards urbanisation. Since there was relatively little non-agricultural production, most people had some direct involvement with agriculture, although everyone did not necessarily labour at it. As far as we can ascertain all were highly stratified societies in which literate people, at least, were aware of the stratification and in which regulation of social relationships normally took place with reference to it; compensation for damage, for example, was assessed in accordance with the status of the man damaged. Slaves formed the lowest element in the hierarchy. Social support and social regulation was to some extent provided by family structures, both nuclear and extended, and to some extent by the political relationships implicit in the notion of lordship; the relative significance of family and lord varied from area to area, as did the manner of operation of lordly support and control. Indeed, the greatest (or at least the most obvious) differences between the regions lay in the level and manner of their politicisation. Ireland had a relatively large number of small kingdoms, associated in a complex structure of overkingships, and it had an aristocracy with considerable political power, shared with kings. In Wales there were several kingdoms, of larger size, whose interrelationships resulted in the long term in the elimination of some and expansion of others. Scotland was notable for a Pictish kingship in the East and an Irish kingship in the West until the ninth century, when the two merged to support the single, precocious, monarchy of Scotland. Cornwall (and Devon till conquered by the English) may have been a single kingdom. In Brittany, on the other hand, there was no kingship until the mid-ninth century and it only occurred then under the exceptional circumstances of invasion and the reaction to this; until then there were certainly aristocrats who wielded more or less personal political power but they had extremely varied relationships with local populations; there may also have been very small-scale local rulers acting for village communities. In addition to these differences between states, the nature and function of law varied from region to region, as did the relationship between political authorities, judgement and law. Hence Celtic societies in the early Middle Ages may have had rural and agrarian and some social aspects in common but they differed considerably from each other in political respects.[3]

The other necessary preliminary is to comment briefly on sources. The available evidence is almost entirely written, surviving in later manuscript copies. There is some archaeological material (relating to secular settlement and the church) and an extremely important corpus of (largely funerary) inscriptions on stone, of which the greater proportion comes from Wales. The written sources are extremely varied in character, although they include very few histories and very few letters, and nothing which approximates to government records. There are narrative records in the form of annals, and pseudo-historical accounts within the Lives of Saints (Welsh Lives date from the eleventh century and later, but sometimes have earlier elements). Records of family relationships, or supposed relationships, are preserved in genealogies, and of transactions in charters (although there are very few Breton genealogies and very few Irish charters). There is an extremely large corpus of early Irish secular law tracts, a much later (late medieval) corpus of Welsh law books and a negligible amount of collected Breton legal material. The content of the Welsh legal material is noted in this paper, although late, since some proportion of it is likely to derive from the early Middle Ages. Ecclesiastical legislation survives from Brittany, Wales and Ireland, although there is far more from Ireland than elsewhere, and ecclesiastical calendars and martyrologies also figure prominently in the Irish collections. There is Irish and Welsh vernacular poetry and prose story material (although records of vernacular Welsh prose do not begin until the late eleventh century); story material also survives in Latin in the Saints' Lives of all areas. The remaining written material consists of scholarly works, religious tracts and commentaries and glosses on the Bible.[4]

This material is not easy to use and almost every source produces problems of interpretation occasioned by the uncertain context of its production. Especially problematic, in the present context, is the legal evidence, ecclesiastical and secular: it is very difficult to know if the rules as formulated reflect practice or aspiration, and this applies as much to the multiple provisions of Irish property law as to the prohibitions of Christian penitentials. The material is also extremely uneven in its distribution, geographical and temporal. For example, Breton material is rich for the ninth century, but thin before. This means that it is often impossible to compare like with like, and therefore to make general comments of relevance to all areas. Moreover, obviously the nature of the sources does not lend itself to statistical analysis. There is far more Irish material of the early Middle Ages than material from the other areas, and correspondingly far more modern comment on Ireland. There is therefore some temptation to assume that the Irish pattern must be applicable everywhere, in default of appropriate evidence; given the observable differences between Irish societies and others it hardly needs emphasising that the temptation needs to be strongly resisted.

Despite the limitations of the source material — and it perhaps needs pointing out that in quantity it amounts to far more than survives for some of the societies discussed in this book — there *is* enough suitable material to justify comment on a number of key aspects of the role of women in society in Ireland, Wales and Brittany, to which areas the survey will be confined.[5] These aspects are legal subjection, politics, property, marriage and sex; there is also material bearing on the impact of Christianity and on the social change associated with it (a matter of especial interest in the early Middle Ages, particularly in the context of the rights and powers of women). Indeed, the interaction between Christian and non-Christian, clerical and secular, forms a constant background to social change in these areas at this period, and presents a constant problem in assessing it (see too Harvey, Herrin, this volume).

The survey will deal predominantly with the sixth to ninth centuries inclusive; although this is dictated by the available primary source material, major social and political changes are evident in all areas from the ninth century and there is therefore good reason to treat the succeeding centuries separately.

Legal Subjection

It is scarcely remarkable that these societies, like most others, were dominated by men: men were the actors in public life; they had powers over persons, themselves and others; they negotiated, bargained and made transactions; descent was normally, though not invariably, traced through males and affiliation expressed with reference to fathers; and men are mentioned far, far more often than women. Both Irish and Welsh material clearly suggests that women were considered subject to men, a woman being subject to her father until marriage, to her husband after marriage and to her sons or her father or her nephew when the marriage ended: 'Quid uult pater efficiat uirgo, quia capud mulieris uir'. So too an Irish king was lord (*comdiu*) of his queen, and expected adoration and obedience; later, in Welsh law, a woman's protector (male) received a payment (*amobr*) in token of that protection on her marriage, her married status was determined by that of her husband, and her honour price was less than that of a male of the same status.[6] There are no explicit Breton statements on this matter, but since a notion of legal power and consequent subjection (*potestas*) clearly existed (cited with reference to a man's capacity to choose a marriage partner) it is not impossible that women were also considered subject in that region; the question, however, remains open.[7] What did this subjection mean in practice, apart from an implied restraint on freedom of action? Since women clearly could have sole powers over property (see below), and some had the power to make gifts, the practical significance of the notion appears to lie with the individual's capacity to perform legal actions. Irish law classified women among the 'senseless' persons, who could not make contracts nor engage in sale and purchase, and Irish ecclesiastical legislation of the late seventh century included women among the group of slaves, foreigners and imbeciles who could not stand as sureties. Where there is charter evidence (Wales and Brittany), women did not normally act as witnesses to transactions; women did not act as sureties nor put down pledges; women did not give evidence in dispute proceedings nor witness settlements of them.[8] The evidence that we have is consistent in suggesting the exclusion of women from the performance of public legal acts, thereby effectively denying them a public legal personality. Women, as such, were not lawworthy, not 'suitable'. Since, however, in some circumstances they were involved in property transactions in their own right, and therefore party to public procedures, denying women legal capacity created something of an anomalous situation. The anomaly was effectively admitted in the Irish ecclesiastical legislation which specified that women were not qualified to act as sureties, although a woman who was a *domina* (lord) might do so.[9]

Politics

Since public office was virtually nonexistent in these societies it is inappropriate to ask if women were eligible for it. State development was too limited to support much in the way of state officers and some royal agents, of undifferentiated function, are the most that can be identified; they do not include women.[10] In the absence of state apparatus, community organisation, insofar as it can be perceived, seemed to operate on the basis of joint action by respected community leaders — elders — rather than through appointed officers responsible to the community; the elders did not include women. There is one clear exception to this, an exception in two senses, for there existed in ninth-century Brittany an hereditary and propertied officer for village business, called the machtiern, who dealt mostly with the regulation of transactions. This position was in one case held by a woman, the *tiranissa* Aourken of Pleucadeuc, the wife of the machtiern of the next village.[11] Although their number was small a few women presumably played a direct part in politics when they had control of large properties and when the course of politics was directly related to property interests. This may well be the underlying reason for Aourken's unusual position, for her husband's family had property in Pleucadeuc and her father-in-law had previously been machtiern there. However, political women are more likely to have operated in Ireland than elsewhere, for the leaders of some powerful religious communities there were women. It may also be of political significance that the deaths of some queens were noted from the eighth century in the Irish Annals.[12] On the whole, however, the absence of reference to women in politics is much more striking than their presence and it is difficult to escape the conclusion that they had very little to do with the conduct of public life.

Property

Ownership of property is not a straightforward concept and there are many aspects of it which vary. Land may be inherited or acquired by other means, such as purchase or gift. If it can be inherited, there are usually strict rules determining those who may qualify to be heirs, and often rules about the order in which they may make a claim to the inheritance; it is unusual to be able to choose an heir. Heritable land may or may not form an indivisible (and therefore inalienable) part of an inheritance. The power to alienate land is therefore a critical aspect of ownership: a person may have total power over property but no power to give it away. Modes of alienation, where permissible, in themselves vary: they may be possible in life or at death (bequest), or both; they may apply to acquired but not inherited land; there may be limitations on the persons to whom land can be alienated, and so on. Further, in the past the rules governing landed property were usually different from those governing movable, and in many societies the landed property assigned to a couple on marriage for the support of themselves, their household and their children could be distinct from other property owned by either one of the couple.

In all Celtic areas under discussion here property was clearly dominated by men, but it was not exclusively in their power. Movable property, as distinct from landed property, appears to have been relatively easily acquired, inherited and passed on by women.[13] There is considerable variation, however, in the way that portions were allocated, in the order in which different degrees of kinship were involved and in provisions for particular circumstances. In early Ireland there is a large corpus of legal material which attempts to provide a prescription for every eventuality, and these do not always appear to be mutually consistent. A father's inherited land was in normal circumstances inherited from him by his sons. In some tracts, in the absence of sons the land went to his daughters; but in others, in the absence of sons it went to his brothers and uncles, and only if there were none of those did it go to his daughters.[14] In any case, in most circumstances the daughters could only have a life interest in the property and could not pass it on to heirs. Now, a father's acquired land tended to be shared between offspring of both sexes and it is clear that women could receive gifts of landed property and could purchase and alienate it in perpetuity. Indeed some of the late seventh-century ecclesiastical records suggest that — contrary to the rules formulated in the secular law tracts — women could bequeath land to women, who could themselves make bequests in perpetuity.[15] There is therefore no doubt that in a range of circumstances, whether married or not and whatever the arrangement about the marriage portion, Irish women could have full and independent control over landed property. The indications are, however, that it was exceptionally difficult for a woman to pass on more than a life interest in her property, and therefore that the totality of her ownership was limited. Effectively this means that a woman *could* have full power over property in her lifetime but that her powers of alienation were extremely limited.

Most of the Welsh evidence comes from late in the medieval period, but there is a little relevant charter material from the early Middle Ages. The (late) law texts record that a father's land normally went to his sons, and only to daughters if there were neither sons nor cousins surviving him (although provision was made for a daughter's dowry); no inherited land was alienable. Earlier charters do indicate that women with surviving brothers shared their portions of land, and it is perfectly clear that women could receive gifts and alienate them. (Sale is only rarely evidenced in early Wales and may have been exceptional.)[16] In Brittany the evidence comes from charters rather than law texts, that is from records of transactions rather than from formally stated rules; the records are primarily concerned with peasant affairs. Here it would appear that although, as elsewhere, land was normally passed from male to male, women could in some circumstances inherit landed property. We therefore find them laying claim to property by stating their genealogies; inheriting from a mother; deciding — in the absence of sons — to pass inherited land to a body other than daughters; and sharing an inheritance with brothers.[17] Inherited land was not merely alienable in practice — by women as well as men — but one lady actually commented, with reference to her own bequest, that nobles were free to dispose of property as they wished.[18] Land could also clearly be acquired by women through gift and purchase and as security for loans; and acquired land was alienable, by gift and sale, and could be used by them as security for loans. The evidence, which is extremely detailed for the ninth century and which indicates that there was considerable movement of property at that period, is perfectly clear that women made these transactions alone, although they also sometimes did so jointly with their husbands.

The evidence which bears upon the question of proprietorship is exceptionally complex and is difficult to treat briefly. However, although there are obviously differences between regions there is quite enough evidence to demonstrate that women *could* have full powers of control over landed property in all areas, and that in some circumstances they could inherit it and in some alienate it. Of course, as in all parts of Europe in the early Middle Ages, the desire to make permanent gifts to religious institutions, and the church's encouragement of this, increasingly influenced and complicated practice concerning alienation of property, and this may account for some of the apparent inconsistencies in rulings. One part of the problem is that, since the inheritance structures were conceptualised as passing through males, women — strictly — could not have heirs; since, at the same time, some women *did* have full powers over property, circumstances were bound to arise in which they needed powers of alienation. The way that the several societies accommodated this need may constitute one of the main areas of difference between them. Indeed, it is the differences in the potential powers of women that are particularly interesting: in broad terms, Breton women had the greatest potential freedom in handling property and Welsh women the least. It is unlikely that this contrast reflects disparate source material rather than actual practice since there is a reasonable corpus of charter material from both early Brittany and early Wales, and charter evidence is especially valuable in recording practice as opposed to ideal rules; it may also be relevant that the powers of Welsh women were still relatively limited when the law texts were recorded several centuries later.

Marriage

In all of these societies, as in most ancient societies, marriage was a matter of arrangement between families, and to a greater or lesser extent constituted an alliance between them and a means of controlling the movement of property. Payments might include support for the new household unit from the bride's family, for the use of one or both (dowry); from the husband's side might come compensation to the bride's family or her protector for the loss of her virginity (brideprice) or payment in recognition of their protection of her virgin state (maiden fee), and/or a gift to the bride by her husband in recognition of *her* gift of herself (morning gift).

The clearest evidence about non-propertied women is that slave women tended to change owners together with their fathers or husbands — they were treated as appurtenant to a male — but our evidence is almost entirely confined to the marriage practices of propertied families. In the latter, marriages were negotiated, the agreement often being marked by a betrothal. They were negotiated by near kin, especially by fathers and in the case of remarriage by sons.[19] Correspondingly kin were involved in settlements following cases of abduction. Female kin members were not involved in these processes in any cases evidenced, although one sixth- or seventh-century Irish canon prescribed that a father should consult his daughter before finalising the marriage arrangement.[20] Again, there is considerable difference in practice between different regions, and there are also considerable differences in the amount of surviving information: most of the Welsh material is late and there is extremely little from Brittany. The early Irish legal material is once more full, with prescriptions for a range of variables. Irish law tracts in fact recognised several different types of marriage, the differences largely depending on the allocation of control of property and on the relationship of wives to each other in a polygamous family unit. These types included the marriage of 'joint contribution', in which each partner contributed to the common marriage stock and retained ultimate ownership of his/her portion, although no decisions about any of it were taken without consultation of the other. Other types included marriages in which one or other partner provided most, and powers over the common stock then varied (not necessarily strictly) in accordance with original contributions. Other regulations provided for apportionment between wives of higher and lower status in a family unit and between their respective children.[21]

The Irish evidence about payments made at the time of marriage is not always clear and would well repay further attention. Most consistently it is suggested that the husband, or his family, made a payment to the bride's father, or her kin (*coibche*, but also *tin(n)scra* in some texts, and *dos* in Latin); the term *coibche* either changed its meaning or this payment could make its way from her father to the bride, for we sometimes find women in control of the *coibche*, giving it a 'dowry' as well as a 'brideprice' element in some circumstances. There are occasional references to other payments: the bride sometimes took chattels with her, consisting of household items and/or cattle, which therefore comprised her family's contribution to the new household economy (*tinoil*).[22] There is also the question of kinship after marriage: perhaps unexpectedly, women did not change kin after marriage but stayed within the kin group into which they were born, i.e. their father's kin. Indeed, according to the law tracts, her own kin had some liability for a woman after marriage and a right to a proportion of the compensation if she was damaged.

Early Welsh evidence about marriage practice is almost nonexistent, but it is notable that charters associate royal husbands and wives in some transactions; this suggests that both might sometimes have shared control of the common marriage property. Hagiographic material instances the involvement of males in the arrangement of marriages, fathers bestowing their children and a nephew his aunt. By the time that law texts were being collected the structure of marriage payments was very clear and three or four different types of payment normally changed hands. The *argyfrau* was taken by the bride, from her kin (cf. dowry) and remained for her use; the *amobr* (maiden fee) was paid by the husband to the bride's lord (possibly her father in earlier times) in recognition of his protection of her virgin status until marriage; the *cowyll* (morning gift) was paid to the bride by her husband. Provision for a fourth payment, to be made in the event of failure of the marriage within seven years (*agweddi*), appears to have been made at the time of marriage. Maternal kin bore a share of responsibility for a son's offences and had a right to a share in compensation payments; females too might receive a share of these payments.[23]

In early Brittany, the very limited evidence indicates that a bride's father received a payment (*dos*) from the husband (and sons did in the case of remarriage) and that the bride received a morning gift (*enepuuert*) from her father-in-law or husband. In later texts a Middle Breton word for 'dowry' is found — *argobrou*, *argourou*, cf. W. *argyfrau*. Joint action by husbands and wives suggests that both might have had an interest in the common marriage property.[24]

In Irish and Welsh cases marriage and the procreation of children was clearly considered to be the normal state in adult life and a desirable one. Legal texts devote some space to responsibility for child-rearing, although it is difficult to differentiate between financial responsibility and practical child-care; fosterage appears to have been favoured by aristocratic families. Separation after marriage seems to have been relatively easy, and the law texts prescribe clear rules for such cases, including specification of the circumstances which justified separation — by either party — and of division of property between them (or provision for the woman). Remarriage was possible, and if anything encouraged, and there is also Breton evidence for this last point. Clearly Christian conversion and teaching introduced different values and in the long term it is likely that large-scale conversion to Christianity occasioned changes in pre-Christian marriage customs, though it should not be forgotten that horror was still expressed by English churchmen over Welsh marriage customs in the late Middle Ages.[25] Christian values took a long time to change established practice, but it is nevertheless clear that the seventh and eighth centuries (and probably the sixth too) saw a vigorous assault by missionaries and clerics on insular customs and values.

Sex

Legal material and incidental references suggest that virginity was considered essential in a woman until her first marriage and therefore that, since marriage itself was negotiated and controlled by the male members of her family, sexual experience for non-slave women was under family control. Since ecclesiastical legislation several times prohibited copulation with female slaves there are hints that they were used for sexual purposes by the free male population.[26] In contrast, Irish vernacular stories lay some stress on the sexual appetite and activity of free women and in some tales suggest that they consciously used their sexuality to win supporters, as Queen Medb offered herself and her daughter Finnabair to the warriors of Ireland.[27] By such means were (short-term) alliances made. Of course, Christian teaching had its own distinctive values in this respect and these are clearly, even forcibly, expressed in all regions. Christian values in some ways reinforced secular attitudes and practices, but in others they clearly ran counter to them. The penitential collections give evidence of a prescribed code of behaviour for Christians, clerical and lay, a code which was strongly against sex, homosexual and heterosexual, within marriage and without: the ideal and best way was to lead a life committed to celibacy. The earliest Irish ecclesiastical legislation prescribes heavy penalties for lapsed virgins, although there are some indications that virginity was perceived as a mental rather than a physical state – a holy woman who had a child could become virgin again after seven years penance. But for those who could not or would not opt for celibacy the early Christian legislators provided rules ranging from the complete abandonment of intercourse to the elaboration of long periods of abstention:

> a woman, if she has been sent away by her husband, must not mate with another man so long as her former husband is in the body, but should wait for him, unmarried, in all patience and chastity, in the hope that God may perchance put penance in the heart of her husband . . .
>
> We prescribe and exhort that there be continence in marriage, since marriage without continence is not lawful, but sin . . . Married people, then, should mutually abstain during the three forty-day periods in each single year . . . that they may be able to have time for prayer for the salvation of their souls; and on Sunday night or Saturday night they shall mutually abstain; and after the wife has conceived he shall not have intercourse with her until she has borne her child.

Heavy penalties were prescribed for rape and abduction, and overall there was a considerable emphasis on monogamy: ecclesiastical legislation forbade adultery, remarriage, separation (even in the case of childless marriages).[28] This idealisation of virginity, and at the least continence, must have run counter to secular principles, especially in the polygamous society of early Ireland; and the frequent repetition of the prohibitions is some indication that, despite increasing conversion to Christianity, all converts did not follow all aspects of the newly prescribed code. A corollary of the Christian advocacy of chastity appears to lie in the Christian attitude to widows, women regarded as especially worthy of respect and deserving special protection.[29] Perhaps this was a means of reconciling the competing ideologies: the widow had experienced the married and maternal state, and yet her present state was chaste.

The Impact of Christianity

The changes occasioned by the spread of Christianity in Europe have been a subject of scholarly interest for centuries, and writers of the present generation have taken some care to point out the increasing influence of the Christian ideal of celibacy in late Roman and Byzantine Europe, and its effects upon marriage, property and the status of women. To put it briefly, many men and women opted for chastity, and there seems to have been some drop in birth rate and consequent concentration of property in a smaller number of hands; the church was one beneficiary of this concentration, for not only were gifts made to it but those committed to chastity also tended to take property with them if they joined religious institutions. Chaste women might thereby find themselves in control of considerable properties for their institutions, and with considerable status too. At the same time, for connected or unconnected reasons, the capacity of women to make bequests was changing in their favour and their subjection to family control was loosening in the sixth century in the East.[30]

The overall impact of the Christian message that celibacy was desirable is impossible to assess in Celtic areas, although it is quite clear that some people (male and female) took a decision to become perpetual virgins, and there are indications that many may have done so in sixth- and seventh-century Ireland. (It is conventional to assume that there was a drop in population, but the evidence for this is not at all precise; if true it may have more to do with plague than with chastity.) On the other hand, there were always married clergy and married clergy with offspring, and before long there were non-celibate abbots.[31] In secular society it is impossible to know whether any or many were influenced by the rules about continence, although it is notable that anecdotes of parental opposition to celibacy appeared in the literature for centuries after the conversion. Women did become holy virgins − nuns − and may have done so despite strong family opposition, taking Christ as their bridegroom, as is explicitly stated; the persistence of young girls in their commitment to virginity against family wishes became virtually a topos in Irish − as in Byzantine − stories. The topos is significant even if it evidences attitudes rather than actual events. Hence, as early as the seventh century Muirchú wrote of the girl Monesan, who was beaten by her parents and drenched in water because of her determination to become a Christian virgin; eventually she was baptised, but immediately dropped dead, though her relics were preserved and known to Muirchú. Fainche jumped into the sea rather than marry. The vernacular Life of St. Brigit included the story of Brigit's refusal to marry: her brothers, who were poor, urged her to do so for they wanted the payment (*tinscra*) made to her family by the husband; Brigit, however, determined to outwit them and pulled out her eye so that she would be blemished and no one would want her as wife.[32] Evidence that women became nuns is very much fuller for Ireland than elsewhere: I know of none before the eleventh century in Brittany, despite the existence of sources that might be expected to make incidental reference to them, and only a few in Wales.

Not only did women become nuns, they also became holy and were venerated as saints. This happened at a very early date in Ireland, for it is likely that cults of Brigit and Ita were already in existence by the end of the sixth century; by 800 the feast days of dozens of women were acknowledged by the martyrologies, which record that a female saint was commemorated on almost every day of the year. These included both continental and local women, but the number of local saints is very striking.[33] It is also striking, for different reasons, that the cult of the Virgin Mary figures prominently in the Irish material from the seventh century, a rather early date for the occurrence of this cult in Western Europe. Brigit and other female Irish saints were sometimes identified with Mary.[34] Again, these trends are much more marked in Ireland than elsewhere; I know of no reference to local Welsh female saints before the eleventh century, although the cult of Brigit was certainly known in Wales by the ninth century and that of the Virgin Mary by the tenth. There is no good evidence of local female saints in Brittany before the twelfth century (and only a few appear in the late Middle Ages), apart from a monastery church in honour of an unknown S. Leupherina, to the north of Ruffiac (Morbihan), c. 830; she does not reappear after the ninth century. Dedications in honour of the Virgin feature from the mid-ninth century and the cult of Brigit seems to have been known in Brittany by the early tenth century.[35]

The attributes of female saints are many and various, but their powers were often associated with healing (a characteristic that was very rare in Celtic male saints) and also fasting; Brigit was also associated with the provision of plenty. There is, perhaps unexpectedly, some stress on the real or substitute maternal qualities of these holy virgins, particularly expressed in their fostering of children. This is most extremely demonstrated in the story of St. Ita, who, deprived by her nuns of the penitential beetle to which she was extremely attached, demanded a foster child, and was rewarded by the arrival of the infant Christ to foster. The commentary on her feast day in the *Martyrology of Oengus* includes a ninth- or tenth-century poem attributed to her, prefaced with the words 'Christ came to Íte in the form of a child, and then she said':

> It is little Jesus who is nursed by me in my little hermitage. Though a cleric have great wealth, it is all deceitful save Jesukin.
> The nursing done by me in my house is no nursing of a base churl: Jesus with Heaven's inhabitants is against my heart every night . . .
> It is noble angelic Jesus and no common cleric who is nursed by me in my little hermitage — Jesus son of the Hebrew woman.

A concern with the maternal side of sainthood is also expressed in an interest in the mothers of saints, whose festivals were frequently noted by the martyrologies, while the qualities of Mary that were stressed are her motherhood of Christ rather than her virginity. Paradoxically, then, though female saints reached sanctity through virginity, the non-virgin aspect of womanhood was a source of continuing veneration. The influence of the Virgin Mary ideology seems extremely powerful.[36]

Despite their place in the array of Christian saints, women did not normally have any part in Christian ritual, although there are tales of the ordination of Brigit and her consecration as bishop, by mistake, and complaints in sixth-century Brittany about priests who allowed women to assist in administering the mass. These were very clearly exceptions. By contrast, women were seen by some church authorities as practitioners of magic.[37]

There is also a sense in which the Christian church stood as a champion of women's rights, and in some sources this was clearly asserted. The best-known text, *Cáin Adomnáin*, purports to record a 'law' agreed in Ireland *c.* 700. It presents the church of Iona as the protector of women and claims that — as women — they are owed special protection. The rule prescribed that in practice women should not fight in battle and that extra penalties should be suffered if damage (wounding, rape, insult, etc.) were done to them. Later prologues added to the text elaborate these notions in an extreme manner, indicating that the writers believed that the formulation of *Cáin Adomnáin* represented a change from earlier practice and attitudes: women used to go to war with their husbands, so they maintained, and were indeed egged on by their husbands from behind; but everything was changed by Adomnán and peace was brought to women.[38]

Discussion

The preceding survey has concentrated on those aspects of women where comment can be made on more than the isolated case. Much, of course, relates to propertied women and there are severe limitations imposed by the available evidence, not least by its uneven distribution. Nevertheless, some general observations are possible: although women *could* exercise considerable powers over property and even (through property) politically, nevertheless they remained a 'subject' group; that subjection was especially manifest in their exclusion from the conduct of ordinary public affairs, in their inability to take part in legal proceedings and dispute settlement procedures, and in the control of their marriage (and sexual experience) by men. None of that is surprising within the conspectus of ancient and early medieval societies, although the details provide some variants on common patterns. More interesting are the problems posed by the areas on which there is inadequate comment. There are several important aspects of woman's role in any society about which these sources say little or nothing: women's quarters, the literacy and education of women, and above all their labour. There are occasional references to women and embroidery, and Irish material, especially, tends to assign home crafts to them — food preparation and clothing; indeed Irish ecclesiastical legislation cited St. Augustine to the effect that woman's place was in the home. Fosterage may have been important for aristocratic Welsh and Irish families, but some women are associated with child care; female slaves are reported performing dairy work, labouring outside with spade and quern, and making clothing.[39] All of this is interesting and relevant but it really is not sufficient to permit comment on the norms for women's labour in any area or at any period: until we know if all women or only certain groups of women did home chores, until we know what proportion of labour in the home was performed by slaves, and until we know how child care was managed, it is impossible to determine how the labour of women was used and how they fitted into the work pattern of the total society.

The image of woman in these societies, as conveyed by their records, is of interest; it is also perplexing, for there was not one image but many, and they are extremely difficult to relate to the social realities.

In Irish and Welsh material of all languages the image of woman as seducible and desirable is powerful and indeed so marked that events — like the wooing of Étaín — can hang on the pursuit of them. If we ask 'what was their view of woman?', one might answer 'an object of desire'. But the active aspect of this largely passive sex role is equally strongly expressed: woman as temptress, sexually and otherwise, and woman as the source of evil. The notion that Eve was the characterisation of womankind, leading man to sin, is sometimes explicitly expressed and occurs in all areas, and Breton saints' lives especially expressed the idea that purity came through masculinity: Landévennec was holy because nothing female had ever been there. The attitude is at least reminiscent of Byzantine approaches to sanctity, achieved through maleness, although I know of no stories of Celtic transvestite saints.[40] Now some parts of these two images are complementary, but others are contradictory: woman is desirable, but desire is bad; hence, sometimes, woman is bad. There is an obvious strand of Christian ideology, but it is difficult to disentangle the Christian from the non-Christian, and to unravel the ambiguities of the Christian attitude itself. Indeed, some Christian writers were themselves aware of the ambiguity, as expressed succinctly in an early poem, possibly written by St. Columbanus:

On Women

Let everyone who is dutiful in mind avoid the deadly poison
That the proud tongue of an evil woman has.
Woman [Eve] destroyed life's gathered crown;
But woman [Mary] gave long-lasting joys of life.[41]

Could woman overcome the evil inherent in her nature by opting for virginity? Some work on women as healers — a female attribute common to Christian saintly literature and also to vernacular stories, where it is sometimes associated with desirable women too — may perhaps assist here.

This brings us to the problem of change, including change from pre-Christian to Christian, of particular interest given the well-evidenced changes that occurred in the late Roman world. Christian literature suggests some present change from warlike to unwarlike, as well as advocating change from sexuality to chastity, for most records were made by clerics and even *Cáin Adomnáin*, with its explicit pre-Christian import, must reflect Christian views and attitudes.[42] The notion that these Christian writers clearly favoured was that Christianity had brought a change in the status (? and nature) of women from being sexual, sometimes warrior, images of fertility to passive, chaste symbols of maternity. Of course, in the absence of pre-Christian records these issues are extraordinarily difficult to assess. In the case of Irish marriage and property law it is conventional to argue that there was a considerable extension of female rights and powers between the sixth and tenth centuries, and to place this in the context of the spread of Christian values and changes in family structure.[43] Since it is so difficult to assign precise dates to the law tracts it has been argued that differences and contradictions must represent *successive* stages; different forms of marriage, for example, have thereby been assigned a place in a sequence. These suggestions may well be sensible; they do not, however, constitute in themselves evidence of changes. So we must still ask if the status of women changed in all or some regions over these centuries, and try to devise a means of assessing and measuring it.

Though they share some characteristics the different emphases of Irish and Breton material are notable and possibly helpful here: the Breton emphasis on sanctity through maleness is not a distinctive Irish characteristic, and the Irish (and to a lesser degree Welsh) stress on the virtues of motherhood is not characteristic of early Brittany (although some expression of this appears in the late Middle Ages). Both extremes, however, share common attitudes to chastity and to the inherently if ambiguously evil nature of woman. Indeed, the contrast between the package of female rights and powers in one region with the package in another is interesting and potentially instructive. It would appear that in early medieval Breton society women had relatively great powers over property and freedom of independent action, while they had no tendency to become nuns and society as a whole apparently had little tendency to venerate women as saints; in Ireland, by contrast, the sanctification of women was marked, while their powers over property seem less than in the Breton case. The contrast will bear more investigation. If there is a relationship between these aspects, then not only should it be possible to understand more of female roles in early Celtic societies but it may also be possible to investigate whether consistent causal factors were in operation, both here and elsewhere.

Notes

1. I am extremely grateful for the comments on this paper made by Averil Cameron, Donnohadh Ó Corráin and Morfydd Owen, and for their patience in

answering the naive questions of one who is unaccustomed to writing women's history. I am also indebted to Pádraig Ó Rúain for helpful conversations about Celtic saints. I have tried to cite recent comment, where such exists; where it does not I have given a selection of references to primary sources. These do not pretend to be exhaustive.

2. For a treatment of grammatical relationships see Lewis and Pedersen (1974); for history of the languages see Jackson (1953); Ó Cuív (1969).

3. There are relatively few works that can serve as an introduction to early medieval social structures in these areas that will also meet the standards of modern historical scholarship, but the following are of some value: La Borderie (1896-1914) vol. 2, for Brittany; Hughes (1966), Mac Niocaill (1972), Ó Corráin (1972) for Ireland; Duncan (1975) for Scotland; Davies (1982) for Wales; and perhaps Pearce (1978) for south-western Britain. Material from the Isle of Man is too fragmentary to permit general comment.

4. Principal sources which are relatively or very easily available are as follows (unless otherwise stated they have English translations): *Annals of Ulster*; Bieler 1979, *Vitae Sanctorum Britanniae*, *Vitae Sanctorum Hiberniae* (no translation), *Lives of Irish Saints*, 'Vita Winwaloei' (no translation); Bartrum (1966), O'Brien (1962); *Cart. Redon, Lib. Landavensis*; *Corpus Iuris Hibernici* (no translation), Wade-Evans (1909); Bieler 1963, *Coll. Canonum Hib.* (no translation); Gantz (1981), Gantz (1976); Stokes and Strachan (1901-3). Further guidance may be found in Bromwich (1974); Davies (1982) (Appendix); Fleuriot (1980); Hughes (1972).

5. I thereby omit the important issue of matrilineal succession to the Pictish kingship in sixth-, seventh- and eighth-century Scotland; for this, see Anderson (1973), Boyle (1977), Jackson (1971), Miller (1982).

6. 'What the father wishes a girl must do, for man is the head of woman.' Pa. II, 27 (Bieler, 1963, p. 194); Stokes and Strachan (1901), vol. 1, p. 222; *Life of Columba*, II.41; Jenkins and Owen (1980), pp. 42-4, 73-5, 190. Cf. Binchy in Binchy (1936), pp. 211-13; Simms (1978), p. 14f.; Ó Corráin (1978a), pp. 9f.

7. Can. Wall., A60 (Bieler, 1963, p. 148). In all of this cf. *patris potestas* in classical Roman law.

8. *Coll. Canonum Hib.*, XXXIV.3; see Binchy (1936), pp. 211-13 and Owen (1980), pp. 42-4.

9. *Coll. Canonum Hib.*, XXXIV.3; Binchy in Binchy (1936), p. 233. The import of *domina* is presumably 'landlord'.

10. See Davies (1982), p. 131; Jones (1972), pp. 373-5; Ó Corráin (1978b), pp. 26-9. It might be argued that Irish legal experts held public office, with responsibility to peoples rather than governments.

11. *Cart. Redon.*, CCLVII.

12. *Annals of Ulster*, s.a. A.D. 731, 733, 757, 794, 939 etc.; see Ó Corráin (1978a), pp. 10f.

13. See Dillon (1936), pp. 133-5; cf. Additamenta, 11.4 (Bieler, 1979, p. 174) and *Bethu Brigte*, ch. 22.

14. Dillon (1936), pp. 133-40; *Coll. Canonum Hib.*, XXXII.9.

15. Additamenta, 11.1-3 (Bieler, 1979, p. 174); *Coll. Canonum Hib.*, XXXII.20 and XLI.10; cf. *Bethu Brigte*, ch. 44.

16. *Lib. Landavensis*, nos. 140, 190b, 207; 'Vita Cadoci', ch. 68 (*Vitae Sanctorum Britanniae*, p. 134); cf. Davies (1978), p. 56, and Davies (1982), pp. 79f.

17. *Cart. Redon.*, CIX, CLXXXIV, CCXXXI, CXXXI; cf. 'Vita Pauli', ch. 10.

18. *Cart. Redon.*, CIX.

19. Thurneysen (1936), pp. 109-12; McAll (1980), pp. 13-16; cf. *Bethu Brigte*, chs. 13-14.

20. Davies (1982), pp. 74, 136; Pa. II,27 (Bieler, 1963, p. 194).

21. Thurneysen, Dillon and Power in Binchy (1936); cf. *Cáin Adamnáin*, ch. 5.
22. Thurneysen (1936), pp. 113-24; Power (1936), pp. 100f.; cf. Pa. I,22 and Penit. Columbani, 14, 16 (Bieler, 1963, pp. 56, 102) for payments *to* the bride's family; cf. Additamenta 11.3 (Bieler, 1979, p. 174) for a possible payment *from* the bride's family. I am obliged to Professor F.J. Byrne for pointing out the value of the Additamenta passages. Note that *dos* does not have the sense of *dos* in classical Roman law.
23. Davies (1978), p. 56; *Vie de S. Samson*, ch. 1; 'Vita Cadoci', ch. 25 (*Vitae Sanctorum Britanniae*, p. 80); Jenkins and Owen (1980), *passim*.
24. Can. Wall., A47 (Bieler, 1963, p. 144); *Cart. Redon.*, CCXXXVI; *Cart. Landevenec*, XLIV; Fleuriot (1964), 111; Loth (1890), p. 128. *Enepuuert(h)* – literally 'honour price' – presumably originated as compensation for her shame at the loss of her virgin state; for the importance of the idea of shame in the Welsh law of women see Owen (1980). The Breton terminology would repay fresh examination: if, as appears to be the case, Middle Breton *enebarz* also signifies 'dowry', then the implied semantic shift may have implications for social change too.
25. See Conway Davies (1948), pp. 460-68.
26. Penit. Vinniani, 39, 40; cf. Can. Wall., A59 (Bieler, 1963, pp. 88, 148).
27. *Táin*, pp. 168ff.
28. Penit. Vinniani, 21, 45, 46 (Bieler, 1963, pp. 80, 90-92 and *passim*).
29. *Vie de S. Samson*, ch. 30; Gildas, ch. 32: *viduitatis castimoniam*.
30. See Patlagean (1969); Ashbrook Harvey and Herrin in this volume.
31. The evidence essentially consists of records of succession to office in monasteries by the sons of former abbots; although some of these were undoubtedly lay abbots, it is clear that others – and their offspring – were full members of religious communities; see Hughes (1966), pp. 161-9; Davies (1978), pp. 128-30.
32. Pa. II, 14 (Bieler, 1963, p. 188); Muirchú, I.27 (Bieler, 1979, p. 98; cf. St. Patrick's 'Confessio', ch. 42; Hood (1978), p. 31); *Mart. Oengus*, pp. 50f.; *Bethu Brigte*, chs. 14-16.
33. *Mart. Oengus*; *Mart. Tallaght*.
34. *Cáin Adamnáin*, ch. 33; *Mart. Oengus*, Prologue, lines 56, 129, 148, 251, 338; *Bethu Brigte*, ch. 11.
35. Davies (1982), p. 174; Davies (1978), p. 132. *CR* 33, 272, 276, 152, 154. Brigit seems to have been known and venerated at Landévennec in the late ninth century since she is included in the calendar of appropriate readings for festivals attached to the late ninth-century Gospels of Landévennec, Gougaud (1936), p. 23, Morey, Rand and Kraeling (1931), pp. 264, 273f.; she may have been known at Rhuys before the departure of the monks of St. Gildas in the early tenth century if traditions about the translation of relics from Rhuys are to be believed, Duval (1977); cf. Laurent (1971).
36. *Mart. Oengus*, pp. 42-5; the translation is that of Murphy (1956), pp. 26-8. *Cáin Adamnáin*, chs. 4, 33; cf. *Mart. Oengus*, pp. 68ff. (Darerca, who mothered 17 bishops).
37. *Bethu Brigte*, ch. 19; *Mart. Oengus*, pp. 64-7; La Borderie (1894-1914), vol. 2, p. 527; Penit. Vinniani, 18, 19 (Bieler, 1963, p. 78); Padel in this volume (on Greek women).
38. *Cáin Adamnáin*. Máirín Ní Dhonnchada is preparing a new edition of and commentary upon this text.
39. Mulchrone in Binchy (1936), p. 190; *Life of Columba*, II.41; *Coll. Canonum Hib.*, XXXII.18; *Vie de S. Samson*, ch. 6; *Cáin Adamnáin*, ch. 33; Owen (1980), p. 43; Wade-Evans (1909), p. 46.
40. See, for example, Penit. Vinniani, 16 (Bieler, 1963, p. 78); *Lib*.

Landavensis, nos. 231, 259, 271; Gantz (1981), pp. 39-59; Patrick, 'Epistola', ch. 13 (Hood, 1978, p. 37): 'Vita Winwaloei', II.5: 'Atque hoc quoque ex eo die privilegium semper usque nunc habet, quod nunquam femineus eundem locum cum omnibus septis ejus late per circuitum, quasi lege ex ore Sancti Winwaloei sancita, temeravit introitus.' There is, however, a *citation* of Eugenia who dressed up as a male in Egypt and became monk and then abbot: *Mart. Oengus*, p. 98f. The stereotyping of woman as sexual temptress is expressed very well by the story of St. Scothíne, who slept between two women every night as a test of his ability to overcome temptation: *Mart. Oengus*, p. 40f.

    41. Walker (1957), p. 214f.

    42. E.g. *Táin*, pp. 28-34; *Cáin Adamnáin*, chs. 3, 7; cf. MacCana (1970), pp. 86-90.

    43. Ó Corráin (1978a), pp. 9-11.

List of Sources

Annals of Ulster	*Annals of Ulster* I, ed. Hennessy, W.M., 1887, Rolls Series, Dublin
Bethu Brigte	*Bethu Brigte*, ed. Ó hAodha, D., 1978, Dublin
Cáin Adamnáin	*Cáin Adamnáin*, ed. Meyer, K., 1905, Oxford
Cart. Redon.	*Cartulaire de l'Abbaye de Redon*, ed. de Courson, A., 1863, Paris
Cart. Landevenec	*Cartulaire de l'Abbaye de Landevenec*, ed. La Borderie, A. de, 1888, Rennes
Coll. Canonum Hib.	*Die irische Kanonensammlung*, ed. Wasserschleben, F.W.H., 2nd ed., 1885, Leipzig
Corpus Iuris Hibernici	*Corpus Iuris Hibernici*, ed. Binchy, D., 6 vols., 1978, Dublin
Lib. Landavensis	*The Text of the Book of Llan Dâv*, ed. Evans, J.G. and Rhys, J., 1893, Oxford
Life of Columba	*Adomnan's Life of Columba*, ed. Anderson, A.O. and M.O., 1961, London
Lives of Irish Saints	*Bethada Náem nÉrenn. Lives of Irish Saints*, ed. and trans. Plummer, C., 1922, 2 vols., Oxford
Mart. Oengus	*The Martyrology of Oengus the Culdee*, ed. Stokes, W., 1905, Henry Bradshaw Society 29
Mart. Tallaght	*The Martyrology of Tallaght*, ed. Best, R.I. and Lawlor, H.J., 1931, Henry Bradshaw Society 68
Táin	*The Táin*, trans. Kinsella, T., 2nd ed., 1970, London
Vie de S. Samson	*La Vie de Saint Samson*, ed. Fawtier, R., 1912, Paris
Vitae Sanctorum Britanniae	*Vitae Sanctorum Britanniae et Genealogiae*, ed. Wade-Evans, A.W., 1944, Cardiff
Vitae Sanctorum Hiberniae	*Vitae Sanctorum Hiberniae*, ed. Plummer, C., 2 vols., 1910, Oxford
'Vita Cadoci'	*Vitae Sanctorum Britanniae*, pp. 24-140
'Vita Pauli'	'Vie de Saint Paul de Léon', ed. Cuissard, C., 1881-83, *Revue celtique* 5, pp. 417-58
'Vita Winwaloei'	ed. de Smedt, C., 1888, *AB* 7, pp. 167-249; also by La Borderie in *Cart. Landevenec* (see above)

Further Reading

The following works will be of use in providing general historical and social context:

Byrne, F.J. (1973), *Irish Kings and High-Kings*, London
Davies, W. (1982), *Wales in the Early Middle Ages*, Leicester
Fleuriot, L. (1980), *Les Origines de la Bretagne*, Paris
Henderson, I. (1967), *The Picts*, London
Hughes, K. (1966), *The Church in Early Irish Society*, London
Mac Niocaill, G. (1972), *Ireland before the Vikings*, Dublin
Ó Corráin, D. (1972), *Ireland before the Normans*, Dublin
Planiol, M. (1953), *Histoire des Institutions de la Bretagne*, 3 vols., Rennes, vol. 2 especially

The remaining works are especially relevant to the question of women:

Binchy, D. (ed.) (1936), *Studies in Early Irish Law*, Dublin
Jenkins, D. and M.E. Owen (eds.) (1980), *The Welsh Law of Women*, Cardiff
MacCurtain, M. and D. Ó Corráin (eds.) (1978), *Women in Irish Society. The Historical Dimension*, Dublin
Power, P.C. (1976), *Sex and Marriage in Ancient Ireland*, Dublin, is a popularising treatment, and slight, but does cite some of the relevant material.

11 IN SEARCH OF BYZANTINE WOMEN: THREE AVENUES OF APPROACH*

Judith Herrin, Princeton, New Jersey

It is now widely recognised that the analysis of male-dominated societies should not be undertaken as if men alone counted in their histories. Women can play a significant role economically and culturally, even if it is only the exceptional individual — usually the wife of a ruler — who manifests overt political power. Female influence is doubly veiled from us: it is often silent, unvoiced by the women themselves, and frequently ignored, either deliberately or as a matter of course in the sources written by men. A full theory of the potential role of women in large pre-industrial societies will require evidence drawn from many in such a fashion that systematic comparisons can be made. The nature of the source material means that this will have to be a collective effort, mounted on the basis of different specialist contributions. Here I will examine some of the roles of women in early medieval Byzantine society, hopefully in a manner that will make contrasts with other social formations a future possibility.

Obviously, any search for Byzantine women must take account of the fact that they lived in a military society where men inevitably exercised power. Their political influence was therefore limited, and I shall not pursue the case of those unusual women who managed to overcome obstacles and prejudice to attain prominence. Although the case of the Empress Theodora is well known, it is also highly eccentric: after all, Justinian first noticed her in a popular entertainment connected with the Hippodrome and in order to marry her regulations preventing actresses from marrying into the senatorial class had to be changed.[1] It would be quite wrong to conclude that many made this extraordinary move from the lowest into the ruling circles of the empire. Theodora remains an exception. Yet many a modern historian has been seduced by the 'grandes dames et belles dames' of Byzantium in a way that is both misleading and deceptive for any study of women in general.[2]

So I propose to follow three particular avenues of approach, devised as a means of identifying the positions, activity and authority of women in Byzantine society. The first is to pick up chance references to female activity in the sources written by men, especially those which occur spontaneously in narratives unconnected with women, incidental remarks and stray observations. The second seeks to document the ingenuity with which women exercised their limited legal rights and is therefore dependent upon the case law that survives – the *Peira* (Teaching) of Eustathios Romaios is the outstanding example. The third approach attempts to outline the significance of ecclesiastical institutions and Christian beliefs for women, an area in which female subjectivity is perhaps most closely revealed. The overall aim of these avenues is to illuminate a practical reality rather than a legal ideal. Women's status and rights were clearly defined in the Code of Justinian and revised, restricted and elaborated in a series of subsequent rulings.[3] But these do not necessarily indicate what women actually did or thought they could do. Of course, the evidence for the period *c.* 600-1100 is scrappy and inconclusive, but it can yield results which bring us into contact with some of the realities of female existence.[4]

Almost none of the materials basic to a study of women survive; no parish church archives of births, deaths and marriages, few landholding records and hardly any personal documents. And the character of those chronicles, saints' lives and legal records that have been preserved severely limits their usefulness for a study of the female half of the population. They all share that element of bias inherent in male authors who note the most outrageous, miraculous and in other ways unexpected aspects of female life, rather than its regular achievements and routines. These sources make it relatively easier to document women with unusual wealth and members of the imperial families than the great majority of females. In particular, they provide extremely little evidence for rural Byzantium, where the greater part of the medieval population lived and worked. Hagiographic texts and monastic documents shed some light but we shall probably never be able to reconstruct the lives of the poorest country men and women. Those who have made their mark on the historical records of the countryside are probably untypical and correspond to a very small fraction of the total. They are women who can utilise written documents, recording their bequests and defending their property, participating in the life of the church and attending to their children's education. Clearly, these are not the wives and daughters of illiterate subsistence farmers; some are familiar with monastic life, others with urban institutions, and most are aware that they have certain rights. Below this level, however, it is almost impossible to tabulate and measure female activities.

Urban women can be glimpsed more frequently through city-based records and the poor are better represented here than their rural counterparts. They feature amongst the crowds who enjoyed races in the Hippodrome and the processions associated with court ceremonies and church feasts; they witnessed public executions, shared in charitable distributions of food and participated in rioting and looting. Women were allegedly foremost in the protest against the removal of the Christ icon from the Chalke Gate of the palace in 726, and several maintained their devotion to icons through the two periods of iconoclast persecution.[5] This greater visibility of city women, especially those of the capital, reflects the dominance of urban life in Byzantium. Although the complex forms of the late antique *polis* were drastically shaken by seventh- and eighth-century economic decline and insecurity, the ideal of city life was not lost. The traditional wealth and variety of facilities and institutions continued to act as a magnet for the countryside, drawing people to the hospitals and healing shrines, to charitable services, schools, government positions, markets and long-distance trade, employment in noble households, public buildings and places of entertainment — in short to all the sights and wonders of civic centres. Constantinople was the sole megalopolis which maintained these and other possibilities, but even provincial capitals, ports and smaller towns held markets and fairs, and could provide opportunities for urban occupations. Because the Byzantines considered it a more desirable and advanced form of social existence, urban dwelling continued to dominate, and the records reflect this situation. City inhabitants are much better documented than the rural population.

The survival of ancient traditions of city life perpetuated public institutions and habits which influenced female behaviour in the early Byzantine period despite the disapproval of the church. Thus attendance at the races, pantomimes and other forms of entertainment, and particularly visits to the baths, were regularly condemned by ecclesiastics to no avail. Paradoxically, the classical pattern of segregation, which effectively kept women apart from men other than their immediate family, also created openings. For in every institution for women, such as the public bath, there had to be female attendants, and these are well documented. The development of private and domestic baths never removed the need for larger public establishments, although fewer and less well maintained than in ancient times.[6] A tenth-century patrician justified his daughter's weekly trip on the grounds that her beauty was related to cleanliness, but made sure that she went out veiled and suitably chaperoned.[7] Other public roles open to women, those of midwife and doctor, reflect the fact that it would have been improper for men to attend to feminine bodily matters.[8] These can hardly be said to constitute a sphere of public employment comparable to that for men: women clearly did not pursue 'careers'. But some were involved in commercial activity, working in small businesses or running them from their homes; selling prepared food on the streets and marketing produce grown in and around the city. Amongst shopowners in tenth-century Constantinople there is evidence of two aristocratic ladies, Eudokia Hetairiotese and Sophia, the wife of a patrician, who might possibly have employed city women in their boutiques (one appears to have been devoted to the production of garments made of goats' hair).[9] Entertainment remained one sector open to women and one in which a certain skill could bring fame and notoriety — hardly a public career though a very public activity.

Maintaining an independent and respectable life in Byzantine cities was, however, a tough business. The church lent its weight to civilian proscriptions of behaviour deemed anti-social, and urban women were certainly caught in a trap created by continuing classical urban traditions and medieval disapproval. Actresses, mimes, dancers and other entertainers were treated almost like prostitutes by law, indeed there can have been only a narrow dividing line between the two. So there was a serious danger for women involved in legitimate public work of being equated with these libertines, a danger exacerbated by the poverty endemic in Byzantine as in all medieval cities. Despite civic distributions of bread and ecclesiastical charity, hunger frequently forced women into prostitution. Those thus reduced to selling themselves were joined by an organised supply of young girls, purchased in the countryside and brought to the cities by pimps and procurers. Some must also have used the opportunity to take their chance of attracting an urban husband; however degrading, the established tradition of courtesans and mistresses offerred a promise, if rarely fulfilled, of marriage. Throughout the Byzantine period there is evidence of a concern to redeem these women. Empress Theodora's attempt to get prostitutes into decent monastic homes was no more or less successful, one suspects, than that repeated in the eleventh century. But an element of more voluntary reform is evident from one of the miracle stories associated with the shrine of Ss. Cosmas and Damian, just outside the walls of Constantinople. There an ex-prostitute, Martha, used to sit behind a curtain fixed up at the left door of the entrance to the church and invite other poor women to resist temptation. Her own release from the madness which had induced her libertine behaviour may perhaps have influenced them as they went into the shrine. But probably of greater weight was Martha's subsequent cure by the saints themselves of her 'persistent headaches'; this finally allowed her to give up her daily vigil in favour of a weekly visit of thanks.[10]

Closely related to the institution of prostitution was that of concubinage, both feeding on the large numbers of female slaves in Byzantine cities. These women were totally dependent upon their owners and sometimes succeeded in making a lasting alliance, legalised by their freedom and marriage.[11] But most were quite unable to alter their servile status and were lucky if their masters arranged to marry them to other slaves and to provide for their children until they too started to work. Personal slaves were regularly freed on the death of their owner, who might also endow them with a legacy which acted as a dowry. Without a dowry their chances of making an honourable marriage were negligible (see below). Within wealthy households female slaves worked in routine domestic jobs and also wove and sewed, frequently under the direction of their mistress, sometimes assisted by a eunuch. There is little evidence for the treatment of slaves, but Christian influence may have improved the conditions of female domestic servants.

The recognised role of eunuchs in Byzantium established this 'third sex' as men with a privileged access to women: they threatened neither the master's authority nor the mistress's purity. While those in the lower levels of society were often slaves or captives, the fact that a whole range of court positions was reserved for the 'beardless men', and that higher echelons in the ecclesiastical administration were theoretically held only by celibate men, meant that in many aristocratic families one son would be destined for such a career. Castration shortly after birth was the normal preparation; the operation was also performed as a method of preventing the sons of ambitious individuals from aspiring to the throne. Eunuchs dominated the personal activity of the imperial couple as wardrobe officials, chamberlains and treasurers, and played a similar role in wealthy households. They were a regular feature of ecclesiastical institutions and city life, and seem to have formed contacts with women that would certainly have been condemned in normal men.[12] Unfortunately it is impossible to put a figure on the number of this group of neutral men, but they were an accepted component of Byzantine society. Their relations with women are particularly visible when they filled the role of 'spiritual father' (see below). In society at large, however, their function was to reinforce the separation of the sexes and the enclosed women's world of domesticity. Within this limited parameter a woman might organise her own household, oversee the family fortunes and take full responsibility for the children. A poor widow who did not have sufficient money to pay the high fees demanded by doctors for a treatment of her nine-year-old son's illness, consulted the healing St. Artemios and offered to sell her sole asset, perhaps a small business that she had inherited, if only her only child could be cured.[13] (Needless to say, the saint spurned her money and performed the cure.) But beyond this essentially domestic sphere, women had few opportunities, especially if they aspired to a position of status and honour. The greater their social standing, the stronger the segregation. Only among those without the means or pretensions to grandeur could the strict separation of men and women be ignored.

Women were clearly at risk in this society, vulnerable to all kinds of slurs if they did not fulfil the prescribed roles of wife and mother. The association of women with superstitious practices, such as the wearing of amulets or incantation of magic spells in order to obtain supernatural assistance, may have been due in part to the difficulties inherent in these roles. Not all poor women could expect to get married, and among those that did the problem of poverty often remained. But in addition, the acknowledged role of women as midwives brought them into intimate contact with the mysteries, and often fatalities, of child-birth. In the absence of medical expertise, midwives regularly employed ancient customs closer to pagan superstition than birthing folklore. The same traditional means were used when women wished to conceive sons rather than daughters, or when young girls wanted to have their chances in love predicted. Women presided over these highly personal and signi-ficant matters and were regularly condemned by both the civil and ecclesiastical authorities for perpetuating pre-Christian beliefs. Although pagan cult observance was almost extinguished by the sixth century, old habits persisted; lighting bonfires at the new moon and jumping over them was one condemned at the Council in Trullo (691/2).[14] And through such activities considered both irreligious and antisocial in some instances, it was a short step to the connection with similar super-stitions involved in the much more serious business of birth. As the chief practitioners of these arts, part astrological, part inherited medical folklore and part outright witchcraft, women were easily associated with anti-Christian belief and heretical ritual.

A measure of the desperation felt by women when things did not work out according to the recommended path of marriage and child-bearing may be gauged from several factors, for example, the frequency of infertility, a source of tremendous shame. The history of Maria as recounted by a ship's captain in the early seventh century is also revealing. It is told in the first person singular in a series of edifying moral tales collected by John Moschos.

I, the wretched one, had a husband and two children by him, the one nine years old and the other five, when my husband died and I remained a widow. A soldier lived near to me and I wanted him to take me as his wife, so I sent some friends (women) to him. But the soldier said, 'I am not taking a wife who has children by another man'. Then, as I learned that he did not want to take me because of the children, and because I loved him, I, the wretched one, killed my two children and told him that now I did not have any. But when the soldier heard what I had done about the children, he said, 'May the Lord God who lives in heaven above abide, I will not take her'. And fearing that this dreadful thing should become known and I should die, I fled.[15]

Maria's situation is probably typical of the poor Byzantine widow, economically insecure, who craves the protection and security of marriage. Her negotiations with the soldier are conducted by other women who understand her predicament. The first proposal does not appear to be received with any sense of outrage and is rejected, formally, on the grounds of the children. The whole incident indicates the frequency of remarriage, a step condemned by the church but regularly practised, judging by the number of legal rulings made to protect the rights of children of previous marriages. Indeed, Byzantine law stipulated that step-parents were obliged to adopt such offspring as their own, which may have been the reason for the soldier's refusal. This law is confirmed by many cases of precisely this type of adoption, where provision of a dowry for daughters is also laid down.[16] Maria, however, tried to remove the obstacle which prevented her from remarrying, and of course the point of the story as related by a clearly prejudiced male source, is that she was eventually punished for this crime. But her tale reveals the immense significance of marriage for women and the 'dangers' posed by widows for men.

Marriages depended upon many factors, not least the dowry. Even between families of modest means a marriage alliance united a certain amount of property in the hands of the new couple, with contributions from both parties. As far as the bride was concerned, what became hers at marriage was normally hers to dispose of, so dowries and wills are related legal documents providing evidence of female ownership and control of wealth. This material facilitates the second avenue of approach, for it permits a fairly realistic appraisal of what individual Byzantine women with a certain amount of property could call their own. While it is true that such acts 'are not the best means of self-expression',[17] neither should they be overlooked. In addition, the role of mothers and grandmothers in the arrangement of marriage contracts, reveals a heavy female influence in what was a key family matter. As young girls could be married at 12 and were often abducted or illegally married below that age, their engagement in suitable alliances was sometimes undertaken early in life. Older female relatives could not be held responsible for subsequent failures: when a man tried to divorce his wife on the grounds that his grandmother had signed all the marriage documents, the court stated that her arrangements were not in question and that she did not have to appear. He, however, had to pay compensation to the bride's family.[18] An active female role in marriage contracts can also be seen in the identification of objects and property as part of a mother's dowry, which is passed on to her daughter, thus preserving inheritance in the female line (also visible in wills). What the bride's family provided as her dowry largely determined the match she would make, as the groom had to contribute an equivalent value. The terms of one particular *proikosymbolion* (dowry contract) are spelled out in a South Italian document of 1097.[19] The bride's mother (probably) fulfilled her daughter Alpharana's obligations by presenting the groom with an *antiproikion* of household equipment, including the bed complete with pillows, and her daughter with the dowry proper (*prix*, normally *proix* or *proika*) consisting of the wedding trousseau and the share in family property. On the male side, Basil, brother of the groom, John, established the three distinct parts which made up his contribution: the *progamaia dorea* (betrothal gifts) of John's fraternal share in the family lands; the *theoretron* or *hypobolon* (bride price, there called *theorethron*), of two *modia* of land at Kalavros and personal gifts, clothes, shoes and jewellery. Of these, Alpharana gained full control only over her maternal inheritance and the personal gifts of Basil, though the *theoretron* was probably in her name. John's inheritance only became hers at his death, and in this sense the dowry contract must be seen rather as an insurance against poverty through bereavement than a transfer of property to a female.[20] A slightly later act follows exactly the same pattern, except that the groom's father stipulates an *hypobolon* of one *nomisma* (gold coin), and a *theoretron*, composed of the fourth part of his property, which he continues to hold until his death.[21] Such arrangements for the legal transfer of wealth only after the donor's death are a regular feature of these acts and confirm the permanent nature of the alliance between families.

The young wife was thus endowed with the basic necessities of her wardrobe and household equipment, possessions which she in turn bequeathed to her own children or to any other person. Her husband administered the property established in the possession of the couple, guided by a series of legal rulings to prevent him from in any way diminishing the value of the dowry lands and goods. This legal protection meant that state officials could not expropriate a woman's dowry even for the payment of her husband's debts. There are cases where she was persuaded to give her consent to such an action, which effectively disinherited her. In many cases, however, the regular transfer of maternal inheritance from one generation to the next occurs peacefully, and in one case a widow is prevented from leaving all her property to a monastery as this will create a penniless orphan. The maternal inheritance is especially mentioned, *tois metroois autes pragmasi*, as something the girl should not be deprived of.[22]

From the few surviving wills drawn up by Byzantine women one can trace the same mixture of personal effects and property that they brought to or gained at their marriage. An undated document of the eleventh century reveals the last wishes of Serika, the daughter of Mavros, from the castle of Stilo in Calabria.[23] She appears to have been childless and to have lived a lonely life since the deaths of her husband and brother. Her entire possessions, movable and unmovable, at Stilo and within the castle, she bequeathes to the lady Helen, wife of John, who also receives the sum of 20 *nomismata*, half from Serika's personal fortune and half from her late husband's. The final provision concerns her slave, Pitzoulos, who is to be freed and treated as a Byzantine citizen, *polites Romaion*. The will is written by Eustathios the priest, witnessed by several local officials and finally Serika signs with her own hand.[24] A will from Tarento of 1044 goes to the other extreme in listing the detailed distribution of every item owned by Gemma, widow of Nikèphoros, a local official and record keeper.[25] The main beneficiary is the church of St. Bartholomew; her nephews also gain substantial portions of her extensive property, and several servants, male and female, are given the houses in which they live, vineyards and other land, as well as personal belongings. Gemma was clearly the owner of a well-run estate, scattered with cottages and patches of vines. She also owned casks and vessels, presumably used in the making and transporting of wine; livestock; grain fields; sheep (unless the skeins of wool to be woven into curtains for the church did not come from her own sheep); and an oven. Her favourite nephew, Leo, is appointed *epitropos* (executor) of her estate and is allotted the ancestral home, half of all the scattered property not otherwise covered, a special dish (*lekanes*), and the table and two goblets which are to be used in a service of *kolybon*, the distribution of wheat to the faithful in the first week of Lent. One female slave, Risa, is given permanent ownership of the house she lives in as a legacy, as well as a vineyard.[26] Another is to be freed at Gemma's death and given the bed she sleeps in and four measures of grain from the next harvest. Permission to live in the cottages they inhabit until their deaths is granted to two other female servants; one of them, Oulita, also receives a chest and stool. Several pieces of furniture as well as some vines, two asses and an unknown number of cattle, are to be sold and the profits divided between the poor and the priests, or to be set aside for the salvation of this generous lady's soul. Only her clothing, jewellery and bed linen is missing in this long list of bequests.[27] One of the nephews, Genesios, later decided to enter the monastery of St. Batholomew, and drew up his own will in which several of Gemma's gifts feature. They are still identifiable 40 years after her own testament in a document of 1086, which further changes Genesios's dispositions.[28]

Clearly, both dowries and wills take on greater importance when greater quantities and values of goods are involved, and are more likely to be found in the upper echelons of Byzantine society than among the poor. But even modest families tried to give their children the basic necessities for setting up home, and women frequently wished to dispose of their shawls, woollen belts, head scarfs and particular cooking utensils to female relatives. Among the same women who knew the use of written documents we also find an awareness of feminine rights in law and the administration of justice. It is, however, unusual to read of women taking their brothers to court, as Theodote did in 1093.[29] She declared: 'My father, that Gannadeos, held these lands and possessed them as master and owner, and gave them to me as my dowry [*proix*]', and brought expert witnesses to support her claim, the local bishop, Mesemerios, Maleinos, the *protospatharios* (a military officer), a certain Erminnon and the other leaders (*archontes*) of Stilo.[30] Once they had declared 'with one voice, speaking in truth and clearly', that Theodote's father had indeed bequeathed the lands at Pilikkeanos to her, the brothers' claim to them was lost. The court ordered these to be returned to Theodote and her sister, declaring that the brothers had usurped them illegally. This female initiative may be compared with another South Italian document, in which Alfarana, widow of an imperial judge of Bari, Petrus, records his will.[31] She takes the step of having it read out publicly, eleven years after his death, in order to confirm her position as executor (*epitropissa*) with supreme authority over her two sons, two daughters, who are to be properly dowered like their elder sister, and all the family property. Presumably the young men were now chafing at her control and needed to be reminded of her legal rights over them until they reached maturity. Petrus had stipulated that his wife was to govern everything as he did.

These two cases present examples of women of one particular Byzantine province as independent property owners, defending their claims in the law courts of Stilo and Bari against any infraction by their male relatives. A more common occurrence is the appearance of a woman accompanied by her husband or another family member. As in all medieval societies, where the possession of land is a major source of wealth, family disputes over inheritance and the division of property were frequent. And although women legally had certain rights, they were rarely able to exercise them effectively. The most frequent means of avoiding quarrels while guaranteeing female control of property was for the immediate kin to give their agreement as witnesses to any alterations in family land holding. An early example is provided by the very first document in the huge archive of the Athonite monastery at Lavra, dated 14 March 897.[32] In this, the Tzagastes family led by the widow Georgia, sells four separate plots of land to Euthymios, abbot of the St. Andrew monastery at Peristerai. One of these plots at Pisson, east of Thessalonike, has a house, well, vineyard and press attached; another has a mill. Georgia's seven children concur in this sale and in the enfranchisement of a personal slave, George, who receives a legacy. Of the six sons, two are monks, and Maria, the only daughter is a nun. Two other sons add to this act their bequest to Euthymios of an enclosed vineyard with its own entrance, which they inherited from their father. This document illustrates one of the central roles for women in Byzantine society: the legitimate transference of property. As in other regions of the medieval world, east and west, women played a major part in building up and disposing of family fortunes. To analyse how great a part, one must distinguish between acts such as the one cited, where women initiate legal activity (either alone, or in the company of their children), and those in which a woman is associated with her husband or some adult male relative. The latter clearly reflect a male initiative, to which the woman's agreement is necessary.[33]

As an example of the sort of research which must be done before one can gauge the precise degree of female independence in these matters, a brief survey of one collection of private legal documents is summarised.[34] Of the 57 documents all dating from the eleventh century, 14 concern women as agents (25 per cent), but only six are initiated by women (10 per cent). These six, reflecting the independent legal activity of women, comprise the following: one court action brought by a woman against her brothers (this is the case of Theodote described above);[35] one sale of land to a monastery by a widow;[36] one gift of land to a monastery made by a single woman, Yakintha, on condition that she be buried close to the church;[37] and three further gifts made by two widows and another single woman, also a nun.[38] One of the widows, a nun called Helen, donates to the monastery of the Holy Trinity, in the castle of Salerno, her family's monastic foundation complete with all its possessions, land, vines and livestock. Her daughter, Meleto, and son Eustathios, together with his wife, give their consent to this rich gift; the document is also witnessed by two of Helen's male relatives, Euthymios Agkenarisis (from her side of the family) and Nikolaos Maravilias (from her husband's side).[39] A more modest donation is made by the widow, Domna, who bequeaths the land she inherited from her parents to a different monastic church, for the redemption of her sins.[40] Again two male relatives are present to agree to this act, but the fact that none of them are identified by family names suggests that they may all come from a less prestigious stratum of society than the nun Helen.

From this very limited examination, it is evident that a significant number of women chose to present their property to the church at the expense of their families. The nature of the documentation, deriving from monastic archives in the main, clearly reinforces this impression, but it also reveals family agreement to such alienations and support for a particular motivation. Lea and her nephew, Nikolaos Portaritès, stipulate that their gift of lands is made on account of the sins of their parents and their own sins and for the salvation of their souls.[41] In documents of 1012 and 1016 Glykeria gave all her property on the island of Skyros to her spiritual father, Eustratios, who was a monk and later abbot of the monastery of Lavra.[42] The support and assistance she had received from Eustratios, especially in the trying circumstances since her husband's death which had brought her to loggerheads with her local bishop, made him a worthy recipient in her view, but she also expected to derive considerable spiritual profit from this close association. Similarly, a childless couple who donated lands to Lavra identified themselves as children of the monastery; thus they transformed their own sterility by becoming the offspring of a distinguished religious institution.[43] This assumption, certainly not restricted to women, that charitable bequests to the church furthered the spiritual progress of the donor, was widespread in Byzantine society. But it perhaps had a special appeal for those whose capacity to order and control their own lives was in reality quite limited. It seems to have been spread evenly throughout society, though our evidence naturally comes largely from the wealthier sectors who had gifts worth recording to make. There can be no doubt that propertied women could alienate their inheritance and that this is a productive field for future work relating to their economic and social roles.

The final avenue of approach to be pursued is that of the influence of Christianity on Byzantine women, for it is in the religious sphere that their subjective feelings can be most closely identified. In their Christian commitment one can get an impression of female force, and in the way this was handled by society one senses a male appreciation of something with potentially dangerous proportions. Although it is frequently assumed that early Christian monasticism was an exclusively male activity, women also shared in the movement to withdraw from the world and lead a celibate life. Like those young men who fled from arranged marriages or announced their intention of abstaining from all physical contact on their wedding night, some women saw their commitment to the faith as a superior alternative to marriage. Fewer may have been able to insist upon this negation of a regular feminine role but some succeeded and are commemorated in apocryphal and hagiographical accounts and moral tales such as those collected by John Moschos.[44] The element of transvestism which pervades this literature often distracts attention from one basic and very obvious fact: that apparel, far more than physique, identified a person. The monastic disguises adopted by women who were able to pass as eunuchs permitted them to simulate a holiness reserved by male ecclesiastical authorities to men only. To the church fathers the very idea of a holy woman was a contradiction in terms, which women could only get round by pretending to be men. Yet the existence of female martyrs gave women a model to follow. Later, the church appears to have recognised the potential of female religiosity by creating ways of channelling it into specifically feminine types of expression. It supported the establishment of convents, the devotion of young girls and widows to celibacy against the social pressures of marriage, and the practice of the spiritual marriage, whereby a couple might decide to deny their marital rights and live in a non-physical union. These developments gave women new possibilities for expressing female sanctity within society and even within marriage, possibilities which were quickly exploited.

The impact of Christian celibacy represents one of the most potent forces at work in Byzantine society. It escaped the church's attempt to control and direct it, producing a number of spiritual practices occasionally condemned by ecclesiastical authorities. The most excessive self-denial of certain column saints lay uncomfortably close to a Manichaean renunciation of the body and all material things, which in the eyes of the church led only to heresy. Similarly, as women increasingly sought an autonomous sphere in Byzantine spiritual life by founding their own monasteries, the male hierarchy of the secular church expressed concern. Since by the sixth century the sole institutional role open to women was the insignificant order of deaconesses, female houses represented a means of exercising Christian devotion in a serious and demanding fashion. Joining a religious community guaranteed a woman a greater degree of self-control than in any other spiritual practice. Therefore it is hardly surprising to find the church trying to insist that the local bishop shall have the right to enter a local convent, or that the priest who must be employed to administer the sacraments shall be appointed by some ecclesiastical authority.

Women with sufficient means to establish their own monasteries were usually able to resist such pressures and devised methods of maintaining their control as founders. St. Anthousa, for example, committed herself to the celibate life while she was still very young, making a vow to her spiritual father who directed her religious development and instructed her as to the site of her foundation dedicated to the Virgin. It was built on an island in Lake Daphnousios some time in the mid-eighth century, that is, during a period of iconoclast persecution. Later Anthousa constructed a monastery for men on the shores of the lake; this she also ruled; and in both the tradition of venerating icons was maintained.[45] In the case of these and many other monasteries, whose history can not be traced for more than a few generations, we seem to be dealing with a spontaneous expression of celibate practice. Unlike the imperial foundations of Constantinople and the major houses of Mouth Athos, no foundation charters (*typika*) survive and so there is no evidence for their scale, organisation or administration. They were probably not equipped to accommodate large numbers or to deal with the medical needs of local people. But they created a focus for female ascetic life and attracted women to them for a whole variety of motives.

For St. Martha, for instance, the convent of the Virgin in Monemvasia was a haven to which she withdrew, probably quite early in her life. She suffered from a constant haemorrhage which must have seriously reduced her chances of leading a normal existence. From the tenth-century description we learn that the nuns chanted the services themselves and had servants who assisted in the work of running the house.

One day Martha was miraculously cured by St. John the Evangelist, who appeared to her in a vision, disguised as the priest who officiated for the nuns. He, however, was away in Thessalonike at that time, which was how Martha recognised the miraculous quality of her vision.[46]

For St. Theodora of Thessalonike the existence of a local convent confirmed her determination not to remarry after the death of her husband. Instead, she sold her property, freed all her slaves except three who accompanied her into the house, gave away two-thirds of her fortune and presented the rest to the community she joined.[47] While resisting parental pressure to marry must have been especially difficult for young heiresses, there is considerable evidence for their absolute refusal to give up the relative independence gained on becoming widows. Not all entered monasteries; some were able to devote themselves to charitable works, caring for the poor, building hospices and endowing churches.[48] In this resistance to remarriage the church gave its support to widows, by insisting on the holy sacrament of marriage as a commitment for life. As civil wedding services were no longer recognised as valid by the ninth century, and ecclesiastical ceremonies had probably accompanied most marriages for centuries before that time, ecclesiastical authority sustained a slightly higher status for the pious widow and widower. This additional weight of canon law stressed the impropriety of second and third marriages, and indirectly assisted the independence of women bereaved and those who managed to remain single by choice.

While some couples adopted a spiritual marriage after the birth of their children and practised a self-imposed chastity (see Harvey, this volume), others decided to part and enter separate monastic institutions. The parents of St. Theodore Studites illustrate this procedure.[49] It was probably reserved to the wealthy few who could provide for their children as well as taking part of the family inheritance with them into their respective houses. While it is not clear whether women of no means but strong convictions could gain entry, the established monasteries of the capital probably restricted their intake and expected novices to add to the foundation's resources. In contrast, the less organised rural houses whose history is very fragmentary and discontinuous, may have been prepared to accept those women who proved themselves truly committed to the celibate life. In the case of married women who fled to monasteries to escape from their families, an eleventh-century ruling insists that they must serve a trial period of six months before taking their vows, and that their husbands must be allowed to see them before the final step is taken. If they then remain obdurate, they must be granted their dowries, which will serve as a material basis for their new celibate lives.[50] This seems to confirm the suggestion that women of property would be expected by the houses they entered to bring some wealth as a condition of their acceptance.

In listing the different motivations which might lead women into monasteries, it is important not to overlook the involuntary path imposed on women convicted of adultery, prostitution and other crimes. From the ninth century onwards the traditional practice was established as law; these women should be sent to convents, where the shining example of Christian women who were there by choice might influence them for the better. They were probably forced to do the most servile tasks in the community, under strict supervision and with no prospect of release.[51] The only improvement in their situation would presumably arise from a heartfelt conversion to the celibate life, but this is not recorded. Rather, a contrary determination to break out of what were in effect female prisons seems to have been the normal reaction of women so confined.

The ideal model of holiness, virginity and purity and the practical life of celibate nuns are both related to particular Byzantine cults: that of the Virgin (which gradually developed from the time of the Council of Ephesos, 431) and that of icons.[52] Both also gained an established place in Byzantine religious life in the early seventh century and neither was restricted to women alone. While the veneration of icons may have had a special importance for women,[53] the relationship between female religiosity and the cult of the Virgin is a problematic one. There is hardly a shred of evidence in the Gospels for the powerful authority of the Virgin; this cult was built up by theologians and (one suspects) by popular devotion to create a novel type of feminine sanctity.[54] This elevated model of total purity and virginity, holiness in a maternal guise, presented women with a new example of Christian womanhood. By imitating the Virgin, women could justify their participation in the life of the church. But the new cult also emphasised the fate of those who failed to live according to its precepts; it strengthened the ancient misogynist condemnation of woman as Eve, and forced the great majority to accept this dichotomy. Thus while a few women might succeed in breaking away from the routine life of marriage and child-bearing by professing a virtuous and respected commitment to celibacy, many more would be even more downtrodden as the unalterable embodiment of disobedience, lust and all the sins which Eve brought into the world.

While there can be no doubt as to the rapid spread of this cult and its central position in the Byzantine church by the early seventh century, the mechanism by which it grew is unclear. Three hypotheses may be considered: first, that it represented a purely theological development related to the protracted debates over the nature, or natures of Christ. Second, that it was promoted by the exclusively male hierarchy of the church to create an acceptable model of female purity. In this case it would have been devised to fill an ecclesiastical need. Third, that it was championed by women whose institutional roles within the church were minimal and who needed an outlet and an identification for their Christian convictions. The persistent devotion of empresses from Pulcheria and Eudokia to Sophia in the late sixth century to the cult of the Virgin must have been important. In this final case, the development would represent a pressure from outside the organised structure of the church, which was incorporated as a means of channelling female piety. Probably all three contribute to the explanation of this complex process, which resulted in the institutionalisation of female benefactors (otherwise excluded), while providing women with a viable means of expressing their faith and churchmen with a respectable image of feminine religiosity. However it was constructed, the cult of the Virgin became an abiding feature of the Byzantine church and one which gained special adherence among women at all levels of Byzantine society.

In pursuing this attempt to identify the influence of Byzantine women, it is necessary to emphasise the military nature of their environment, which clearly imposed wide restrictions on their activity. But unlike their counterparts in Islamic or Western Europe states, specific factors in the Byzantine context permitted certain forms of female self-expression. Inherited urban traditions, access to written documents and law courts, patterns of segregation and the influence of eunuchs, all set Byzantine women apart from their contemporaries. Even the poor who had no education and were forced to work could still participate in fairs such as that held on S. John's feastday in Ephesos or that of S. Demetrios in Thessalonike. Their situation changed in the early Byzantine period, reflecting the economic shrinkage of the seventh and eighth centuries and the subsequent expansion and prosperity of the late ninth and tenth, as well as the development of new forms of Christian institutions.[55] Politically women might have little influence, depending on their male relatives, but in cultural terms they always played an important role, not only domestically but also in the life of the church.

With these general impressions in mind, it is interesting to return to the question of those exceptional women, such as Theodora, who wielded considerable power. Nearly all of them gained such authority by marrying emperors and by becoming the mothers of imperial princes. That is, they were outsiders, not born 'in the purple' (a reference to the purple chamber where empresses gave birth and thus a description of imperial credentials). In contrast, many of the princesses of purple birth were sacrificed to dynastic alliances which often took them away from Byzantium and the imperial court. Neither the Empress Theodora in the sixth century, nor Irene in the eighth or the second Theodora in the ninth, were prepared during their childhood for the role of *Augusta*, they were all catapulted into it by marriage. Yet the position of imperial consort and widow commanded such respect that empresses were very rarely rejected (though Sophia, widow of Justin II, was thwarted by his successor, Tiberius II, 578-82). They may have been maligned, misinterpreted and frequently condemned, but seldom deposed from positions of great influence and patronage. They regularly exercised decisive choice in the matter of the succession, by selecting another consort to share the throne in the Roman fashion of fifth-century empresses, Pulcheria and Ariadne (a similar procedure was used, incidentally, by Queen Theodolinda of the Lombards in 590), or by acting as guardian for a young son. During the early Byzantine period these undefined but generally accepted rights were tested by several ambitious and intelligent women.

Irene and the ninth-century Theodora, for instance, were both widowed in circumstances that permitted them to reign as regents for minors. Both put their portraits on the coinage, presided over important ecclesiastical councils and retained a good deal of independence by not remarrying. Irene went so far as to dispense with her son, the senior emperor, by having him blinded — a fact which disqualified him from ruling. She then reigned alone for five years with the assistance of two eunuchs, whom she played off against each other. As sole emperor she signed at least one official act as *Basileus*, though using the feminine *Basilissa* (or *Augusta*) on her coins.[56] Theodora was not quite so ambitious. She ruled for her young son for 14 years before being removed by her own brother. During that time, however, she had controlled the court with the aid of a trusted adviser, and she even emerged from eight years of confinement in a nunnery to resume the title of *Augusta*. Such positions in the imperial hierarchy were important because they involved particular ceremonies, public roles at the major events in the political and ecclesiastical life of the empire. They also commanded funds, costumes and servants all linked to the titles. Both Irene and

Theodora (and other empresses) manifested an adroit understanding of these factors.

Even if these exceptional women had no direct influence on others, their presence and the fact that they were accepted in Byzantine society was influential. That some women could be accorded supreme powers, even of life and death, that they were commemorated as rulers on coins, acclaimed in public ceremonies and held responsible for official documents and imperial policy, made them identifiable symbols of female leadership. They were probably more visible than their counterparts in the medieval west and the Muslim east, especially to the population of Constantinople. Throughout their society the histories of these women must have reinforced the powers accorded to widows, notably in the guardianship of children, and their relatively privileged status. Young girls from wealthy families may well have dreamt of exercising the power of an empress, perhaps by being selected in a beauty contest like the second Theodora. Despite the unlikelihood of making such a transition, the fact that imperial brides were not normally chosen from the established families at court (during this period) meant that it was a real possibility, if a remote one. Curiously, although Byzantine women were more effectively excluded from public life, shrouded in Christian roles and reduced to a very private existence during the transition from late antiquity to medieval Byzantium, imperial widows extended their powers after *c*. 600 AD.

The empresses, however, occupied an exceptional position. The position of Byzantine women overall was manifestly subordinate. It was mainly in monastic institutions, often founded on inherited wealth and thus not very numerous, that women could exercise authority directly over men. Yet they had a discernible influence upon the religious ideology and practice of their society, and for those with means it was possible to fight for their rights, particularly as widows. A combination of factors, specific to the early medieval Byzantine empire, allowed women to break through the silence of the historical records to a remarkable degree, one not matched by their sisters in the Muslim, Jewish and Western Christian worlds of the time. Among these factors the acceptance of female heads of state in a world overwhelmingly dominated by male authority deserves emphasis. For the fact that such exceptions were admitted perhaps demonstrates the wider extent of feminine influence — institutionalised and expressed in the ways described above — which was in turn reinforced by the empresses themselves.

Notes

1. Procopius, *Secret History* IX.1-34, 47-54; X.1-18: the law, *CJ* V.4.23.
2. Diehl, 1906-8, is a distinguished example of such an approach and includes a study of female piety (the mother of S. Theodore of Stoudion) as well as portraits of empresses and imperial princesses. More recently, the excellent survey by Grosdidier de Matons (1974) tries to avoid this context but is forced to utilise the same limited source material in general.
3. See for example Beaucamp, 1977.
4. The study by Laiou (1981) wisely concentrates on the later period, eleventh to fourteenth centuries, when documentary evidence becomes more abundant. The image is nonetheless dominated by high-born women of the capital. An instructive contrast is provided by the same author's reconstruction of a peasant woman's life (Laiou, 1977, pp. 294-8).
5. See Herrin (1983).
6. For a seventh-century example, see the *Miracles of S. Artemios* (Papadopoulos-Kerameus, 1909), no. 11 (11-12); cf. Mango (1980), p. 79.
7. Kurtz (1899), p. 3. I cite this aristocratic text to draw attention to what is implied rather than stated, namely the existence of female public baths and non-aristocratic bath attendants at this date, but cf. Mango (1981), pp. 339-41.
8. Cf. *Peira* XXX.11, 79; XLIX.36 (where a bride's virginity has to be attested in court by women). On the frequent mention of women as midwives, Laiou (1981), p. 245, n. 62.
9. Oikonomides (1972), pp. 345-6.
10. Deubner (1907), pp. 128-32; French translation, Festugière (1971), pp. 120-5.
11. E.g. the slave of Kamelavkas, a high-ranking official (*protospatharios*), whom he married and established in her own home; *Peira* IV.25.
12. On the position of eunuchs at court in the late Roman empire see Hopkins (1978), pp. 172-96.
13. *Miracles of S. Artemios* (Papadopoulos-Kerameus, 1909), no. 36, 57-9; the asset is called 'oiktra pragmatidia'.
14. Mansi, XI, col. 973, canon 65.
15. John Moschus, *Pratum Spirituale* 76, *PG* 87, col. 2929. Women feature in many of these stories, often as resilient and faithful wives and Christians; some indeed are given an almost heroic role, cf. chs. 170, 179 and 189. But there is also a sprinkling of typically misogynist comments, including one of the Sayings attributed to the Desert Fathers, ch. 217, col. 3108: 'Salt is from the sea and if it gets close to water it dissolves and disappears. Similarly, the monk is from woman, and if he goes near a woman, he dissolves and ceases to be a monk . . .'.
16. See for instance *Peira* XIV.16 and a rather later document of adoption from southern Italy, Trinchera (1865), no. 177. This collection of extremely important Greek documents from S. Italian and Sicilian archives is gradually being replaced by modern critical editions by A. Guillou. While accepting the latter's harsh judgement on the appalling quality of Trinchera's edition (see *Byzantion* 24 (1954), 6) I have been obliged to use it. Similar arrangements for adoption exist in Jewish medieval legal practice.
17. Laiou (1981), p. 259.
18. *Peira*, XVII.19 (an aristocratic marriage between families of patrician rank, in which a lot of property might have been involved). In a related case, XLIX.26, a mother breaks off her son's betrothal because in the three years since the contracts were exchanged the bride's family has become too poor to fulfil the terms. The children were aged nine and seven at the time of the engagement. For

penalties imposed on those who married girls under 12 years old, see XLIX.22 and 34; Dölger (1924-65), III, nos. 1048, 1116 and 1167.

19. Trinchera (1865), no. 63 (1097); unfortunately the document is not fully preserved. On marriage in Byzantine Italy, Guillou (1977). A detailed and complete contract from the eastern part of the empire is edited by Reinach (1924). Although drawn up in Greek and corresponding quite closely to Byzantine customs, the groom is Jewish and presents a larger amount of jewellery, much of it gold, than is commonly mentioned in the more modest documents from southern Italy. It resembles tenth-century contracts from the Jewish community in Damascus published by S. Assaf, *Tarbiz* 9 (1937), pp. 11-34 (in Hebrew), and partly translated in Ashtor (1961), especially pp. 66-8. For a helpful analysis of the differences between Christian and Jewish customs, see Goitein (1967-78), III, pp. 47-159.

20. Robinson (1929), no. 66 (1108) records the donation made by Trotta of the land at Myromana, which she held as her *theoretron*, to Abbot Neilos of Carbone. Cf. the case of a widow taking possession of her *theoretron*, in order to sell it, Guillou (1963), no. 7. The widow, Theodote, obtains the consent of her daughter, Kale, and her brother-in-law, Theodore, in this alienation of 175 feet of vineyard, which constituted her dowry. Another document reveals a wife assigning to her husband 'all my dowry' (*theoretron*) in her will, see Trinchera (1865), no. 192.

21. Trinchera (1865), no. 170, of 1166. Here the trousseau is listed more fully and includes a quantity of bed-linen, covers, sheets, pillows, etc.; dresses and pieces of linen; cooking equipment; three doves, one tame and two wild; and her mother's share in the house, lands, vines and trees which she owns, excepting one holding at Tympa with a mill.

22. *Peira* XIV.22.

23. Nitti di Vito (1900), no. 46.

24. One of these witnesses is Nikolaos, *ekprosopo Bareos*, perhaps the 'Nicola, hecprosopo Bari' known from an act of 1034, see Nitti di Vito (1900), no. 23. The Byzantine title of *ek prosopou* originally designated any representative standing in for another official, but gradually took on a specific meaning. In eleventh-century Southern Italy it probably indicates the chief civilian official either of a province, or as in this case, of a city; see von Falkenhausen (1967), pp. 107-8.

25. Robinson (1929), no. 53 (1044).

26. Cf. the will of Clementza, wife of the judge, Laurentios Kaballarios of 1226, Trinchera (1865), no. 274.

27. The dowering of freed slaves was a prerequisite for their chance of marrying, see *Peira* XLIX.6; Trinchera (1865), no. 24 (1033). Similar provisions occur in the Jewish Geniza documents of this period, see Goitein (1967-78), I, p. 145.

28. Robinson (1929), nos. 59 (1076) and 61 (1086).

29. Trinchera (1865), no. 56.

30. Some of these witnesses belong to important local families, see von Falkenhausen (1967), p. 141. Theodote herself comes from an established background; the Gannadeos family is represented by Gregorios, recorded as *protospatharios* and judge in Mesiano, Calabria, in a case of 1095, witnessed by men from Stilo, see Guillou (1963), no. 2; two further male relatives are active near Messina in Sicily in 1135 and 1189 (see no. 5 and appendix II).

31. Nitti di Vito (1900), no. 27 (1039), in Latin.

32. Lemerle, Guillou, Svoronos, Papachryssanthou (1970), I, no. 1. This document was probably drawn up at the moment when Georgia decided to follow her children into the monastic world, and therefore comes very close to being a

will. As the imperial monastery of S. Andrew was for men only, it was possibly to a convent attached to it or to the church of S. Nikolaos (the only other beneficiary named) that she would have retired.

33. This problem is recognised and tackled by Laiou (1981), pp. 234, 239 (tables I and II), but with insufficient clarity. Principal donors appearing in a significant role must be separated from interested parties and cases involving women, as in Wemple (1981), p. 110, table 3.

34. Again the Trinchera collection is employed, however inadequately edited (see n. 16 above).

35. Trinchera (1865), no. 56 (1093).

36. No. 33 (1042).

37. No. 51 (1089).

38. No. 29 (1034), see below on Lea and her nephew.

39. No. 49 (1086).

40. No. 46 (1063).

41. No. 29 (1034).

42. Lemerle, Guillou, Svoronos, Papachrysanthou (1970), I, nos. 16 and 20 (1012 and 1016). Taken with no. 1 (see n. 29), these three acts are the only ones from the 48 covering the period 897-1198 initiated by women (not counting the imperial *chrysoboulla*, which feature so prominently).

43. No. 18 (1014), cf. no. 40.

44. The experience of these women is illuminated by Patlagean (1976) (repr. Patlagean, 1981). Cf. Anson (1974) and Davies, this volume. A parallel case in Gaul: Gregory of Tours, *In gloria confessorum*, 16.

45. For the *Life of Anthousa,* see now C. Mango, 'St Anthusa of Mantineon and the family of Constantine V', *Analecta Bollandiana*, 100, (1982), pp. 401-9.

46. *Acta Sanctorum*, May V (1866), pp. 425-7.

47. Kurtz (1902), p. 12.

48. For example, S. Anna of Levkos and the widow of S. Philaretos, see *Acta Sanctorum*, July V (1969), pp. 486-7; Fourmy and Leroy (1934), 165-67.

49. See the funeral oration for his mother by S. Theodore, *PG* 99, cols. 884-901.

50. *Peira* XXV.4.

51. John of Ephesus cites a particularly strict nunnery at Chalcedon that was used as a prison for three noble ladies in the late sixth century. When they refused to accept the imperial definition of orthodoxy, they were shorn of their hair, dressed in black robes and forced to do the most menial chores, even cleaning the latrines; *Ecclesiastical History* II.12.

52. This is not to suggest that the cult of the Virgin was confined to Byzantium; on the contrary, its early appearance in Celtic Ireland (Davies, this volume) indicates what a powerful appeal it had in regions remote from the eastern Mediterranean.

53. Cf. p. 169 above and n. 5.

54. Averil Cameron (1978); Wenger (1955). The dedication of the Emperor Justin II and his wife Sophia to the cult of the Virgin represents a powerful stimulus to an already popular pressure.

55. The improvement in source material which becomes apparent in the late eleventh and twelfth centuries corresponds to a fundamental change in Byzantium, recognised by most historians. The 'quickening of urban life' documented by Laiou (1981), pp. 241-8, is matched by an influx of Western contacts that internationalise the world of Constantinople and other major cities exposed to Crusader and Norman influence.

56. On the powers of empresses see Maslev (1966); Bensammar (1976),

especially p. 250. For their use of the coinage, Grierson (1973), pp. 336-7, 347-8, 452-4.
* I should like to thank Professors Raymond Crew and Geoff Eley for their valuable comments on an earlier draft of this paper.

Further Reading

Beaucamp, J. (1977), 'La situation juridique de la femme à Byzance', *Cahiers de civilisation médiévale* 20, 145-76
Buckler, G. (1936), 'Women in Byzantine law about 1100 AD', *Byzantion 11*, 391-416
Diehl, C. (1906-8), *Figures byzantines*, 2 vols., Paris
Grosdidier de Matons, J. (1974), 'La femme dans l'empire byzantin', in Grimal, P. (ed.), *Histoire mondiale de la femme*, Paris, III, 11-43
Herrin, J. (1983) 'Women and the faith in icons in early Christianity', in Samuel, R., Stedman Jones, G. (eds), *Culture, Ideology and Politics*, London, 56-83
Laiou, Angeliki E. (1981), 'The Role of Women in Byzantine Society', *XVI Internationaler Byzantinistenkongress, Akten I/1*, 1981, Vienna (= *JOB* 31.1, 233-60)

PART SIX: THE ECONOMIC ROLE OF WOMEN

Male tactics for the deployment of women within the economic structure of their societies, and the roles open to rich women within that structure

12 BRIDEWEALTH AND DOWRY IN NUZI[1]

Katarzyna Grosz, Copenhagen

Introduction

In 1896 T.G. Pinches published a cuneiform tablet of a hitherto
unknown type differing from all other cuneiform documents by its
peculiar onomastic and dialect (CT II, pl. 21). Soon, tablets of the same
type, acquired at the antiquities market in Kirkuk, began to appear in
European museums. The 'Kirkuk tablets' aroused considerable scholarly
interest but it was soon evident that a more regular acquisition of tablets
through archaeological excavations was out of the question because of
the modern occupation of the site.

In 1925 E. Chiera, then the annual professor of the American
Schools of Oriental Research, learned that the 'Kirkuk tablets' did not
come from this city after all, but from a site some 16 km south-west of
it. The tablets were found in a small mound situated at the foot of a
large *tell* called Yorghan Tepe. Chiera at once started the excavations
which were carried on through subsequent seasons until 1932 (Starr,
1937 and 1939). In their course over four thousand tablets were
unearthed.[2]

The history of Yorghan Tepe falls into two main periods: the
Akkadian and the Hurrian. In the Akkadian period the majority of the
population bore Semitic names, the language written was Old Akkadian
(*c.* 2400-2250 BC) and later Old Assyrian (*c.* 2000-1850 BC) and the
city's name was Gasur (Meek, 1935, vii-xvi). The overwhelming majority
of tablets, however, come from the period 1500-1350 BC, when the
city's name was Nuzi and its population Hurrian. Nuzi was part of the
kingdom of Arraphe (modern Kirkuk) which in its turn was part of the
kingdom of Mitanni. Thus some time between 1800 and 1500 the
Hurrians not only infiltrated the area but also became the largest ethnic
group in the city itself and in the countryside.

The Hurrians are attested in cuneiform sources as early as the third
millennium BC. In Mesopotamia they appeared to be indigenous to the
Habur area whence they spread southwards. They are well attested in
Mari on the middle Euphrates in the Old Babylonian period (*c.* 1800
BC), but their main concentration lay north-west of the Tigris where
they formed the kingdom of Mitanni, one of the chief political factors

193

in the Near East in the period 1550-1300 BC. The capital of this state has not yet been found and all information about Mitanni is derived from Egyptian, Hittite and Babylonian sources. The Assyrian sources from this period are extremely scanty and consist first of all of royal building inscriptions which do not deal with political matters. Assur was at this time a vassal of Mitanni; the extent of the Assyrian principality is unknown, but it is generally believed that the end of the Hurrian occupation of Nuzi, marked by a great fire and general destruction, is to be linked with the Assyrian struggle for independence from Mitannian domination. The city never recovered after the great disaster which happened around 1350 BC. It seems that the Hurrians were subsequently assimilated by the Assyrians, the whole area becoming part of the Assyrian homeland.

In this situation it is interesting to observe that the Semitic influence in Nuzi is of Babylonian rather than Assyrian origin. Personal names are composed with Babylonian rather than Assyrian theophorics, the scribal families were of Babylonian origin and, most important of all, the written language was a dialect of Babylonian. The presence of Assyrians was limited to refugees seeking employment with private citizens of Nuzi and to small groups of palace personnel.

The textual material from Nuzi is characterised by certain peculiar legal documents, the most famous of which is the sale adoption, in reality a camouflaged sale of land. In this fictitious adoption the seller adopts the buyer and bequeathes to him a piece of property as his inheritance share. The buyer in return gives the seller a 'present' which corresponds to the value of the immovable. The buyer is explicitly released from ordinary filial obligations, such as obedience and performing burial rites after the parent's death, and also from carrying out the *ilku* obligation.[3] In the whole corpus of Nuzi texts there are hundreds of sale adoptions but not a single outright sale of land. Once Assyriologists became convinced that the sale adoptions must have covered up the sale of land (Steele, 1943), several scholars attempted to explain the apparent inalienability of immovables in Nuzi.

Two theories must be mentioned here: according to the first, Nuzi represents a feudal system in decay (Koschaker, 1928). Thus all land belonged originally to the crown and was parcelled out in return for the *ilku* obligation. In our period the system was dissolving, possession of land had become hereditary, and the owner could dispose of his plot by the device of adopting the seller. However, he still had to perform the *ilku* obligation.

The second theory sees in Nuzi a decaying system of extended family communes (Jankovska, 1969a; 1969b). Originally, all land belonged to the family communes and could not be acquired by strangers. With time the rigid system of family ownership was relaxed, the family members could own plots of communal land privately, and a buyer could acquire immovables if he was adopted fictitiously into the family. That the adoption *was* purely fictitious is clear because it did not entail performing burial rites or carrying out the *ilku* obligation which, according to this theory, was an obligation towards the family commune.

Since the sale adoption is a phenomenon unique in Mesopotamia and characteristic of Nuzi alone, it has often been explained as an expression of the ethno-cultural differences between the Hurrians and the Semites. I feel, therefore, that it is imperative to stress that: 1) a 'feudal system' (in Assyriology this means a system of land tenure held against an obligation, often, but not necessarily, of a miliary character towards the crown) of a kind existed in Babylonia and Assyria as well; 2) the most recent studies indicate that when land was privately held, it was often sold between family members only, and it seems that in some periods at least it was impossible to sell land outside the family; 3) it is not possible to point out any specific item of the material culture of Nuzi as specifically Hurrian. It is therefore my opinion that extreme caution should be exercised whenever an attempt is made to explain some apparently peculiar social or legal practice by ethnic factors alone.

The textual material from Nuzi falls into two groups: palace and private archives. The palace archives consist of administrative documents such as ration lists, lists of personnel, census lists, etc. (Mayer, 1978). They were found in the palace area of the *tell* and their number is relatively small for a 150-year-long occupation. Also, some typical text groups, of which letters are the most conspicuous, are missing. It is therefore probable that the palace was evacuated before its destruction and the important part of the archive was transferred to some safer place.

The overwhelming part of the private archives from Nuzi do not come from the main *tell* but from a small mound at some distance from it. The mound contained ruins of two extensive house complexes in which two large archives were found. One of them belonged to a prince and contained, apart from private juridical documents, administrative tablets of the same type as those found in the palace. It is, therefore, probable that the prince played an important role in the administration of the city.

The second private archive, with over a thousand documents, is

among the largest in Mesopotamia (Maidman, 1976). It consists of juridical and administrative documents, while tablets dealing with private
family matters, such as wills, marriage and divorce tablets, records of
divisions of property, etc., are conspicuously absent. The economic
activities of five generations of this extremely successful family of
ascending large estate owners are well documented in the records. Their
large and elaborate house, just next to the prince's mansion, bears
witness to the importance of this family.

The private documents from the main *tell* deal chiefly with family
matters — wills, divorces, marriage contracts, etc. — are amply represented here. Administrative documents of the same type as those from
the palace were also found. The inhabitants of the private quarters of
the *tell* were therefore certainly closely linked with the palace administration. Probably they did not possess land, or if they did, it was not
the chief source of their income. Some of the private quarters of the
city inhabitants must have belonged to the scribes who worked for the
palace and for the private population of Nuzi.

Although the excavations of Yorghan Tepe were terminated in the
thirties, the last major publication of cuneiform texts from this city
appeared only in 1962 (Lacheman, 1962), and there are still some 700-
900 unpublished tablets. The editors of the Nuzi tablets have followed
the usual custom of grouping documents according to the legal category they represented rather than to their archival context. This practice has resulted in a series of excellent studies of the legal customs of
Nuzi, but it also has a drawback — the homogeneous archives, sometimes illuminating a continuous period of up to five generations, were
split up and a Nuzi scholar today is faced with the tedious and at times
impossible task of trying to reconstruct the original archival context for
each text.

With the loss of context for each document it became more difficult
to study the social system of Nuzi and some important aspects of it are
still either disputed or not researched at all. The family structure and
the kinship system, the system of land ownership, the importance of
irrigation, the relationship between the palace and the population —
these are but a few examples of the neglected yet extremely important
aspects of Nuzi studies.

The field of women's studies is among the most neglected. Scientific
interest in Mesopotamian family law made it necessary to investigate
some social practices in which women were directly involved — marriage
and divorce, the rules of inheritance, etc. However, there exists no
study directly concerned with the position of women — their role

within the family, their contribution to the economy of the family or that of the palace. And yet the sources for an investigation of these topics are adequate. Over 300 private documents deal with the position of women within the family and more or less the same amount of tablets concern their role in the palace. My own study of the institutions of bridewealth and dowry was based on the private archives alone — I hope to investigate the palace archive in the near future.

Bridewealth and Dowry: Theoretical Considerations

The textual corpus for the study of the institutions of bridewealth and dowry consists of over 100 private legal and economic documents, such as marriage contracts, receipts of bridewealth or dowry, testaments, and a number of economic documents pertaining to the economic activities of women.[4]

The bridewealth and the dowry become manifest at the moment of marriage; the bridewealth travels from the bride-taking to the bride-giving family, while the dowry moves the opposite way. The Mesopotamian law codes often mention the dowry and the bridewealth within the same law paragraph,[5] as though they always occurred within the same marriage. This, however, does not seem to have been the case in Nuzi. The marriage contracts mention either the bridewealth or the dowry, and they both occur together only in the case of indirect dowry, i.e. when a part of the bridewealth is turned over to the bride as her dowry. Historians of Mesopotamian law consider the dowry an expression of women's inheritance rights. It represented the inheritance share to which the bride was entitled from her paternal home. It is much more difficult to establish the function of the bridewealth and scholars differ considerably in their interpretations.

The commonest theory is that the bridewealth represents the price paid for the bride, the Mesopotamian marriage being thus a marriage by purchase (Koschaker, 1917, ch. 2). Another theory sees the bridewealth as a fossil from the proto-literate period. Only when a sum of money was paid for the bride was a union of two people considered to constitute a lawful marriage. Thus the bridewealth was the institution whereby simple cohabitation became wedlock. In time a written contract took over the function of bridewealth which thus became an anachronistic and purely symbolic gesture (van Praag, 1945).

The institutions of bridewealth and dowry have been subject to a close scrutiny by social anthropologists and there exists today a vast theoretical framework for further study of both these payments (Boserup, 1970; Goody and Tambiah, 1973; Goody, 1977; Gomaroff, 1980).

Bridewealth

Bridewealth is a transaction between two families — that of the groom and that of the bride. It is given by the bride-taking family to the bride-giving family, so that the latter can acquire wives for themselves (Goody and Tambiah, 1973, p. 5). One may say that the bridewealth is a compensation for the loss of a female worker and the money used to acquire another one. In some societies the payment is made in commodities which in themselves have no intrinsic value but are exclusively used for bridewealth transactions. People practising bridewealth in our day also explicitly stress the non-commercial purpose of the transaction. It seems, therefore, that the primary goal of a bridewealth transaction is to establish certain social links rather than economic gain.

The amount of bridewealth varies depending on the amount of prestige which the bride's family commands and on her own merits. The sum is paid in movables, often by instalments stretching over a period of years. In case of divorce the bridewealth may or may not be returned to the groom's family.

From my study of the Mesopotamian law codes I have gained the impression that in Mesopotamia the bridewealth was not returned if the reason for the divorce was the husband's dislike for his wife or his wish to marry a different woman. Such a divorce can be interpreted as a grave loss of prestige for the wife and her family; the bridewealth then constituted perhaps a compensation for the 'loss of face'. If childlessness was the reason for divorce the bridewealth was returned.

Dowry

Social anthropologists recognise the dowry as an expression of women's inheritance rights (Goody and Tambiah, 1973, p. 17). Sons are as a rule required to wait for their share until the death of their father, even if it means that they live under the paternal roof long after they have become adult, are married and have children. Daughters, on the other hand, receive their share of the patrimony at the moment of marriage and are thus 'paid off'. The transfer of dowry is a transaction between the bride and her father and it takes place within one family (even though the groom's family may have a say in the matter). The dowry remains a distinctive unit throughout the marriage. Thus a husband cannot sell his wife's dowry without her consent, but neither can she lightly dispose of it – it is ultimately destined for the children. If a childless marriage is dissolved the wife takes her dowry with her.

The contents and size of a daughter's inheritance share, or dowry, can differ considerably in different societies. Sometimes daughters and sons have equal inheritance rights, but often a daughter's share is smaller than a son's. Daughters may or may not have inheritance rights to land. Even if they do, the father may still prefer to equip his daughter with money and movables rather than with land, thus avoiding excessive division of immovables between too many heirs. After all, when the daughter moves in with her husband their main income will be derived from his share of patrimony. Her brother, on the other hand, will have to support his wife and children on his share of inheritance.

India is one of the countries in which both the bridewealth and the dowry exist simultaneously (Goody and Tambiah, 1973, p. 59ff). A marriage with dowry is considered the highest form of matrimony and it is reserved for the highest castes. Bridewealth is given among the poor; it is considered a child-sale by the higher castes and despised as such. In some cases a part of the bridewealth is turned over to the bride as her dowry – this practice of indirect dowry is perhaps an effort to disguise the fact that the bridewealth is being paid.

Bridewealth and Dowry in Nuzi

Bridewealth

The textual material concerning the bridewealth falls into three groups: adoptions of girls, marriage contracts, and receipts of various goods received as instalments on the bridewealth.[6]

The adoption contracts contain as a rule stipulations guaranteeing that the adoptant will marry off the adopted daughter. There exist four types of adoption of women and their function is still disputed; unfortunately, the limits of this paper do not permit any discussion of the tablets themselves or even the briefest presentation of the problems involved.[7] Suffice it to say that the majority of contracts contain clauses concerning the bridewealth, conforming with the data gathered from other types of documents.

A typical marriage contract is drawn up between the groom or his father, and the father of the bride, who is mentioned by name but does not take active part in the transaction.[8] Only when the bride is given away by her brother does the contract contain her declaration that she is marrying of her own free will. Such a declaration is never included in the contract where the bride is represented by her father, which indicates that whereas the father had absolute authority over his daughter, the brother's authority over his sister was limited.

A marriage contract usually forbids the groom to take another wife, unless the present one proves barren. However, if the barren wife was an heiress to her parents' whole property, or if she was a princess, the prestige attained by the marriage offset the disadvantage of childlessness. A wife of high status could also provide her husband with a slave girl for the purpose of bearing his children.

At the end of a marriage contract the amount of bridewealth is often stated, as are sometimes also the terms of payment. The document ends with a list of witnesses and their seals.

In the receipts of goods paid as instalments on the bridewealth the following items are listed: the commodity, its value in silver, name of the payer, and sometimes also the outstanding amount.

Out of a total of 20 documents dealing with the bridewealth the father or brother of the bride is the recipient in 19 cases. The full amount of the bridewealth is very seldom transferred at once; unfortunately, the terms of payment must have been agreed upon orally in the majority of cases because they are missing from the documents. The commodities transferred are livestock, textiles, copper, and sometimes silver.

The amount of bridewealth seems to have been fairly stable — 40 shekels of silver is the average. This uniformity is rather surprising because the size of the bridewealth should vary according to the bride's social position, her beauty, diligence at work, etc. It is possible that the bridewealth in Nuzi was a fixed, symbolic amount — as it happens, it corresponds fairly well with the value of a female slave. It is also possible that the bridewealth tablets from Nuzi concern women belonging to the same social group and thus to the same 'price class'.

It is impossible to establish how often marriages were accompanied by bridewealth agreements. Out of 20 marriage contracts, ten contain mentions of bridewealth and there are ten receipts of bridewealth payments. However, transfer of movables did not necessarily require a written document and many bridewealth transactions could thus have gone unrecorded, especially if the whole amount was paid at once.

Dowry

It has already been stated that the institution of dowry is an expression of women's inheritance rights and that unmarried daughters are provided for in their father's will.

In Nuzi daughters are mentioned in nine testaments out of a total of about 50. In all other cases we must assume that either the daughters were already married or that the testator only had sons.

A daughter's share is usually much smaller than a son's — she may be given a small plot of land, or a house — the dimensions of the smallest one were 8,75 sq. m. Such a small inheritance share was not sufficient for an independent existence, nor was it meant to be — the girl's share would be added to the plot of land which her future husband would inherit from his parents. Should the girl remain single, one of her brothers would most probably manage her inheritance for her and she would live with him and his family.

In one testament the daughter is not explicitly given any property at all but is instead made guardian over her brothers. This means that she enjoyed the usufruct of the property and managed the household without having been given the right to alienate any part of the family's possessions. The position of guardian was as a rule entrusted to the testator's wife; in this case we must assume that the wife was dead and the daughter considerably older than her (minor) brothers. She was obviously not expected to marry. The institution of guardianship served not only to provide the women of the family with means of sustenance, but also to keep the property undivided as long as possible — usually until the death of the guardian.

There exist six documents recording the transfer of dowry — the amount of land corresponds very closely to that mentioned in the wills. Stipulations concerning dowry never formed part of the marriage contract itself, because the dowry was a transaction between the bride and her father and not a transaction between two families, as in the case of bridewealth. The documents recording transfer of the dowry holdings constituted the title to the property in question and were carefully preserved through generations. Should the property be sold, all tablets concerning it would be transferred to the new owner and included into his archive. (This explains why so many apparently unrelated private family documents were found in the archives of rich land owners.)

A very special situation arose when the daughter was the only heir to the property. The father's lineage was thus automatically ended, because children belong to their father's lineage and his daughter's children would thus belong to the lineage of their father. The heiress's property would also pass over to her husband's family. In order to avoid this the father of the only daughter could adopt his son-in-law. In this way he would acquire an adoptive male heir and his grandchildren would stay in his own lineage.

Four documents deal with the above situation. They are formulated as a combination of marriage and adoption, where the groom is adopted by his father-in-law. He is forbidden to take another wife and to alienate any part of the property under pain of expulsion from the household. Thus a man could marry a rich heiress and be adopted by her father if he forever relinquished the prerogative of becoming a full master of his household, even after the death of his father-in-law. In some documents the father-in-law was obviously still hoping for a son of his own; the tablet declared that, should he beget a son, this son would become the chief heir to the property.

Allowing for the accidental character of our sources, the scarcity of documents dealing with dowry is still surprising, especially in view of the fact that all transfer of immovable property required a written document. We must therefore assume that either the institution of dowry was not widespread in Nuzi (an improbable assumption because we know that women had inheritance rights and the dowry is an expression of them), or that the dowry only exceptionally consisted of immovables. Our dowry tablets would then concern only exceptional cases of this institution, while the usual practice would call for dowries composed of movables. The transfer of these movables would not necessarily be recorded in writing.

There are several indications that the dowry in Nuzi could consist of movables. In the four attested cases of indirect dowry a part of the bridewealth was turned over to the bride. The amount ranged from the whole bridewealth to an unspecified 'rest'.

In all documents recording transfer of dowry the bride gives a gift to the person who is giving her away. The gift consists of textiles, blankets, livestock or silver, and it represents a considerable value. I have called this gift a 'counter dowry payment' and I believe that it represents what a girl traditionally could expect to receive from her paternal home. When given land she relinquishes her claim to the movables and 'gives' them to her guardian. It is possible that these movables were considered the bride's personal property already before marriage, especially if she had participated in their production through spinning, weaving and tending animals.

There exists very little evidence illuminating the problem of administration of dowry during marriage. The dowry formed a part of a family's property and the system of administration of private property within a household (be it the dowry or any other kind of private possession) is unknown. The law codes do not give any direct information about this subject, but it seems clear that all property was at least nominally under the authority of the head of the family. Apart from this general rule a great variety of arrangements certainly existed.

In some testaments from Nuzi the testator states: 'I hereby release my sons' and my wife's private accumulations', thus relinquishing his authority over the private acquisitions of individual family members. Whether the wife's 'private accumulations' included also her dowry is unknown. It seems certain that the dowry was at some stage assimilated to the rest of the family's property — were it not so, we would expect testaments in which women disposed of their own possessions. The only testaments made by women dispose of the family's property which each of these women held in her capacity as guardian. In one case, where the husband's testament is also preserved, it is possible to check that the widow is making disposition exactly according to her husband's wish.

It is my belief that the dowry stayed as a separate unit until children were born. Up to then the wife would take her dowry with her in case of divorce. When the children were born the dowry was assimilated to the rest of the property, although it is possible that the wife still retained some nominal authority over it. The divorce at this stage was either impossible, or at least very difficult. The wife had earned the right to a lifelong support in the conjugal household, while her dowry formed part of the patrimony which the children would inherit in due course. Although the husband most probably administered the dowry, especially if it consisted of immovables, it is still possible that he could not sell it without his wife's consent. We know of very few sale adoptions in which the sellers are a married couple. Where such cases occur, I believe that the alienated property was originally the wife's dowry and by her participation in the transaction she expressed her consent to the sale. There is no reason for the wife's presence in the transaction otherwise.

In the few cases when women appear as sole sellers of immovables they are always designated as 'FN, daughter of PN', which indicates their unmarried status. The plots sold are always much larger than the usual inheritance share and I conclude therefore that these women were sole heiresses to their father's property. Sometimes they sold it in return for a lifelong support in the buyer's household. Such women obviously did not have any relatives at all.

Women were also engaged in purchase of land, and as a matter of fact, the fortune of the already mentioned family of big estate owners seems to have been established by the mother of the family, who was active in over 30 land purchases. The provenance of her funds is unknown.

All testaments from Nuzi explicitly forbid the wife to bequeath any property to strangers, even if she is made guardian over the household. The penalty for disobedience is expulsion from the household without any financial compensation.

Thus on the one hand women's possibilities of disposing of their private property seem to have been very limited indeed, but on the other hand tens of business documents attest the economic activities of women designated as 'FN, wife of PN', therefore either married or widows. Every type of economic transaction is represented, from slave sales to acquisition of immovables. Were these women's funds derived from their dowries or from their position as guardians? Were the wives or widows allowed to dispose of their private acquisitions as long as the transactions did not entail losses for the family? Unfortunately the economic archives of these women are not matched by any private documents and the legal position of these female business tycoons will thus always be subject for conjectures.

Conclusions

The aim of this paper was to present the institutions of bridewealth and dowry in Nuzi and to apply to them the social anthropological theory concerning these two payments. It was my hope to demonstrate that a theoretical framework constructed on the basis of modern data could with profit be applied to ancient oriental sources as well, because certain social institutions, or customs, remain basically the same over the ages.

If these social phenomena, hitherto partly incomprehensible to an Assyriologist working along more orthodox lines, could be understood more easily with the help of social anthropology, then the same approach could perhaps also be applied to other ancient oriental sources. It must be stressed, however, that caution should be exercised when applying social anthropological models to cuneiform sources, which by their nature are fragmentary and often inconclusive. The greatest advantages of the social anthropologist – that of studying a living society and the possibility of re-examination and cross-checking the data, or the model, against the existing situation – are absent in studying cuneiform sources. Their inconclusiveness can sometimes be used to prove completely divergent models.

In my own research of the bridewealth and dowry systems in Nuzi I have consecutively constructed two different models, and although I am convinced that the one presented in this paper is closer to the truth, the nature of my sources does not permit a completely positive identification. The use of social anthropology, however, has permitted a closer definition and a better understanding of the system of bridewealth and dowry than would have been possible if using other methods. It has also put this system in a wider perspective.

This is especially apparent in the case of bridewealth, because a lack of understanding of this payment has influenced the Assyriological interpretation of Mesopotamian marriage as marriage by purchase, the bridewealth being the price, and the marriage agreement not much different from a slave sale. The social function of the payment was thus completely lost. Also the custom of indirect dowry was misunderstood, leading in one case to a theory that the bridewealth was a fund destined for the wife (Cardascia, 1969, p. 196).

I believe that the system of bridewealth and dowry in Nuzi resembled that found in India today, where the dowry is given by the highest strata of the society (Goody and Tambiah, 1973, p. 68ff). The bridewealth is practised by the poor, while those who are a little better off and conscious that the bridewealth-marriage is despised by the rich and regarded as a child-sale resort to the indirect dowry, enabling them to equip the daughter with a dowry and keep a part of the bridewealth.

In support for this reconstruction I cite the fact that Nuzian princesses and rich women married with huge dowries, while the bridewealth is most often mentioned in tablets recording marriage between free women and slaves of influential persons. It is quite plausible that only economic duress would induce a man to marry his daughter to a slave, and the bridewealth marriages could thus be interpreted as marriages in the lowest and poorest strata of the society.

It must be pointed out, however, that dynastic marriages between the pharaohs and Mitannian princesses attested in the royal correspondence from Amarna, involved both the bridewealth and the dowry, and ferocious haggling between the two courts is recorded with respect to the size of these two payments. I believe that royal marriages between monarchs of the same rank required even more care about the matters of prestige than matrimonial agreements between ordinary citizens. The marriage payments accompanying such marriages must have been matching, because any other arrangement would involve a loss of face for the party who payed more. It is therefore possible that the royal marriages can be completely excluded from our considerations as atypical.

Notes

1. This article represents a further elaboration of a theoretical approach presented by me for the first time in the article 'Dowry and Brideprice in Nuzi', in *Studies on the Civilization and Culture of Nuzi and the Hurrians In Honor of E.R. Lacheman*, M.A. Morrison and D.I. Owen (eds.), Winona Lake, 1981. Since it is based on the same textual corpus, available in cuneiform copies only, I have avoided exact references to texts or quotations from them here. Readers wishing to consult original sources are therefore referred to this publication for detailed bibliographical references and tables.

2. For a bibliography of published texts cf. Wilhelm (1970), pp. 2ff.

3. The *ilku* obligation, attested throughout almost the whole of Mesopotamian history, was a duty connected with land tenure. It was owed to the king and could be both military and non-military in character. The exact nature of this obligation is still disputed, and it is possible that it varied from period to period. For a discussion of the term cf. *RLA*, vol. 5, s.v. *ilku*.

4. These documents are, with rare exceptions, available only in cuneiform copies.

5. Cf. §138, §§ 163-4 of the Code of Hammurabi (Driver and Miles, 1955).

6. The documents are available in cuneiform copies only.

7. For a presentation of these adoptions cf. Koschaker (1928), pp. 82-91; Cardascia (1959).

8. For a transliteration and translation of a marriage contract cf. Pfeiffer and Speiser (1936), p. 55.

13 INFANTICIDE IN HELLENISTIC GREECE[1]

Sarah B. Pomeroy, New York

The subject of infanticide has been frequently explored by historians and philosophers both in antiquity and the present. More than many topics in ancient history, it is likely to elicit an emotional response and to reveal a writer's biases and values. All discussions of the practice which admit that it existed are either neutral or condemnatory; no one praises this form of population control. Greek and Roman authors used infanticide as a topos of social criticism. They reported that it was practised by their own corrupt compatriots, but not by aliens including Egyptians and Jews (Cameron, 1932). Infanticide is not only a secular issue. Before Islam, it is said, unwanted females could be buried alive (Saleh, 1972, p. 124). But the extent of this practice was doubtless exaggerated by those who wished to demonstrate the benefits of Islam. Catholic scholars too have found much to condemn in this practice. To the Greeks and Romans abortion was the same as late contraception (Hopkins, 1965, pp. 136-42). To press this line of reasoning one step further — infanticide is simply late abortion. In antiquity it was certainly preferable to late abortion from the standpoint of the mother's health.

Infanticide is thus a form of family planning, but unlike any other device available before the invention of amniocentesis, it permits parents to select the offspring they will raise on the basis of their sex. The Greeks did have their methods for determining the sex of the foetus *in utero*. They believed that the male was more active than the female, that the male quickens after 40 days and the female after 90, that the male foetus leans to the right, the female to the left (Aristotle, *GenAn* IV 6 775a, *HA* VII 3 583b), and that a pregnant woman has a good complexion if the foetus is male, a poor complexion if it is female (Hippocrates, *Aphorisms* 48, 42). These signals were probably considered by women contemplating whether to carry a pregnancy to term. When they proved incorrect, as they frequently must have done, infanticide was an option. We should also observe that of all the forms of family planning (contraception, abortion and infanticide) it is infanticide that is most likely to involve the father, for he is the parent who must decide whether or not an infant is to be a member of his family. Children belonged to their fathers, not their mothers. Greek and

Roman law codes stated that when a father died, a newborn infant must be offered to its father's family. Only after its agnates refused it, might the mother dispose of it as she pleased (Pomeroy, 1975).

Among social historians, those who study women's history have been especially interested in this topic, since infanticide affects women as mothers and since it selects more daughters than sons. Moreover, the subject of infanticide raises a variety of discomforting questions about the value of women. Myths about Amazons may tell of women warriors who preferred girl babies to boys. When a son was born he was either killed immediately or sent to his father. But the evidence of history and anthropology tells a different story. No known society positively prefers girl babies to boys (Dickemann, 1979).

Even where infanticide is not explicitly practised, neglect of female children by the denial of adequate care produces the same result. Everywhere more boys are born than girls, but in developed countries the survival rate and life-expectancy is higher for girls than for boys. Yet in countries like India more young girls than boys die. Since this sex ratio is contrary to the dictates of physiology, other factors must be operating. Some demographers explain this sex ratio by the preference for sons and the reluctance to raise daughters. Others believe that girls are not killed or neglected and propose that women, like other underclasses, are not adequately counted by the census (India, 1974). If this be the case it gives yet another example of the neglect of women in such countries; for those who are not counted are those who 'do not count'; and who therefore do suffer neglect.

Literary evidence for infanticide from classical antiquity is abundant.[2] The sources range from authors like Plato, Plutarch, Apuleius and Seneca (to name just a few) down to a letter written on papyrus in 1 BC from a soldier in Alexandria to his wife in Oxyrhynchus in which he instructs her that if she gives birth to a son she should rear it, but if she has a daughter she is to expose it (*P. Oxy.* 744). These bits of written testimony demonstrate in themselves a tolerance of infanticide in classical antiquity (Pomeroy, 1975).

But the major challenge confronting the historian who would discuss the subject of infanticide in Greek antiquity is the lack of census data comparable to that available from modern India. Sources that can yield statistics for the study of the demography of the ancient world are rare. Few numbers are large enough to impress a modern cliometrician. For the study of Roman demography historians can analyse census data, tax rolls, tombstones and figures for the army and slave familia, but there is little such material available for the Greeks. Athens, as usual, has provided most of the data. Using inscriptions and literary evidence (especially private orations), historians have been able to trace the genealogy of families who are wealthy and noteworthy enough to get into such sources. Because of the Athenians' well-known reluctance to give the names of respectable women in public, women who must have existed are not mentioned. Thus the stemmata published in J.K. Davies' *Athenian Propertied Families* (1971) realise the hopes of Hippolytus or Zeus that children be born from fathers alone, for often descent is traced solely through the male line. Earlier generations of historians, including J.J.B. Mulder (1920) and A. Zimmern (1931), used material of this nature as the basis of demographical studies.[3] Not only are the sources defective, but the historians themselves did not divulge their methods. For example: Did they allow for a sister whenever a brother-in-law is mentioned? Did they add a mother to every group of children? On the other hand, to have supplied missing women could have been to inflate the number of women without justification. Many upper-class women, especially those of proven fertility, married more than once, some even three times (Thompson, 1972). Nevertheless, their names are not known (Schaps, 1977). A thrice-married anonymous woman would thus show up as three women.

Another body of evidence derives from a set of inscriptions from Miletus (*Milet* 3, 34-93). Most of these date from 228 to 220 BC. Others come from the end of the third century and the beginning of the second. A few are later. Miletus was prosperous and did not suffer from the urban decline that beset many of the older Greek cities in the Hellenistic period. The magnificence of the public buildings and the employment of mercenary soldiers, from time to time, to maintain an offensive in external relations bear testimony to the wealth of the city.

In the Hellenistic period, the Milesians hired mercenaries from the Greek islands and from Ionia, from south-west Anatolia and other areas in the Greek world. The majority of those whose place of origin is known came from Crete, famous as a nursery for Hellenistic mercenaries. The mercenaries were enrolled as Milesian citizens and were settled nearby in Myus, a city under Milesian control.

The names of the immigrants were inscribed on the walls of the Delphinion, the sanctuary of Apollo. The Delphinion inscriptions differ from the Athenian sources in the obvious respects that they derive from a different period and not only from a different place but from a different sort of place, for Crete and the other places of origin of these mercenaries were provincial backwaters compared to Athens. Moreover, the Athenian material largely reflects those groups wealthy or influential enough to get into the historical sources. There is no specific information on the class from which the soldiers derive. But from the fact that they are mercenaries to whom citizenship in Miletus offered upward social and economic mobility, it may be deduced that they are members of a lower class than the Athenians.

The lists of immigrants provide the largest single body of statistics available for the study of demography in Hellenistic Greece. W.W. Tarn examined inscriptions in *Milet* 3, 34-93 and reported the following results:

> [For] the prevalence of infanticide . . . for the late third and second centuries the inscriptions are conclusive. . . . Of some thousand families from Greece who received Milesian citizenship *c.* 228-220, details of 79, with their children remain; these brought 118 sons and 28 daughters, many being minors; no natural causes can account for these proportions (1952, pp. 100-1).

M.I. Rostovtzeff (1941, pp. 1464-5) accepted and cited Tarn's work, and such is the authority of Rostovtzeff that his work is still being quoted in turn — for example by E. Will (1975, p. 512, n. 2). Tarn's work is referred to in a recent study by R.P. Duncan-Jones (1982), and it apparently served as the inspiration for Claude Vatin, who wrote:

> en 228/227 et en 223/222, quinze puis vingt et une familles crétoises ont été admises à bénéficier du droit de cité à Milet. [*Milet* 3, 34, 38] . Ces trente-six familles ont, au total, soixante-trois enfants; sept d'entre elles ont plus de trois enfants, douze ont deux enfants; ce taux de natalité est déjà légèrement insuffisant pout maintenir la population a son niveau; mais surtout on constate qu'il y a deux fois plus de garçons que de filles: quarante-deux contre vingt et un (1970, p. 231).

The inscriptions are fragmentary. In their publications neither Tarn nor Vatin indicate whether or how they took cognisance of the lacunae. The editors of the inscriptions state that a total of more than 1,000 people were enfranchised in the decrees of 228/227 and 223/222 (*Milet* 3, p. 75 [199]). Tarn's allusion to 1,000 *families* is a major mistake (but if correct it would have strengthened his argument). Although there is space for more than 1,000 names, owing to the fragmentary condition of the inscriptions, fewer than 1,000 are totally, or even partially, extant. Some people are listed as individuals and some as members of family groups. The members of a family are with very few exceptions listed in the same formal order: husband, wife (her name followed by *gunē* 'wife'), male children, and, last, female children. The lists are continuous, and are not skewed — as are some lists on papyrus[4] — by a recurrent loss of the names of females listed on the bottom. Because of the pattern in which family members were listed, it has been possible to reconstitute some families by adding people who were problematic insofar as their names or family roles were fragmentary or totally absent. Sex was deduced from the name, family relationship and physical placement in the inscription. The results of this study appear in Tables 13.1 and 13.2; (pp. 220-22).

The most striking feature of the Delphinion population is the disproportion between the sexes, with males outnumbering females by more than two to one. The sex ratio is more skewed among the children than among the adults. The small number of daughters contributes to a second noteworthy phenomenon: the small size of families. Several hypotheses can be presented to explain the sex ratio.

The first hypothesis is that suggested by the census report from India discussed above: the daughters existed but were not counted. Women are usually undercounted in census-type lists, but the difficult problem is how to assess how far the tendency can go. The recorded sex ratio in a list like the one on the Delphinion results from the interests of the heads of household giving the information and of the government officials taking it down. Historians and anthropologists have noted many characteristics of Greek society that might lead a father to omit mentioning a daughter or two. The ambiguity of the Greek language fosters the invisibility of women (Pomeroy, 1977, p. 52; 1982a, pp. 3-4). *Pais* means both son and child of either sex. To be really specific about a daughter, she would have to be called *thugater*. When fathers in rural Greece nowadays are asked how many children (*paidia*) they have, they may enumerate only the sons. The engendering of sons is a tribute to a man's masculinity; a father may wish to conceal a proliferation of daughters. Thus, in Table 13.2, line 11, it may be observed that only eleven fathers dared to list a daughter when they had no sons at all. On line 16, 15 fathers are listed with unspecified children. These may simply be fathers who failed to show up on the appointed day to make their report, or they may be men who are ashamed of having two or more daughters and no sons. Similarly, the higher valuation placed on males than on females could have led the magistrates to be more careful about recording the names of boys than of girls, even when the information was given to them.

These arguments are, however, general in nature. The specific situation in Miletus was such as would motivate a father to list all his daughters. These inscriptions record grants of citizenship and women were the recipients of such grants in the Hellenistic period. From the fact that adult women who are alone are inscribed as citizens, it may be deduced that girls and boys are listed not merely as daughters and sons of citizens, but as citizens in their own right. In imitation of the Athenian citizenship law, citizenship in many Hellenistic cities depended upon descent from both a citizen father and mother. The enrollment of some of the new immigrants with the label 'nothē' or 'nothos' suggests that the double parent requirement existed in their cities of origin. *Nothos* is often translated 'bastard'. All these *nothoi* do have patronymics, and the only *nothos* who is married named his son for the child's paternal grandfather (*Milet* 3, 78). However, all the *nothoi* lack ethnics. It is likely that *nothos* in these inscriptions, as in Demosthenes and elsewhere, refers to a child of a citizen father and an alien mother.[5] The second-class status of such children is indicated by the fact that the only married *nothos* and *nothē* are married to each other (*Milet* 3, 78). The *nothoi* who came to Miletus then had a good deal to gain in the form of citizenship in a leading Greek city. The Delphinion inscriptions themselves, by the very fact that they list women, often carefully identified by patronymic and ethnic, indicate that the double citizen-parent requirement existed at Miletus. Therefore, fathers who, as new immigrants, had little standing in the community would certainly want to leave no ambiguity about the status of their daughters. What might happen otherwise is made clear by the case of Neaera, from fourth-century Athens. Neaera was accused of having been born a slave, moving to Athens from Corinth, and then having the audacity to pass herself and her daughter off as Athenian citizens ([Demosthenes], 59). It would be impossible to so challenge the citizenship of any woman whose name was inscribed on the Delphinion.

Only one of the families has two daughters and none have more than two. This statistic is not surprising. Among the Greeks, a large number of daughters was a rarity. It was a manifestation of great wealth and pride on the same scale as owning horses that raced at pan-Hellenic festivals. The Athenian Callias, who won three victories in chariot racing — two of these in a single year — had three daughters. Themistocles had five. Adimantus, commander of the Corinthian fleet at Salamis, had three.[6] Two of the highest-ranking members of the Ptolemaic aristocracy also had a remarkable number of daughters. Polycrates had three, and he was so wealthy that not only did he own racehorses himself, but his wife and daughters had horses which won at the Panathenaia some time after 197 BC. Later on in the second century, Theodorus, who like Polycrates served as a governor of Cyprus, had a family that included at least three, and probably four, daughters. Dryton, a well-to-do reserve officer who lived in Pathyris in the second century BC, had five. In contrast, families with three or more sons were common enough. Even Socrates, who advertised his poverty, had three.

The figures from Miletus may be evidence for selective female infanticide, but they need not be a direct numerical reflection of it. The life cycles of girls and boys are different. The official designations of a boy as *anēbos* (prepubertal) or *hēbon* (mature) and of a girl as *korē* (maiden), marked the different stages. Offspring, designated simply as *huios* (son) or *thugater* (daughter) without qualifying titles, may be beyond the ages covered by them. The age at which boys changed from *anēboi* to *hēbontes* at Miletus is not known. In fact, the official age of maturity for boys, even for a city like Athens where there is ample documentation, is a matter for debate (Golden, 1979). If the Milesians followed the Athenian practice, then the boys presumably became *hēbontes* after their *ephēbeia*, or sometime between 18 and 20. If, on the other hand, *hēbon* was not an official age class at this time in Miletus, but simply connoted a male who manifested the outward signs of puberty, then boys as young as 14 might have been so designated.[7] Girls leave their families of origin for marriage at 14 more or less. Before this they are called *korai*. Starting from equal numbers, if we allow for both boys and girls to be counted up to 14, we would expect equal numbers. If boys are counted up to 18 and girls up to 14 we would expect one and one-third as many boys as girls. If boys are included up to 20 and girls up to 13 we would expect one and one-half more boys. These are artificial and mathematically convenient postulates. Daughters of migrants might have been married at even earlier than usual ages, before the departure of their parents, since the pool of old friends and relatives among whom bridegrooms would be found would be larger in one's native polis than in Miletus. The average age at which women will marry for the first time is due partially to the sex ratio in a given society. Where women are in short supply, they will marry young.

On the other hand, the figure of 14 as the age of menarche[8] and marriage in antiquity comes to us from medical and literary sources that are biased toward the upper classes. Menarche is related to nutrition. Xenophon (*Lac. Pol.*, I 3) reports that among Greeks, only the Spartans nourished girls as well as they did boys. Aristotle (*HA* IX 1

608b) asserted that women need less food than men. Among the upper classes, Greek girls probably were well fed; but the daughters whom mercenaries left at home or took along with them in their campaigns were less well-nourished than, say, the wife of Ischomachus in Xenophon's Athens, and may have reached maturity later in their teens. If the figures from Miletus include daughters up to the ages of 16, 17 or 18, they must indicate a high rate of infanticide. We could easily play around with different ages for girls and boys, but there is no reasonable combination that will account for the sex ratio among the children at Miletus.

Another factor of note is how few the children are in proportion to the entire population. It must have been difficult for children to survive the rigorous life endured by these people before they settled in Miletus. Moreover, husbands who are absent on campaigns cannot impregnate their wives. Most important is the consideration that many women will not have completed their childbearing years at the time of the migration. The couples without children noted in Table 13.2, line 1, are either infertile or are upwardly mobile young couples. They are not likely to be elderly folks with an empty nest, for older people without the security of children are not eager to undertake changes. Moreover, that most of the parents are young is suggested by the infrequency of broken marriages, although the completed families could be the result of remarriage after the death of a former spouse.

Knowing what we do of Greek life expectancy,[9] we must assume that most of the parents and the children who came to Miletus were young. If there had been a large number of sons designated as *hēbontes* we would have to assume a large number of fathers who were at least 40. There is only one *hēbon* (and he is part of an extended family group including his parents [*Milet* 3, 62]), who is married, he is unusual. Generally, Greek men married around 30. Thus only the men who are fathers of *hēbontes* were definitely over 40. Therefore we ought not explain the sex ratio by the fact that men in antiquity enjoyed a longer life span than women and posit that the single men are elderly widowers. A migrant population tends to be comprised of young male adults (Sorre, 1955, pp. 198-9). The Delphinion inscriptions do record twice as many males as females among the adults. Doubtless these men were young.

We should also ask ourselves whether families with the good fortune to have more sons than daughters were more likely to migrate to Miletus, leaving behind their hypothetical statistical counterparts in which the daughters outnumbered the sons. Of course we can only speculate about whether the group would have been self-selecting in this way. It is certainly possible that families that happened to have many sons, but insufficient resources, would want a fresh start in a pre-eminent city that offered them a brighter future. Moreover, it is conceivable that parents, bolstered by the security of many sons, would venture to leave their ancestral home. Yet there is no evidence, not even a plot of new comedy, that may be adduced to corroborate the existence of such an attitude. Moreover, if the departure of young single men created a surplus of unmarried women in their places of origin, the existence of such women would have discouraged parents from raising daughters. No Greek society ever had room for respectable spinsters.

There are two categories of parents whose special experience affected the sex ratios of their children. The first of these are the ones who probably had led a harder life than the rest. Crete was the place of origin for most of the migrants whose ethnics are known.[10] Since ten men are listed twice, once alone and once with their families, it appears that they had left their families behind when they undertook military service on behalf of Miletus (*Milet* 3, p. 47 [171]; Launey, 1949, p. 256). When they accepted the Milesians' offer of citizenship they brought their families from Crete in several large contingents. In contrast to the women and children who simply had to make one voyage from Crete to Miletus in the company of compatriots are those from Caria, Anatolia, and more distant places in the Greek world. There are 23 such married couples who did not come from Crete, and whose place of origin is known. They may have started out as members of a cohort of soldiers all from the same neighbourhood, for mercenaries were often recruited in groups. But by the time they showed up at Miletus, they appear as the sole couple from a particular city. Most of these people had probably travelled about a great deal. Mercenaries lived like nomads, bringing their families and all their material property along with them wherever they went. Female infanticide is a characteristic of migratory people (Sorre, 1955, p. 45). Thus the sex ratio is more skewed among the children of parents whose ethnics are given and who do not come from Crete than among the rest of people listed on the Delphinion. The 21 families with children have among them 37 sons and five daughters.[11]

Life in a Hellenistic army must have been unfavourable to the raising of female children. There was little incentive for a professional soldier to raise a daughter. On a farm, a daughter could be helpful doing women's work, but in an army she was simply another mouth to feed.

In a settled community it might be useful to have a daughter so that one might make a marriage alliance with another family, but for a soldier to provide a dowry for a daughter whom he was likely to marry off to another soldier was tantamount to throwing his money away. Among the intangibles to consider is the negative effect that being in an intensely masculine milieu like an army has on the value of a daughter.

Another group of parents whose special experience affected the sex ratio of their offspring were those without spouses. The only single mothers are part of extended family groups. One is a mother of two sons accompanied by her own father and mother, and the other migrated with her adult son and his wife. Both these women are probably widows. According to Greek law, in cases of divorce the children belong to the father not the mother. Thus the single mother with two sons must be a widow and have them by default. There are eight single fathers with children; only one single parent has a daughter, and they are members of a large extended family group (*Milet* 3, 62). It is important to observe that all the other children of single parents are male. Then, as now, it must not have been easy to be a single parent. Under the pressure of raising children without a spouse, parents divested themselves of daughters, perhaps leaving them at home in the care of relatives or friends, or perhaps taking more drastic measures.

Thirty-six children lack a family and are listed as individuals. These are probably orphans who remained with the group of mercenaries after their fathers died. The hazards of a military career added to the normally low life expectancy of people in antiquity will have left many children as orphans. Since according to Greek law they inherited their father's property — at the very least a suit of armour, a wagon, draught animals and their own household equipment — they were not poor. The Greek word '*orphanos*' means a fatherless child. The existence of a mother does not affect the status of an *orphanos* (Pomeroy, 1982a). Because new citizens at Miletus are listed with patronymics not matronymics, it is impossible to determine whether any *orphanos* actually had a living mother.

Despite the presence of single fathers, who, presumably, should be eager to remarry, and the abundance of single men, there are a surprising number of unmarried women. These are the 11 adult daughters in families and another 17 women travelling alone. The latter group are probably, for the most part, widows, left stranded with the contingent of mercenaries when their husbands died.

Among the Greeks there is a long tradition of caring for a soldier's orphans, and at times for his parents as well, but ignoring his widow

(Pomeroy, 1982b). In the funeral oration, Pericles comforted the parents of the dead, and he declared that orphans would be supported at the expense of the state. But to the widows all he could say was that the greatest glory of a woman is to be least talked about by men, whether in praise or blame. In a settled community, a widow would return to the care of her natal family, who would find another husband for her. Of the 11 Athenians who are known to have remarried after the death of their spouses, eight were women (Thompson, 1972). But the widow of a Hellenistic mercenary was in a more vulnerable situation since she lacked male relatives who could arrange another marriage. Unlike an orphan, a widow did not inherit from her husband unless he had left a will with a specific bequest for her, and she probably had to spend her dowry when she was left a widow. An impoverished widow was not an attractive bride, certainly not in the Hellenistic period, when many men chose not to marry at all. The spectre of these unmarried women must have discouraged soldiers from raising daughters.

Mark Golden (1981) has recently postulated a female infanticide rate of 10 per cent or more for Athens, arguing that otherwise there would have been an oversupply of marriageable women. A general rate of female infanticide for Hellenistic Greece has not been established, but even a rate as high as the one suggested by the Delphinion inscriptions need not have been suicidal for the people concerned.[12] Such a rate among isolated endogamous people like the Inuit or Bushpeople, it is true, would cause a population to die out eventually. But limited populations of Greeks living in attractive locations could be replenished in a variety of ways. On a small scale there was seepage from the lower strata of a population into the citizen group. Neaera and her children furnish an example of such seepage (see above, p. 212). If the woman had not been so notorious and if her male friend did not have political enemies, she could well have gotten away with it in a period when there was laxity regarding the roster of citizens. States dealt with their changing population needs by legislation either accepting or rejecting as a citizen a child born of the union of a citizen and a non-citizen. All the known cases involve a citizen father and an alien mother. Thus another solution to the shortage of women was simply to marry a foreigner. Mass enfranchisements, whether of slaves (as following the battle of Arginusae, after Athens had sustained heavy casualties at the end of the Peloponnesian War), or of freeborn people (as in Miletus) were not uncommon. Immigration was another means of replenishing citizen rosters. Doubtless Greek immigrants flocked to Miletus because they wanted to live the kind of life in which they would be able to raise all the children born to them, for painful as it is to study infanticide, it must have been far more painful to be forced to practise it. Thus although a population decline is well attested for the Greek world in the Hellenistic period, a prosperous state like Miletus need not have suffered from it.

The Hellenistic period may be characterised as the age of the deracinated Greek and of the mercenary soldier. Thus the people who were enfranchised by Miletus were not atypical. Mercenaries did not live on the fringes of society, but exerted great influence, not only in military and political spheres, but in cultural and social life as well (Launey, 1949). Because mercenaries travelled extensively and then often settled down in military colonies, or (as in Miletus) in one of the older cities, their way of life was revealed to sedentary people. The people whose names appear on the Delphinion gave preference to males, and exposed or neglected their female offspring, and such practices were not anomalous in Hellenistic Greece.

Notes

1. A shorter version of this paper was presented at the Berkshire Conference of Women Historians, Vassar College, 17 June 1981. I am grateful to Ernst Badian, Stanley Burstein, Valerie French, William Harris and Cynthia Patterson for their comments, and to the Research Foundation of the City University of New York for a grant which supported research for this paper.

2. For surveys of such evidence see Glotz, 'Infanticidium' and 'Expositio' in Daremberg and Saglio (1877), Golden (1981), and Eyben (1982).

3. For criticism of Mulder and Zimmern see Gomme (1933), p. 80.

4. For the effect of the mutilation of papyri on demographic statistics see Hombert and Préaux (1952), p. 157.

5. See Liddell-Scott-Jones, *s.v. nothos*.

6. Plut., *Mor.* 871. I am grateful to R. Merkelbach for this suggestion.

7. I am grateful to R. Merkelbach for this suggestion.

8. See Amundsen and Diers (1969).

9. On longevity in antiquity see, e.g., Samuel, Hastings, Bowman and Bagnall (1971) and Duncan-Jones (1982).

10. At least 283 Cretans are listed in *Milet* 3, 38 alone (*Milet* 3, p. 74 [198]).

11. No children: (72), (86). Sons: 2(41), 6(45), 2(46), 2(50), 2(57), 6(64), 1(65), 3(66), 3(67), 2(70), 1(74), 2(75), 2(77), 1(79), 2(82). Daughters 1 each: (41), (46), (70), (75), (77).

12. See Harris (1982) and Golden (1981) for well-argued criticism of the model conceived by Engels (1980).

Further Reading

Brunt, P.A. (1971), *Italian Manpower, 225 B.C.-A.D. 14*, Oxford
Eyben, Emiel (1982), 'Family Planning in Greco-Roman Antiquity', *Ancient Society* (forthcoming)
Menander, *Perikeiromene* (The Girl who Gets Her Hair Cut Short), *Aspis* ('The Shield')
Préaux, Cl. (1978), *Le monde hellénistique*, 2 vols., Paris

Appendix

In the following tables the numerals in the left-hand margin refer to the paragraphs following the tables. These paragraphs give the citations on which the tabulations are based. The following abbreviations have been employed:

A = *anébos*
D = daughter
E = *hébon* (mature youth)
F = single adult woman
H = husband
K = *koré* (maiden)
M = single adult man
N = *nothé* or *nothos* (non-citizen)
S = son
W = wife

Table 13.1: Total Population[a]

	TOTAL PEOPLE			766
	Adult females		147	
	Adult males		401	
		Adults		548
	Girls		46	
	Boys		168	
		Children		215
	PEOPLE WITH PARENT, CHILD AND/OR SPOUSE			
2-15)	Nuclear[b] families with specified			
	number of children		91	
	Within these:			
	Daughters			34
	D K		23	
	Other D		11	
	Sons			131
	E		26	
	A		88	
	Age unspecified		37	
	Children with two parents			165
18)	Single parents with specified number			
	of unmarried children			10
	Single mother		1	
	Single father		8	
	S		13	
	D		1	
	Children with single parent			14
16)	Other fathers		15	
2-15, 18)	Mothers			92
2-16, 18)	Fathers			115
1)	W not mothers			37
1)	H not fathers			37
	PEOPLE WITHOUT PARENT, CHILD AND/OR SPOUSE			
19)	K without parents (not N)		7	
20)	A without parents (not N)		10	
21)	N A		14	
22)	N K		5	
	Children without parents			36
23)	N F		1	
24)	N M		6	
25)	F (not N or mothers)		17	
26)	M (not N or fathers)		243	
23, 25)	F			18
24, 26)	M			249

Notes: a. These figures are approximate because of fragmentary inscriptions and restorations and because of inscriptions that say 'autos kai ekgonoi'. b. Extended families are broken down into components for this calculation.

Table 13.2: Family Groups[a] (including fragmentary and/or problematical)

1)	H W[b]	37
2)	H W 1S A	20
3)	H W 1S E	0
4)	H W 1S unspec.	2
	[H W 1S total]	[22]
5)	H W 2S A	16
6)	H W 1S A, 1S	1
7)	H W 2S E	1
8)	H W 2S unspec.	5
	[H W 2S total]	[23]
9)	H W 3 or more S	3
10)	H W more than 1S	10
11)	H W 1D	11
12)	H W 1S 1D	8
13)	H W 2S 1D	10
14)	H W 3 or more S 1D	3
15)	H W 1S 2D	1
16)	Head of household and children (autos kai ekgonoi)	15
17)	Extended family groups	9

Notes: a. These figures are approximate because of fragmentary inscriptions and restorations and because of inscriptions that say 'autos kai ekgonoi'. b. Extended families are broken down into components for the calculation of 1-16.

Tabulation of Family Groups

1)   H W: 2 (34a); 2 (34b); 1 (34h); 2 (34i); 3 (34p); 1 (38r); 1 (38s); 2 (38t); 1 (38u); 3 (38v); 1 (38x); 2 (38y); 2 (38bb); 2 (38dd); 2 (38hh); 1 (38ii); 3 (61); 1 (62); 1 (68); 1 (72); 1 (82); 2 (86) = 37

2)   H W 1S A: 1 (34d); 1 (34h); 1 (38q); 1 (38s); 1 (38u); 3 (38z); 1 (38aa); 1 (38bb); 1 (38ff); 1 (38ii); 1 (41I); 1 (65a); 1 (67); 1 (72); 1 (74); 1 (78); 1 (79); 1 (81) = 20

3)   H W 1S E: none

4)   H W 1S (unspec.): 1 (68); 1 (82) = 2

5)   H W 2S A: 1 (34a); 1 (34h); 1 (38x); 1 (38ff); 3 (45); 1 (50); 1 (57); 3 (64); 1 (65a); 2 (74a); 1 (76) = 16

6)   H W 1S A 1S E: 1 (34b)

7)   H W 2S E: 1 (38q)

8)   H W 2S (unspec.): 1 (38ee); 1 (62); 1 (67); 1 (81); 1 (96) = 5

9)   H W 3 or more S: 1 (62) H W 2S A 2S E; 1 (66) H W 1S E 2S A; 1 (34) H W 3S A = 3

10)   H W more than 1S (number uncertain because of frag. inscr.): 1 (34i); 1 (38o); 1 (38ff); 1 (65a); 2 (68); 2 (74a); 1 (81); 1 (93) = 10. Note: For these families 20S (unspec.) have been added on Table 13.1

11)   H W 1D: 1 (34a) daughter has 2 sons mentioned with her; 3 (34e) K; 1 (34h) K; 1 (38aa) K; 1 (38ee) K; 1 (65) if restored correctly); 1 (86); 1 (90) = 11

12)   H W 1S 1D: 1 (34e) HW 1S A 1D K; 1 (34i) H W 1S A 1D K; 1 (38r) H W 1S A 1D; 1 (38r) H W 1S H 1D K; 1 (38u) H W 1S A 1D; 1 (38v) H W 1S A 1D K; 1 (38cc) H W 1S 1D; 1 (41) H W 1S A 1D K = 8

13)   H W 2S 1D: 2 (34d) H W 2S A 1D; 1 (34h) H W 2S A 1D K; 1 (38hh)
    H W 2S 1D K; 1 (46) H W 1S H 1S A 1D K; 1 (62) H W 2S A 1D K;
    1 (70) H W 2S 1D K; 1 (75) H W 2S A 1D K; 1 (77) H W 2S A 1D;
    1 (81) H W 2S A 1D K = 10

14)   H W 3 or more S 1D: 1 (38q) H W 3S A 1D K; 1 (62) H W 1S H 3S A
    1D K; 1 (84) H W 1S H 2S A 1D K = 3

15)   H W 1S 2D: 1 (38ff) H W 1S A 2D K

16)   Men listed as heads of households but names of other members
    omitted: 1 (42); 3 (44); 7 (54); 1 (58); 3 (63) = 15

17)   Extended family groups (counted as separate units in 1-16 above):
    1 (34a) H W D her 2S A; 1 (34a) H W 3S A 1 sister; 1 (34i) H W
    mother; 5 (61) groups of brothers and sisters; 1 (62) three-
    generation complex = 9

18)   Single parent, child(ren): 1 (34a) F 2S A; 1 (38p) M 1S A; 1 (41) M 1S
    A; 1 (50) M 2S A; 1 (50) M 2S E; 1 (55) M 1S A; 1 (61) M 1D;
    1 (66) M 2S A; 1 (69) M 2S E = 9

19)   3 (38ii); 1 (38 11); 1 (77) adopted daughter; 1 (80); 1 (89) = 7

20)   A without parents: 1 (41); 1 (45); 1 (55); 1 (65a); 1 (66); 1 (70);
    1 (75); 1 (79); 1 (80) = 10

21)   NK: 1 (45); 1 (64); 1 (76); 2 (79) = 5

22)   NA: 1 (51); 1 (65); 2 (65a); 2 (70); 2 (76); 1 (77); 1 (79); 1 (82);
    2 (87); 1 (89) = 14

23)   NF: 1 (46) = 1. Note (78) NW mother

24)   NM: 1 (45); 1 (65a); 1 (67); 1 (72); 1 (74); 1 (74a) = 6. Note 1 (41) N
    father and 1 (78) NH father.

25)   F (not N): 1 (34b); 2 (38kk); 1 (45); 1 (48); 1 (56); 1 (59) (note: her
    husband's name and his genealogy are listed here too); 1 (65);
    2 (65a); 3 (72); 1 (77); 2 (80); 1 (84) = 17

26)   M (not N) excluding men whose names appear again in family groups
    and those mentioned with *ekgonoi* (offspring): 2 (34a); 4 (34b);
    3 (34d); 1 (34h); 1 (34i); 93 (38a-n); 6 (38o); 2 (38p); 6 (38s);
    4 (38t); 1 (38u); 5 (38x); 1 (38z); 2 (38aa); 2 (38bb); 3 (38cc);
    5 (38gg); 2 (38ii); 8 (38kk); 8 (41); 5 (45); 2 (46); 1 (47); 3 (49);
    1 (51); 1 (52); 7 (54); 1 (55); 1 (60); 3 (61); 1 (64); 2 (65); 4 (65a);
    5 (66); 3 (67); 2 (68); 2 (69); 3 (70); 4 (72); 5 (75); 3 (76); 1 (78);
    7 (79); 1 (80); 2 (82); 3 (84); 3 (85); 3 (86); 2 (87); 3 (89) = 243

14 WOMEN AND WEALTH[1]

Riet Van Bremen, London

An inscription from the city of Megalopolis in the Peloponnese, dating from the second century BC, commemorates a woman, Euxenia, for her public benefactions. The first half of the inscription informs us about her ancestry (she was related to Philopoemen, the great general of the Achaean League — maybe his granddaughter) and tells us that she was priestess of Aphrodite in Megalopolis. The last four lines of the inscription sing her praises as follows:[2]

> For a sturdy wall around the temple she built
> For the goddess, and a house for the public guests.
> That a woman trades her wealth for a good reputation,
> Is not surprising, since ancestral virtue remains in one's children.

Some three centuries later, in the Pisidian city of Sillyon, four lengthy inscriptions record the activities, wealth and reputation of Menodora, daughter of Megacles.[3] We are told that she belonged to an illustrious family of local benefactors and magistrates. Menodora herself has worked her way through a series of magistracies, priesthoods and liturgies.[4] In one of the inscriptions she has in fact just completed her term as *dekaprōtos*, member of a committee of ten concerned with public revenues and the collection of taxes.[5] Menodora distributed large quantities of wheat and money amongst the inhabitants of Sillyon,[6] as 'payment' for her own public posts and for those of her children. She also donated, in the name of her son, a sum of 300,000 denarii, to be used as a fund for the *alimenta* of the *paides* in Sillyon.[7] One of the inscriptions provides us with the reason for the institution of such a fund: Megacles, Menodora's son had recently died.[8] To commemorate his death his mother built a temple with several cult statues in it, one of them a large gold and ivory statue of Fate personified. A statue of the deceased boy stood also in the temple.[9] Menodora herself received a number of statues, which, together with their lengthy and explicit inscriptions, served as permanent reminders to the passer-by of her reputation and public-mindedness, telling him how she had offered her money and her services to the public good.

223

I have chosen these two examples because of the connection between wealth and public image they show. Despite the fact that three centuries separated Menodora and Euxenia, it can be said that both were typical representatives of the wealthy elite in Greek cities. One of the most striking features of Greek urban society in this period, i.e. from about the second century BC to the third century AD, is the prominent public role played by female members of these elites. In Asia Minor, where city life was most developed in this period, the phenomenon is more widely attested, but it is by no means confined to that area. In order to explain what I mean by 'public role' I shall sketch briefly the evolution of public life in the Greek cities from the early Hellenistic period onwards.[10] In these Greek cities a group of notables emerged, a wealthy elite, whose members drew their wealth largely from the land they possessed, but who preferred to be defined by their political activities. Gradually they monopolised political bodies like council and assembly, as well as public offices, and used their wealth solely in the context of those magistracies and other posts for the benefit of the city, thereby combining the 'spontaneous' benefactions they had formerly bestowed upon their cities with liturgies and generosities previously given in the context of magistracies – the so-called benefactions 'ob honorem'. Originally a clear distinction had existed between the various municipal offices and liturgies. Eventually, this distinction became blurred, simply because both tended to be performed by members of the same wealthy elite. Magistrates often paid the extra costs of their offices and came to consider it a matter of honour not to touch the public funds reserved for a certain post, but to pay all the costs out of their own pocket. They added splendour to their office by spending more than was required, and tried to outdo each other in lavish benefactions, buildings, public meals and distributions, and many other things, stimulated by an elaborate complex of honours emanating from the city. Eventually, liturgies were even turned into elected posts. All this is reflected in an increasingly confusing terminology in the inscriptions honouring the wealthy benefactors-politicians.[11] Later in the Imperial period, when cities had come to rely entirely on the system, we hear of obligations to pay a fixed sum upon entry into the council, of reluctance to accept a costly post and of dividing up ruinous annual posts into months, weeks and even parts of a day.

It is in the context of this system, often labelled 'euergetism',[12] that we see women playing important public roles. As is well known, the only public roles women could be seen playing throughout the Greek world from the archaic period onwards were those of priestesses and similar religious functionaries. There is a striking contrast with the type of participation in public life of women like Euxenia and Menodora. In the many, almost exclusively epigraphic documents that illustrate the latter, women appear to have rendered the same social, political and financial services to their cities as their male fellow citizens and they were honoured for those services in much the same way.[13] Women thus seem to have encroached upon the traditionally sacrosanct, male-dominated sphere of public life and city politics. Many public offices and liturgies performed by men were also performed by women.[14] Women were also active from an early period onwards as 'spontaneous' benefactors; they competed with men in the building of temples, theatres, public baths, and in many other types of benefactions. There were, of course, still numerous women in priestly offices, but the role of priesthood in public life had greatly increased since the Classical period, and many now had public rather than merely religious functions. The holding of a priesthood often involved spending large sums of money on festivals, banquets and games in honour of the gods, and it was common enough for priests to take on the building or restoring of a temple. The sale of priesthoods, too, became more common in the course of the Hellenistic period, especially in Asia Minor, and priesthoods tended to run in one specific family.[15]

Why did women enter the traditionally male sphere of public life? Did the equally traditional and well attested Greek view that women's place is in the home, confined to a female sphere of activity,[16] not hold for this period, in this context and area, and if not, why not? There are many ways of approaching these questions. In this paper I have chosen to concentrate on one theme, that of wealth, for two reasons. First of all, because in most of our evidence the public role women played appears to be so inextricably tied up with the wealth they possessed that it seems crucial to try and establish the exact nature of that wealth where women are concerned. If we are to assume, as the inscriptions appear to imply, that these women were spending their own fortunes, then we have to ask how normal it was that Greek women were in a position to own considerable sums of money and other property. Could these women inherit, buy and sell? How independent were they in those matters, did they need a male guardian, a *kyrios*, whenever they were involved in legal transactions, as appears to have been the case in Classical Athens? I have furthermore chosen to focus on wealth because it has been implied by several scholars that changes in the legal and economic sphere were responsible for the prominent position of women in Greek cities in the Hellenistic and Roman periods. This theory has been conveniently summarised by S.B. Pomeroy in a chapter on Hellenistic women:

> Here we have one of the main reasons for the increased importance of women: the acquisition and use of economic power. A slow evolution in legal status, particularly in private law, can be traced. This change can be seen more in the areas newly Hellenized through Macedonian conquest than in the old cities of the Greek mainland. In this milieu of deracinated Greeks, lacking the traditional safeguard of the polis, a Greek woman might not have easy recourse to the protection of her male guardians, and hence she required both an ability to safeguard herself and an increased legal capacity to act on her own behalf.[17]

A second theory which attempts to explain the public role of women and in particular the phenomenon of female magistrates, proposes that women's participation in public life was caused by the growing economic decay of the Greek cities in the course of the second and third centuries AD and thus presupposes that wealth was the main element in determining what roles women were to play inside their cities. When pressure on the wealthy to spend their money in costly offices and social obligations grew; when, in other words, men were being pressed harder for financial contributions and were often unable or reluctant to pay up, it was time for women to be drawn in. 'Les magistratures féminines s'expliquent toujours par des raisons d'argent', writes P. Veyne.[18]

In what follows, I will first consider the problems involved in determining the nature of women's wealth and its legal implications. I will then discuss the two theories set out above, arguing that neither theory manages sufficiently to explain the prominent public role of women like Euxenia and Menodora, but that a more satisfactory explanation might be found if we take into account the social and ideological as well as the economic components of the system of euergetism. Within the scope of this paper the discussion will necessarily be a limited one, mainly aimed at providing some more general — and tentative — answers about the relation between women's legal and economic position and her image in society.[19]

Most of the material informing us about women's wealth and its legal implications in our period, is epigraphic. The inscriptions are practically always honorific ones, either private or public. References to wealth are mostly in the form of explicit descriptions of the benefactions made; their type and size, sometimes giving the actual monetary value. None of the typical documents of the Euxenia-Menodora type mention any legal details, not even the presence or absence of a guardian. By their very nature honorific inscriptions omit such basic details, which makes them virtually useless as a source of legal information. Elsewhere, in literary or legal authors, or in a few more specific, non-honorific inscriptions, there are snippets of information on the actual legal facts of the relation between women and property. The latter add valuable details to the general outline derived from the bulk of the epigraphic material, but on their own they could never provide us with a consistent picture of this aspect of the life of Greek women in the Hellenistic and Roman periods.

Let us first look at the nature of women's wealth. It hardly needs stressing that most wealth in antiquity was derived from the land. Urban elites in Asia Minor who, in the inscriptions, define themselves mainly by their political activity, owned vast estates in the territories of their own and that of other cities.[20] If we look at the whole range of gifts and distributions women gave to cities, we see that apart from gifts of money there were many gifts in kind. A number of those, to judge from their nature, are likely to have come from the estates of the bene-factor. In Sillyon, Menodora gave measures of wheat to the members of the council, the *gerousia*, the assembly and to other groups of citizens and non-citizens.[21] Such distributions of wheat are paralleled by those of women in other cities of Asia Minor.[22] To illustrate, I will give just one example. In Termessos, a woman, Atalanta, made a promise to provide a yearly distribution of wheat to the 'mass of the people'. That promise was made, so the inscription records, after a famine had struck the city.[23] Atalanta, who is called 'modest' and 'adorned with every feminine virtue', had often before benefited the city, in the tradition set by her ancestors, with great and splendid gifts, with loans of money, contributions, sacred offerings, etc. In return for all these benefactions, the people of Termessos honoured Atalanta with a bronze statue and a gold crown and they decided to set up her statue in the 'most con-spicuous place in the city, near the stoa of Attalos, against the south wall'.[24]

By far the most frequent liturgy in Greek cities, the *gymnasiarchy*, practically always involved the provision of olive oil for use in the gymnasium or during the games. It could be such a costly liturgy that its tenure was often divided up into months, weeks, or even days. Sometimes, as in Menodora's case, the addition: *elaiou thesei*, 'for the provision of oil', was added specifically to the post. Some inscriptions even mention simply: *aleipsās(a)*, 'having provided oil'.[25] Wheat, wine, oil, and occasionally meat, all feature in inscriptions for female benefactors as frequently as in those for men. They suggest that women owned grainland, vineyards, olive groves and pasture land.[26] It is impossible to determine exactly the extent to which women were involved in and profited from the ownership of land. Even in the case of male landowners we cannot do more than speculate on the size and extent of landed wealth, the exact nature of profits and the amount of involvement of a landowner in his estates and their products. In both the earlier Greek material and in the Hellenistic and Roman evidence we see women owning, buying and selling land. From the early Hellenistic period there are some scattered attestations of female landownership; women owned almost two-fifths of the land in fourth-century Sparta, according to Aristotle.[27] They appear in various land registers.[28] The size of most of the plots known from the early Greek material is relatively small; to my knowledge the largest single plot of land owned by a woman is recorded in a land register from Larisa, where a woman owned 250 plethra, that is 53 acres.[29]

Epicteta of Thera, who lived around 200 BC, talks about 'the estates in my possession, which I myself bought'.[30] Although she does not specify their size, they must have been considerable if we can judge by the rest of the inscription, which clearly shows her to be a wealthy woman. If we move to Asia Minor, the size of estates owned by women is larger. An early, though not necessarily very representative, piece of information is given by Xenophon.[31] He tells us of the vast estates owned by Mania, the widow of Zeuxis, collector of revenues for the Persian satrap Pharnabazos, in the fourth century BC.

Most of the examples I want to discuss here date however from the three centuries when city life was at its most prosperous, the first century BC and the first two centuries AD, which is also the period when the public role of women was most in evidence. Cicero's *Pro Flacco* mentions the estates near the city of Apollonis, belonging to the mother-in-law of Amyntas, a wealthy landowner and 'the most important man in his city'.[32]

In several areas of Asia Minor we hear of *oikonomoi* and *pragmateutai* (slave agents or stewards of large estates), specifically in connection with a female patroness-landowner. There are examples from Sardes, Tralles, Pinara,[33] and a further one from Termessos which is worth discussing more fully for its references to the woman's role in public life. An agent-freedman of Artemis, wife of Meidianos Platonianos, set up a statue for his mistress. In the inscription she is called 'mother of the council', 'perpetual *gymnasiarchos*' and '*ktistria*' ('founder' or 'builder') 'of the gymnasium'.[34] The statue of Artemis was set up by Aurelius Molos Diskos, 'to his *patronissa*'. A second statue base is dedicated to the husband of Artemis, Meidianos, but it is explicitly set up by a (different) freedman of his wife!

A female Lyciarch[35] from Sidyma, M. Aur. Chrysion Nemeso, is known to have taken care of a promise of land, which her son had made previously to that city. He had determined that some of his estates around Mount Cragus (in the south-west corner of Asia Minor) should be given to the city. His mother executed her son's wishes and divided the land up into separate plots for the benefit of the citizens of Sidyma. There is no reason to assume from the inscription (or from other, related, ones) that the husband of Chrysion was dead at the time.[36]

The mother of one of the greatest benefactors in the Greek world, Opramoas of Rhodiapolis, famous for the huge inscription on his tomb, in which many of his benefactions to the cities of the Lycian League are recorded, appears to have possessed estates near the city of Korydallis. From an inscription we know that she was a citizen of that city and Opramoas, in another inscription, is said to have owned estates there *kata diatheken*, 'inherited', presumably from his mother.[37]

Women also matched men in the straightforward financial activity of moneylending, either to individuals or to cities. Examples are not very plentiful in either case, simply because this type of activity tends not to be recorded other than in perishable archives; unless, as we will presently see, the sums involved were so large that it appeared necessary to write down the agreements (or disagreements) for everyone to inspect. How many loans ended up as 'gifts' or 'benefactions' is difficult to say, but there were presumably quite a few. Two women who received grazing rights for their flocks in the small town of Copae had previously lent money to that town and subsequently remitted the town's debts. Nicareta,[38] a woman from the town of Thespiae in Boeotia, was involved in legal skirmishes with the neighbouring town of Orchomenos in the early second century BC. The latter was clearly in great difficulty to pay back the sums of money it had borrowed from Nicareta on several occasions. No remission of debts took place here, as the lengthy inscriptions documenting the case show. Nicareta was finally persuaded to accept a repayment, which was presumably smaller than the actual sum due. She had lent the total sum of 17,585 dr. while the eventual agreement lists a sum of 18,833 dr. It would, however, be another year before Nicareta finally received her money back.[39] In

Termessos, Atalanta had provided the city with loans of silver money,[40] and in Aphrodisias a woman bequeathed money to the city council, 'to be collected from my debtors'.[41]

The size of women's benefactions, although hard to quantify, does not differ considerably from that of benefactions given by men. Menodora's 520,000 den. do not quite equal Opramoas's enormous gifts, but then few others do.[42] She, along with several other women, ranks high on the benefactor scale. It can, on the other hand, not be overlooked that the ratio of women to men in honorific inscriptions is highly in favour of men, that women always formed a minority in land sale records, in lists of benefactors and similar documents.[43] It has to be asked, too, whether the frequently occurring formula: *ek ton idion*, 'out of her own funds', means exactly what it appears to be saying. If a family owned and had owned estates in a certain area for a considerable time and if several of its members, male and female, were benefactors of the city on whose territory their estates were situated, performing liturgies and holding magistracies, some of which ran in the family, as in the case of Menodora, and if, to make it even more complicated, both men and women were said to have performed their liturgies *ek ton idion*, then there is no way in which we could possibly establish the division of wealth between the members of the family, between husband and wife. Should we assume that estates were naturally in the hands of the head of a family? Were female benefactors always widows or only children? Were sums of money spent by women and distributions made in their name only nominal ones, actually paid for by their fathers or husbands? These questions are perhaps too sceptical; the evidence does suggest that women could and did own land and other forms of property in their own right. In order to answer them, moreover, it would be essential to have information about the exact nature of the systems of inheritance in different Greek cities, the ways in which Greek women acquired their property, the ratio of men to women within Greek families and many more, similarly vital but unascertainable factors.

The implicit starting point of what I will call the 'deracination theory', which postulated a growing legal and economic freedom for women in order to explain their increased social prominence, is the fifth-century Athenian situation, about which we are relatively well informed. The economic role and power of women in that society appears to have been extremely restricted.[44] Compared with their Athenian predecessors most Greek women in the cities of Asia Minor in the Hellenistic and

Roman periods appear extremely 'liberated'. But how valuable is such a comparison? What can we say about a possible evolution in women's legal and economic status on the basis of a comparison between the earlier Greek material and our Hellenistic and Roman evidence?

A recent study[45] has investigated the relation between women and property in Classical and early Hellenistic Greece in the whole of the Greek mainland. The author has examined most of the evidence available on women's legal and economic position from the sixth to the second centuries BC, confining himself to mainland Greece and the Aegean Islands. The evidence, outside Athens mainly epigraphic, is extremely scattered and very difficult to interpret. Schaps himself ventures little generalisation, but a few general patterns emerge nevertheless with reasonable clarity. Outside Athens women seem to have wielded more control over their property. They could inherit and bequeath property and could exercise control over their dowries.[46] Women manumitted slaves and could therefore own them, they could sell and buy land, lend and borrow sums of money. They could and did donate gifts in many forms and sizes.[47] It appears that in some parts of Greece women did not need the assistance of a male guardian when entering upon legal transactions. If they did, his assistance often seems to have been a mere formality; it was the woman who performed the transaction in the presence of her guardian. Why the institution seems to have been unknown in certain areas is not at all clear.[48] On the basis of these general conclusions it is clearly unnecessary to postulate a further evolution in women's status in order to explain the phenomenon of the wealthy, independently acting woman. The situation on the Greek mainland in the Classical and early Hellenistic periods as described by Schaps and others already shows a considerable freedom of action for Greek women. We could drop the idea of such an evolution without getting into too much trouble. If we wanted to compare in a more precise way the already tentative conclusions from the early Greek material with what little we can establish about the later period in Asia Minor, we would face insoluble problems. The nature of the documents varies considerably, there will never be sufficient evidence to account for the differences that are likely to exist between cities and there are many more problematic aspects. What I will attempt to do here is to match in a very general way the pattern established by the studies of Schaps and others for the earlier period with some of the evidence available for our later period. In doing this I mainly want to try and see whether Schaps's careful and tentative conclusion, that within his chosen period and area he has not been able to detect any evolution in the status or legal freedom of women,[49] could be extended still further to apply to the later period in the Greek East.

The presence or absence of a male guardian whenever a woman entered upon a legal transaction, was, as we saw, a main element in the deracination theory. We have already noted that the institution may not have been common to all Greek states even in the earlier period, or may not have been considered worth mentioning in official documents in those areas for some unknown reason. The same ambiguity is present if we look at the later evidence. There are two statements made by Roman observers, one of them Cicero and the other the lawgiver Gaius. Cicero, in the *Pro Flacco*, in a passage on the ownership of an estate near the town of Apollonis, remarks that 'under Greek law a guardian has to be appointed for women involved in the sale of an estate'.[50] Gaius, commenting on the Bithynians, is quoted as having said the following: 'There, women and children are held not as by us in tutela, but in *quasi tutela*' (the latter refers to the practice of appointing a guardian only in the case of legal procedures). According to Gaius it was customary that the husband or the eldest son acted as guardian for a woman.[51] These two observations are supported by scraps of evidence from inscriptions. Land sale documents from Mylasa and Olymos show women partaking in sales with the assistance of a *kyrios*; in one case the father, in another the son of the woman involved. There are further similar examples.[52] The evidence is slight, but the essential point is surely that in Hellenistic and Roman times the assistance of a male guardian seemed still required. A total silence in all our sources and remarks from Cicero and Gaius about Greek women not requiring a guardian when they were involved in the sale of an estate would have given us more reason to assume that a significant change had taken place. I venture to suggest that the *kyrios* was in all likelihood just as common in second-century Asia Minor as he was in mainland Greece in the second century BC.[53]

Women's right to inherit is referred to incidentally in some inscriptions. A woman gave a benefaction 'out of the property left to me by my husband'.[54] Another woman is called *kleronomos*, 'heiress', of her husband's property.[55] There is evidence for women leaving their property to their children,[56] female landownership is well attested, and women slave owners were certainly no exception.[57] There is, of course, more research to be done in this area than is possible within the scope of this paper, but my main purpose in this brief overview has been to investigate whether there is any ground for explaining the prominent position of women in the Hellenistic and Roman periods in terms of an evolution of their legal and economic status. Even after a summary enquiry, I think that the answer will have to be no. The theory seems to me to create more problems than it is capable of solving. We have no ways of finding out whether there was a significant evolution in women's legal rights or in their relation to property in the course of the Hellenistic period. If we could learn anything at all from comparing the evidence of the Classical period on the one hand and the Hellenistic and Roman periods on the other, it would be that there seems on the contrary to be a remarkable similarity between the two periods. What may at first sight appear to have been an improvement in women's status, is in reality not so much a difference in women's status as merely a rather spectacular difference in the size of the fortunes owned by women. But the latter is a consequence of the enormous difference in wealth between Hellenistic and Roman Asia Minor and mainland Greece in the Classical period, a difference which does not entirely disappear in the later period.[58]

It is the relation between this vastly increased wealth in the hands of women and their status and image in society which I wish to consider next. The explanation, given by several scholars, attributing the prominent role of women to the decay of city life in the second and third centuries AD, is inadequate if we look at the chronology of female participation in public life. Some of our earliest examples date from the second century BC and their number increases steadily during the next three centuries. There is certainly no dramatic increase in the number of female benefactors, officeholders and liturgists in the late second and early third centuries AD. It is, in fact, during the first and early second centuries AD, when the Greek East was at its wealthiest and there were no signs of decay yet, that we encounter the largest number of women in public positions. The evolution of women's benefactions, liturgies and offices followed more or less along the lines of the general evolution of the system of 'euergetism'. Wealth, power and prestige had been inextricably and increasingly linked ever since the beginning of the Hellenistic period, but that had been the case for women as well as for men. It was, therefore, not the needs and demands of a society in trouble which prompted women to exchange their traditional female sphere of house and family for that of public life and civic interests.

Before looking at an alternative explanation for the relation between woman's wealth and her image in society, it is necessary to look more closely at some aspects of that image. There is no space here for a full and detailed discussion; in what follows I mainly want to stress in a very summary way the ambiguity between what seems to me a remarkable continuity in the way women were perceived – the ideology and mentality regarding women – and the prominent public role wealthy women could be seen playing in their cities. In literary and philosophical sources of the Hellenistic and Roman periods dealing with the subject of women, to name but a few, Stoics like Antipater of Tarsus and Musonius Rufus, Plutarch, some Neo-pythagoreans,[59] the dominant theme is that of the virtuous, modest wife, whose main task it is to care for her husband and children, who is pious and silent. According to Plutarch 'the speech [of a virtuous woman] ought not to be for the public, and she ought to be modest and guarded about saying anything in the hearing of outsiders . . .'.[60] There is in fact a remarkable preoccupation with women and marriage in the sources of this period. These 'traditional' ideas about women are, however, not just the hobbyhorses of a few moralists, out of touch with reality. They are, to a great extent, mirrored in the language used in our inscriptions. In seeming contradiction to the public activities and independent behaviour of these women, the most frequent epithets used for women are to be found in exactly the traditional feminine area of modesty, loving dedication to husband and family, piety, decency, etc., an ideology which also pervaded the numerous funerary inscriptions from all over the Greek world, set up by 'ordinary' Greeks.[61] In short: qualities associated with domestic life and affection.

In some Greek cities women went about veiled,[62] and Menander of Laodicea tells us that 'many cities elected officials to control women, . . . in others . . . it is thought wrong for a woman to keep shop or do any other market business; at some festivals, as at Olympia, women do not appear at all'.[63] We have seen that in the Hellenistic and Roman periods a male guardian was still required to assist in legal transactions entered upon by women. His presence or absence does not appear to have been of great consequence as far as the actual transaction was concerned; he appears as a mere token figure most of the time, but ideologically the persistence of the idea that a woman needed a male guardian is significant. In short, without going into more detail here, I believe that there is, in the different sources, a strong suggestion that traditional ideas on women had changed little in the course of the Hellenistic and Roman periods.

The hundreds of inscriptions recording the activities and position of women in many Greek cities as benefactors, in offices, performing liturgies and receiving public honours in return, seem to tell a different story. Women's prominence, as well as their intrusion of the traditionally male, public sphere of *agora*, *gymnasium*, of the whole physical centre of public life and politics, may be shown most convincingly by looking at the profusion of statues and inscriptions set up for women in all parts of the city. The 'physical' presence of female benefactors in the form of statues must have been quite impressive.[64] Greek cities were filled with statues of wealthy men and women. Those of women stood not just in or near temples; the only area of public life traditionally belonging to women as well as men, but in conspicuous places all over the city. In Kyme, in the second century BC, Archippe, who had built a council house and had given all sorts of distributions to the inhabitants of Kyme upon its completion, received a statue in the market-place. The statue represented Archippe, being crowned by a colossal personification of the 'People'.[65] In Cyzicus, some women appealed to the council to be allowed to set up a statue of the priestess Kleidike 'in the men's agora'.[66] In Perge, at least part of the city was dominated by the building activities of one woman, Plancia Magna, daughter of M. Plancius Varus, governor of Bithynia.[67] She built the magnificent gate complex at the south entrance of the city, its walls lined with the statues of the Imperial family, the founders of the city, and Plancia's own ancestors. Three statue bases were found which once served as pedestals for statues of Plancia herself. One of the statues has been recovered and is now in the Antalya museum. It shows Plancia, dressed in the robe of priestess of the Imperial family.[68] Thus the presence of female benefactors was constantly felt inside the cities. In addition to the statues there were the conspicuous inscriptions and monumental buildings to remind one of the greatness and goodness of important men and women.

The ambiguity set out here can only be solved by trying to find different reasons for women's prominence from the ones invoked in the two theories I referred to earlier. After all, women could have spent their wealth silently, via their fathers, brothers or husbands. They did not have to 'go public' and imitate men.[69] I believe that more profitable explanations are to be found in the social and ideological components of Greek urban elites, and, more precisely, in the relation between public and private spheres. It is an important feature of the full-grown system of euergetism that the distinction between private and public life disappears; the private, domestic sphere, in all its aspects, overlaps increasingly with that of politics and public life.[70] The overlap is visible in the attitude of the notable towards his city, the growing importance of dynastic elements in actual politics as well as in ideology, and it is reflected in a most telling way in the vocabulary used to describe the relation of the benefactor-politician to his city. Mutual concern and affection are expressed in a way usually reserved for the family context and the affectionate emotions associated with it.[71] Important citizens could, for instance, be adopted by their cities as 'fathers', 'mothers', 'sons' and 'daughters of the city'. And whole cities could be seen mourning publicly the death of a member of one of their ruling families.[72] Those attitudes and concerns were mirrored by equally familial attitudes on the side of politicians and public figures towards their cities. Patriotism was often, and more and more frequently, expressed in terms of paternalism and familial affection. So women's private, domestic sphere was no longer very private; it had become a centre of attention. The families of benefactors, including their wives and daughters, had become essential elements in the dynastic, self-justificatory ideology of these elites. Women were important assets to their husbands and fathers, because they were the means to enforce the continuity of a leading family and thus safeguard its social superiority. But the social distance between upper-class women and their less-well-off sisters was of course hardly noticeable if they shared a traditionally secluded female life inside the house, occupying themselves with typically female tasks. So they followed their male relatives out on to the public stage and imitated men's paternalistic involvement in civic life, using their wealth in an equally magnanimous, civic way for the benefit of their cities, still praised for their traditionally feminine qualities, but now in public, visibly and conspicuously.

Women could only act within the framework created by their male relatives. An imitation of socially accepted and honourable activities of men seemed all that was possible, and then only to a certain extent; the outer limits were formed by the types of activity of male benefactors, the inner ones by the ever present ideology of the modest, silent, loving wife. Priesthoods had been, and continued to be, traditionally 'safe' and accepted transitional areas for women, but we saw that these had become associated with other public posts and liturgies and were now part of that whole area of civic posts and services. Activities requiring action in the form of travelling, deliberating, voting, etc., remained closed to women. Paradoxically, the disappearance of a clear distinction between private and public life enabled women to move outside their traditionally female sphere into the male world of public life and politics, but their behaviour in public was still defined and constrained by the same traditional ideology. It cannot be denied that conditions created by this system must have given upper-class women greater actual freedom to move about, increased visible presence and importance within their cities, and greater practical independence. The possession of wealth and the apparent freedom to use that wealth inside a sufficiently flexible and tolerant legal system, were clearly essential preconditions for that independence. But they were not *in themselves* sufficient factors to bring about the prominent position enjoyed by these women. The wealth factor has to be seen in a wider context; as the crucial element which secured not only the political power of these local elites, but also their prestige and superiority in every other aspect of life. The important public role played by female members of these elites has to be understood rather as a result of the social and ideological components of the system of euergetism than as a direct consequence of changes in women's legal and economic freedom. In that context, too, the apparent contradictions between the ideology regarding women and their actual position in society disappears.

Notes

1. I should like to thank Averil Cameron and Simon Price for comments on an earlier draft of this paper.

2. *IG* V. 2. 461. For the date of the inscription and for Euxenia's relation to Philopoemen see Wilhelm (1934).

3. *Ed. princ.* Lanckoronski (1890), nos. 58, 59, 60 and 61. Nos. 58, 59, and 60 also: *IGR* III, 800-802. Nos. 60 and 61: *BCH* XIII (1889), 486-7. There is no translation available of the inscriptions. See also: Magie (1950), p. 1519. For a further inscription, mentioning Menodora's son and her husband, see: *BE* (1967), 606.

4. Liturgies were financial duties expected of the rich. From fourth-century Athens they are already well known. The Greek world never knew a system of direct or wealth tax, and this was an indirect way of tapping the resources of the rich. The system expanded greatly in the course of the Hellenistic period. See further e.g. Davies (1971) pp. i-xxi, de Ste Croix (1981), pp. 305-6, and Rostovtzeff (1941), pp. 619-21, and see Veyne (1976) on the different meaning of 'liturgy' in the Classical and Hellenistic periods.

5. On *dekaprotoi* in Greek cities see: Magie (1950), 1516-7, n. 48 and p. 648. The essential requirement for the post was solid wealth, which could serve as a guarantee in case not enough tax was collected.

6. A list of Menodora's further offices and liturgies: high priestess of the emperor cult, priestess of Demeter 'and all other gods', *hierophantis* (religious office) of the ancestral gods, *decaprotos*, *ktistria* ('founder', 'builder' or 'restorer'), *demiourgis* (an eponymous office) and *gymnasiarch* 'for the provision of oil'. To pay for her 'everlasting' *demiurgy* she left a sum of 220,000 den. to the city. With the 300,000 for her son, that makes 520,000 den. as total expenditure in cash. The extent of her other benefactions is more difficult to assess (but see Note 8).

7. Magie's translation: 'the support of destitute children' is clearly wrong here (Magie (1950), p. 658). *Alimenta* were distributions of food to children, better known from the west, but the *paides* in a Greek city were always a well-defined social category, not just all children, and they were certainly not destitute. See now the discussion by Balland (1981), pp. 194-202, with a second Lycian example of an *alimenta* fund (by Opramoas).

8. From the last sentence of inscr. no. 58: 'All this in memory and honour of her son'. The statue of Fate is another wry reminder of his death. A similar gilded statue of Fate, set up by Opramoas in Myra, cost more than 10,000 dr. See Balland (1981), pp. 192-3.

9. There are many examples of honorific inscriptions set up by mothers for their deceased children and of foundations instituted in their honour; see e.g.: Reinach (1893) in Iasos; Laum (1914), n. 111 (translated) in Aphrodisias, and see Robert (1966), p. 84, n. 1.

10. The following summary is necessarily very limited and cannot do justice to all aspects of the process. A much fuller account is given in an important recent study of euergetism in the Greek as well as in the Roman world. Veyne (1976), esp. chs. 1 and 2, on the Greek cities. De Ste Croix (1981) has an excellent appendix (4) on the process of destruction of Greek democracy in the Roman period, pp. 518-37; see also Garnsey (1974) on the later Roman period.

11. See Veyne (1976), pp. 271-98; 'spontaneous' and 'ob honorem' are terms used by Veyne.

12. From the Greek *euergetès*, 'benefactor', frequently used in the inscriptions. See Veyne (1976), pp. 215-16, for a precise definition of the term.

13. A very convenient collection of some of the more interesting inscriptions is Pleket (1969). Several of these texts have been translated in Lefkowitz and Fant (1982).

14. *Gymnasiarchy*, *agonothesy*, *strategy*, *prytany* and *demiurgy*, to name but a few, were all held by women. For the meaning of these terms see, e.g., Jones (1940). See further the lists in Paris (1891), Braunstein (1911), and Magie (1950), pp. 1518-19, n. 50.

15. For the sale of priesthoods see Nilsson (1961-7), pp. 77-82, with examples. For priesthoods running in one family see, e.g., the article 'Hiereis' in *RE* bd. VIII.2.

16. See for a summary of that view, e.g.: Pomeroy (1975), ch. 4, and Gould (1980), both with references to previous works.

17. Pomeroy (1975), p. 126. A similar explanation is put forward in Wolff (1975). Compare Pomeroy in *AJAH* 1-2 (1977), p. 51: 'The Hellenistic period was one which witnessed many social and economic changes for women . . . the transformation was so profound that, to cite the most dramatic evidence, for the first time in history women even appear as magistrates in Greek cities and are granted civic honours.'

18. Veyne (1976), p. 357, n. 261, a view shared by Jones (1940), p. 175, and Chapot (1904), p. 163, amongst others. The above is rather a simplistic rendering of often more subtle arguments, but the whole is undoubtably seen as part of a 'degradation' of public life.

19. I intend to do this more fully in a Ph.D. thesis, which I am at present preparing.

20. Dual (or triple, etc.) citizenship often suggests that the owner had estates in the territory of both/all those cities. See for instance *Rev. Arch.* (1978), pp. 277ff. on an Ephesian woman with citizenship in Apollonia. See in general on landed wealth: MacMullen (1974), index, s.v. 'wealth, basis in agriculture'; de Ste Croix (1981), ch. 3; and Finley (1973), *passim*; Broughton (1938), pp. 599-695; Rostovtzeff (1941), pp. 805-26 and notes; Robert (1937), pp. 240ff.

21. The quantities of wheat explicitly specified for the different social groups, on which see: de Ste. Croix (1981), pp. 196-7 and 179.

22. The problem with wheat in particular is that apparently the landowners were not always able to produce sufficient quantities of grain. Often wealthy citizens provided money for the purchase of grain, or they held the office of *sitones*, charged with procuring grain for the city. See: Magie (1950), pp. 1512-13, n. 42, and p. 646, for Lycia in particular see now the interesting discussion by Balland (1981), pp. 211-22.

23. *TAM* III 1, nos. 4 and 62, and see: Heberdey (1929), p. 135.

24. The stoa of Attalos is indeed in the very centre of public life, next to the agora, near the theatre and several temples.

25. See, e.g., Pleket (1969), nos. 13 (Arneai) 18 (Aphrodisias; *aleipsása* in 1. 9) and for further references the lists in Paris (1891), pp. 43-8; Braunstein (1911), pp. 28-35; Magie (1950), pp. 1518-19, n. 50. See also Robert (1966), pp. 83, n. 7 and 84, n. 1.

26. For distributions of wine and/or meat e.g.: Archippe in Kyme, late second century BC in Pleket (1969), n. 3 (wine and meat), and on Syros, distributions of wine: *IG* XII.5, 659, and *CIG* add. 2347k.

27. Aristotle, *Pol.* 1270a. 23-5.

28. Like those from Olymos, Mylasa and Larisa. Olymos: Le Bas Waddington (1870), 323, Mylasa: *BCH* XII (1888), esp. n. 9 on p. 26 and Robert (1945), pp. 75-6, Larisa; see the following note.

29. Habicht (1976), p. 158, 1.5, around 200 BC. There are more women in this register.

30. Translation, Greek text and commentary in Laum (1914), pp. 43ff. no. 43 (German), and in Dareste Haussolier (1904), pp. 79ff. (French).

31. Xen. *Hell.* III. 1. 27-8, cf. de Ste Croix (1972), pp. 38-9.

32. Cic. *Pro Flacco*, 71-72. (Loeb, ed., vol. 10).

33. Sardes: *A.M.* (1896), p. 112, no. 1. Pinara: *TAM* II 518. Tralles: *ILS* 8836, cf. Jahreshefte (1907), 295ff. See also: *BCH* LII (1928), 412-13, and Rostovtzeff (1957), 655 n. 5. In general on slave agents of large estates: Robert (1957), pp. 241-2.

34. *TAM* III 123 and 58. See also: nos 122 and 57, and see Robert (1966), pp. 86 n. 5.

35. On Lyciarchs and the Lycian League see now Jameson (1980), but with the remarks of Balland (1981), pp. 8-9, on the 'Lyciarch-archiereus' question.

36. *TAM* II, nos. 188, 189, 190. See Jameson (1980), p. 848, on the problem of Chrysion's husband who was apparently not a Lyciarch himself. Against the independence of female Lyciarchs, assumed by Jameson, see Balland (1981), p. 9 with n. 85, who is clearly right.

37. *TAM* II.578 (Opramoas). *TAM* II.916 (Aglais, his mother).

38. *SEG* XXII (1967), 432.

39. *IG* VII 3172. Translation, Greek text and commentary in Dareste Haussolier, vol. I, pp. 275-310. Nicareta was assisted by her kyrios.

40. See Note 23.

41. *CIG* 2817.

42. See *TAM* II 3 no. 905 occupying more than 20 pages of text, and see now Balland (1981), pp. 194-224. On Opramoas as perfectionist-benefactor: Veyne (1976), pp. 295-6.

43. See, for instance, the Mylasa and Olymos records and, for lists of benefactors, e.g.: *BCH* X (1886), p. 199, on Rhodos, second century BC; or *CIG* 3148 in Smyrna, Benndorf Niemann (1884), nos 86-8, in Aperlai; and Le Bas Waddington (1870) 678, in Iulia Gordos.

44. See Pomeroy (1975), chs. 4 and 5, with references, and her bibliography in

Pomeroy (1973). The number of books and articles on the position of women in Classical Athens is enormous. See for a more balanced view, Schaps (1979), *passim*, and esp. his conclusion.

45. Schaps (1979).

46. Schaps (1979), s.v. 'inheritance' and 'dowry', and see Schaps (1975).

47. Schaps (1979), s.v. 'manumission', 'land', 'loans', 'gifts'.

48. Schaps (1979), s.v. *'kyrios'*. See also Babakos (1964) on Kalymnos, and Babakos (1962) on the apparent lack of a *kyrios* in Thessalian inscriptions from the third century BC to the third century AD. On the *kyrios* see esp. Beasly (1906) (cases with and without *kyrios*), and see Taubenschlag (1938).

49. Schaps (1979), pp. 96-7, stressing the different situation in Egypt. His, and my, generalisations do not include the Egyptian material.

50. Cic. *Pro Flacco* 71-72.

51. Gaius, *Institutes* I, p. 193, c.f. Marshall (1968), pp. 106-7.

52. See Beasly (1906) for examples; see also *SEG* XII (1955) 258, in Gytheion (41) 2 A.D., *SIG* 1234, in Myra-Teichiussa.

53. Confirming Schaps's opinion on pp. 96-7, Schaps (1979). There are several attestations of women acting as guardians (*epitropoi*) for young children. An example from Thessaly is given in Babakos (1962), pp. 318-20, with several further examples; from Erythrae where the woman herself is assisted by her *kyrios*, and some Egyptian evidence. The female *Lyciarch* Chrysion, who executed her son's wishes, may have acted in a similar capacity. Another example, from Xanthos, is commented on by Balland (1981), pp. 254-6, who gives further attestations and discusses the phenomenon in general.

54. *TAM* II.1, no. 394, in Xanthos.

55. *I. Priene*, no. 255 and the remarks of Robert, *BE* (1973), 375, p. 141.

56. See Note 30; Epicteta to her daughter, and Note 37, Opramoas's mother.

57. The *pragmateutai* inscriptions mentioned in Note 33 are only a few examples of both land ownership by women and of women slave owners. There are many more examples of inscriptions set up for a woman by her freedman.

58. An inescapable impression one gets when looking at Schaps's material, is that the largest part of his evidence deals with relatively small-scale transactions; modest plots of land and small gifts. The few exceptions to that rule date from the late third and second centuries BC.

59. Antipater of Tarsus (second century BC): in Von Arnim (1905), fr. no. 63 (= Stobaeus, *Florilegium*, LXVII.25), no translation available. Musonius Rufus: in a convenient translation, Lutz (1957) esp. nos III, IV, XIIIa and b, and XIV. Plutarch, the protagonist *par excellence* of the value system of Greek elites in our period, on women and marriage, esp. in *Praecepta Coniugalia*, *Consolatio ad Uxorem* and *Amatorius*. See Panagopoulos (1977), and Goessler (1958). Neopythagoreans: in Thesleff (1965-8), esp. the female Neopythagoreans; Melissa, pp. 115-16, Perictione, pp. 142-6, Phintys, pp. 153-4. On the date of these texts see Thesleff. There is a translation of a fragment by Perictione in Pomeroy (1975), pp. 134-6.

60. Plutarch, commenting on an incident when Theano, Pythagoras's wife, exposed her arm when putting her cloak around her: 'A lovely arm', someone exclaimed. 'But not for the public', she said. *Praecepta Coniugalia*, *Moralia* 142 C-D, 31-2.

61. Evident from the collection by W. Peek (1955), and see Pleket (1974), and Robert (1965), esp. pp. 34-41, and 317-24. See also Vatin (1970), pp. 31-3, for the preoccupation with marriage since the early third century BC.

62. See Robert (1948), p. 66ff, with references, and MacMullen (1980), p. 208.

63. Menander, 227, in Russell and Wilson (1981). But there seems to have been no uniform custom as to the actual physical presence of women in Greek

cities. Priestesses had specially reserved seats in the theatre. See, e.g., *Arch. Delt.* (1967), 452-7, in Mytilene, *I. Didyma*. no. 50, in Didyma, *REG* XIX (1906), p. 98, in Aphrodisias, *TAM* III.1, 870 and 872, in Termessus. I think that female agonothetes too may well have attended their 'own' games.

64. See on statues for private individuals Pekary (1978), and see Gordon (1979). An example of a woman who received a multitude of different types of statues: *BCH* XLIV (1920), p. 77, no. 8, in Lagina. (*I. Stratonikeia* II.1, 536.)

65. *I. Kyme* no. 13, and see Pleket (1969), no. 3, with references. Reference to the statue in C., lines 1ff.

66. *CIG* 3657 and see *A.M.* VII (1882), pp. 151-9.

67. *IGR* III.794 (= Le Bas 1371). *Arch. Anz.* (1956), pp. 117-18, and see *BE* (1957), 496. On the Plancii in general (and on Plancia) see Jameson (1965), Mitchell (1974), and Jones (1976).

68. Photograph and description of Plancia's statue: *Arch. Anz.* (1975), pp. 74-6, and in Inan-Alföldy-Rosenbaum (1979), vol. I, no. 225 (Description); vol. II, pl. 158, 1-3; 159; 160, 2; 271, 4.

69. On imitation of men, explicitly referred to in inscriptions, see e.g. the decree for Aba from Histria, Pleket (1969), no. 21, lines 17-21, and in Mantinea, *BCH* XX (1896), pp. 124-31, lines 39-40 of the inscription. In an inscription from Knidos, a woman is said to have wanted to do well: 'just like her father and brothers' (*akolouthos*). See (provisionally) *AJA* 76 (1972), pp. 393ff. Also see Robert (1965), pp. 220-7.

70. See in general for what follows the excellent account in Veyne (1976), pp. 104-25, 236-7 and 256-71, and, for a similar theory explaining the separation of private and public life, but concentrating on Classical Athens, Humphreys (1978).

71. See Panagopoulos (1976) for a comparison of that vocabulary in Plutarch's *Praecepta Coniugalia* and the language used in public decrees.

72. Examples for women abound. See, for instance a recent example in Tios, *ZPE* 24 (1977), pp. 265ff., and in general Robert (1966), pp. 85-6 and Robert (1969), pp. 317-29. The earliest example of a woman called 'daughter of the People' is from Kos; it dates from the second century BC; *P. del Pass*. XIII (1958), pp. 418-19. A striking example from Cyzicus is the public mourning upon the death of a woman, Apollonia, *SEG* XXVIII (1978), 953, paralleled by *BCH* XV (1891), no. 2, pp. 575-8 in Aigiale.

Further Reading

Very little has been written on the role of women in Greek cities in the Hellenistic and Roman periods. What follows is just a small selection of works that may be useful.

Braunstein, O. (1911), *Die politische Wirksamkeit der griechischen Frau*, Diss. Leipzig

Jones, A.H.M. (1940), *The Greek City from Alexander to Justinian*, Oxford

Lefkowitz, M.R., and Fant, M.B. (1982), *Women's Life in Greece and Rome*, London

Macmullen, R. (1980), 'Women in Public in the Roman Empire', *Historia* 29, 208-18

Mitteis, L. (1891), *Reichsrecht und Volksrecht in den östlichen Provinzen des römischen Kaiserreichs*, Leipzig

Pleket, H.W. (1969), *Epigraphica, vol. II. Texts on the Social History of the*

Greek World, Leiden

Pomeroy, S.B. (1973), 'Selected Bibliography on Women in Antiquity', *Arethusa* 6, 125-57

Pomeroy, S.B. (1975), *Goddesses, Whores, Wives and Slaves. Women in Classical Antiquity*, New York

Schaps, D. (1974), *Economic Rights of Women in Ancient Greece*, Edinburgh

Vatin, Cl. (1970), *Recherches sur le mariage et la condition de la femme mariée à l'époque hellénistique*, Paris

Veyne, P. (1976), *Le Pain et le Cirque. Sociologie historique d'un pluralisme politique*, Paris

PART SEVEN: WOMEN IN RELIGION AND CULT

A cultural sphere open to female influence and the consequent male
efforts to control it

15 GODDESSES, WOMEN AND JEZEBEL

Peter R. Ackroyd, London

From somewhere back in a remote past, in the thirties or forties, I recollect somewhat imperfectly an account of the death of Jezebel included in a book of schoolboy howlers. It may be that in relating this I am supplementing at some points: the story has now passed through yet another stage of transmission. But, as I recall, we begin with Jehu approaching Jezreel, and Jezebel at the window. In response to his shout of 'Who is on my side?'

> there looked out two or three unicorns. And he said: Throw her down; and they threw her down. And he said: Throw her down again; and they threw her down again. And they threw her down unto seventy times seven. And they gathered up of the fragments twelve baskets full.

I do not believe that was ever a schoolboy howler; if it has a genuine basis in reality, it has undergone several stages of elaboration before reaching the form in which I recollect it: the unicorns and the numbers are certainly part of the tradition, but literary, stylistic and source analysis would suggest at least the hand of an editor. In its essentials, however, it remains close enough to its biblical source. No one could doubt that the portrayal of Jezebel accords with the general impression created by the biblical narratives in I and II Kings. Jezebel, according to almost everything in our sources – and we have no others – was the biblical equivalent of the 'bad thing' of *1066 and all that*. She is uniformly described as engaged in nefarious practice of one kind or another. She appears as the alien Sidonian wife of Ahab, and his worship of Baal is immediately mentioned in the same breath (I Kings 16.31); she massacred the prophets of Yahweh (18.4); she maintained at her royal table 450 prophets of Baal and 400 prophets of the goddess Asherah (18.19 – even for Jezebel, the men exceeded the women); she threatened Elijah with death, and he ran away in terror (19.2f.); she suborned witnesses to contrive the death of Naboth so as to obtain his vineyard for her shilly-shallying husband (21); and perhaps we might add that her daughter Athaliah usurped the Judaean throne for seven years, and, though it is not explicitly stated, was apparently considered responsible for a temple of Baal in Jerusalem (II Kings 11). Jezebel's husband Ahab is described as having done even worse than the previous rulers of the northern kingdom of Israel by his involvement with Sidon and with the worship of Baal (I Kings 16). In one prophetic version of the theme of judgement upon Judah, the accusation is that the Judaeans have 'kept the precepts of Omri; what the house of Ahab did, you have done; you have followed all their ways' (Mic. 6.16).

But there is, surprisingly, one contrasting moment. In fact, both Ahab and Jezebel have one moment of heroic quality. I Kings 22 relates how Ahab met his death, and we have a vivid picture of the severely wounded king, propped up in his chariot facing the enemy, while the blood flowed down upon the floor of the chariot; and in the evening he died (22.34f.). It is true that the association of this story with Ahab has been doubted, but this is what tradition has come to say of him.

The Jezebel story is equally striking. When the army commander Jehu, encouraged by a prophetic messenger and the royal officers, took over the kingship and murdered all the members of the royal house, Jezebel is described as having heard the news at Jezreel. When Jehu arrived, she had painted her eyes and dressed her hair, and she stood looking down from a window. As Jehu entered the city gate, she said — ironically, scornfully, we may assume — 'Is it peace, you Zimri, murderer of your lord?' It does not matter for our discussion whether we are dealing with a constructed story rather than with exact history. The story as told portrays here, rather unexpectedly, a woman, the queen mother — a figure of status in both Judah and Israel, the *gebirah* the 'great lady' (Ahlström, 1963, pp. 61ff.; de Vaux, 1961, pp. 117-19) — who taunts the rebel claimant to the throne, when all the power is in his hands, with being nothing but an upstart like the Zimri who assassinated the king of Israel, Elah. The mention of Zimri is interesting, since the story as told in I Kings 16 goes on to relate the actions of another military commander, Omri, who overthrew the rebel Zimri and another claimant to the throne, and took it for himself. He was Jezebel's father-in-law. Whatever else tradition has said about Jezebel, and all of it negative, it records a courageous woman, with the dignity to face certain death with no loss of face. And according to the story, Jehu, having seen her to her death, gave orders that 'this accursed woman' should nevertheless be buried, 'for she is a king's daughter' (II Kings 9.34). He gave his orders too late; the scavenger dogs had left nothing but skull, hands and feet, though perhaps this is to be seen rather as the precision with which the narrator aligns the fate of Jezebel to the prophetic judgement attributed to Elijah — 'dogs shall devour the flesh of Jezebel; her corpse shall be like dung upon the ground' (II Kings 9.36f.; cf. I Kings 21.23f., and also II Kings 9.9f.). And there is hesitation here since the same prophetic judgement, differently attributed, is used of the dynasty of Jeroboam I (I Kings 14.11); and also of that of Baasha (I Kings 16.4). The stylised use of the same prophecy suggests a patterning of events to fit a theological interpretation (Ackroyd, 1962, pp. 7-11).

To begin thus with Jezebel is to take up the wrong end of my title first; but I may perhaps be allowed to give this paper a chiastic structure. We shall return to Jezebel in due course.

If our priorities are right, we ought, I suppose, to begin with the goddesses; though here there are problems in view of the universal hostility to goddesses — and indeed to all other gods — within the pages of the Old Testament. The hostility to goddesses is such that mention of them is very limited and — an important point this — for the most part their mention is closely associated with alien rulers, alien queens, with practices which ought not to have occurred. But even this general statement admits of some qualification; and a closer consideration of biblical and non-biblical evidence raises some difficult but important questions.

I

We may take first two pieces of clear non-biblical evidence: clear, that is, in its statements, though less certain in its interpretation. The first has now been known for many years, and is to be found in the collection of papyri in Aramaic found at Elephantine in Egypt and belonging to the fifth century BC. Two points about these texts may be recalled. They derive from a community which described itself precisely as 'the Jewish force' (*hyl' yhwdy'*). The terms used are quite clear: the military term is familiar in its Hebrew form (*hyl*) in various senses, but one is 'army'. In this context we might speak of a military post or a military detachment, clearly placed at Elephantine for border control duties. The indications are that it was there for more than a century, since it traced its history back to the time at least of Cambyses (Pap. 30.13, 530-22 BC) and the latest documents point fairly precisely to the last years of the fifth century and to the probability of extermination at the hands of Egyptian nationalists. The adjective Jewish or Judaean is also explicit; this community described itself as deriving from Judah, otherwise it would not have used such a term. The comment is obvious; but the reason for stressing it will become plain.

The second point concerns the later history of this community, as the rising tide of Egyptian nationalism threatened. When their temple was destroyed, they appealed for help and protection to the Persian authorities; and they appealed both to Jerusalem and to Samaria. In this there are problems, and they concern both the political organisation of the Palestinian area in this period and the nature of the relationship religiously between Jerusalem and Samaria. It is an anachronism to speak of 'Samaritans' as that term is later used, for the emergence of the Samaritan religious community and its relationship to the Jerusalem community come later (cf. e.g. Coggins, 1975). We may observe, for what it is worth, that the governors in Samaria, two or perhaps three of whom bore the name Sanballat, familiar from the book of Nehemiah where one such appears as Nehemiah's opponent (Neh. 2.19, etc.), could give their sons names indicative of adherence to a religious belief in which the deity Yahweh was prominent and probably central: Delaiah and Shemaiah, two sons of Sanballat I, who appear in the Elephantine papyri; and a Hananiah who appears in the fourth century, son of Sanballat II (Cross, 1975, 5 (188)). More important, we find that the Jerusalem authorities gave assurance of their support, recognising, it would appear, the propriety of the appeal and the religious status of the Elephantine community. It can be argued that the reply imposes some restriction on forms of worship, but a possible explanation of the restriction could be that the Jewish community at Elephantine was being enjoined to avoid practices which would give offence to the religious susceptibilities of their Egyptian neighbours. Now the emphasis on these points is relevant, since in these documents it becomes clear that this Jewish community, claiming and being accorded recognition by Jerusalem, included among the objects of its reverence not only Yahweh (the name appears in a form *Ya'u* (Yahu or Yaho), which might in fact be nearer to the real pronunciation than the debatable Yahweh of modern convention), but also other deities entitled Anath-bethel, Anath-Ya'u, Ishum-bethel and Herem-bethel (Cowley, 1923, pp. xviiif.; Porten, 1968, pp. 151-79). The interpretation of these titles or names is not entirely straightforward; but one point is clear, namely that a title or name Anath-bethel can only denote a female divinity. Ishum-bethel and Herem-bethel have been understood as alternative titles of Yahweh. But this could hardly be said of Anath-bethel. Even more clearly Anath-Ya'u would appear to be the consort of Ya'u.

Ishum(Eshem)-bethel (*'šmbyt'l*) raises another question. The Old

Testament provides evidence suggesting that the use of the word *šēm*, name, particularly but not solely in the Deuteronomic writings, may represent a tendency towards hypostatisation. The 'name of God' appears often to be virtually equivalent to the person of God. Comparison may be made with a north Syrian deity *'ašîmā'* (II Kings 17.30; cf. also *'ašmat šōmᵉrôn*, Amos 8.14), which appears to be connected with an Old Aramaic word for name, *šm*. Some Ugaritic texts refer to Astarte as *šm b'l*. (For this and related material and a useful discussion, see Mettinger, 1982, pp. 129-88.) This raises the question whether one way in which a female consort of Yahweh became absorbed into the male deity was by a process of treating the female divinity as a hypostasis of the male rather than as having independent status. It would suggest (see further below) that the concept of deity in Israel includes both male and female elements. An eventual monotheism must by some process eventually move beyond male and female distinctions.

These last points must be tentative and open to fuller discussion. What is clear at this stage of the discussion is that the evidence from Elephantine opens up questions which have not yet been fully resolved. For the moment we may simply note that to those who have noted the hostility with which goddesses are treated in the Old Testament, the picture of religion in a Jewish community in Egypt, with close contact with Jerusalem, may come as something of a shock. It is hardly surprising that attempts have been made at explaining away the evidence. But here, it appears, we have a Jewish community which worships a god and a goddess.

The second piece of evidence comes from some relatively new material found at the site known as Kuntillet 'Ajrud in the Sinai. I have seen only brief reports, photographs of inscriptions and drawings, some discussion of the buildings (Meshel, 1978, 1979). It is clear that there are many unresolved questions. The pictures portray divine figures and symbols, including what may be a representation of the Egyptian god Bes (but cf. Emerton, 1982, p. 10), perhaps not altogether surprising in an area between Palestine and Egypt, though such figures are found more widely in the Levant (cf. e.g. *ANEP*, pp. 663f.). But the texts are quite explicit, even though fragmentary: thus, for example, after a broken opening, 'may you be blessed by Yahweh, our protector, and by his Asherah'; and another 'Amaryau said to my lord . . . may you be blessed by Yahweh and by his Asherah. Yahweh bless you and keep you and be with you'. The two publications of the finds are very sketchy; essentially they say the same thing, but there are one or two curious points.

In the first of the texts quoted, the word translated 'our protector' consists of the four consonants *šmrn* — which may quite properly be construed as a participle with suffix. It also happens to be the group of letters which form Shomeron, the Hebrew for Samaria. Meshel comments that the name Yahweh is never followed by a proper name, and only in the title Yahweh Sebaot does it appear closely linked to a following word 'Yahweh of the armies' denied by Cross who renders 'he creates the hosts' (Cross, 1973, p. 65). Emerton (1982, p. 9f.) draws attention to another text with 'Yahweh of Teman and his Asherah'; but Teman is an area (the south) rather than a place, and we might compare 'Yahweh of the south' (cf. Hab. 3.3) with the place-name Baal-Zaphan 'Ba'al of the north' (e.g. Exod. 14.2). (A fuller discussion of the connection of the deity name with a place-name is given by Emerton (1982, pp. 3-9).) Meshel may have wished to see a reference to Samaria so that the clearly stated association of Yahweh with Asherah could be associated with the alien north. He does in fact argue for a northern provenance of the people responsible for this material: the particular form of the divine name Yahweh which appears as the affix in proper names such as Amaryau has its analogies in the northern material, for example in the Samaria Ostraca of about 800 BC: the form uses the affix *-yw*, not *-yhw* which is common in Judah. Is this a clue which points away from Judah? I think it doubtful if it can be too firmly maintained. Thus a fourth-century BC coin from the province Yehud, Judah, has *yhzqyw hphh* (Stern, 1982, p. 224). Meshel also seems to use both the term 'Phoenician script' and 'Early Hebrew script': it is not clear whether these are intended to be differentiated. My limited skill in epigraphy would suggest that no such differentiation is to be made. Is this another way of implying, in rather popular publications, that these people, whoever they were, could not have been proper Judaeans — though all the historical analogies rather simplistically introduced into the discussion point in fact to Judaeans rather than anyone else? Again we may note that Asherah in the context most naturally suggests a deity: but in one rendering he adds: his *asherah* (using a small letter where Yahweh is rendered by God with a capital) — cella or symbol; in another he queries whether Asherah is deity, tree or shrine (for discussion see Emerton, 1982, pp. 15-18). The Old Testament material makes it clear that Asherah can be a deity — as also in the Ras Shamra texts — but also a symbol of a deity, and perhaps of wood, sometimes at least seen beside a *massebah*, a pillar of stone. It has often been assumed, and probably rightly, that we have here symbols of a male and a female deity. Furthermore, the appearance of cow/calf imagery in the pictures suggests a comparison with the tradition of calves set up in the northern kingdom by Jeroboam I, interpreted in polemical manner as representations of a deity or deities; but bull symbolism is used of Yahweh, described as the *'abbîr*, strong one = bull.

Now my concern is not here with the detail of either of these pieces of evidence. The Elephantine material has been discussed many times and very fully, and though problems remain, the texts are understood clearly enough. The publication so far of Kuntillet 'Ajrud is popular and incomplete: a detailed study is much to be desired. But two points emerge: one is that in both cases there are indications, indirect or direct, that the deity Yahweh had a female consort; the other is that in both cases discussion of the texts has involved some endeavours at evading the clear meaning of the material, or at attributing it to a non-Judaean source, and thereby making a claim for the purity of the religious tradition which stems from there. The possibility of a male and female deity pair in the Old Testament period, except as an aberration, offends the susceptibilities of both some Jews and some Christians. It should not surprise us when we consider the wider religious background and the degree to which ideas and practices have changed over the centuries. The evidence of these texts points clearly to the existence in ancient Judah of such apparently aberrant beliefs and practices. The biblical evidence confirms this, but almost always in a polemical context; and it is this that we need now to examine.

II

The discussion of the biblical references to goddesses opens up a wide area involving the Near Eastern background and in particular the evidence of the Ras Shamra texts and of later material which points to the continuance of what are termed 'Canaanite' beliefs (Oden, 1979, who particularly stresses the cult of Asherah). I do not propose to enter into the details of this area; it is sufficient here to observe that the range of information, in texts and in representations, is now very substantial, so that comments on biblical references to the religion of the area may be set in context. We are no longer dependent on a merely polemical presentation of Canaanite religion; we can draw on the rich and complex evidence available, with the result that both greater clarity and a realisation of greater complexity is apparent.

So far as the biblical material is concerned, it is evident that of the three specific goddess names familiar from the Canaanite material — Asherah, Ashtoret, Anath — the first two appear, the third can be said to be attested but only indirectly. The title 'Queen of heaven' in Jeremiah 7 and 44 probably refers to one of these goddesses; we may observe that the question of identity is less important than the likely assumption that such a title is to be set alongside the title given to Yahweh as 'God of heaven' (e.g. Ezra 1.2) and the use for him of the title 'king', *melek* (e.g. I Sam. 12.12). The 'queen of heaven' may be assumed to be consort of the 'king of heaven', though this latter phrase does not appear in the biblical text.

Asherah appears commonly enough, either as a deity name or as a symbol of the deity, made of wood — so indicated by the reference to the offering of a sacrifice on the wood of the Asherah in Judg. 6.26, and in other references to burning and cutting down. The distinction between goddess and symbol is not always completely clear.

Ashtoreth appears, often alongside the masculine Ba'al and often in the plural, to denote the alien deities (so most clearly in Judg. 2.13) which Israel worshipped on forsaking Yahweh. The name appears also in place-names, and as a noun with 'flock of sheep' in the sense of 'sheep-breeding' or the like (Delcor, 1974).

Anath does not occur as the name of a goddess but it appears in proper names, both of places and people. Thus Anathoth is the home of Jeremiah (Jer. 1.1). One of the judges is called Shamgar ben Anath (Judg. 3.31 and 5.6): he is a problematic figure, since in the second passage he would be more readily understood as an oppressor, and his name Shamgar is usually thought to be non-Hebraic. The apparently plural form, Anathoth, also appears as a personal name (I Chron. 7.8; Neh. 10.19), and a man named Anthothiyah appears in I Chron. 8.24 with the same derivation: it seems at least possible that this latter name means 'Yahweh is my Anath' (the form would be plural, as in the place-name). This last provides a point of contact with an ingenious textual emendation, proposed though purely conjectural, to the obscure text of Hosea 14.9 (English 14.8). The text runs 'O Ephraim, what have I to do with idols? It is I who have answered (*'ānîtî*), I who have watched over him (*'ᵃšûrennû* or perhaps 'who have affirmed it' NEB). I am like an evergreen juniper/fir'. The sense is not at all clear. The emendation proposed: 'It is I who am his Anath (*'ᵃnātô*) and his Asherah (*'ašrātô*)', is very close to the received text. Such a proposal is attractive though purely hypothetical; but alongside the proper name Anthothiyah, and in the light of the strongly sexual imagery of the book of Hosea, the claim that Yahweh is himself the female consort, i.e. that he incorporates the female as well as the male aspects of deity (cf. de Boer, 1974, pp. 38-49; Trible, 1976), is appealing. To this we may add the contention, which seems probable, that the verbal root *'nh*, used frequently for example in Hos. 2, means 'to love' rather than 'to answer' (Deem, 1978), suggesting that the material here too may be making deliberate allusion to the goddess and to some process of rethinking the relationship between people and deity which incorporates the ideas which belong to the concept of god and consort.

A less precise attachment to this kind of thought — with some overlap of language — may be detected in the Song of Songs; the unresolved debates about both origin and interpretation make its evidence uncertain (for full recent discussion, see Pope, 1977). The 'Queen of heaven' in Jeremiah presents a further aspect of the thought, for here, in chapter 44, we may observe not only reference to worship being offered to her, with emphasis on the part played by women in this worship but with clear indication of the involvement of men as well, but see a skilful element of polemic in that we are presented with people who claim, reversing the normal statement, that it is neglect of the Queen of heaven which has brought disaster; the prophetic judgements of apostasy are turned upside down.

The biblical evidence in regard to goddesses is thus patchy and clearly incomplete; filling of the gaps is to some extent a matter of conjecture. To do this involves recognition of the nature of the evidence as polemical, directed towards stressing the undesirability of certain religious beliefs and practices. (It may be noted that later tradition, expressed in the actual form of the text, was concerned to suggest that the title 'queen' (*malkāh*) should be replaced by 'work', i.e. product of human activity (*m^eleket*). Cf. also the polemic in Isa. 44. against idols made by human craftsmanship.)

Thus we may observe that the Jeremiah material falls into two parts. In Jer. 7, a comment is offered on religious practice in Jerusalem, where members of the community engage in the worship of the 'Queen of heaven'. This is part of a homiletic section, extending through chapter 7 and into chapter 8, largely concerned with the condemnation of the whole people, the justification for the destruction of the Jerusalem temple, on the basis of long-standing apostasy and improper religious belief and practice. It is an example, in specific terms, of an explanation of the disaster to Judah in 587 BC as judgement, and reflects subsequent exposition of the message of Jeremiah in the light of that disaster. Like comparable comments on apostasy and the like in the books from Deuteronomy to Kings (the so-called Deuteronomic

History), it offers a rationale of the disaster, directed towards the rethinking necessary in the aftermath and with a view to the future. Jeremiah 44 offers a use of the same motif, but here with a slightly different aim: it portrays a refugee group in Egypt, which has been shown to go there contrary to the divine word mediated by Jeremiah, engaging in the same practices, with an upside-down theology to justify themselves. It is part of a reworking of Jeremiah material designed to demonstrate that the hope for the future cannot lie with such refugees in Egypt; that the future in Judah is already lost; that hope rests in Babylon alone, in the exiled Jews there. It is a demonstration eventually to be brought to its logical conclusion in the writings of the Chronicler some two centuries later in which the future can only be thought of in this way because Judah itself was left totally depopulated during the exile – a view which clearly lacks historical basis, but represents a significant theological pressure, and relates, as does the Jeremiah material, to the problems of the rehabilitation of the Judaean community under Persian rule. It must be doubtful how far this evidence can be used to reconstruct actual religious ideas and practice, and how far it represents projections into the Jeremiah material of a specific localising of religious failure understood as responsible for disaster.

In the main passages which deal with condemnation of the people – both Israel and Judah – in the period of the monarchy, Ashtoreth (or Ashtaroth in the plural) appears with reference to alien religious practice, either alongside reference to Ba'alim (e.g. I Sam. 7.4) or in explication of reference to other gods (so perhaps I Sam. 7.3; cf. Judg. 2.13, 10.6) or in reference to a shrine connected with non-Israelites at Beth-shan (I Sam. 31.10); or, in I Kings 11.5, in reference to the goddess of the Sidonians in a passage which deals with the many wives of Solomon, and includes also reference to the god of the Ammonites, named as Milcom (11.5), though this is probably a title, as is also Molech (11.7), and to the god Chemosh of the Moabites (11.7), known directly from the Moabite Stone (cf. *ANET*, 320).

Asherah appears in connection with an image made by Maacah, mother of king Asa of Judah (I Kings 15.13); with prophets of Asherah and of Baal in the Jezebel narrative, already noted (I Kings 18.19); with an image put in the Jerusalem temple by Manasseh (II Kings 21.7); and with the removal of the worship of the goddess under Josiah (II Kings 23.4, 7), in which some detail is given of the vessels and garments or shrines made by the women in the Jerusalem temple. II Kings 13.6 refers to the Asherah in Samaria in a comment on the continuing evil practices of the northern kingdom (see also below). In all these instances reference is to undesirable introduction or approved abolition of a cult of the goddess. From the viewpoint of the writers of the books of Kings, the practices of the north were all religiously wrong, so that the presence of the Asherah at Samaria is merely another example. The presence of such practices in Judah is attested by the reference to abolition, but here the Josiah reference belongs in the context of the picture of a reforming ruler, directly contrasted with his grandfather (and effective predecessor) Manasseh: it owes something at least to a patterning of the narratives in which good and bad kings alternate over the last century of Judah's existence. The Maacah reference is slightly out of step, but since the same name appears as non-Israelite in connection with Absalom, it is often inferred — though the chronology seems a little difficult — that we are dealing with same alien family, and that the Asherah was a foreign introduction. The prominence given to Jezebel as a foreign princess provides the clearest and fullest presentation of the theme that the worship of the goddess was a foreign import.

But is this true? If we take all the evidence, the worship of a goddess — with one or more names or titles — is clearly associated with a native king, Manasseh, and with Judaeans/Jerusalemites. If we add yet one more piece of evidence, this point is underlined. For one passage has so far been untouched, that in Judg. 6 which tells the first part of the story of Gideon. This relates how Gideon was both divinely designated as leader — a theme to be developed in the second part of the story — and commanded to pull down the altar of Baal and to cut down the Asherah, both to be found in the possession of Gideon's father. The status of Gideon's father is unclear, but since the altar and symbol of the god and goddess are evidently regarded highly by the people of the place (6.28), and Gideon is threatened with death for his sacrilegious action (6.30), it is hardly likely that this is a private shrine; and since the name of Gideon's father is Joash, in which the divine name Yahweh appears as the prefix, it is clear that he is to be regarded as a worshipper of Yahweh. The inference is that this altar and symbol were associated with Yahweh and a consort Asherah, the former being designated, as may be seen from other evidence, quite normally as Ba'al, lord.

A further pointer may be seen in the statement in II Kings 13.6, that Jehu, who is clearly described in II Kings 10 as having destroyed the temple of Baal and its worshippers, had evidently not removed the Asherah which stood at Samaria. 'The conclusion must be that Jehu and his time did not regard the *asherah* as being a "non-Israelite" phenomenon' (Ahlström, 1963, p. 51). The point is not absolutely secure, since the summary of the reign of Ahaziah to which 13.6 belongs cannot be regarded as providing certain evidence about Jehu, and in any case uses some of the conventional language condemnatory of all northern kings. But the singling out of this one item is noteworthy.

III

The interpretation of the evidence as normally offered runs along two lines (for other and wider aspects of the discussion, see Smith, 1971, esp. chs. 2 and 4). First, it is maintained that the worship of a goddess within the Israelite/Judaean communities is due to foreign influence. Even Patai, whose study *The Hebrew Goddess* (1967) contains a mixture of useful information, simplistic account and unproved assumption — often entertaining, but not always reliable — manages to maintain, from comparison with evidence of identifications of deities, that 'Asherah, Astarte and Anath . . . arrived, at different times no doubt, among the Hebrews, and, although foreign in origin, they soon adopted the Hebrews as their children . . .' (p. 26). So the alien goddess, as he goes on to say, became a Hebrew goddess, fully adopted into the religious life of the people. But she is defined as alien in origin. In this line of interpretation, Jezebel becomes a type; into her figure is projected in detail the hostility to what is believed to be alien practice. Significantly, she becomes the embodiment not only of what is alien to Hebrew religion, but also of what is alien to Hebrew law. The Naboth story, it is often argued, shows that kings outside Israel did not have the understanding that Israelite kings did, namely that the king was as much subject to the law as the ordinary member of the community. The fact that kings are shown as promulgators and upholders of law throughout the ancient Near East makes it doubtful if such a view can be maintained. It is more natural to suppose that kings, in Israel as elsewhere, were not always prepared to accept the dictates of the law which they claimed to uphold. Numerous examples appear in the biblical narratives of kings castigated for wrong social behaviour, as well as wrong religious behaviour. Jezebel is depicted as the stronger character; but Ahab accepts responsibility for the infringement of law, escaping the judgement by his penitent attitude (I Kings 21.27-9). We may very properly ask how far the whole portrayal of Jezebel is part of a stylised piece of polemic designed to demonstrate that such religious practices as are here indicated do not belong in Israel; that they are alien. This is not genuine religious history: it is arguing against what, on other grounds, has become unacceptable. The archaeological evidence, particularly that of Kuntillet 'Ajrud, especially if it is to be assigned to an early date, shows the presence of the concept of Yahweh and his Asherah as consort over a very long period of time. We may see, both in Hosea and in the Deuteronomic History, indications of the polemic against such a concept of deity. I suspect that the Gideon story is part of that polemic; it is unlike any other of the judge presentations, and in fact appears to argue both the case against the female consort and subsequently the case against kingship (so Judg. 8 and its sequel in Judg. 9).

The second line of interpretation is to argue that it was on entry into Canaan that Israel, with its Yahwistic faith from the wilderness period, encountered for the first time a religious culture in which male and female divinities existed side by side. In fact such an encounter is, in Numbers 25, projected into the wilderness period itself, before the actual entry: no detail is given, but the implications of sexual practice suggest the presence of male and female deities. This interpretation is itself part of a much wider concept, in which the contrast drawn between Israelite religion and Canaanite is sharpened. There are two problems about such a line of thought, though it must be recognised that the biblical material has so conditioned its readers to the acceptance of this line, that it is not easy to see how to break away from it. One is that it is recognisably on a par with other aspects of idealisation of the past which can be found in other religious traditions. In the biblical material, the ideal past is projected into the patriarchal period in Genesis, or into the wilderness period as a bridal period; it is also projected into the earliest stages of the primeval story. It has a further effect in the picture of the period of David, and more especially of Solomon, as an ideal one, in spite of much evidence to the contrary. In the formation of such idealisms, the actual facts, if they are discernible, do not do much to undermine the view. The idealisation of David, for example, is amply countered by the narratives of II Samuel, but this has not prevented a picture emerging at variance with that evidence.

The other problem centres on the extreme difficulty of defining the Israel of the pre-settlement period, and of knowing where the wilderness and exodus traditions are to be placed in relation to the subsequent development of the community. The problems of the so-called settlement period are so difficult to resolve that while it would be oversimple to move to the kind of portrayal which pictures Israel as arising out of internal movements within Palestine, it is equally oversimple to speak in terms of a radically different group coming from outside (for a recent assessment, see Ramsey, 1981). Some element of reinforcement for such simple idealism has come from the assumption – found for example in T.E. Lawrence – that the nomad Arabs of the desert represent a cleaner and more invigorating atmosphere, congenial to particular types of religious development: a view which is as romantic as that which supposes that Hebrew is by its very nature a language peculiarly adapted to religious thought.

These wider issues are not susceptible to easy resolution. They are an expression of an anxiety which I feel about the ease with which biblical scholars and adherents of the religious traditions which stem from the biblical materials emphasise the distinctiveness of those materials in contrast with a partly imagined outside world, while increasingly the relationship between the biblical and non-biblical has come to be clear. The differences – and these are still to be explained – lie in the fact that the biblical material itself is not simply the product of the context in which it originated, but is the result of the long process of interaction between tradition and the thought of the community, in the course of which many changes took place. It is somewhere within that interaction that the undesirability came to be accepted, generally if not universally, that an adequate concept of God demands uniqueness and onliness.

IV

I am well aware that I have said something about Jezebel and something about goddesses, but not much about women. But in part this has been implied by what amounts not to a defence of Jezebel but to an attempt to understand the projection into her figure of antagonism to the worship of a goddess as consort to Israel's god. It is possible here to wonder whether one of the details of that vivid description of the last scene of her life means more than is at first sight clear: when she paints her eyes and dresses her hair and looks down from the window, she appears rather like the portrayal of the 'woman at the window', a familiar symbol of ancient Near Eastern art, and held to represent the goddess as sacred prostitute (*ANEP*, 131). It is almost as if she is being presented, and rejected, as the goddess herself. The projection of antagonisms into female figures is to be found not only here but also in the opening chapters of Genesis and in the portrayal of 'dame folly', the seductress, in the opening chapters of the book of Proverbs (e.g. Prov. 5; 7). But if that one-sided picture has sometimes seemed to dominate, we may recall that the biblical material portrays a 'dame wisdom' also in Proverbs (e.g. Prov. 1.20ff.; 8), as well as an ideal woman in the final chapter of the book (31.10-31); it portrays heroines of war like Deborah in Judg. 4-5 and Judith in the book of that name, and of loyalty like Esther, and prophetesses like Huldah (II Kings 22); and equivocal characters like Bathsheba, the adulterous wife of Uriah the Hittite who was also the mother of the ideal king Solomon. And perhaps it is not altogether amiss to recall that the genealogy of Jesus in Matthew I has room within it for the heroic but ambivalent Tamar of Genesis 38, of Rahab the harlot the mother of Boaz the ancestor of David by Ruth (Ruth 4.17, 18-22), as well as that 'wife of Uriah', here so described rather than named.

Further Reading

Ahlström, G.W. (1963), *Aspects of Syncretism in Israelite Religion*, Horae
    Soederblomianae, 5. Gleerup, Lund
De Boer, P.A.H. (1974), *Fatherhood and Motherhood in Israelite and Judaean
    Piety*, Leiden
Cowley, A. (1923), *Aramaic Papyri of the Fifth Century B.C.*, Oxford
Porten, B. (1968), *Archives from Elephantine. The Life of an Ancient Jewish
    Military Colony*, Berkeley and Los Angeles
Smith, Morton (1971), *Palestinian Parties and Politics that shaped the Old
    Testament*, New York and London
Trible, P. (1976), 'God, Nature of, in the Old Testament', *Interpreter's
    Dictionary of the Bible*, Abingdon, Nashville and New York, Supplement,
    pp. 368f.

16 THE NADĪTU WOMEN OF SIPPAR

Ulla Jeyes, London and Copenhagen

Introduction

The *nadītu*s were a very special group or institution of women, dedicated to the sun god Šamaš, who lived in the city of Sippar in northern Babylonia. They were housed within a walled area, the *gagûm* ('the Locked House') in the temple of Šamaš. *Nadītu* possibly means the 'fallow' or 'barren' one. This institution is peculiar to the Old Babylonian period and is recorded from *c*. 1880-1550 BC. It had special links with the rulers of the 1st Babylonian dynasty and its heyday was under Hammurapi and his son Samsuiluna, i.e. 1792-1712 BC.

The City of Sippar

Sippar had come under the supremacy of Babylon, which is only about 70 km to the south, from the onset of the 1st Babylonian dynasty in the early nineteenth century BC (Harris, 1975, pp. 1ff.). However, during the reign of Sumulael of Babylon (1880-1845 BC) there are records of three local rulers. In the 29th year of Sumulael the wall of Sippar was built, or possibly rebuilt, and to the end of the 1st Babylonian dynasty the kings of Babylon maintained the defences of Sippar and the cult of Šamaš. Under Hammurapi (Harris, 1975, pp. 86ff, 146-7) the cult of Marduk, the city god of Babylon, was introduced to Sippar and military garrisons were stationed there. The temple administration and the judicial system came under royal supervision and the number of central government bureaucrats and tax collectors were increased (Harris, 1975, pp. 40ff; 1968, pp. 727ff.). The walled Sippar consisted of Sippar proper and two satellite towns which originally had been nomadic settlements. Its population has been estimated to be about 5000 (Scheil, 1902, p. 23). Land was owned mainly by the temple and by a few wealthy families, a general pattern in the Old Babylonian period. Sippar was an important city of trade (Harris, 1975, pp. 257ff.) and from the reign of Samsuiluna the local government was headed by a 'Harbour' (*kārum*) and 'the Overseer of Merchants' instead of, as formerly, by a 'Council of Elders' chaired by a lord mayor.

The Sources

The source material from Sippar amounts to more than 500 texts, mostly published in cuneiform copies only and a large number of unpublished texts (Harris, 1969, p. 133). The published documents deal almost exclusively with the economic affairs of the *naditu*s: sale, lease, loan, inheritance, adoption and lawsuits in connection with the latter two. Furthermore, letters found in Sippar and elsewhere and 12 paragraphs of the famous law code of Hammurapi add to the material (Driver and Miles, 1955, § §40, 110, 137, 144-7, 178-182).

However, this substantial material does not render itself to a balanced study of the *naditu* women in general and their role in society in particular. The archaeological history of Sippar will illustrate this point: in 1880 Hormuzd Rassam (Rassam, 1897, pp. 397ff.) began searching for the mound of the biblical Sepharvaim as he had been told that it contained a golden model of Noah's Ark. With his usual good luck he was able to identify the mound of Abu Habba with ancient Sippar in 1881. He had happened upon the temple compound of Šamaš itself and he remarked that this compound which he reckoned to be 3500 sq. yards was 'divided into two distinct buildings, one for religious purposes and the other for the habitation of priests and royalty', and that 'each block of buildings was surrounded by a breastwork'. These two building complexes were to be identified with the temple É.BABBAR ('the White House') for Šamaš and his consort Aja and the adjacent living quarters of the *naditu* women, the *gagûm*, which will be referred to as 'the cloister'. Rassam also found a great number of tablets and in fact he published a plan of what he called 'the palace and temple' (Rassam, 1897, p. 407). In his absence the site became the object of many clandestine diggings, Baghdad being only about 30 km away. Thus a large number of tablets ended up on the market in Baghdad and some were bought by the Englishman E. Wallis Budge in the 1890s. In 1894 the Frenchman V. Scheil excavated in Sippar, concentrating his efforts like Rassam on the temple area. Since 1978 the site has been under excavation by a team from the University of Baghdad.

Thus the discoveries from these excavations have practically all been made in the temple area and in the houses of the *naditu* women in particular, but due to the unscientific character of the excavations only the house of one *naditu* has been identified (Scheil, 1902, p. 25; Harris, 1962, pp. 10-11).

The drawbacks and limitations of the textual material can thus be summarised as follows: Firstly, the *naditu*s are seen to play a disproportionately large role in the community, e.g. in about 70 per cent (Stone, 1982, p. 50) of all contracts from Sippar at least one party is a *naditu*. That a group of 100-200 women should dominate business life to that extent in a city with a population of over 5000 is unlikely and indeed the material from the city of Nippur (Stone, 1982, p. 51), which also had a *naditu* institution, provides a much more balanced picture. Secondly, because the texts have nearly all come from the houses of the *naditu*s the documents are of a kind which their owners would find it in their interest to keep safe: proofs of purchases, owed interests in barley or silver or successful court cases. Thus the *naditu*s might well appear more active and successful in their business life than is necessarily the case. Thirdly, the textual material might also give a distorted picture overstressing their business activities at the expense of their religious duties.

Status and Tradition of the Cloister

With these reservations in mind it can still be maintained that the *naditu* institution in Sippar was one of wealth and status. It was instituted for Šamaš who together with Marduk held the highest-ranking positions in the Old Babylonian pantheon and whose cult centre in Sippar was one of major importance. The institution also received royal patronage which is best illustrated by the fact that three princesses (Harris, 1964, p. 123; 1969, p. 140) became *naditu*s of Šamaš: Ajalatum, daughter of Sumulael, a daughter of Sin-muballit, Hammurapi's sister Iltani and another Iltani, daughter of either Samsuiluna or Abi-ešuh (1711-1684 BC). In the year formulae of Hammurapi the 4th year is called 'the wall of the *gagûm* was built'. Later in his reign Hammurapi reinforced that wall (Harris, 1963, p. 122).

The earliest record of the cloister can be traced back to Immerum (Harris, 1975, p. 10), one of the three local rulers of Sippar in the early nineteenth century BC. According to the so-called cruciform monument of Maništušu (Sollberger, 1967-8, pp. 50ff.), the third ruler of the dynasty of Akkad who reigned in the 23rd century BC, this king claims to have built the *gagûm* for Šamaš and Aja. Under Nabonidus (555-539 BC) the *naditu* institution in Sippar was revived and possibly this document, a contemporary forgery, was fabricated during his reign to endow the cloister with a tradition.

The Background of the Naditu Women

*Naditu*s were dedicated to male deities other than Šamaš in Sippar, e.g.
to Marduk in Babylon and to Ninurta in Nippur (Renger, 1967, pp.
175ff.), but possibly only those in Sippar lived in a cloister since all
but few references to a *gagûm* (*CAD*, G, 10-11) in the Old Babylonian
period are made to the one in Sippar. However, there is evidence that
the Šamaš *naditu*s were the highest in rank (Harris, 1975, pp. 315-16)
and they were certainly recruited from the wealthiest of families, not
just in Sippar but also from other cities in Babylonia (Renger, 1967,
pp. 150ff.). Foreigners who had settled in the Sippar area are also
reported to have sent their daughters to the cloister (Harris, 1976b,
pp. 150-1).

It was probably decided at the birth of the oldest daughter within
such a wealthy and influential family that she should be dedicated to
Šamaš or, as the expression goes, be 'raised to the god' (Renger, 1967,
p. 153). This decision was reflected in the name (Harris, 1964, pp.
126ff.; 1972, pp. 102ff.) given to the girl. Some but not all *naditu*s in
Sippar carried names which have not been found elsewhere, e.g. Amat-
Šamaš ('the servant girl of Šamaš') or Erišti-Aja ('Aja's desire'). There is
no evidence that there was a change of name at the initiation of the girl
into the cloister. Sometimes girls were referred to as *naditu*s of Šamaš
years before their initiation (Harris, 1964, p. 114), an indication that a
girl was intended for *naditu*-ship at birth or at least an early age.

The Initiation of a Naditu

It is not altogether certain at which age the girl took part in her initiation ceremony or whether that event always coincided in time with her
leaving her father's house and moving into the cloister. But as the initiation in some respects was comparable to a marriage settlement it seems
reasonable to assume that a girl became an initiated *naditu* when she
reached the nubile age of about 15. Shortage of accommodation
(Harris, 1963, pp. 124ff.; 1975, pp. 24-5) within the cloister might be
the simple explanation why some *naditu*s did not move into the cloister
immediately after their initiation. The living space within the walls of
the cloister did not expand with the increased prestige of the institution
under Hammurapi and his successor and living conditions for some of
the *naditu*s do appear to have been rather cramped. The houses within
the cloister were expensive and some *naditu*s only rented a house or a

part of a house. The wealthy *nadītu*s on the other hand could own more than one house. The suggestion of a noviceship which has been put forward by R. Harris (Harris, 1962, pp. 3-4; 1964, p. 114) seems less likely.

The initiation ceremony (Harris, 1964, pp. 112ff.) took place once a year during the first three days of the tenth month of the year, Tebet (December-January). There is sparse evidence as to what happened then but on the first and third day offerings were given to Šamaš and Aja. The second day was dedicated as a memorial day to the deceased *nadītu*s and this festival was evidently concluded with a banquet. As regards the new *nadītu*s themselves there is evidence that during the festival somebody put 'the thread of Šamaš' on their hands, symbolising, one would imagine, their future affiliation with Šamaš. One letter (Harris, 1964, p. 118) from a *nadītu* refers to when she first entered the cloister and saw the face of her lady, an indication that the new *nadītu* was led into the presence of the goddess Aja. When the younger Iltani, the princess, was initiated she was 'sprinkled' and an extispicy was performed (Goetze, 1948, p. 104). The Old Babylonian omen literature (*CAD*, E, 172-3) confirms that divine consent was sought for the consecration of a high-ranking priest or priestess. For the *nadītu*s, however, there is no evidence that an extispicy was performed at every single initiation and it is possible that this ritual was reserved for the exalted figure of a princess.

Economic transactions comparable to those of a marriage settlement were carried out between the head of the *nadītu*'s family and the cloister. First of all the girl received a dowry. Lists of items (Dalley, 1980, pp. 53ff.) which made up such a dowry give clear evidence that the *nadītu*s were recruited from very wealthy families. One list mentions, e.g., 9 slave-girls, 24 garments, 42 headdresses and even a shroud. *Nadītu*-ship obviously was for life. Other items on those lists are jewellery, furniture, crockery, weaving equipment, cows and sheep. Another part of the dowry was a share of the paternal estate. The paragraphs 178-180 of the Laws of Hammurapi which have been shown to merely sanction already common practice (Harris, 1961b, pp. 164ff.) give three options for the administration of that share:

1) The brothers of the *nadītu* could manage her share for her, in which case they were obliged for the rest of her life to supply her with food and clothing. If they failed in their obligations she had a right to choose a new manager for her share.

2) The *nadītu* could manage her share herself and in this case, unlike in 1), she could bequeath in her will this share to 'whomever she likes', if

her father had stated so in writing at the dowry settlement. The brothers would not be able to raise any claim.

3) In the case where the *nadītu* received no share in the paternal estate she would share equally with her brothers at the death of the father. In this case a *nadītu* of the cloister is clearly favoured in the Laws of Hammurapi in comparison with a *nadītu* of Marduk who would get a share amounting to only a third of her brother's.

The *nadītu* of Šamaš is also favoured in comparison with a woman given away in marriage who could never administrate her share of the paternal estate herself and after her death it had to go to her sons or, if there were none, back to her father's family (Driver and Miles, 1952, pp. 344ff.; 1955, pp. 62-3). Furthermore, unlike the woman given in marriage, the *nadītu* at her initiation got 'ring money' (Renger, 1967, p. 161) over which she had full rights to make her own arrangements. This sum could amount to as much as ten minas of silver.

The cloister also incurred expenses at the initiation. It paid out a 'betrothal gift' (*biblum*). According to a text (Harris, 1964, pp. 111-12) which lists the items of food, drink and silver which made up this betrothal gift the brother of the *nadītu* got one šeqel of silver and a vessel of grain only and the rest seems to have gone towards paying the expenses in connection with the initiation ceremony. Another text (Harris, 1964, pp. 114-15) lists items of food, drink and silver given as a 'bridal gift' (*terhatum*) by the cloister on the day the thread of Šamaš was placed on the hand of the new *nadītu*. Apparently, in this case too the items stayed in the cloister and were not, as a bridal gift usually is, given to the girl's father. Generally it appears that an attempt was made in the chosen terminology to draw parallels between the initiation of a *nadītu* and a marriage settlement, although the actual financial transactions carried out in these two cases were not identical.

The Nadītu's Relationship to Šamaš and Aja

Both the goddess Aja and the initiated *nadītu* were called the *kallatum* (*CAD*, K, 79ff.) of Šamaš. This term is the designation for a young girl who goes to live and be provided for in her father-in-law's house some years before the consummation of her marriage to the son of the house. Therefore *kallatum* can mean 'daughter-in-law', 'sister-in-law', 'betrothed', 'bride' or 'bride-to-be' depending on the context in which this term occurs. Virginity (Finkelstein, 1970, p. 246) is implied in all cases and if a *kallatum* did not stay chaste her betrothal could be called off by her father-in-law.

The very title, *nadītu*, may reflect a lifelong virginity, *nadītu* having the meanings of 'fallow', 'unsown' or 'barren' (*CAD*, N, pp. 63ff.). *Kallatum*, when applied to the *nadītu*, I would prefer to translate as 'betrothed' and not as 'daughter-in-law' of Šamaš, as maintained by R. Harris (1975, p. 308), because this latter interpretation would imply that the *nadītu* was intended for a non-existent son of Šamaš.

But as Šamaš has a father, the moon god Sin, it is possible to understand Aja as both the daughter-in-law of Sin and the 'bride or fiancée' of Šamaš as suggested by R. Harris (1975, p. 315). Aja and the *nadītu* were in the same position in their relationship to Šamaš and there is evidence that the latter looked up to Aja almost as an older sister, referring to her as 'my goddess' (Harris, 1964, p. 120) and giving her special presents (Schorr, 1913, pp. 47-8) apart from the obligatory offerings.

The *nadītu* was in a different position to her god from the priestesses, who in the course of their religious duties had sexual relations. To that group belonged the *entum* ('high priestess') and the *ugbabtum*. The *entum* was the higher-ranking one and there is evidence (*CAD*, E, 172-3) that the *ugbabtum* could aspire to become an *entum*. Both words can be written with the Sumerogram NIN.DINGIR and in this case it is not always entirely clear which one is meant. In the relationship to their god both were comparable to a man's wife as is indicated in paragraph 127 (Driver and Miles, 1952, pp. 275-7; 1955, pp. 50-51) of the Laws of Hammurapi. According to this paragraph a man stands to suffer severe punishment if he spreads false slanderous rumours about either a NIN.DINGIR or a man's wife. In a passage from the Old Babylonian account of the Flood it is said about the *entum* and the *ugbabtum* that (sexual relations with men) are taboo and they must not bear children (Finkelstein, 1970, p. 246). Unfavourable apodoses from the omen literature refer to the NIN.DINGIR conceiving, having unorthodox sexual relations in order not to conceive or dying from venereal disease (*CAD*, G, 10; E, 172-3, 325).

This evidence shows that it was considered a sacrilegious offence and a perfect scandal if an *entum* or *ugbabtum* did not stay chaste and as with an adulterous wife they could undoubtedly expect the death penalty. There is no evidence of a *nadītu* fulfilling the role of either an *entum* or an *ugbabtum* and the repercussions for the *nadītu* who did not stay chaste might have been less severe. Paragraphs 155-156 of the Laws of Hammurapi (Driver and Miles, 1952, pp. 318ff.; 1955, pp. 60-61) may be relevant to this argument. They state that a man stands to receive the death penalty if he sleeps with his son's *kallatum* after the son has slept with her but if the man sleeps with her before he shall merely pay in compensation an amount equal to the bridal gift and the betrothal is broken off.

Although the chaste state of the *nadītu*s is not disputed in so far as they did not generally have children there are two cases (Finkelstein, 1976, pp. 187ff.), both dating from the reign of Hammurapi, in which a *nadītu* of Šamaš is in possession of a newborn infant and arranges for it to be nursed. Since there is no mention of anybody else who could figure as the natural mother of those infants it is difficult to conclude otherwise than that they were born by *nadītu* women. It is noteworthy that the *nadītu*s in question kept their titles and in witnessed documents brought their childbearing out in the open. There is no evidence of any punishment or even social disgrace.

There is just one mention of an *entum* (Harris, 1975, pp. 312-13) of Sin in Sippar but there is no evidence of her having any connection with the cloister. *Ugbabtu* priestesses (Harris, 1975, pp. 314-15), on the other hand, are recorded to have lived in the cloister and in paragraph 110 of the Laws of Hammurapi (Driver and Miles, 1952, pp. 205ff.; 1955, pp. 44-5) the death penalty by burning is prescribed for a '*nadītu* or an *ugbabtum* who does not live within the cloister' if she 'opens a tavern from inside or enters a tavern' and, by implication, becomes involved in prostitution which was associated with such a place. Apparently, it was not thought to impair the respectability of a *nadītu* if she owned a tavern or a part of a tavern as this is recorded on two documents (Scheil, 1902, pp. 98-102, 119-120; Harris, 1975, pp. 20-21), one of which is dated to the reign of Hammurapi's father, Sin-muballit.

However we interpret the relationship between the *nadītu* and her god it remains a paradox to us that she could marry so long as she did not have children. It is generally maintained though that the *nadītu*s of Šamaš, in contrast to those of Marduk, were not allowed to marry and it is also assumed that when the Laws of Hammurapi refer to *nadītu*s marrying, those from the cloister in Sippar were excluded (Harris, 1964, p. 108; 1975, pp. 315-16). When a *nadītu* married she could, according to the Laws of Hammurapi, acquire for her husband a second wife whose role as childbearer to her husband and servant to the *nadītu* is stated in one marriage contract (Schorr, 1913, pp. 10-12). Apparently, the second wife was often recruited from the lowest rank within the cloister and temple hierarchy, being a so-called 'lay sister'. Hammurapi's Laws (Driver and Miles, 1952, pp. 290ff.; 1955, pp. 56-7) state that under no circumstances should she consider herself equal to the *naditu*. Married *naditu*s of Marduk are reported to have lived in Sippar (Renger, 1967, pp. 174-5). We must conclude that as long as the marriage of a *naditu* represented a mere social and economic arrangement it was not seen as interfering with her relationship to her god.

The Religious Duties of a Naditu

There are a few scattered references which give a picture of the *naditu* in constant attendance to Šamaš and Aja in their temple adjacent to the cloister. There is mention of twice daily offerings (Harris, 1964, p. 121) and of a special offering, *the piqittum* (Harris, 1963, pp. 149-50; 1964, pp. 128-30) ('the delivery') which consisted of oblates, cuts of meat and beer. If a *naditu* for various reasons did not manage her estate herself it was the duty of the executor to supply this offering which possibly was brought on the 20th of each month, the number 20 being sacred to Šamaš. Apart from this monthly festival and the aforementioned one when the new *naditu*s were initiated about six other festivals (Harris, 1975, pp. 199ff.) of which very little is known took place. It is possible that the *naditu*s went to the temple in a procession for at least some of those festivals and took part in banquets.

The Organisation of the Cloister

The cloister was to a large extent an autonomous and self-contained body. The world outside its walls was simply referred to as 'the outside' (Harris, 1964, p. 131). The cloister was also inhabited by some members of the administrative staff which, except in the earliest period of the history of the cloister, was male (Harris, 1964, p. 132; Renger, 1967, pp. 157-8). From the reign of Sumulael onwards this staff (Harris, 1963, pp. 131ff.) at any one time was headed by a maximum of three *waklū* ('stewards') and a maximum of four *atû* ('gate keepers'). A 'judge of the cloister' is recorded as well but it is uncertain whether he was permanently appointed or just brought in to judge the internal affairs of the cloister. Some administrators had inherited their offices and their daughters often became *naditu*s. The administrative centre of the cloister was the 'house of the *gagûm*' (Harris, 1963, pp. 128-9). Apart from a contemporary lexical text which mentions a 'mother of the *naditu*s' (Harris, 1963, pp. 141-2) there is no evidence of a mother supreme within the cloister. Eight *naditu*s were scribes (Harris, 1963, pp. 138-9), albeit not very productive as such. Apparently only one was in action at a time. The cloister had a granary (Harris, 1963, pp. 129-130) and employed a female domestic staff of weavers, millers and cooks (Harris, 1963, pp. 142ff.). Generally there is not much evidence of communal activities but the 'house of the *gagûm*' (Harris, 1963, p. 154) served as a communal store for safekeeping. Possibly the *naditu*s paid an annual revenue in barley to the cloister and a 'tax for the gate' as well (Harris, 1963, p. 155). These might have been collected by the aforementioned gatekeepers.

The Cloister and the Temple

Officials from the temple are known to have entered the cloister when acting as witnesses to the business transactions of the *naditu*s. These were conducted at the gate of the cloister (*CAD*, G. 10; Harris, 1963, pp. 155-6; 1964, pp. 130-1). Lawsuits of the *naditu*s were held in the temple in the presence of the divine symbols of Šamaš and witnessed by temple officials.

The temple was a rich and important institution in its own right. It owned vast estates and during the reign of Sin-muballit it employed 850 workers (Harris, 1968, p. 729). It played an important social role as well, lending money to the poor (Harris, 1960, pp. 126ff.). However, the sources give no information about the economic relationship between cloister and temple.

The cloister as a whole was under the authority of the temple. The highest-ranking temple official, the *šangûm* (Harris, 1961a, pp. 117ff.; 1975, pp. 154ff.) was above the *waklû* of the cloister in rank. The temple and cloister became the objects of Hammurapi's efforts towards centralisation (Harris, 1961a, pp. 118ff.; 1968, pp. 727ff.). From his reign onwards the temple officials were entitled 'servant of RN' and not, as formerly, 'servant of É.BABBAR'. Judges became 'judges of Sippar' instead of 'judges of É.BABBAR'. The *naditu*s were not exempt from paying a royal tax (Harris, 1963, p. 154; 1968, p. 729).

Social Conditions Within the Cloister

Between 100 and 200 *naditu*s (Renger, 1967, p. 168) lived within the cloister at the same time. The kinship links (Harris, 1962, pp. 1ff.; 1964, pp. 125-6; 1969, pp. 133ff.) which have been traced amongst them are those of sisters, paternal aunts and nieces or, in a few cases, great nieces. Thus it was a family tradition to send the oldest daughter to the cloister. In some cases *naditus* were related to lower ranking priestesses who also resided within the cloister (Renger, 1967, p. 152).

As the *naditu* did not have children herself she was allowed to make provisions for her old age by adopting (Harris, 1962, pp. 1ff.; 1964, p. 122; 1969, pp. 133ff.; 1976b, pp. 150-51) one or more younger *naditus* with whom she often but not always was related. The adoptee should according to the adoption document provide for her adoptive mother as long as she lived, treat her respectfully and fulfil the obligation of the aforementioned *piqittum*-offering for her. In return the adoptee could expect an inheritance such as a house within the cloister but if she failed to live up to her obligations the adoption document could be invalidated. There were other reasons for an adoption: an old and, one must assume, destitute *naditu* adopts, in one case, a younger one to pay off her debt (Harris, 1976a, pp. 131-2). In another case a *naditu* adopts a slave-girl and her infant and decides that her adoptee should be set free after her death (Schorr, 1913, pp. 53-5). In return for this act of charity the slave-girl should look after the *naditu* for the rest of her life. Thus the adoption procedures served as a kind of social security within the cloister.

There is no proof that the *naditus* were banned from leaving the cloister but because of their religious duties it is unlikely that they absented themselves for longer periods or left the city of Sippar. They did evidently visit or receive visits from their relations.

Not surprisingly the life expectancy of a *naditu* was very good (Renger, 1967, pp. 166-8). The younger Iltanti, the princess, was a *naditu* for a record period of over 60 years. When a *naditu* eventually died it could be expressed by the following euphemistic phrase: 'After her gods have invited her (to a feast)' (Harris, 1964, p. 120). At least some *naditus* were buried in the graveyard of the temple which was discovered by Scheil (Scheil, 1902, pp. 21-9).

The Business Enterprises of the Naditus

The *naditus* acted as private individuals in their business transactions, never as representatives for the cloister or the temple and, unlike the temple loans, there does not seem to have been any element of charity in the lending business of the *naditus*. There is no doubt that some did very well with their initial assets, their dowry and 'ring money' and they increased their property of land, houses, slaves and silver (Renger, 1967, pp. 161ff.). Their business transactions involved silver and barley lending and lease of fields, orchards, houses, barns, shops, slaves and oxen (Harris, 1962, pp. 1ff.). During the reign of Hammurapi the owner's share of the yield of a field became fixed at one third (Harris, 1968, p. 728). One *naditu* did trade in tin (Harris, 1976b, p. 150) but any travelling was undertaken by a male employee. A sailor working for the cloister is also recorded (Harris, 1963, pp. 146-7). The *naditus* were occupied by spinning and weaving (Harris, 1964, p. 132) as well but that does not seem to amount to much more than occupational therapy. The wealthiest of them all appears to have been the younger Iltani (Harris, 1962, pp. 6-8), the princess, whose large estate was run by an estate manager. Another *naditu* is recorded to have employed 117 workers (Harris, 1964, p. 133). There is some evidence that the *naditus* co-operated in their business life inasmuch as they tended to own and buy up land next to each other (Harris, 1962, p. 8; 1963, p. 153; 1975, pp. 214ff.). A field could also be jointly owned by two *naditus* and probably joint arrangements were made for such things as transport of produce.

The Naditu and her Family

In her own family the *naditu* often seems to have played the role of the aunt from whom her relations had expectations. Her next of kin and heirs (Harris, 1962, pp. 1ff.; 1976a, pp. 129ff.) were her father, brothers, paternal uncles, nephews and cousins. In most cases, though, her brothers and nephews, both of whom were called *ahhū* ('brothers'), would inherit from her either equally between them or, if there was a stipulation in her will, a favourite brother or nephew could be her sole heir. If there was an adoptee she would according to the adoption document be an heir as well. The property which the *naditu* received in her dowry should, unless stipulated otherwise, go back to her kinsmen after her death and it was likely to do so after it had been increased due to often successful business transactions of the *naditu*. Sometimes she had conveniently bought up land adjacent to the paternal estate (Harris, 1962, pp. 2, 9-10).

However, a *naditu* was allowed to bequeath in her will property which she had earned herself to an adoptee to whom she was not related (Harris, 1969, pp. 138ff.). This gave rise to some bitterly contested court cases (Harris, 1963, p. 125; 1969, pp. 138ff.) and in one case (Schorr, 1913, pp. 359-61) the unrelated adoptive daughter was accused by the heirs of a deceased *naditu* of having fabricated a will according to which she would inherit a house within the cloister.

The Naditus and their Community

There are very few references about the attitude of society towards the *naditu*s but it appears that they were looked upon as a group and not always without resentment. Letters testify to *naditu*s being beaten up by men with whom they had had business dealings (*CAD*, N, 63-4; Renger, 1967, pp. 158-9).

The reasons (Harris, 1976a, p. 132; Stone, 1982, pp. 50ff.) behind establishing an institution like the cloister in Sippar are religious as well as social. Undoubtedly it was regarded as an act of worship by a well-established family to consecrate a female member to an important cult centre like the Šamaš temple in Sippar. Thereby the family ensured a close link with the deity and his consort to whom the *naditu* would pray and give offerings on behalf of living as well as dead family members. In a community where the privately owned estates were in danger of being split up into increasingly smaller strips of land because each son received an equal share it was beneficial for a family to provide for a daughter in a way so that her share returned to the paternal estate.

For the community as a whole the cloister institution was a measure against overpopulation. For the *naditu*s themselves the cloister provided status, mutual support, social security and, exceptional for the society in which they lived, a measure of financial and therefore also personal freedom.

17 THE ROLE OF JEWISH WOMEN IN THE RELIGION, RITUAL AND CULT OF GRAECO-ROMAN PALESTINE

Léonie J. Archer, Oxford

In the first century AD, the historian Josephus wrote:

> There is endless variety in the details of the customs and laws which prevail in the world at large ... some people have entrusted the supreme political power to monarchies, others to oligarchies, yet others to the masses. Our lawgiver, however, [that is, Moses] was attracted by none of these forms of policy, but gave to his constitution the form of what may be termed a 'theocracy'. ... He did not make religion a department of virtue but the various virtues ... departments of religion.

Thus, Josephus declared, 'Religion governs all our actions and occupations and speech; none of these things did our lawgiver leave unexamined or indeterminate.' The historian concluded his description of the all-embracing character of Jewish religious law in the life of Hellenistic Palestine with the statement: '... even our womenfolk and dependants would tell you that piety must be the motive for all our occupations' (*Con. Ap*. II:164f.). The aim of this paper is to examine the extent to which women were permitted to give public expression, through participation in the nation's religion, ritual and cult, to the piety which governed their lives. In order to gain the fullest appreciation of their role in the religion of Hellenistic Palestine (*c*. 300 BC-*c*. AD 200), however, we must first pause and briefly trace the history of their involvement in the centuries which preceded the period under consideration.

From the earlier strands of the Old Testament, it is apparent that women in the pre-exilic period of Hebrew history (i.e., before 587 BC) enjoyed a certain active involvement in the nation's religious affairs. In the biblical narratives they appear together with men at public assemblies and expositions of the Law (see, e.g., *Ex*. 35:1f.; *Deut*. 29.9f., 31:12-13), participate fully in the annual cycle of festivals (e.g., I *Sam*. 2:19; II *Kgs*. 23:21; II *Chron*. 35), often in the role of singers and dancers (e.g., *Ex*. 15:20-21; *Judg*. 21:21; *Jer*. 31:4; *Ps*. 68:12,

26-27), feature as prophetesses (e.g., *Judg.* 4:4f.; II *Sam.* 20:16f.; II *Kgs.* 22:14f.) and as persons who generally have a special association with the holy men (*Judg.* 13:6f.; II *Kgs.* 4:23f.), and are seen in attendance at shrines and sanctuaries as sacred prostitutes and in other cultic capacities (e.g., *Gen.* 38; *Ex.* 38:8; I *Sam.* 2:22; *Hos.* 4:13-14).[1]

Significantly, however, the period to which these texts refer was one in which that rigid monotheism so characteristic of later Judaism had not as yet developed. Polytheistic, or rather Baalistic, belief and worship flourished and shrines to the various deities, Yahweh included, dotted the countryside. Prominent among these deities were the goddesses, who included in their number Anath (the Queen of Heaven), Asherah and Ishtar, and it was with these cults that women were especially associated (e.g., *Judg.* 3:7; I *Kgs.* 11:5f., 15:13; II *Kgs.* 23:7; *Jer.* 7:18, 44:15f.). In the course of time, however, the monotheistic principle began to assert itself. Gradually (see also the paper of P. Ackroyd, this volume) the god Yahweh was elevated to a position of supremacy over all other deities. With this rise to power of a single male deity and the concomitant lessening in status of the other members of the Israelite Pantheon (especially its female members), the role played by women in public religion began to diminish. The first step in that direction was taken when the early Hebrew legislators, in a deliberate move intended to establish the worship of Yahweh, forbade the practice of sacred prostitution, this ritual being fundamental to the non-Yahwistic cults and also one in which women played a central role (*Deut.* 23:18-19. Cf. I *Kgs.* 15:12; II *Kgs.* 23:7). Women were further removed from cultic activity when the Yahwists forced the abolition of all rural shrines and centralised worship at the Temple in Jerusalem, a move which was again designed to rid the land of undesirable cults (cf. I *Kgs.* 6ff.). At this central sanctuary there was no place for female officiants as the Temple's affairs were regarded as the sole responsibility of an organised, hereditary male priesthood dedicated to the service of Yahweh.[2] The fact that only men could serve as priests was of course the result of the rigid patriarchy which by this time structured and organised the lives of the Jewish people. Under such a social system all positions of leadership — in government, religious life, tribe and family — lay in the hands of men and passed along the male line.

But Yahweh's victory was not won overnight. The books of *Kings* and II *Chronicles* bear witness to the way in which, as late as the sixth century BC, worship of the old gods and goddesses continued throughout the land of Israel, and even, on occasions, at the Temple in Jerusalem itself. Ironically, Yahweh's final victory came with the destruction of

His Temple at the hands of the Babylonians in 587 BC. For generations prior to this calamity, the prophets of Israel had been warning the people that if they did not abandon their syncretistic ways, the wrath of the one true God would descend upon them. The destruction of the Temple and the exile to Babylonia were thus viewed as the dramatic realisation of these doom prophecies and as final proof of the absolute power of the jealous God, Yahweh.

The traumatic events of the sixth century thus occasioned a fundamental rethinking of the position of the Hebrews *vis-à-vis* their God and His Covenantal Law and marked a watershed in the history of Judaism. Convinced that their present tragedy was the result of God's righteous wrath, the exiles set about ridding themselves of all impurity in an effort to regain His favour. To this end, all records of the past were zealously preserved and older, more primitive legal traditions extensively reworked and edited in the light of their developing concepts and attitudes. Innovatory ideas emerged such as that of Israel being the suffering servant of the Lord, a people with a special mission in the world. Monotheism was rigorously reaffirmed, God's power and majesty underlined, and stress laid upon the peculiar relation which existed between God and His chosen people.[3] Of particular significance and far-reaching consequence to the lives of women was the exilic legislators' obsession with ritual cleanness. In order to create a people which was truly holy to God, the religious leaders of the time formulated a complex of laws whose specific purpose was the encouragement of purity on both an individual and communal level.[4] The primitive blood taboo which lay behind so many of the Hebrews' ideas about purity led to women being declared unclean for a large part of their lives in consequence of the blood of childbirth and of the menstrual cycle. The exilic book of *Leviticus* dealt in detail with the pollution which resulted from contact with women during these periods and prescribed vital purification rituals to avert danger. Further precautions were taken by severely restricting the movement of women during their times of uncleanness. In particular, no one in a state of ritual impurity was allowed to enter the Temple or participate in cultic activities. Thus *Lev*. 12:2f. decreed that, 'If a woman be delivered and bear a man-child, then she shall be unclean seven days ... and she shall continue in the blood of purification thirty-three days; she shall touch no hallowed thing, nor come into the sanctuary, until the days of her purification be fulfilled. But if she bear a maid-child, then she shall be unclean two weeks and shall continue in the blood of purification sixty-six days.' During the time of menstrual uncleanness — which consisted of the days of bleeding plus seven days purification — women were similarly forbidden to enter the Temple, for as Yahweh declared in *Lev.* 15:31: 'Thus shall ye separate the children of Israel from their uncleanness; that they die not from their uncleanness when they defile my Tabernacle that is in the midst of them.'[5]

The time to begin putting these new ideas into effect came with the emergence of Cyrus (539-30 BC) who, in the first year of his reign, issued a decree ordering the restoration of the Jewish community and cult in Palestine (*Ezra* 1:1-4, 6:3-5). By 515 BC the restored community had re-established the centralised worship of Yahweh and had rebuilt the Temple in Jerusalem. Some years later, under the inspiration of the scribal priest Ezra, a huge assembly of both men and women was called, and the Law as revised and edited during the time in exile was publicly read. At this public reading, to use the words of Nehemiah, '. . . all those that had separated themselves from the peoples of the lands unto the Law of God, their wives, their sons, and their daughters, everyone that had knowledge and understanding . . . entered into a curse, and into an oath, to walk in God's Law, which was given by Moses the servant of God, and to observe and to do all the commandments of the Lord . . .' (10:29f.). To ensure that the people did not revert to their old ways, the start of this Second Temple period also saw the beginning of a programme of formal education which in the course of the next few centuries was to develop into a comprehensive system of schooling designed to bring knowledge of the Torah to all members of the Jewish community, rich and poor, aristocrat and ordinary citizen alike. As we shall see, however, women were not destined to be a part of this education programme.

Another move which was to have far-reaching consequence for women's role in religion was the development of a different familial structure. Again to make the Torah a living force in the land and to guard against assimilation and idolatrous practice, the post-exilic community sought to strengthen its inner bonding by reinforcing the basic social unit of the family. As a result of the increasing sophistication of Hebrew life and thought monogamous unions were encouraged, married children were urged to set up separate households, and archaic practices such as concubinage and the levirate virtually disappeared. In other words, the older system of the extended patriarchal family gave way to the nuclear family.[6] With this move towards the nuclear structured family, there developed an increasing rigidity in attitude towards and definition of function within the family group: the woman's role was placed firmly in the private sphere of activity as wife, mother and homemaker, whilst that of the man was located in the public sphere as worker and family supporter and as active participant in social, political and religious affairs (see *Prov*. 31:10f.). These two post-exilic developments − that is, the concentration upon ritual purity and the sharp differentiation in male-female social function − were gradually to exclude women from nearly all public expressions of piety.

By the time we reach the Hellenistic period (from *c*. 300 BC), therefore, Yahweh's rule was firmly established and the Torah, as formulated in the exile and beyond, dominated the lives of the Jewish people − to such an extent that in the first century AD, Josephus was able to coin the term 'theocracy' to describe their state of polity. It might, however, be more exact to use the term 'nomocracy', for the Torah as delivered by God to Moses was essentially a holy Law, a Covenant whose basic element was the commandment, or rather a series of commandments designed to encompass the Israelites' every moment.[7] According to later Jewish thinkers the enumeration of these commandments was as follows: 'Six hundred and thirteen precepts were given to Moses − three hundred and sixty five of them are negative commandments, like the number of days of the solar year, and two hundred and forty eight are positive commandments corresponding to the parts of the human body' (*Makk*. 23b). Although this figure should not be taken too literally (as demonstrated by the obvious artificiality of the equation), the statement does indicate the all-pervasive nature of the commandments in Jewish life.[8]

The question which we have to ask is, were women obliged to observe all these commandments? The answer to this is no, for although in principle fulfilment of the Law in its entirety was laid upon both men and women (witness the way in which women were present at the original delivery of the Law at Mount Sinai and at its public reading under Ezra where they, together with their menfolk, entered into the curse already mentioned), the rabbis of our period declared women exempt from nearly all of the positive precepts whose fulfilment depended upon a specific time of the day or of the year (*Kidd*. 1:7). Thus, for example, women were under no obligation to circumcise their sons or to take them to the Temple for the ritual redemption of the first-born (*idem*); they were exempt from making the thrice yearly pilgrimage to Jerusalem at the feasts of Passover, Pentecost, and Tabernacles (*Hag*. 1:1); from living in the ceremonial booths which were erected at the feast of Tabernacles (*Sukk*. 2:8); from shaking the Lulab (Tos. *Kidd*. 1:10); sounding the Shofar at the new year (Tos. *R.H.* 4:1); reading the Megillah at Purim (Tos. *Meg*. 2:7); and from making the daily affirmation of faith, 'Hear O Israel, the Lord our God, the Lord is One' (*Ber.* 3:3). Women's exemption from these time-geared precepts was the direct result both of their extensive periods of ritual impurity and of their designated role as closeted homemakers. Unclean and in a state of domestic seclusion, they thus became increasingly less involved in matters of public religion, and the situation quickly developed wherein their non-participation was viewed in terms of exclusion rather than mere exemption. Out of consideration of these various factors, women were also exempt from the one general precept whose fulfilment was central to the entire religious system — study of Torah.[9] Women thus had no share in the system of formal schooling which flourished in Palestine during the Hellenistic period, and in consequence of their ignorance of the Law, were further removed from the possibility of giving public expression to their piety.[10] We might also note that even if women did observe the commandments from which they were exempt, then it benefited them nothing, for the rabbis placed them in the category of 'one who is not commanded and fulfills', a Talmudic expression meaning that the action was without value (*Sot.* 21a). Women were, however, subject to all of the negative commandments and failure to observe those resulted in the full weight of the penal code descending upon them (*Kidd.* 35a; *Pes.* 43a).

If women did accompany their menfolk to the Temple when the latter were fulfilling the command to appear before the Lord, then their role was one of passive onlooker rather than active participant, for they were not allowed into the inner precincts where the main activity of the cult, that is, sacrifice, was conducted. Indeed, they were often not even allowed into the outer courts, for as Josephus writes: 'All who ever saw our Temple are aware of the general design of the building and the inviolable barriers which preserve its sanctity. It had four surrounding courts, each with its special statutory restrictions. The outer court was open to all, foreigners included; during their time of impurity women alone were refused admission. To the second court all Jews were permitted and, when uncontaminated by any defilement, their wives; to the third, male Jews [alone], if clean and purified; to the fourth, the priests ...' (*Con. Ap.* II:102f. Cf. *Ant.* 15:418f.; *B.J.* 5:193f., espec. 227; *Kel.* 1:6-9). The system of court within court, each gradually increasing in holiness, eventually led to the sanctuary itself which was situated in the centre of the Temple complex and was called the Holy of Holies. Only the High Priest was allowed to enter that area, and then only once a year (*Kel.* 1:9). The business of sacrifice was conducted in the Court of Priests, and to this court male Israelites were permitted to bring their private offerings, which were then sacrificed by the priests at the altar of unhewn stone (*Kel.* 1:8). Only rarely were women granted admission to this inner court for, as the Mishnah records, 'The rites of laying on of hands [on the beast's head before its slaughter], of waving, bringing near [the meal-offering], taking the handful and burning it, wringing the necks of the bird-offerings, sprinkling the blood [of the offerings on the altar] and receiving the blood . . . these are performed by men but not by women, excepting in the meal-offering of the suspected adulteress and of the female nazirite for which they themselves perform the act of waving' (*Kidd.* 1:8).[11] It is possible, however, that even for these exceptions women were not allowed into the inner area, for *Sot.* 1:5 records that at least in the case of the suspected adulteress, the offering was to be made at the Eastern Gate which lay over against the Gate of Nicanor, the latter being the entrance which separated the Court of Women from the Court of Israelites. We might also note that nazirites (dedicated ascetics) were by this time something of a dying breed and so the other exception listed in the Mishnah might not have had any reality.[12] Women were also disqualified from making the avowal at the offering of first-fruits and from sprinkling the water and mixing the ashes at the ceremony of the Red Heifer (*Bikk.* 1:5; *Parah* 5:4, 12:10), and from eating hallowed things in the Temple (*Bikk.* 4:3). Occasionally, however, and despite the mishnaic ruling, women were permitted to perform the ritual of laying on of hands — presumably on those occasions when the offering was of a particularly personal nature (such as a sin offering or the sacrifice demanded for the purification after childbirth), but the comment of the Gemara (the post-AD 200 commentary on the Mishnah) regarding this practice was: 'Not that it was customary for women, but that it was to appease the women' (*Hag.* 16b). In the main, where sacrificial ritual was concerned, women in the formula of the Talmud were coupled with gentiles, slaves, children, imbeciles, deaf-mutes, and persons of doubtful or double sex, all of whom were excluded from participation in the Temple's cultic affairs. They remained in the outer, less hallowed, area of the so-called Court of Women (a title which was in fact something of a misnomer as men had free access to this precinct), removed from the activity of the inner recesses of the Temple proper.[13]

It is moreover possible that on one occasion in the year women were further distanced from the ceremonial, for included in the Mishnah's account of the celebrations which took place at the close of the first day of the feast of Tabernacles is found the following report: 'Before-time [the Court of Women] was free of buildings, but [afterward] they surrounded it with a gallery, so that the women should behold from above and the men from below, and that they should not mingle together' (*Midd.* 2:5. Cf. *Sukk.* 5:2; Tos. *Sukk.* 4:1). From this gallery, according to *Sukk.* 5:4, women watched as the men below celebrated the feast's water libation to the accompaniment of music, songs, dances and illuminations. The reason given at a later date by the rabbis for this segregation of the sexes was the fear that the feast's riotous nature would encourage immoral behaviour among the participants (*Kidd.* 81a). However, too much stress should not be laid upon the existence of this gallery, for the evidence regarding it is both meagre and confused.[14] In any case, there seems to be no indication in the sources that this gallery — even if it existed — was used at any other time in the year, despite the confident assertions to that effect by some scholars.

We may now turn to examining the role of women in the synagogue, an institution of very different character to that of the Temple. Whatever the exact origins of this institution — and conjectures on that subject differ enormously[15] — it is certain that by the late Second Temple period (the Second Temple period lasting from the sixth century BC to AD 70) it was a well-established feature of Jewish religious life, for rabbinic sources, the New Testament and Josephus all bear witness to the existence of synagogues throughout Palestine by the first century AD.

The primary function of the synagogue was to serve as a place for public reading of the Torah, and the main day upon which people assembled to hear the Law was the Sabbath, though readings also took place on Mondays, Thursdays and high holidays. As these Scripture readings, which followed a cyclical sequence, were intended to be instructive rather than merely devotional, they were accompanied both by an interpretative translation from the Hebrew and by a sermon. The synagogue thus served as a central element of the Jewish educational system.

As a general extension of women's exemption from the time-geared precepts and in consequence of their non-obligation to study Torah, women were not required to attend the synagogue. Only men could make up the quorum of ten which was necessary for a service, and if less than ten men were in attendance, even though women were present, then the congregation, to use the words of Mishnah, '. . . may not recite the Shema with its benedictions, nor may one go up before the Ark, nor may they lift up their hands, nor may they read [the prescribed portion of] the Law or the reading from the Prophets . . .' (*Meg.* 4:3).[16] Similarly, only men were allowed to read from the Torah scroll, for although women were in theory eligible, it was not customary for them to obey the public call to read. Thus the Talmud declared that, 'All are qualified to be among the seven [who read on sabbath mornings] , even a minor and a woman, but a woman should not be allowed to come forward to read out of respect for the congregation' *(Meg.* 23a). The reason for this exclusion on the grounds of 'respect for the congregation' is nicely analysed by R. Loewe who writes that,

> . . . the ineligibility of women . . . (to act) . . . as leaders in prayer for congregations including men (rests) on the principle that whereas obligation may be fulfilled by a plurality of those liable to it acting cooperatively, one of their number taking the lead and the others consciously fulfilling their obligation in unison with him, the situation would be quite otherwise were the quasi-representative figure not under an obligation of precisely analogous quality to that of the remainder of the congregation.[17]

Loewe also points to the significant fact that the Hebrew expression for 'officiant' at a service literally means 'agent of a group'. In consequence of their non-obligation, therefore, women were unable to act in this capacity.

It is also likely that women sat apart from the men who were conducting the service, for a characteristic of the Second Commonwealth (i.e. the Second Temple period) was an increased morbidity where free mingling of the sexes was concerned.[18] We cannot say, however, exactly what form this probable separation of the sexes took. Many modern scholars have argued for the existence of special women's galleries or for the presence of lattice-work screens, but their conclusions rest heavily upon meagre evidence imaginatively manipulated in the light of present-day Jewish practice. Thus, for example, Avi-Yonah, writing of the excavations at Beth Alpha — a Galilean synagogue of basilica design, late 5th or 6th century AD — says: 'The remains furnish no evidence that would establish the existence of a second storey, but it is reasonable to assume that there was one and that a women's gallery was built on top of the two colonnades and above the vestibule.'[19] Similarly, the archaeologist Sukenik was so convinced that this synagogue had a women's gallery that he even drew into his ground plans a special access stairway without its actually existing and assumed the existence of a similar staircase for the basilica synagogue of Chorazin (3rd-4th century AD).[20] Of the synagogue at Hammath by Gadara (4th century AD), the same scholar — although admitting that the remains were practically confined to the foundations and that it was consequently impossible to hazard a restoration of the superstructure – stated that: 'It may, however, confidently be inferred that the basilica was provided with a gallery for women worshippers, from the massive pillars at the north eastern and north western corners of the colonnade . . .'.[21] From these and other sites Sukenik concluded that '. . . most [Palestinian] synagogue ruins have preserved unmistakable traces of a gallery'. In fact, however, of the Galilean synagogues thus far excavated, only Susiya (4th-5th century AD) has remains of stairs appropriate for a gallery and possibly Kefir Bir'im (3rd-4th century AD) (but here they appear with a question mark in the restoration plan).[22] In the oldest synagogue so far revealed, that of Masada (1st century BC), there is no trace of steps, galleries or screen bases, a point of some significance when one recalls that this synagogue was used for some time by religious zealots. And, of course, even if it could be proved that galleries were common in ancient synagogues, that fact alone would not mean conclusively that their purpose was to provide for women at worship. Our literary sources, even those as late as the Middle Ages, remain silent on the whole subject of galleries, screens or other areas specifically designated for female worshippers. Abrahams advances the theory that such special areas arose in the late thirteenth century when it was customary for men and women to spend the night of Yom Kippur in the synagogue.[23] From the evidence so far available, therefore, it is impossible to say what form the segregation of the sexes took, though the likelihood that they were segregated – for the reasons already mentioned – remains. Possibly women simply sat at the back of the synagogue quietly observing the service in progress. Whatever the answer to these problems, however, it is certain that women's role was once again that of passive onlooker rather than active participant. An order issued by St Paul to disciples in Corinth bears witness to the attitude current among the Jews of the first century. He wrote: 'As in all the churches of the Saints, the women should keep silence . . . they are not permitted to speak, but should be subordinate as even the Law says. If there is anything they desire to know, let them ask their husbands at home' (I *Cor.* 14:34-36. Cf. I *Tim.* 2:11-14). It is likely that in any case domestic duties, in particular the care of young children, frequently prevented women from regularly attending the synagogue. And here we might remember that the Law did not allow mothers to carry their infants outside the privacy of the home on the sabbath (*Shabb.* 18:12). An obvious consequence of this ruling was that women were housebound on precisely the day when the main assembly and exposition of the Law took place.

In the ritual of the home women also had little role to play. They could not make up the number needed for the common grace or that required for the slaughter of the passover offering (*Ber.* 7:2; *Pes.* 8:7). Prayer was led by the men of the household, and in all matters of home ceremonial it was sons rather than daughters whose active participation was encouraged. This was in order to train boys to the observance of those commandments whose fulfilment would be their responsibility on reaching adulthood. An example of this differentiation in involvement is found in the Mishnah's description of the Seder ritual. As part of this ritual, the Bible made express provision for ceremonial questions on the history and meaning of the service to be asked by children of their parents. Significantly, this duty fell only to sons and never to daughters (*Pes.* 10:4). Women were, however, involved to some extent in the ritual which surrounded the weekly celebration of the Sabbath. The rabbis gave them the responsibility of lighting the lamps which heralded the start of the holiday and the duty of baking the two loaves which were required for the Sabbath's inaugural meal (*Shabb.* 2:6; *Ber.* 31a). The blessing of the loaves, however, was the men's responsibility.

All in all, about the only privilege left to women in Hellenistic Palestine was that of weeping – in other words, their one official position was that of publicly mourning the dead at funerals, an office common to women throughout the Near East (*Moed Katan* 3:8-9; *Ket.* 4:4. Cf. *Judg.* 11:40; II *Sam.* 14:2; II *Chron.* 35:25). They were also involved in certain other activities associated with the dead (I *Sam.* 28:7f.; *Mk.* 16:1; *Lk.* 23:55, 24:1). With regard to their ability to act in this capacity, however, two points must be made. Firstly, although women were prominent at funerals, they were not responsible for the mourners' benediction or for the performance of other religious duties (and I stress the word religious) designed to ensure the smooth passage of the dead. These duties were incumbent upon men alone (*Meg.* 4:3. Cf. *Tob.* 6:15; *Ahikar* 1:4-5). Secondly, those ritual areas of death in which women were involved belonged primarily to the shadowy region of popular superstition and were not the concern of Judaism proper (hence my earlier stress upon men's *religious* duties). Indeed, as Segal points out, the law codes contain conspicuously few references to such matters, the reason being that these practices, arising as they did from isolated events which could not be inserted into the recurrent cycle of an annual calender, were the concern of individuals rather than the representatives of the official cult. Segal further suggests that it was precisely the fact of women's involvement on these occasions which encouraged the silence in our sources.[24] We should also remember that many of the mourning rites, inherited as they were from earlier more primitive days, were deemed incompatible with the official religion, ritual and cult of Hellenistic Palestine, and as such were frequently condemned (see, for example, *Lev.* 26:28; *Deut.* 14:1, 18:11; *Ps.* 106:28; *B.S.* 30:18-19; *Jub.* 22:17; *Ep. Jer.* 31:32).

Excluded from all official means of religious expression, women turned to magic — or rather continued the magical tradition which had been theirs in the early period of Hebrew history.[25] Although time does not allow us to enter into a discussion here of the magical practices of Hellenistic Palestine, a couple of points should be noted. Firstly, according to our sources, it was especially women who were associated with magic. Thus, for example, the great religious leader Hillel declared on one occasion: 'The more flesh, the more worms ... the more women, the more witchcrafts' (*Aboth* 2:7), and later Jewish thinkers, when pondering the Bible's specific condemnation of sorceresses rather than sorcerers (*Ex.* 22:17), reasoned that this was 'Because mostly women engage in witchcraft' (*Sanh.* 67a).[26] The second point is that women were especially associated with sinister or base magic (hence the references to them as witches and sorceresses), and with simple, super-stitious folk practice. They were precluded from activity in the higher, more powerful magical arts, for these required an esoteric knowledge gained through immersion in a mystical lore from which women were barred. Thirdly, many of the magical practices in which women were involved were vigorously opposed and condemned by the religious leaders of the time in consequence of their incompatibility with the true worship of Yahweh (*Lev.* 19:26f.; *Deut.* 18:9-11; *Ezek.* 13:17f.; *B.S.* 34:1-8; *Sanh.* 7:7, 11).[27]

Overall, therefore, the position of women in Jewish religion, ritual and cult may best be summed up by the Mishnah's constant coupling of women with minors and slaves, and by a statement of Josephus that, in the eyes of the Law, '... the woman ... is in all things inferior to the man' (*Con. Ap.* II:201). Throughout their lives, women's personal vow of valuation to God was reckoned at roughly half that of men (*Lev.* 27:2f.),[28] and it was in the light of these facts that men each morning offered the following prayer of thanksgiving: 'Blessed art thou, O Lord our God, King of the Universe, who has not made me a woman.'[29]

Abbreviations used in the Text

B.B.	Baba Bathra	*Midd.*	Middoth
Ber.	Berakhoth	*Naz.*	Nazir
Bikk.	Bikkurim	*Ned.*	Nedarim
Erub.	Erubin	*Pes.*	Pesahim
Hag.	Hagigah	*R.H.*	Rosh ha-Shanah
Hall.	Hallah	*Sanh.*	Sanhedrin
Kel.	Kelim	*Shabb.*	Shabbath
Ket.	Ketuboth	*Sot.*	Sotah
Kidd.	Kiddushin	*Sukk.*	Sukkah
Makk.	Makkoth	Tos.	Tosefta
Meg.	Megillah	*v.*	Jerusalem Talmud
Men.	Menahoth		

Notes

1. Women acting in public capacities: Astour (1966), pp. 185-96; Brooks (1941), pp. 227-53; Peritz (1898), pp. 111-47 (though this article goes somewhat overboard in assuming a total involvement for women at all levels of religion and cult).

2. For these various developments, see Segal (1979), pp. 121-37.

3. These ideas are to be seen especially in the writings of Deutero-Isaiah (*Is.* 34-35, 40-55, parts of 56-66). For the effect of the exile on Jewish life and thought, see conveniently Bright (1960), pp. 323-55.

4. For the equation by the legislators of ritual cleanness with holiness, see Neusner (1973), pp. 18f.

5. The Priestly Code also itemised certain states of male impurity (*Lev.* 15:2f.). These, however, arising as they did from no regular bodily cycle, were not nearly as restrictive or immobilising as those decreed for women.

6. Here one might contrast the descriptions of family life in the early biblical narratives with the last chapter of *Proverbs* (a post-exilic work) which neatly depicts the ordering of a nuclear family. For the move toward monogamy, note the constant coupling of husband and wife, father and mother in the post-exilic writings; for married children leaving their parents, see *Ahikar* 2:45; *B.B.* 6:4; *B.S.* in *B.B.* 98b; for the disappearance of concubinage (the obligation of marriage with the widow of a childless brother, the eldest son of the union succeeding to the deceased's estate), see Epstein (1942).

7. Thus the rabbis characterised God as the one 'who sanctified us with His commandments and commanded us' (Tos. *Ber.* 7:9), and declared that 'a man performs ten precepts before ever he eats a piece of bread' (v. *Hall.* 58a).

8. For details of the domination of Jewish life by the commandments, see Urbach (1975), pp. 315f.

9. On the importance of education in the lives of the Jewish people, see, e.g., *Ber.* 47b; *Men.* 110a; *B.B.* 12a; especially *Kidd.* 1:10: 'He that has no knowledge of Scripture and Mishnah . . . has no part in the habitable world.' For women's exemption, *Kidd.* 29b; cf. *Naz.* 29a; *Erub.* 27a. Contrast *Kidd.* 1:10 with 'Better

to burn the Torah than to teach it to women' (y. *Sot.* 3:4).

10. The rabbis found scriptural authority for the view that women were intellectually incapable of coping with the demands of an education in Torah and should instead concentrate upon household affairs: 'There is no wisdom in woman except with the distaff. Thus also does Scripture say: "And all the women that were wise-hearted did spin with their hands" (*Ex.* 35:25)' (*Yoma* 66b). On the incorrectly held assumption that Beruriah was a woman of learning (and that thus other women possessed educational opportunities), see Goodblatt (1977).

11. For details of the offerings made at the Temple, see *Lev.* 1:3ff. and Barton (1927), pp. 79-89.

12. For a description of the lifestyle of the nazarites and of the reasons for their decline, see Robertson Smith (1894), pp. 324f., 482; Fohrer (1973), pp. 153-4; Bonsirven (1931), p. 188. We should also note that even if a woman did decide to become a nazarite, her husband had the right to revoke her vow (*Num.* 30:3f.; *Naz.* 4:1-5, 9:1; *Ned.* 1:9).

13. A further reflection of the non-status of the female in the Temple cult is to be seen in the exilic legislators' specification that all important sacrifices be of male victims (*Lev.* 1:3f.). According to Philo, the reason for this rule was because 'the male is more complete, more dominant than the female, closer akin to causal activity, for the female is incomplete and in subjection and belongs to the category of the passive rather than the active' (*Spec. Leg.* I.198f.).

14. For a survey of the evidence available, see Hollis (1934).

15. See, for example, Finkelstein (1930), pp. 49-59; Gutman (1981); Morgenstern (1956), pp. 192-201; Zeitlin (1931) (all of differing opinions).

16. Note that the rabbinic definition of what constituted a town (as opposed to a village) was a community in which there lived ten unoccupied men (who could be counted on to form a quorum) (*Meg.* 1:3).

17. Loewe (1966), pp. 44-5.

18. See Epstein (1948).

19. Avi-Yonah (1975), I, p. 187.

20. Sukenik (1932), pp. 15f.

21. Sukenik (1935), p. 72.

22. See S. Gutman *et al.*, 'Excavations in the Synagogue at Horvat Susiya', in Levine (1981), p. 124, and Seager (1975) (contains material on Galilean synagogues). Z. Ma'oz remarks: 'The view that synagogues of this period did not contain a women's gallery is supported by the synagogue at Gamla where no traces of any separation are found' (Levine, 1975, p. 39). We might also note that the excavators of Capernaum, which was once thought to have stairs appropriate for a gallery, are now convinced that there was no gallery (ibid., 100).

23. Abrahams (1932), pp. 39-40.

24. Segal (1976), pp. 2, 5.

25. Trachtenberg (1961), part I.

26. The Mishnah records the fact that Simeon ben Shetah had 80 women from Ashkelon hanged in one day (*Sanh.* 6:4). According to the Jerusalem Talmud these women were witches (y. *Hag.* 2:2, 77d; *Sanh.* 6:9, 23c).

27. Significantly, the Priestly Code's prohibitions on magical practices appears together with the ban on prostitution and mourning rites (*Lev.* 19:26f. cf. *Nahum* 3:4).

28. Regarding this differentiation, Philo wrote: 'the Law laid down a scale of valuation in which no regard is paid to beauty or stature of anything of the kind, but all are assessed equally, the sole distinction being between men and women, and between children and adults' (*Spec. Leg.* II.32).

29. The use of this blessing may first have been authorised in the second

century AD, either by R. Meir or Judah. Possibly something of the sort was known to St Paul (*Gal.* 3:28). See Loewe (1966), p. 43.

Further Reading

J. Jeremias (1969), *Jerusalem in the Time of Jesus*, Appendix: 'The Social Position of Women', London
S. Safrai (1976), 'Religion in everyday life', 'The Temple', 'The Synagogue', in S. Safrai and M. Stern (eds.), *Compendia Rerum Iudaicarum ad Novum Testamentum*, Amsterdam, sect. 1, vol. II, 793-833; 865-907; 908-44
— (1969), 'Was there a women's gallery in the synagogue of antiquity?', *Tarbiz* 23, 329-38 (in Hebrew, English summary p. 11)
R. de Vaux (1961), *Ancient Israel, Its Life and Institutions*, tr. J. McHugh, London

18 WOMEN IN EARLY SYRIAN CHRISTIANITY

Susan Ashbrook Harvey, Providence, Rhode Island

Early Syriac Christianity presents many problems, especially regarding women. But it may be possible to account for the disparities at least in part by positing a relationship between aspects of the spirituality, and aspects of the Christian society, in the Syrian Orient of late antiquity. To seek the practical results of particular religious ideas is a tenuous business at best, but the attempt itself may raise useful questions.

The term 'Syrian Orient' is here used to include those places where Syriac was spoken as the major language: primarily the Roman provinces of Syria, Osrhoene and Mesopotamia, and their Persian neighbours; but Syriac was also the *lingua franca* of the eastern Roman frontiers in a larger sense. Within this Syrian realm, Greek-speaking cities (like Antioch) displayed more Syrian character than Greek, despite their efforts to conform to 'Hellenism'; and Greek literature of Syrian origin (such as the writings of Theodoret of Cyrrhus) reveals more of a Syrian disposition than is warranted by whatever its format might be. Accordingly, Syriac Christianity is marked from its inception by its distinct circumstances. It developed apart from Graeco-Latin tradition. The parallel experience, for example, of Egypt is not without significance, but the language factor is pivotal. Unlike Coptic, Syriac found space for its own development: it built a rich literary and scholarly tradition of its own. There was little serious Hellenic presence in Syriac culture or thought until the sixth century AD, although influence begins in the fifth century; until then, we have what we may term a 'semitic Christianity'. The differences to the 'mainstream' early church are instructive, and — as in the case of women — set a fresh light on the beginnings of Graeco-Latin Christianity and Christian culture.

The ancient semitic world gave evidence of a religious tradition remarkable for its receptivity and sensitivity towards feminine aspects of the divine. Not until the growth of the Virgin Mary cult from the fifth century AD onwards did the cultural heritage born of the classical world begin to foster a comparable element for Western civilisation. In the Syrian Orient, however, a pattern of powerful female symbols was established long before Christianity's appearance; this may account for the striking tendency of the early Syriac church, in contrast to those of the Graeco-Latin cultures, to encourage feminine symbols in response to Christian revelation.

Its polytheistic past left the heritage of the Syrian Goddess, whose cult eventually spread across the Graeco-Roman world. She survived from the ancient Near East, when she had been known as Ishtar, Ashtoreth and Astarte, to become the Aramaic Atargatis, whose cult endured into the early Christian era. Although her following was never so great as that of the Egyptian Isis, the Syrian Goddess maintained a solemn and influential presence throughout Hellenistic and Roman times, across the Mediterranean cities. In the pagan cosmology of the Syrian Orient, she functioned as part of a 'holy trinity' – a triad of Mother, Father and Son; such a configuration often characterised religious beliefs in the ancient Near East (Isis herself was part of one). Her worshippers recognised her as a universal divine presence, identifying her with Isis, the Phrygian Cybele and Greek Hera, as the Great Mother of creation.

On the other hand, the Syrian Orient was Christianised primarily through Judaism. Judaism offered a practical heritage more organic than that of Greece or Rome. Here, the aggressively masculine imagery used for the God of Israel in the Old Testament worked as just what it was: a consciously contrived imagery, in reaction against neighbouring religious concepts and deities. A delicate underworking of female imagery is also present in the Old Testament: God as midwife (*Ps.* 22: 9-10), God as comforting mother (*Is.* 49:15, 66:13), God travailing in the throes of divine labour pangs (*Is.* 42:14bff.). Such passages served to remind that Israel's portrait of God as mighty and thus male, was in fact an intentional contrivance: no more, but no less (Trible, 1978).

The complementary strains of thought fostered within Jewish monotheism are telling. Most notable is the personification of Holy Wisdom as a female figure: she who sits at the Lord's right hand, the force through whom God creates and acts. Because Wisdom – Hokhma – is a feminine noun in Hebrew, the personification is a natural extension into literary imagery of a linguistic attribute. But more is involved in Wisdom's female persona than the simple extension of a grammatical category. Her articulation fits a pattern. History shows that where a religious spirituality does not incorporate feminine aspects, powerful female symbols will nonetheless be found by the society involved, and not necessarily to the detriment of monotheistic religion. For Judaism, the curtailment of Wisdom speculation during the reign of gnosticism was followed by the development, in the rabbinic period, of another female image — the holy Shekinah, the female personification of God's divine presence, she who is His daughter and bride (Von Rad, 1972; Goldberg, 1969). Neither Wisdom nor the Syrian Goddess represented the dominant theological focus for their respective religions. Yet both, and perhaps the Goddess in particular, were seen to be more powerful than comparable female deities of the Greek or Roman pantheons. Lucian pointed out that one would have to combine Hera, Athena, Aphrodite, Artemis, Nemesis, Rhea, Selene and the Fates, to encompass the power of the Syrian Goddess (*Dea Syria*, 32). It may not be surprising, then, that unlike the Graeco-Latin churches, early Syriac Christianity used female imagery and symbols to explore the divine mysteries.

Thus Syriac tradition at its earliest, and for many centuries thereafter, saw the Holy Spirit as female, following both the instinct of grammar — *rūha'*, Syriac for 'spirit', is a feminine noun — and of inherited religious thought patterns (Murray, 1975, pp. 312-20). The Syrian Judaeo-Christian *Odes of Solomon*, dating probably to the second century AD (Charlesworth, 1977), offer images of the divine that contrast sharply with Graeco-Latin writings of the same time. Not only is the Holy Spirit portrayed in the feminine as the Mother Spirit, but so, too, is Christ at times clothed in feminine images and terms; the striking Ode 19 even hymns God in female form.

Ode 19 has in fact unnerved scholars ever since its discovery at the turn of this century. Its portrayal of a female Holy Spirit, at work with God the Mother (a portrait with no inhibition for anatomical detail) who serves as Mary's midwife, has proved distressing to the sheltered sensitivities of twentieth-century academics. But Ode 19 points to a further contribution in the early Syrian appreciation for the feminine. In it, Mary is hailed in concise yet dazzling terms. She is the 'Virgin Mother of Many Mercies' — a title 'rediscovered' in the tenth-century Latin west — who 'bore . . . without pain'; she 'loved with redemption', 'guarded with kindness', and 'declared with grandeur'. The confidence of this passage exceeds the sparse and reserved picture of Marian devotion in the second century that we draw from other sources, and appears somewhat precocious. The themes touched upon prefigure major Marian doctrinal developments, rarely pursued before the fifth century elsewhere, and some not until medieval times (Graef, 1963). Scholars have suggested that Ode 19 confuses Mary with Isis, but this misses the mark; it is a common excuse for dismissing 'problems' in the development of Mary's cult. In the Syrian Orient of the second century, the Virgin Mother of Many Mercies found in Ode 19 was not an isolated case.

To find Syrian devotion for Mary in the prime of its flourishing, one must jump ahead, but only as far as the fourth century. The hymns of Ephrem Syrus, the greatest of Syriac poets, offer noteworthy tribute (Murray, 1971; Brock, 1979). Ephrem presents a Marion devotion far more developed than what is found contemporarily in the west. Greek orthodoxy would not open similar possibilities until the fifth century — at the earliest with Cyril of Alexandria — and Catholicism in the Latin west would not foster such attitudes for several more centuries after that (Graef, 1973; for Ireland, however, see Davies in this volume). For Ephrem, Mary partakes of and shares in her Son's redemptive role; even more, she, too, is present in the Eucharist, for the body of Christ received in the Eucharist is that very one which he took from Mary. She is essential for, inseparable from, Christ's works. Ephrem's successors followed his lead. But although Ephrem marks the artistic and theological flowering of Syrian veneration for Mary, he could hardly have introduced her cult in such profound proportions to the Syrian church. It had to be there already.

The spiritual kinship bridging Ode 19 and the Marian hymns of Ephrem may add weight to the theory that the *Protevangelion of James* — the singularly influential second-century apocryphal account of the Virgin's life, composed originally in Greek — is a work of Syrian origins (Smid, 1965; cf. Strycker, 1961). More important, however, is the enormous favour it enjoyed with the Syrian Christian communities. The Syriac version is our oldest translation of the work, and its immediate and long-lasting popularity in the Syrian Orient is well attested. Again, an independent but related Syriac *Life* of the Virgin was also in circulation, possibly as early as the mid-second century (Budge, 1899; Lewis, 1902). Certainly, Mary's place in early Syriac Christianity was not regarded with the doctrinal reservations and inhibitions expressed further west before the fifth century.

Thus religious experience in the Syrian Orient both before and after Christianisation reveals an intense presence of powerful female imagery and symbols. This experience was not easily shared with Graeco-Latin culture, despite its fervent reception in Hellenistic times of the Oriental goddess cults. These cults remained external borrowings, even when 'Hellenised' or 'Romanised'; and as such, they remained in fundamental tension with their adopting society. They point to what was lacking in classical spirituality, rather than to what was inherent. So, for example, the western church banned the *Protevangelion of James* as heretical almost as soon as it was published. Again, female imagery of the divine on par with the *Odes of Solomon* for subtlety and poignancy would not appear in the west until medieval times (McLaughlin, 1975). So it was not surprising that Syriac Christianity would eventually find its wings clipped, by the pressures of conforming to 'mainstream' Graeco-Latin Christianity. Syriac theology did not reveal serious Hellenic concessions until late in the fifth century, but a quieter acquiescence begins sooner, in the subversion of symbols natural to the Syrian milieu.

By the year 400, steps had been taken to bring the Syriac concept of the Holy Spirit into conformity with that of the 'orthodox' church. Thus when used to signify the third element of the Trinity, *rūha'* was transformed into a masculine noun — but the change governed only that particular usage of the word. After 400, Syriac writers no longer follow the tradition found uniformly in earlier works, but refer to the Spirit in masculine terms and imagery (although the occasional hymn writer followed the older tradition, apparently for metrical reasons).

In similar manner, the otherwise feminine *meltha'*, Syriac for 'Word', becomes masculine when used to translate the Greek 'Logos', as found in the Peshitta, the Syriac Bible. The case of *meltha'*, Word, is not necessarily so provocative as that of *rūha'*, Spirit, where a clear theological mandate prompted the change: the Holy Spirit was not feminine, and that was that. The transformation of *meltha'*, Word, on the other hand, may reflect problems of translation technique at this time, whereby such an alteration could happen simply in the attempt to render important terminology from another language more faithfully. We do not have examples of the exploration of a female imagery for the Word as we do for the Spirit in the early Syriac Fathers. But the indisputable motivation with regard to the Holy Spirit would suggest that the parallel experience of the Word is too close for coincidence.

The unease evoked for orthodoxy by images drawn from grammatical attributes indicates how charged these basic concepts were for the church: even a linguistic category was not neutral. For its part, the Syrian 'idea' of the Holy Spirit as the Mother Spirit survived amongst those Syrian writers who knew no Greek, despite the measures to eradicate it, and to this day can still be found in liturgical books using the ancient readings.

Deprived of its feminine principle in the Trinity, the Syrian Orient after 400 was left to cultivate its sensitivities through the cult of the Virgin Mary; this it did very well. But the fifth century also saw the passionate emergence of Marian devotion in the wider Graeco-Roman church, quite suddenly a force to be reckoned with — as a recent study on crowd violence at this time has shown (Gregory, 1979). In fact, theologians had their own reasons for dragging Mary into the limelight at this particular point, and none of them had to do with her directly. Their interests were partly Christological and partly political (Sellers, 1953). But the fervour with which the Virgin's popular cult grew indicates that Mary as a symbol in herself touched deep needs in the Christian society.

There are clear echoes here of the reception given earlier to the oriental goddess cults. The heritage of classical antiquity would seem to have left unfulfilled a hunger nonetheless felt by its people. Of course, the mystery religions were attractive to the Hellenistic world for other reasons, apart from the longing for powerful female symbols; Mithraism, for example, does not fit this pattern. But the repetitive features of the goddess cults, and Mary's cult, make such a considera- tion unavoidable. The manner in which Marian devotion, both popular and theological, flourished throughout Christendom belies the con- trived and manufactured 'orthodox' austerity that tried to clamp down on early Syriac spirituality: a spirituality that included an appreciation for feminine dimensions of the divine.

Spirituality can affect a number of things. But the question here is how did it affect the ordinary functioning of society in the Syrian Orient of late antiquity?

As was generally the case for the Roman Empire as a whole, Syrian society before its Christianisation provided for its upper-class women a relative degree of freedom and respect, resulting from and dependent upon the advantages of an affluent society. Again, as was general throughout the Graeco-Roman realm, the basic Christian precepts of equal worth and responsibility for the sexes were received by Syrian society with some ambivalence. There was, however, an important difference of nuance. The Syrian Orient received these teachings in a religious context that instinctively complemented them: it harboured an inherent sense of feminine presence in the experience and perception of the divine. That this was a matter of nuance rather than mandate must be stressed. Nonetheless, religious and societal concepts substan- tiate each other where they coincide; to this extent, Syrian society might have been more receptive to the consequences of Christian teachings towards equality than the less sensitive situation where classical presuppositions held sway. A greater strain on familiar struc- tures would perhaps have resulted.

Such a suggestion is conjectural. But it provides a reasonable explana- tion for what would otherwise appear a puzzling phenomenon in Syriac Christianity: the development of a distinctly misogynist Christian social pattern, far more blatant than in Graeco-Latin culture. The pattern was violently and quickly entrenched, once set in motion. So despite a flourishing wealth of feminine imagery in religious thought, real women soon found themselves in a radically poisoned position. At the same time, we have here a viable measure for the implications of attitudes being fostered in the wider Christian body.

As happened elsewhere, Christianity for the Syrians did not grow up as a unified religion (Wilken, 1979); nor did it display a recognisably 'orthodox' basis, as a dominant position, until late in the fourth century. Prior to that time, a number of conflicting parties were present. Those with the greatest followings, and whose doctrines were sufficiently powerful to affect the texture of the subsequent orthodox Syrian church, were Valentinianism and Marcionism — two movements of wide distribution in the Graeco-Roman sphere, from the mid-second century onwards.

Both of these groupings fall inside the general realm of gnosticism. But their contributions to the eventual Syrian churches were social rather than theological in effect (Vööbus, 1958). Both shared an absolute reliance on dualistic thought. An ascetic understanding of Christian life, and the glorification of celibacy, marked the crucial boundaries within which their followers lived. However, Marcionism was probably the most pervasive form of earliest Christianity in the Syrian Orient (Bauer, 1972); significantly, it offered an understanding of the gospel message that was in essence egalitarian. Its practitioners lived and worshipped according to a literal interpretation of the Pauline doctrine that in Christ there is neither male nor female. Its women were granted the exceptional rights to teach, exorcise, and baptise — a situation that brought scandalised horror from the 'orthodox' (Tertullian, *de praescriptione haereticorum*, 41). The practical consequences of Marcion's preachings against marriage meant that women were not restricted to producing children and serving a family. The Marcionites offered women a role of significance basic to the social rendering of their religion, as much as to its theology: they granted women positions of high responsibility and sacerdotal import. In the Syrian Orient, these ideas would fall on fertile soil, as an extension into the temporal realm of religious concepts already deeply ingrained. Not surprisingly, women were eager converts.

In fact, asceticism coloured the overall development of Christianity in the Syrian Orient, heretical or orthodox, for many centuries (Brock, 1973; Gribomont, 1965). Thus the popularity of celibacy as a response to Christian teaching was ubiquitous (Vööbus, 1951). But differently than in the west, celibacy was consecrated as vital for the lay as well as vocational believer, both male and female: baptism was reserved for the celibate alone. Lay offices for both women and men also required celibacy, and some canonical restrictions — a feature surviving into the Middle Ages. Spiritual marriage, that is, co-habitation in chastity, was widely followed as a solution for combining marriage with a life of faith (cf. Patlagean, 1969). These circumstances preceded the formation of monasticism for women as a separately organised institution. Less extensively than in the Marcionite movement, Syrian Christian society allowed women some options, and the honour of a fundamental affirmation of respect.

But by the late third century, pressure to conform to the Graeco-Latin churches was growing. A major target was the curtailment of ascetic values in the realm of 'secular' society. To do this, the church tried to separate asceticism into a vocation distinctly isolated from the life and practices of the lay community. Spiritual marriage, in particular, was attacked. But the vehicle used to glorify the 'perfect life' of the ascetic was the vilification of Woman. Utter contempt for the physical realm turned to unbounded hatred for the female, as the source of all pollution (Vööbus, 1958). The vitriolic scorn which Syrian Christianity began to heap on women during the third century became a recognised feature of the Syrian churches (Fiey, 1966). As Arthur Vööbus phrased it, the conflicts over forms of celibacy in the Syrian churches resulted in trends that all 'ended in misogyny . . . and had a great future ahead' (Vööbus, 1958, I, p. 83). But there can be little doubt that much of this attitude also showed a backlash against the disconcerting possibilities raised by Marcionism, towards a genuinely changed socio-religious structure — one that would have allowed women new standards of equality.

Tensions between religion and society proved irreconcilable. Women bore the brunt of the damage, just as they had in the case of Syrian spirituality. The fifth century in the Syrian Orient saw a strict limitation in the use of female religious symbols and imagery, with the Virgin Mary left in isolation. The fifth century also saw a rigid restriction of women's place in Syrian Christian society; even ascetic women were viewed now as a source of dreaded danger to men, and the ascetic practice prescribed for women was one that properly complemented their now tarnished social position: in contrast to the outwardly aggressive and exhibitionist asceticism performed by men in this area (it was the Syrian Orient that invented the trend of pillar saints like Symeon Stylites), Syrian women were directed to an ascetic practice that was demure, deferential, unobtrusive, passive – and supervised by men. They were veiled from head to toe; their eyes were ever downcast; they never spoke; they were enclosed; they wept continually; it was an asceticism of repentance (Theodoret, *Historia Religiosa*; Vööbus, 1961).

Two memories from the Syrian Orient of Late Antiquity demarcate the polarities of women's experience at this time. The first pays singular homage to what was possible when spirituality flavoured people's lives. St Febronia was a Syrian nun martyred at the turn of the fourth century around the year 302, by Roman officials (*BHO* 302-3; *BHG*³ 298-9). Her *Life* is an extraordinary piece of hagiography, regardless of its historicity (our earliest manuscript dates from the sixth century). Febronia was raised from birth in a convent near Nisibis, renowned for the erudition and wisdom of its sisterhood. Within this community, Febronia grew to hold a special place on three accounts: for her surpassing ascetic labours, for her capacity to teach others, and for the fact that she had never seen a man or been seen by a man. Both by the women of the convent and the women of the city, Febronia was considered truly blessed. The arrival of Roman soldiers on the scene, however, led to her imprisonment and death by slow torture, much of it sexual, as a warning for other Christians in the area.

The scenes of mourning amongst the women of the region – Christian and pagan, married and unmarried – are hauntingly evoked; they mourn as much for the loss of their cherished one, as for the invasion of her life by men, from whose eyes and whose evils Febronia had always been protected. Her life had been seen as one of true freedom in Christ, not restricted by society's dictates, but devoted instead to education, contemplation and friendship. In fitting tribute, her *Life* claims to have been written by a woman – an event remarkable in itself in antiquity – Febronia's spiritual sister Thomaïs, who became abbess of the convent soon after the saint's death. Febronia's story is also unusual because all the women in it are presented in positive terms. The standard hagiographical practice, whether Syriac or otherwise, is to present women saints as individuals who are exceptions to the rule of their own kind; convents are generally treated as groups of women and thus derided for harbouring institutionally the worst traits of their constituents. By contrast, Febronia is presented as a special woman among many fine women.

Febronia's *Life* is written with a graceful and elegant love: it is a vision of women unstereotyped and unrestricted, and it offers possibilities that do justice to early Syrian spirituality. But although her cult was popular, and remains so to this day (Gülcan, 1977), Febronia's *Life* is a unique piece of literature for its time. However, the Syrian milieu gave rise to another hagiographical motif, which flourished vengefully across the Christian Roman Empire between the fifth and ninth centuries: our second memory, the motif of the transvestite saint (Delcourt, 1961; Patlagean, 1975). These were women who chose to pursue their Christian vocation disguised as monks, and whose sanctity was derived from living, literally, as men. Their ruse was inevitably discovered at their deaths, if not before, and always greeted with shouts of praise and wonder: here, truly, were women who had risen to glory! The roots of the theme date back to the second-century apocryphal *Acts of Paul and Thecla* (Hennecke and Schneemelcher, 1973), in which Thecla had begged to conduct her missionary works disguised as a boy — much to Paul's distress. But the real starting point in popular literature began with the fifth-century Syrian story of St Pelagia, Antioch's most brilliant and breathtaking woman of ill-repute (*BHO* 919; *BHG*[3] 1478-9; Petitmangin *et al.*, 1981). Converted suddenly and in spectacular manner to the life of faith, she had enigmatically disappeared, and secretly lived out her career as a hermit in Jerusalem, renowned as a 'holy 'eunuch monk'. Her real identity was discovered at her death.

Pelagia's tale was captivating, especially to the men who wrote about it; unlike Febronia's story, it inspired many other legends in other languages along the same line (Delehaye, 1962). But these imitations were often blatantly allegorical: these women saints chose to disguise themselves as men, to 'become' men, because they could not serve God adequately as women. Men were worthier than women, monks were holier than nuns. The image summarised the church's stance on women: grace and sanctity were judged according to maleness. Nor was this theme found only in legend: there were real women who followed Pelagia's choice (e.g., St Anastasia, *BHG*[3] 78-9; cf. Piacenza Pilgrim, *Travels*, 34). Although the motif was of questionable orthodoxy — Deut. 22:5 expressly forbids either sex to assume the dress of the other — the theme of the transvestite saint enjoyed a striking popularity throughout Christendom for half a millennium before other ideas of women and sanctity began to gain momentum (Patlagean, 1975).

The extremity of the Syrian imagery in this case clearly tapped an incisive and widespread sentiment. But the image of the transvestite saint served to crystallise the misogynism that had grown to be an integral part of Syrian Christianity.

The tendencies underlying the common developments of the Syrian churches are consonant with those displayed throughout the Graeco-

Roman world. They reflected the consensus of the wider church, perhaps with a more specific articulation. But there is a shrill extravagance to the Syrian situation, as if to indicate that Syrian society had in fact proved genuinely responsive to the implications of its spiritual sensitivities. In any event, the tensions created were too great for the emerging Christian society to accommodate. Once again, women suffered the consequences.

Further Reading

Brock, S.P. (1979), 'Mary and the Eucharist, an Oriental Perspective', *Sobornost* I.2, pp. 50-59

Drijvers, H.J.W. (1980), 'The 19th Ode of Solomon', *JTS* 31, pp. 337-55

Murray, R. (1971), 'Mary the Second Eve in the Early Syriac Fathers', *Eastern Churches Review* 3, pp. 372-84

—— (1975), *Symbols of Church and Kingdom: A Study in Early Syriac Tradition*, especially pp. 312-20, Cambridge

Segal, J.B. (1958), *Edessa: The Blessed City*, Oxford

Vööbus, A. (1958), *A History of Asceticism in the Syrian Orient*, CSCO 184, Sub. 14, 197, Sub. 17, Louvain

ABBREVIATIONS

AASOR	Annual of the American Schools of Oriental Research
AB	Analecta Bollandiana
AfO	Archiv für Orientforschung
AJAH	American Journal of Ancient History
AM	Mitteilungen des Deutschen Archäologischen Instituts. Athenische Abteilung
AMI	Archäologische Mitteilungen aus Iran
ANEP	The Ancient Near East in Pictures Relating to the Old Testament[2], 1969, Pritchard, J.B. (ed.), Princeton
ANET	Ancient Near Eastern Texts Relating to the Old Testament[3], 1969, Pritchard, J.B. (ed.), Princeton
Annales ESC	Annales: Économies Societés Civilisations
ANRW	Aufstieg und Niedergang der Römischen Welt, Temporini, H. (ed.), 1972, Berlin
Anth. Pal.	Anthologia Palatina
AOAT	Alter Orient und Altes Testament
AOATS	Alter Orient und Altes Testament, Sonderreihe
AOS	American Oriental Society
Arch. Anz.	Archäologische Anzeiger
Arch. Delt.	Archaiologikon Deltion
ASA	Association of Social Anthropologists
ASAW	Abhandlungen der philologisch-historischen Klasse der sächsischen Akademie der Wissenschaften
Ath. Mitt.	Athenische Mitteilungen
BA	Biblical Archaeologist
BCH	Bulletin de Correspondence Hellénique
BE	Bulletin Épigraphique (annually in REG by J. and L. Robert)
BHG	Halkin, F. (1957), Bibliotheca Hagiographica Graeca, 3 vols., 3rd ed., Brussels (Subsidia Hagiographica 8a)
BHO	Peeters, P. (1910), repr. 1954, Bibliotheca Hagiographica Orientalis, Brussels (Subsidia Hagiographica 10)
BICS	Bulletin of the Institute of Classical Studies
BSA	British School at Athens, Proceedings of
BSFE	Bulletin de la Société française d'Égyptologie
CAD	Chicago Assyrian Dictionary
CIG	Corpus Inscriptionum Graecarum
CJ	Classical Journal
CPh	Classical Philology
CQ	Classical Quarterly
CR	Classical Review
CRAI	Comptes Rendues de l'Académie des Inscriptions
CSCO	Corpus Scriptorum Christianorum Orientalium
CSEL	Corpus Scriptorum Ecclesiasticorum Latinorum
CT	Cuneiform Texts from Babylonian Tablets in the British Museum
CVA	Corpus Vasorum Antiquorum (continuing series arranged by museum)
DHA	Dialogues d'Histoire Ancienne

DOP	*Dumbarton Oaks Papers*
GR	*Greece and Rome*
HSCP	*Harvard Studies in Classical Philology*
HSS	*Harvard Semitic Series*
IDidyma	*Didyma II: Die Inschriften, von A. Rehm*, Harder, R. (ed.), 1959, Berlin
IGRR	*Inscriptiones Graecae ad Res Romanas pertinentes*, Cagnat, R. *et al.*, 1906-27
IKyme	*Die Inschriften von Kyme*, Engelman, H. (ed.), 1976. *Inschriften griechischer Städte aus Kleinasien Bd. 5*, Bonn
ILS	*Inscriptiones Latinae Selectae*, Dessau, H. (ed.), 1892-1916, Berlin
IPriene	*Die Inschriften von Priene*, Hiller von Gaertringen, W. (ed.)
JAOS	*Journal of the American Oriental Society*
JBL	*Journal of Biblical Studies*
JCS	*Journal of Cuneiform Studies*
JEA	*Journal of Egyptian Archaeology*
JEOL	*Jaarbericht . . . van het Vooraziatisch-Egyptisch Genootschap 'Ex Oriente Lux'*
JESHO	*Journal of the Economic and Social History of the Orient*
JHS	*Journal of Hellenic Studies*
JJS	*Journal of Jewish Studies*
JKF	*Jahrbuch für kleinasiatische Forschung*
JNES	*Journal of Near Eastern Studies*
JOAI	*Jahreshefte des österreichischen archäologischen Instituts*
JOB	*Jahrbuch der österreichischen byzantinischen Gesellschaft*
JRS	*Journal of Roman Studies*
JSS	*Journal of Semitic Studies*
JTS	*Journal of Theological Studies*
JWI	*Journal of the Warburg and Courtauld Institutes*
KZ	*Zeitschrift für vergleichende Sprachforschung*
LÄ	*Lexikon der Ägyptologie*
Mansi	Mansi, J.D. (1759-98), *Sacrorum conciliorum nova et amplissima collectio*, 53 vols., Florence
OA	*Oriens Antiquus*
OLZ	*Orientalistische Literaturzeitschrift*
Or.	*Orientalia*
PAAJR	*Proceedings of the American Academy for Jewish Research*
P del Pass.	*La Parola del Passato*
Peira	Zepos, I. and P. (eds.), 1931, *Peira of Eustathios Romaios, Ius Graeco-romanum* IV, Athens
PG	Migne, J.P., *Patrologia Graeca*
PL	Migne, J.P., *Patrologia Latina*
RA	*Revue d'assyriologie et d'archeologie orientale*
RE	Pauly-Wissowa, *Realenzyklopädie des klassischen Altertums*
REG	*Revue des études grecques*
Rev. Arch.	*Revue archéologique*
RHA	*Revue hittite et asianique*
RHR	*Revue d'histoire des religions*
RLA	*Reallexikon der Assyriologie*
SBT	*Studien zu den Boğazköy-Texten*
SEG	*Supplementum Epigraphicum Graecum*
SIG	*Sylloge Inscriptionum Graecarum*, Dittenberger, W., ed.
SRKK	*Studien zur Religion und Kultur Kleinasiens*, Festschrift F.K. Dörner, 2 vols., Sahin, S., Schwertheim, E., Wagner, J. (eds.),

	1970, Leiden
TAM	*Tituli Asiae Minoris*, Kalnika E. *et al.* (eds.), 1901- , Vienna
TAPA	*Transactions of the American Philological Association*
TLS	*Times Literary Supplement*
UF	*Ugarit Forschungen*
VAB	*Vorderasiatische Bibliothek*
WdF	*Wege der Forschung*
ZA	*Zeitschrift für Assyriologie*
ZAW	*Zeitschrift für die alttestamentliche Wissenschaft*
ZPE	*Zeitschrift für Papyrologie und Epigraphik*
ZSS	*Zeitschrift der Savigny Stiftung*

APPENDICES, ADDENDA AND CORRIGENDA

1. Women: Model for Possession by Greek Daemons
Ruth Padel, London

This field has received the most intensive and sophisticated treatment in the last ten years; particularly important work, that has substantially refined and changed understanding, has been done by Loraux, Zeitlin, Sourvinou-Inwood and, not least, by the contributor herself. We are, therefore, very grateful to Ruth Padel for allowing the text to be reprinted as it stands.

Some of the major bibliographical additions to be noted are:

Carson, A. (1986), *Eros the Bittersweet,* Princeton, NJ
du Bois, P. (1988), *Sowing the Body: Psychoanalysis and Ancient Representations of Women,* Chicago
Just, R. (1989), *Women in Athenian Law and Life*, London, New York
Lloyd, G.E.R. (1990), *Demystifying Mentalities*, Cambridge
Loraux, N. (1982), *Les enfants d'Athena: idées athéniennes sur la citoyenneté et la division des sexes*, Paris
— (1986), *Tragic Ways of Killing a Woman* (trans.), Cambridge, Mass.
Padel, R. (1984), 'A portrait of Teiresias', *Encounter* (November), 44–9
— (1990a), 'Making space speak', in Zeitlin, F., Winkler, J. (eds), *Nothing to do with Dionysos?* Princeton, NJ
— (1990b), 'Reflections on feminism and classical scholarship', *Gender and History* 2/2, 198–211
— (1992), *In and Out of the Mind: Greek Images of the Tragic Self*, Princeton, NJ
— (forthcoming) *Mad, Possessed and Female: Attributes of the Greek Tragic Self*, Princeton, NJ
Parke, H.W. (1988), *Sibyls and Sibylline Prophecy*, London
Sissa, G. (1990), *Greek Virginity* (trans.), Cambridge, Mass.
Sourvinou-Inwood, C. (1990), 'Sophocles' *Antigone* as a "bad woman"', in Dieteren, F., Kloek, E. (eds), *Writing Women into History*, Amsterdam Historische Reeks 17, 11–38
— (1991), *'Reading' Greek Culture*, Oxford
Steiner, G. (1984), *Antigones*, Oxford
Zeitlin, F. (1986), 'Configurations of rape in Greek myth', in Tomaselli, S., Porter, R. (eds), *Rape*, Oxford, 122–51

2. Exit Atossa: Images of Women in Greek Historigraphy on Persia
Heleen Sancisi-Weerdenburg, Utrecht

In the decade since *Images of Women* has appeared, studies on women in Persian society are still strikingly absent. The one exception is Maria Brosius' DPhil dissertation, *Royal and Non-Royal Women in Achaemenid Persia (559–331 BC)* (University of Oxford 1991; to be published in the series 'Oxford Classical Monographs'), which makes full use of the Persepolis tablets. The tablets, including the still unpublished large collection of the Chicago Oriental Institute, contain yet more interesting material. For an overview of this, including bibliographical references, see D.M. Lewis, 'The Persepolis Fortification Texts', in *Achaemenid History IV: Centre and Periphery*, eds H. Sancisi-Weerdenburg and A. Kuhrt (Leiden, 1990), 1–6. Useful information on the economic affairs of Queen Parysatis can be found in M. Stolper, *Entrepreneurs and Empire: The Murašu Archive, The Murašu Firm, and Persian Rule in Babylonia* (Leiden, 1985), esp. 63–4.

E. Hall, *Inventing the Barbarian: Greek Self-Definition through Tragedy* (Oxford, 1989) demonstrates the mechanism by which, in Greek tragedy, barbarians are equipped with characteristics also applied to women and how both are drawn into the same semantic complex (see esp. 206). P. Briant has shown in 'Institutions perses et histoire comparatiste dans l'historiographie grecque' (*Achaemenid History* II: *The Greek Sources*, ed. H. Sancisi-Weerdenburg and A. Kuhrt [Leiden, 1987], 1–10) that the Greek descriptions of Persian history serve, more often than not, to define Greek identity. In the same volume, R.B. Stevenson ('Lies and invention in Deinon's *Persica*', 27–35) analyses the fragments of Ctesias' successor, Deinon. For the essentially novelistic character of one tale involving Atossa and a Greek doctor, see A. Griffiths, 'Democedes of Croton: a Greek doctor at Darius' court', *ibid.*, 37–51.

There is a new French translation of Jacoby's fragments of Ctesias: *Ctésias: Histoires de l'Orient*, trans. and comm. J. Auberger (Paris, 1991). On Ctesias' historiographical qualities, or rather defects, see H. Sancisi-Weerdenburg, 'Decadence in the empire or decadence in the sources? From source to synthesis: Ctesias', in *Achaemenid History* I: *Sources, Structures, Synthesis*, ed. H. Sancisi-Weerdenburg (Leiden, 1987), 33–46.

Much of Elizabeth Carney's criticisms of the conventional treatment of Macedonian royal women ('"What's in a name?" The emergence of a title for royal women in the hellenistic period' in *Women's History and Ancient History*, ed. S.B. Pomeroy [Chapel Hill, NC, 1991], 154–172; 'Olympias', *Ancient Society* 18 [1987], 43–8) are relevant to the study of Persian royal women.

The Persepolis tablets contain material unique for the ancient world and a complete demographic analysis of this remains a desideratum.

4. Influential Women
Mary Lefkowitz, Wellesley, Mass.

This essay was reprinted, with minor revisions, in *Women in Greek Myth* (London, 1986), 80–94. In a thoughtful review in *The Washington Book Review* (May 1987), 18–19, J. Rusten noted that in the literature of the fifth and fourth centuries there was a conscious effort to subordinate the needs of the family to those of the state; hence women who were willing to sacrifice themselves or their children for Athens, such as Praxagora in Euripides' *Erechtheus* or Macaria in the *Heraclidae*, were particularly laudable from the point of view of Athenian males. As Rusten observes, the most extreme expression of this ideology may be found in Book V of Plato's *Republic*, where the notion of family is completely done away with; cf. S. Said, 'La République de Platon et la communauté des femmes', *L'Antiquité Classique* (1986), 142–62, and my 'Only the best girls get to: why Plato wasn't a feminist' *TLS* 5/5–11 (1989), 484; 497. But it would be hard to show that this ideology, however forcefully argued, ever succeeded in making much dent in family values championed by heroines such as the 'revived' Antigone of Sophocles' *Oedipus at Colonus* and Euripides' *Phoenissae*. Although the Greeks refused to give women political and civic rights equal to their own, they were never able (or apparently eager) to silence them, and so long as women could express themselves, even within the confines of the home, they could comment on and influence the action undertaken by men. For their positive moral influence in Homer and Hesiod, cf. 'The heroic women of Greek epic', *The American Scholar* 56 (1987), 503–18 and 'The powers of the primeval goddesses', *ibid*. 58 (1989), 586–91. O. Patterson, *Freedom* (1991), 105, rightly calls attention to the importance of what Greek women say (even in works by male authors), but he gives them too much credit when he suggests that their complaints about their own condition helped call attention to the similar restrictions imposed on slaves.

6. Women and Housing in Classical Greece: The Archaeological Evidence Updated
Susan Walker, London

This paper has generated mixed reactions: an enthusiastic response from an archaeologist directing new excavations of early Islamic houses in the Maghreb must be set against the more cautious reactions of classical archaeologists working in Greece. As yet I have received no comments from excavators of newly discovered classical houses, and it cannot yet be judged how useful an interpretative tool the questions might be. It has been objected that the division of houses represented graphically here is arbitrary and obscures the evidence for other uses of the rooms (Jameson [1990], 172; Jameson [1991], 104 with n. 16). The arbitrariness was intentional: the drawings are no more than a means of encouraging archaeologists to consider house-plans from a point of view given little attention before 1983. The second point is a valid one, and in his two articles on this subject Jameson has assembled much interesting evidence for the varied uses of rooms in classical houses. However, his observation that the classical Greek house, like its modern rural counterpart, expressed the cohesion of the nuclear family and their suspicion of all outsiders (1991, 106) is not well substantiated, and I have yet to be convinced that male/female relations are as spatially insignificant as Jameson suggests.

Since 1983, a number of relevant studies have been published. Of the major publications, Hoepfner and Schwandner (1985) provide splendid illustrations of Greek houses and of the design of towns, though their text is thin on social history. Conversely, Pesando (1987, 1989) has thoroughly mined the literary evidence, but needs Hoepfner and Schwandner to provide a full architectural picture. Jameson's articles, themselves full of interesting detail and well annotated with further references, appear in works that have much to offer the student of domestic architecture in its urban and rural setting.

Select Bibliography

Hoepfner, W., Schwandner, E. (1985), *Haus und Stadt im klassischen Griechenland* (Wohnen in der klassischen Polis, vol. i), Munich

Jameson, M. (1990), 'Private space in the Greek city', in Murray, O., Price, S. (eds), *The Greek City-State from Homer to Alexander*, Oxford, 171–95

— (1991), 'Domestic space in the Greek city-state' in Kent, S. (ed.) *Domestic Architecture and the Use of Space*, Cambridge, 92–113

Pesando, F. (1987) *Oikos e Ktesis: la casa greca in età classica*, Perugia

— (1989), *La casa dei Greci*, Milan

7. Women on Athenian Vases: Problems of Interpretation
Dyfri Williams, London

Addenda to Notes:

p. 105, n. 9: see now H. Immerwahr, 'An inscribed cup by the Ambrosios Painter' *Antike Kunst* (1984), 10–13

p. 105, n. 15: for Kerameikos, Bau Z, see now U. Knigge, *Der Kerameikos von Athen: Führung durch Ausgrabungen und Geschichte* (Athens, 1988), 88–94 (where the building is interpreted as a private house).

Recent Bibliography:

Harvey, D. (1988), 'Painted ladies: fact, fiction and fantasy', in Christiansen J., Melander T. (eds), *Proceedings of the Third Colloquium on Ancient Greek and Related Pottery*, Copenhagen, 242–54
Keuls, E.C. (1985), *The Reign of the Phallus*, New York
Koch-Harnack, G. (1983), *Knabenliebe und Tiergeschenke*, Berlin
Meyer, M. (1988), 'Männer mit Geld', *Jahrbuch des Deutschen Archäologischen Instituts* 103, 87–125
Perschel I. (1987), *Die Hetäre bei Symposion und Komos in der attisch-rotfigurigen Vasenmalerei des 6.–4. Jahrh. v. Chr.*, Frankfurt
Reinsberg, C. (1989), *Ehe, Hetärentum und Knabenliebe im antiken Griechenland*, Munich

8. Bound to Bleed: Artemis and Greek Women
Helen King, Liverpool

Since 'Bound to Bleed', awareness of the medical texts of the Hippocratic corpus as a source for images of women has grown, in line with a wider interest in the history of the body and of sexuality. There are important sections on women and medicine in Geoffrey Lloyd's *Science, Folklore and Ideology* (Cambridge, 1983), while among the recent publications of Ann Ellis Hanson must be mentioned 'Continuity and change: three case studies in Hippocratic gynecological therapy and theory', in *Women's History and Ancient History*, ed. S. Pomeroy (Chapel Hill, 1991) and 'The medical writers' woman', in *Before Sexuality*, ed. D.M. Halperin, J.J. Winkler and F.I. Zeitlin (Princeton, NJ, 1990). On menstruation in particular, see Lesley Dean-Jones, 'Menstrual bleeding according to the Hippocratics and Aristotle', *TAPA* 119 (1989), 177–92; in relation to the hazards of the transformation from *parthenos* to *gynē*, see my own 'The daughter of Leonides: reading the Hippocratic corpus', in *History as Text*, ed. Averil Cameron (London, 1989), 13–32. The cultural representations of virginity have been discussed by Giulia Sissa, *Greek Virginity* (Cambridge, Mass., 1990) and the significance of hanging in relation to female death by Nicole Loraux, *Tragic Ways of Killing a Woman* (Cambridge, Mass., 1987). The companion piece to 'Bound to Bleed' is my article 'Sacrificial blood: the role of the *amnion* in Hippocratic gynecology', *Helios*, 13/2 (1987), and also in *Rescuing Creusa*, ed. M. Skinner (Lubbock, Texas, 1987), 117–26.

9. Hittite Birth Rituals
Jackie Pringle, London

On p. 135, l. 10 it seems preferable to translate as follows:
'And upon him his hands are bound . . .'

10. Celtic Women in the Early Middle Ages
Wendy Davies, London

Corrigenda

p. 145, l. 29 should read '(Cumbric)'
p. 153, ll. 10–11 should read 'from the husband's side might come
compensation to the bride's family or her protector for her loss
(brideprice)'

Additional Bibliography

Bitel, L. (1986), 'Women's monastic enclosures in early Ireland', *Journal of Medieval History* 12, 15–36
— (1990), *Isle of the Saints*, Ithaca, NY
Davies, W. (1989), 'The place of healing in Early Irish society', in Ó Corráin, D., Breatnach, L., McCorie, K. (eds), *Sages, Saints and Storytellers*, Maynooth
— (1988), *Small Worlds: The Village Community in Early Medieval Brittany*, London
Kelly, F. (1988), *A Guide to Early Irish Law*, Dublin
Ó Coráin, D. (1985), 'Marriage in Early Ireland', in Cosgrove, A. (ed.) *Marriage in Ireland*, Dublin

11. In Search of Byzantine Women: Three Avenues of Approach
Judith Herrin, Princeton, NJ

Corrigenda and Addenda

p. 186, n. 5 should read 'Herrin (1982)'. Add: Huxley (1991); Herrin (1992a, 1992b)
p. 186, n. 10 add: on early Byzantine prostitution, see Leontsini (1989)
p. 186, n. 12 add: for the eleventh century treatise on eunuchs by Theophylact of Ochrid, see Spadaro (1981)
p. 186, n. 16 add: on dowry in Byzantium, see Simon (1976); White (1982)
p. 187, n. 23 add: on Byzantine wills in general, see Manaphes (1976), on the will of Kale-Maria Pakouriane, see Lemerle (1977)
p. 188, n. 48 should read 'Leukas' (in place of Levkos)
p. 188, n. 50 add: cf. Fledelius (1982)
p. 188, n. 54 following 'Averil Cameron (1978)', add: Cameron (1989) and

(1991): 97–106, 165–75
p. 188, n. 55 following 'Laiou (1981), pp. 241–8', add: Laiou (1986)
p. 189, l. 3 should read 'Raymond Grew' (not 'Crew')
p. 189, list of further reading, should read 'Herrin J. (1982)' (not '1983')

Additional Bibliography

Abrahamse, D. de F. (1985), 'Women's monasticism in the Middle Byzantine period: problems and prospects', *Byzantinische Forschungen* 9, 35–58

—— (1984), 'Byzantine asceticism and women's monasteries in early medieval Italy' in Nichols J., Shank L.T. (eds), *Medieval Religious Women* I: *Distant Echoes*, Kalamazoo, 31–49

Archer, L. *et al.* (eds) (1993), *An Illusion of the Night. Women in Ancient Societies*, London

Bynum, C.W. *et al.* (eds) (1986), *Gender and Religion: On the Complexity of Symbols*, Boston, Mass.

Cameron, Averil (1989), 'Virginity as metaphor', in Cameron, A. (ed.), *History as Text*, London, 184–205

—— (1991), *Christianity and the Rhetoric of Empire*, Berkeley and Los Angeles.

Carras, L. (ed.) (1984), *Life of St. Athanasia*, in Moffat, A. (ed.), *Maistor*, Canberra

Fledelius, K. (1982), 'Women's position and possibilities in Byzantine society with particular reference to the Novels of Leo VI', *JOB* 32/2, 425–32

Galatariotou, C. (1984/5), 'Holy women and witches: aspects of Byzantine conceptions of gender', *Byzantine and Modern Greek Studies* 9, 55–94

—— (1987), 'Structural oppositions in the Grottaferrata *Digenis Akrites*', *Byzantine and Modern Greek Studies* 11, 29–68

—— (1988), 'Byzantine women's monastic communities: the evidence of the *typika*', *JOB* 38, 263–90

Goody, J. (1983). *The Development of the Family and Marriage in Europe*, Cambridge

Gouillard, J. (1982), 'La femme de qualité dans l'oeuvre de Théodore Stoudite', *JOB* 32/2, 445–52

Herrin, J. (1992a) '*Femina byzantina*: the Council in Trullo on women', *Dumbarton Oaks Papers* 45

—— (1992b), 'Public and private forms of religious commitment among Byzantine women', in Archer *et al.*

Huxley, G. (1991), 'Women and Byzantine iconoclasm' in Perreault, J.Y., *Les femmes et le monachisme byzantin*, Athens, 11–24

Laiou, A. (1985), 'Observations on the life and ideology of Byzantine women', *Byzantinische Forschungen* 9, 59–102

—— 1986 'The Festival of Agathe: comments on the life of

Constantinopolitan women', in *Byzantion: Aphieroma ston A.N. Strato I*, Athens, 111–22

Lemerle, P. (1977), *Cinq études sur le onzième siècle*, Paris

Leontsini, S. (1989), *Die Prostitution im fruehen Byzanz*, Vienna

Manaphes, K. (1976), *Monasteriaka typika-diathekai*, Athens

Rosenqvist, J.O. (1986), *The Life of St. Irene Abbess of Chrysobalanton*, Uppsala

Runciman, Sir Steven (1984), 'Women in Byzantine aristocratic society', in Angold, M. (ed.), *The Byzantine Aristocracy IX-XIII Centuries*, Oxford, 10–22

Simon, D. (1976), 'Das Ehegueterrecht der Peira: ein systematischer Versuch', *Fontes Minores* 7, 193–238

Sorlin, I. (1991), 'Striges et géloudes: Histoire d'une croyance et d'une tradition', *Travaux et mémoires* 11, 411–34

Spadaro, M.D. (1981), 'Un edito di Teofilatto di Achrida sull'eunuchia', *Rivista di Studi Byzantini e Slavi* I, 3–38

Talbot, A.-M. (1985), 'A comparison of the monastic experience of Byzantine men and women', *Greek Orthodox Theological Review* 30, 1–20

Treadgold, W. (1988), *The Byzantine Revival*, Stanford, Calif.

Weyl-Carr, A.M. (1985), 'Women and monasticism in Byzantium', *Byzantinische Forschungen* 9, 1–15

White, D. (1982), 'Property rights of women', *Jahrbuch der Oesterreichischen Gesellschaft* 32/3, 539–48

14. Women and Wealth

Riet Van Bremen, London

The general conclusions of this article stand, and have not been significantly challenged, although some will be modified in my forthcoming book *Women in Public in the Graeco-Roman City*. Corrections are, however, necessary in two cases. First, a mistake in interpretation: in *JHS* 107 (1987), 174 n. 12, J.J. Coulton rightly corrected my reading of *kata diatheken* (p.229 and n. 37): Opramaos bequeathed estates *kata diatheken*, but did not inherit them *kata diatheken* from his mother; although they undoubtedly came from his mother's family they did not necessarily pass from mother to son. Second, my assessment of the role and importance of Menodora, discussed on pp. 223, 230 and in n. 6, has changed significantly: see my article 'A Family from Sillyon', *ZPE* (forthcoming).

From a number of publications on this subject I list here only those that I think have made important additional points to the ones made in my article, or that have added interesting new material.

On matters of inheritance, ownership and other related problems, R. Lane Fox, 'Aspects of Inheritance in the Greek World', in *CRUX: Essays presented to G.E.M. de Ste. Croix* (Exeter, 1985), 209–32, is interesting, as is C. Vial, *Délos indépendante, 314–167 avant J.-C.*, BCH Suppl. X (Paris, 1984); an important study of Delian families within the social and political life of the island. It has many pertinent observations on the role of women. Ph. Gauthier, *Les cités grecques et leurs bienfaiteurs (IVe-Ier siècles avant J.-C.): contribution à l'histoire des institutions*, BCH Suppl. XII (Paris 1985), esp. 39–75, discusses the emergence of female benefactors in the late hellenistic period. Guy Rogers, 'The constructions of women at Ephesus', *ZPE* 90 (1992), 215–23, has interesting points to make, although his main argument is not convincing. There are three new decrees documenting the negotiations between the benefactress Archippe and the city of Cyme (mentioned on p. 235). These new texts, together with the four already known, are now most easily accessible in *SEG* XXXIII (1984), 1035–41.

15. Goddesses, Women and Jezebel
Peter R. Ackroyd, London

(This addendum has been written with substantial help from Richard Coggins, London.)

There has been much recent study by a variety of scholarly concerns of the place of goddesses in the religion of ancient Israel. Part of the interest arises from archaeology, and the concern to understand the significance of the many female figurines that have been discovered. This overlaps with the reconstruction of the history of Israelite religion: was insistence that Yahweh alone was god a long-standing characteristic of Israel or was it a development which took place around the time of the exile? Were the condemnations of the worship of other gods and goddesses aimed at those who should have 'known better', or were they in effect a call to new understanding? Feminist scholarship has also played an important part in tracing the role of the goddess(es); while some attempt has been made to reconstruct an idealised golden age when the goddess was worshipped before the patriarchal dominance of Yahweh took root, other scholars have taken a more nuanced line, setting the role of the goddesses alongside that of Yahweh.

Among books and articles specifically devoted to these themes may be mentioned S.M. Olyan, *Asherah and the Cult of Yahweh in Ancient Israel* (Atlanta Ga., 1988); A. Lemaire, 'Who or what was Yahweh's Asherah?', *Biblical Archaeology Review* 10 (1984); P.L. Day (ed.), *Gender and Difference in Ancient Israel* (Minneapolis, Minn., 1989). In German, U. Winter, *Frau und Göttin* (Freiburg, 1983) was the precursor of a large number of studies devoted to this whole range of topics; several have been published in the same series (Orbis Biblicus et Orientalis), with special attention to the archaeological material. A recent volume of collected essays, assessing the evidence from a variety of viewpoints, is M.T. Wacker and E. Zenger (eds), *Der eine Gott und die Göttin*, Quaestiones Disputatae

135 (Rome, 1991). A substantial bibliography may be found in A.P. Long, *In a Chariot Drawn by Lions* (The Women's Press, 1992), 227–58.

17. The Role of Jewish Women in the Religion, Ritual and Cult of Graeco-Roman Palestine
Léonie J. Archer, Oxford

The words of Josephus from *Contra Apionem*, which open this paper, are a useful starting point for a discussion of women's roles in ancient Judaism. To speak of a 'theocracy' and to present God's law as central to Jewish life and thought is to capture a certain flavour of Jewish existence in Graeco-Roman Palestine, i.e. the dominance of an identifiable and separate belief system. It must be remembered, though, that that religion or belief system was not as monolithic or homogeneous as Josephus, who was writing an *apologia*, might have wanted his readers to think. There was no normative Judaism in these centuries. Old and new orderings and ritual practices co-existed. The rabbinic system of later centuries was but a part of the picture. There was a state of flux.

The oldest extant code of Jewish law, the Mishnah (redacted *c*. AD 200), reflects this flux. It is drawn upon heavily in this paper. The later commentary on the Mishnah, the Gemara, is also used. (The two may be differentiated by the non-specialist reader by the way in which they are referred to: Mishnah is cited by, as it were, chapter and verse (*Meg.* 4:3), Gemara appears by chapter and folio (*Meg. 43a*).) Both were written after the centuries under consideration, but both contain material pertaining to the period. Not utilised here are the so-called intertestamental writings, i.e. the apocrypha and pseudepigrapha, which are not of the same legalistic genre and so not of the same immediate use for an analysis of the woman's prescribed role in public religion. They do, however, offer other insights to the scholar of the period, and my study, *Her Price is Beyond Rubies: The Jewish Woman in Graeco-Roman Palestine* (Sheffield, 1990), which draws heavily on these sources, discusses in greater detail than space allows here such aspects of the woman's life as education, domestic duties, property rights and ritual impurity which were part and parcel of her prescribed religious role and of our understanding of it.

Her Price is Beyond Rubies also deals in some detail with the subject of women and death ritual, and with the general question of female involvement in what was (and still is) seen as popular, and therefore inferior, religion or 'superstition', matters with which this paper closes. Regarding death ritual, such duties as were accorded the woman at the graveside reflected and restated society's belief in her 'otherness', in her uncleanness and her emotionality. They also reflect society's belief in the woman's closer kinship with 'nature' as opposed to the 'higher realm' of 'culture', a matter which I discuss in *Through the Devil's Gateway: Women, Religion and Taboo*, ed. Alison Joseph (London, 1990), 22–49, and elsewhere.

Regarding women's involvement in 'magical' practices and the like, it must be emphasised that the designation 'popular' or 'superstitious' is in line with our received texts (and most secondary commentary). In other words, it comes from texts that are the record of what came to be the dominant and then the exclusive religion, i.e. the religion of Yahweh, a religion, in public manifestation at least, of the male community. Although the texts reveal much about how non-conforming parties (and women) were viewed, they give little hard information about the actual practices or the practitioners which they denigrate. Such was not their purpose. We need to look beyond our sources and ask: what were these women doing, what alternative and co-existent groupings did they constitute? What, for example, was the real story behind the eighty witches hanged at Ashkelon? I tackle some of these issues of alternative communities in an essay that appears in a volume conceived of as a successor to *Images of Women in Antiquity* ('Notions of community and the exclusion of the female in Jewish history and historiography', in *An Illusion of the Night: Women in Ancient Societies*, ed. L.J. Archer, Susan Fischler and Maria Wyke (London, 1993)).

For a discussion of the Jewish woman's role in the religion, ritual and cult of Graeco-Roman Palestine, therefore, it is necessary to consider (a) her involvement (or non-involvement) in what was to be the publicly constituted and formalised religion, (b) her role in rituals that hovered on the edge of acceptability and/or were deemed to be the special domain of women and (c) her possible participation in rituals that ran counter to what the Yahwists sought to promote.

Corrigenda

p. 273, l. 6: read 'polity' (instead of 'policy')
p. 285: in the list of Abbreviations used, the last entry should read '*y.* Jerusalem Talmud' (not *v.*)

18. Women in Early Syrian Christianity
Susan Ashbrook Harvey, Providence, RI

Additional Bibliography

Brock, S.P. (1990), 'The holy spirit as feminine in Syriac literature', in Soskice, J. (ed.), *After Eve*, London, 73–88
Brock, S.P., Harvey, S.A. (1987), *Holy Women of the Syrian Orient*, Berkeley, Calif.
Harvey, S.A. (1990), *Asceticism and Society in Crisis: John of Ephesus and the 'Lives of the Eastern Saints'*, Berkeley, Calif.
— (1993), 'Feminine imagery for the divine: the Holy Spirit, the Odes of Solomon and Early Syriac tradition', *St. Vladimir's Theological Quarterly*

BIBLIOGRAPHY

Abrahams, I. (1932), *Jewish Life in the Middle Ages*, rev. ed. C. Roth (sic), London
Abusch, T. (1974), 'Mesopotamian anti-witchcraft literature, part I. The nature of *Maqlû*', *JNES* 33, 251-62
Ackroyd, P.R. (1962), 'The vitality of the Word of God in the Old Testament', *Annual of the Swedish Theological Institute* 1, 7-23
Adam, J. (1963), *The Republic of Plato*, 2nd ed., Cambridge
Ahlström, G.W. (1963), *Aspects of Syncretism in Israelite Religion*, Lund (Horae Soederblomianae, 5)
Alexiou, M. (1974), *The Ritual Element in Greek Tradition*, Oxford
Amundsen, D.W., Diers, C.J. (1969), 'The age of menarche in classical Greece and Rome', *Human Biology* 41, 125-32
Anderson, M.O. (1973), *Kings and Kingship in Early Scotland*, Edinburgh
Annas, J. (1981), *An Introduction to Plato's Republic*, Oxford
Anson, J. (1974), 'The female transvestite in early monasticism', *Viator* 5, 1-32
Archi, A. (1974), 'Il sistema KIN della divinazione ittite', *OA* 13, 113-33
Ardener, E.A. (1975), 'Belief and the Problem of Women', in Ardener, S. (ed.), *Perceiving Women*, London
Ardener, S. (ed.) (1981), *Women and Space: ground rules and social maps*, London
Arthur, M.B. (1976), 'Review Essay: Classics', *Signs* 2, 382-403
Ashtor, E. (1961), 'Le coût de la vie dans la Syrie médiévale', *Arabica*, 8, 59-73
Aske, M. (1981), 'Magical spaces in the Eve of St. Agnes', *Essays in Criticism* 21/3, 196-209
Astour, M.C. (1966), 'Tamar the hierodule', *JBL* 85, 185-96
Avi-Yonah, M. (ed.) (1975), *Encyclopaedia of Archaeological Excavation in the Holy Land*, I-IV, London
Babakos, A. (1962), 'Vormundschaft im altthessalischen Recht IIIc. BC - IIIc. AD', *ZSS* 79, 311-22
— (1973), *Familienrechtliche Verhältnisse auf der Insel Kalymnos im ersten nachchristlichen Jahrhundert*, Köln
Bachelard, G. (1964), *The Poetics of Space*, trans. N. Jolas, New York
Balland, A. (1981), *Fouilles de Xanthos VII: Inscriptions d'époque impériale du Létôon*, Paris
Balsdon, J.P.V.D. (1962), *Roman Women: Their History and Habits*, London
Bansammar, E. (1976), 'La titulature de l'impératrice et sa signification. Recherches sur les sources byzantines de la fin du VIIIe siècle à la fin du XIIe siècle', *Byzantion* 46, 243-91
Barthes, R. (1960), *Sur Racine*, Paris
Barton, G.A. (1927), 'A comparison of some features of Hebrew and Babylonian ritual', *JBL* 46, 79-89
Bartrum, P.C. (ed.) (1966), *Early Welsh Genealogical Tracts*, Cardiff
Bauer, W. (1972), *Orthodoxy and Heresy in Earliest Christianity*, 3rd. ed., London
Beasley, T.W. (1906), 'The *Kyrios* in the Greek states other than Athens', in *CR* 20, *CR* 249-55
Beaucamp, J. (1977), 'La situation juridique de la femme à Byzance', *Cahiers de civilisation médiévale* 20, 145-76

Beazley, J.D. (1956), *Attic Black-figure Vase-Painters*, Oxford
— (1963), *Attic Red-figure Vase-Painters*, 2nd. ed., Oxford
Beckman, G.M. (1977), *Hittite Birth Rituals*, Ann Arbor
Benardete, S. (1969), *Herodotean Inquiries*, The Hague
Benedetti, B. (1980), 'Nota sulla ^{sal}ŠU.GI ittita', *Mesopotamia* 15, 93-108
Bengtson, H. (1977), *Griechische Geschichte von den Anfängen bis in die römische Kaiserzeit*, 5th ed., Munich (von Müller, I. ed. Handbuch der klassischen Altertumswissenschaft iii/4)
Benndorf, O., Niemann, G. (1884), *Reisen in Lykien und Karien*, 2 vols., Vienna
Bieler, L. (ed.) (1963), *The Irish Penitentials*, Dublin (Scriptores Latini Hiberniae 5)
— (ed.) (1979), *The Patrician Texts in the Book of Armagh*, Dublin (Scriptores Latini Hiberniae 10)
Binchy, D.A. (1936a), 'The legal capacity of women in regard to contracts', in Binchy (1936b), 207-34
— (ed.) (1936b), *Studies in Early Irish Law*, Dublin
Blair, J. (1981), 'Private parts in public spaces: the case of actresses', in Ardener, S. (ed.) (1981), 205-28
Blecher, G. (1905), *De Extispicio Capita Tria*, Giessen
Boardman, J. (1980), *The Greeks Overseas*, 3rd. ed., London
Bonsirven, J. (1931), *On the Ruins of the Temple*, London
Børresen, K.E. (forthcoming), 'The Patristic Use of Female Metaphors Describing God'
Boserup, E. (1970), *Women's Role in Economic Development*, New York
Bouché-Leclerq, F.A. (1879-82), *Histoire de la divination dans l'antiquité*, 4 vols., Paris
Bourgey, L. (1953), *Observation et expérience chez les médécins de la collection hippocratique*, Paris
Boyle, A. (1977), 'Matrilineal succession in the Pictish monarchy', *Scottish Historical Review*, 56, 1-10
Braudel, F. (1975), *The Mediterranean*, trans. S. Reynolds, London
Braunstein, O. (1911), *Die politische Wirksamkeit der griechischen Frau*, diss. Leipzig
Brelich, A. (1969), *Paides e Parthenoi*, Rome
Bright, J. (1960), *A History of Israel*, London
Broadhead, H.D. (1960), *The Persae of Aeschylos*, Cambridge
Brock, S.P. (1979), 'Mary and the Eucharist: an oriental perspective', *Sobornost* 1/2, 50-59
Bromwich, R. (1974), *Medieval Celtic Literature. A Select Bibliography*, Toronto
Brooks, B.A. (1941), 'Fertility cult functionaries in the Old Testament', *JBL* 60, 227-53
Broughton, T.R.S. (1938), 'Roman Asia Minor', in T. Frank (ed.), *Economic Survey of Ancient Rome*, IV, Baltimore
Browning, R. (1971), *Justinian and Theodora*, New York
Budge, E.A.W. (ed. and trans.) (1899), *History of the Blessed Virgin* (in Syriac), 2 vols., London
Burde, C. (1974), *Hethitische Medizinische Texte*, Wiesbaden (SBT 19)
Burkert, W. (1977), *Griechische Religion der archaischen und klassischen Epoche*, Stuttgart
Burnyeat, M.F. (1977), 'Socratic Midwifery, Platonic Inspiration', *BICS* 24, 7-16
Byrne, F.J. (1973), *Irish Kings and High-Kings*, London
Cahen, E. (1930), *Les Hymnes de Callimaque*, Paris
Calmeyer, P. (1976), 'Zur Genese altiranischer Motive. V. Synarchie', *AMI* n.f. 9, 63-95

Cameron, A. (1932), 'The exposure of children and Greek ethics', *CR* 46, 105-14

Cameron, Averil (1978), 'The cult of the Theotokos in sixth-century Constantinople', *JTS* n.s. 29, 79-108

Campbell, J.K. (1964), *Honour, Family and Patronage. A Study of Institutions and Moral Values in a Greek Mountain community*, Oxford

Canivet, P., Leroy-Molinghen, A. (eds. and trans.) (1977-9), *Théodoret et Cyr, Histoire des moines de Syrie*, Paris (Sources chrétiennes 234 and 257, 2 vols.)

Cantarella, E. (1981), *L'Ambiguo Malanno. Condizione e immagine della donna nell'antichità greca e romana*, Rome

Caplice, R. (1970), 'Namburbi texts in the British Museum IV', *Or.* n.s. 39, 111-51

Cardascia, G. (1959), 'L'adoption matrimoniale à Babylone et à Nuzi', *Revue historique de droit francais et étranger*, ser. 4/37, 1-16

Carlier, J. (1980-81), 'Les Amazones font la guerre et l'amour', *L'Ethnographie*, 76, 11-33

Cartledge, P. (1981), 'Spartan Wives: liberation or licence?', *CQ* 31, 84-105

Cassin, E. (1982), 'Le Proche-Orient ancien: virginité et strategie du sexe', in Tordjinian (ed.), *La première fois ou le roman de la virginité perdue*, Paris, 241-58

Chantraine, P. (1946-7), 'Les Noms du mari et de la femme, du père et de la mère en grec', *REG*, 59-60, 219-50

Chapot, V. (1904), *La province romaine proconsulaire d'Asie*, Paris

Charlesworth, J.H. (ed. and trans.) (1977), *Odes of Solomon*, 2nd ed., Missoula

Clark, S.R.L. (1975), *Aristotle's Man*, Oxford

Coggins, R.J. (1975), *Samaritans and Jews. The Origins of Samaritanism Reconsidered*, Oxford

Comaroff, J.L. (1980), *The Meaning of Marriage Payments*, London

Conze, A. (1893-1922), *Die attischen Gabreliefs*, Berlin

Cowley, A. (1923), *Aramaic Papyri of the Fifth Century BC*, Oxford

Cross, F.M. (1973), 'The Religion of Canaan and the God of Israel', in *Canaanite Myth and Hebrew Epic. Essays in the History of the Religion of Israel*, I, Cambridge, Mass., 1-75

—— (1975), 'A Reconstruction of the Judaean Restoration', *JBL* 94, 4-18

Dale, A.M. (1956), 'Seen and unseen on the Greek stage', *Collected Papers* 1969, Cambridge, 119-29

Dalley, S. (1980), 'Old Babylonian Dowries', *Iraq* 42/1, 53-74

Daremberg, C., Saglio, E. (1877-), *Dictionnaire des antiquités*, Paris

Dariste, R., Haussolier, B., Reinach, T. (1890-1954), *Recueil des Inscriptions juridiques grecques*, Paris

Daube, D. (1972), *Civil Disobedience in Antiquity*, Edinburgh

David, T. (1976), 'La Position de la femme en Asie Centrale', *DHA* 2, 129-62

Davies, J. Conway (ed.) (1946-8), *Episcopal Acts and Cognate Documents relating to Welsh Dioceses 1066-1272*, 2 vols. (Historical Society of the Church in Wales)

Davies, J.K. (1971), *Athenian Propertied Families 600-300 BC*, Oxford

Davies, W. (1978), *An Early Welsh Microcosm*, London

—— (1982), *Wales in the Early Middle Ages*, Leicester

de Boer, P.A.H. (1974), *Fatherhood and Motherhood in Israelite and Judaean Piety*, Leiden

Deem, A. (1978), 'The Goddess Anath and some Biblical Hebrew Cruces', *JSS* 23, 25-30

Delcor, M. (1974), 'Astarte et la fecondité des troupeaux en Deut. 7.13 et parallèles', *UF* 6, 1-5

—— (forthcoming), 'Le culte de la "Reine du Ciel" selon Jer. 7.18; 44.17-19, 25 et

ses survivances', in Delsman, W.C. *et al.* (eds.), *Von Kanaan bis Kerala. Festschrift J. van der Ploeg*, Kevelaer, Neukirchen (AOAT 211)
Delcourt, M. (1961), *Hermaphrodite. Myths and Rites of the Bisexual Figure in Classical Antiquity*, trans. J. Nicholson, London
Denyer, S. (1978), *African Tribal Architecture*, London
de Ste. Croix, G.E.M. (1972), *The Origins of the Peloponnesian War*, London
— (1981), *The Class Struggle in the Ancient Greek World*, London
de Vaux, R. (1961), *Ancient Israel: its life and institutions*, London
Detienne, M. (1972), *Les Jardins d'Adonis*, Paris
— (1976), 'Potagenie de femme, ou comment engendrer seule', *Traverses* 5-6, 75-81
— (1977), *Dionysos mis à mort*, Paris
— (1979), 'Violentes "eugénies" ', in Detienne, M., Vernant, J.P., *La cuisine du sacrifice en pays grec*, Paris
Deubner, L. (1903), *De Incubatione*, Leipzig
— (1907), *Kosmas und Damian. Texte und Einleitung*, Leipzig, Berlin
Dickemann, Mildred (1979), 'Female infanticide, reproductive strategies and social stratification: a preliminary model', in Chagnon, N.A., Irons, W. (eds.), *Evolutionary Biology and Human Social Behaviour. An anthropological perspective*, North Scituate, Mass., 321-67
Diehl, C. (1906-8), *Figures byzantines*, 2 vols., Paris
Diehl, E. (1964), *Die Hydria*, Mainz
Diepgen, P. (1937), *Die Frauenheilkunde der alten Welt*, Munich (Stoeckel, W. (ed.), Handbuch der Gynäkologie XII/1)
Dillon, M. (1936), 'The Relationship of mother and son, of father and daughter, and the law of inheritance with regard to women', in Binchy (1936b), 129-79
Dodds, E. (1951), *The Greeks and the Irrational*, Berkeley
— (1965), *Pagan and Christian in an Age of Anxiety*, Cambridge
Dölger, F. (1924-65), *Regesten der Kaiserurkunden des byzantinischen Reiches*, 5 vols., Munich, Berlin
Douglas, M. (1966), *Purity and Danger*, London
— (ed.) (1970), *Witchcraft Confessions and Accusations*, London (ASA 9)
Drews, R. (1974), 'Sargon, Cyrus and Mesopotamian Folk History', *JNES* 33, 387-93
Drijvers, H.J.W. (1980), 'The 19th Ode of Solomon', *JTS* 31, 337-55
Driver, G.R., Miles, J.E. (1952), *The Babylonian Laws vol. 1. Legal Commentary*, Oxford
— (1955), *The Babylonian Laws vol. 2. Text, Translation*, Oxford
Duncan, A.A.M. (1975), *Scotland, the Making of the Kingdom*, Edinburgh
Duncan-Jones, R.P. (1980), 'Demographic change and economic progress under the Roman Empire', in *Tecnologia, Economia e Società nel mondo romano, Atti del Convegno di Como*, 1979, Como, 67-80
Duval, M. (1977), 'La grande vierge des Celtes d'Irlande en Petite Bretagne', in *Actes du 99e Congrès national des sociétés savantes (Besançon, 1974)*, I, *La Piété populaire au Moyen Âge*, 425-44, Paris
Ehrenreich, B., English, D. (1979), *For Her Own Good*, London
Eitrem, S. (1950), 'Some notes on the demonology of the New Testament', *Symb. Osloenses*, fasc. supp., 12
— (1953), 'The Pindaric Phthonos', in *Studies presented to D.M. Robinson*, II, 513-16, St Louis
Ellinger, I. (1953), 'Winged Figures', in *Studies presented to D.M. Robinson*, II, 1180-85, St. Louis
Emerton, J.A. (1982), 'New Light on Israelite Religion: the implications of the inscriptions from Kuntillet "Ajrud" ', *ZAW* 94, 2-20

Engels, D. (1980), 'The problem of female infanticide in the Greco-Roman world', *CPh* 75, 112-20
Epstein, L.M. (1942), *Marriage Laws in the Bible and Talmud*, Cambridge
— (1948), *Sex Laws and Customs in Judaism*, New York
Erikson, E. (1964), 'Inner and outer space: reflections on womanhood', *Daedalus* 93, 582ff
— (1968), *Identity, Youth and Crisis*, London
Etienne, G., Etienne-Germau, J. (1975), *Documents pédagogiques: scènes de la vie quotidienne à Athènes*, Brussels
Evans-Pritchard, E.E. (1937), *Witchcraft, Oracles and Magic among the Azande*, Oxford
Farnell, L.R. (1896-1909), *Cults of the Greek States*, 5 vols., Oxford
Fassbender, H. (1897), *Entwicklungslehre, Geburtshülfe und Gynäkologie in den hippokratischen Schriften*, Stuttgart
Fehrle, E. (1910), *Die kultische Keuschheit im Altertum. Religionsgeschichtliche Versuche und Vorarbeiten 6.6*, Giessen
Festugière, A.-J. (1971), *S. Thècle, Ss. Côme et Damien, Ss. Cyr et Jean (extraits), S. Georges, Collections grecques de miracles*, Paris
Finkel, I. (1980), 'The Fertile Crescent', *AfO* 27, 37-51
Finkelstein, J.J. (1969), 'The Laws of Ur-Nammu', *JCS* 22, 66-82
— (1970), 'On some recent studies in Cuneiform Law. A review article', *JAOS* 90/2, 243-56
— (1976), '*Šilip rēmim* and related matters', in *Kramer Anniversary Volume*, Münster (AOAT 25)
Finkelstein, L. (1930), 'The origin of the synagogue', *PAAJR* 1, 49-59
Fishburne Collier, J. (1974), 'Women in Politics', in Rozaldo, M.Z., Lamphere, L. (eds.), *Women, Culture and Society*, Stanford
Flashar, H. (1966), *Melancholie und Melancholiker*, Berlin
Fleuriot, L. (1964), *Dictionnaire des Glosses en vieux Breton*, Paris
— (1980), *Les Origines de la Bretagne*, Paris
Fohrer, G. (1973), *History of Israelite Religion*, trans. D. Green, London
Foley, H. (1975), 'Sex and state in ancient Greece', *Diacritics* 5/4, 31-6
Fourmy, M.H., Leroy, M. (1934), 'La vie de Saint Philarète', *Byzantion* 9, 165-7
Friedrich, J. (1950), 'Churritische Märchen und Sagen in hethitischer Sprache', *ZA* , n.f. 15, 213-55
Gantz, J. (1976), *The Mabinogian*, Harmondsworth
— (1981), *Early Irish Myths and Sagas*, Harmondsworth
Garnsey, P.D.A. (1974), 'Aspects of the decline of the urban aristocracy in the empire', *ANRW* II/1, 229-52
Geyer, P. (ed.) (1965), *Itineraria et alia geographica* (Corpus Christianorum, ser. lat. 175), Turnholt
Gildas (1978), *The Ruin of Britain and other Works*, Winterbottom, M. (ed. and trans.), Chichester
Gluckman, M. (1970), *Custom and conflict in Africa*, Oxford
Goetze, A. (1948), 'Thirty Tablets from the reigns of Abi-Ešuh and Ammiditana', *JCS* 2, 73-112
Goitein, S.D. (1967-78), *A Mediterranean Society*, 3 vols., Berkeley, Los Angeles
Goldberg, A.M. (1969), *Untersuchungen über die Vorstellung von der Schekinah in der frühen rabbinischen Literatur*, Berlin
Golden, M. (1979), 'Demosthenes and the age of majority at Athens', *Phoenix* 33, 25-38
— (1981), 'Demography and the exposure of girls at Athens', *Phoenix* 35, 316-31
Gomme, A.W. (1933), *The Population of Athens in the Fifth and Fourth*

Centuries BC, Oxford
Goodblatt, D. (1977), 'The Beruriah Tradition', in Green, W.S. (ed.), *Persons and Institutions in Rabbinic Judaism*, Missoula (Brown Judaic Studies 3)
Goody, J., Tambiah, S.J. (1973), *Bridewealth and Dowry*, Cambridge (Cambridge Papers in Social Anthropology 7)
Goody, J. (1977), *Production and Reproduction. A comparative study of the domestic domain*, Cambridge (Cambridge Studies in Social Anthropology 17)
Gordon, R. (1979), 'The real and the imaginary, production and religion in the Greco-Roman world', *Art History* 2, 6-34
Gougaud, L. (1936), *Les Saints irlandais hors d'Irlande*, Louvain, Oxford
Gould, J.P. (1980), 'Law, Custom and Myth: aspects of the social position of women in Classical Athens', *JHS* 100, 38-59
Goussier, L. (1958), *Plutarchs Gedanken über die Ehe*, diss. Basel
Graef, H. (1963), *Mary: A History of Doctrine and Devotion*, 2 vols., London, New York
Gregory, T. (1979), *Vox Populi: Popular Opinion and Violence in the Religious Controversies of the Fifth Century AD*, Columbus, Ohio
Gribomont, J. (1965), 'Le monachisme au sien de l'église en Syrie et en Cappadoce', *Studia Monastica* 7, 7-24
Grierson, P. (1973), *Catalogue of the Byzantine Coins in the D.O. Collection and in the Whittemore Collection* III, Washington, DC
Grosdidier de Matons, J. (1974), 'La femme dans l'empire byzantin', in Grimal, P. (ed.), *Histoire mondiale de la femme*, 4 vols., Paris, 3.11-43
Guillou, A. (1963), *Les Actes grecques de S. Maria di Messina*, Palermo
— (1977), 'Il Matrimonio nell' Italia bizantina nei secoli X e XI', *Settimani di studio*, 24, Spoleto, 869-86
Gülcan, I. 'The renewal of monastic life for women in a monastery in Tur Abdin', *Sobornost* 7/4, 288-98
Gurney, O.R. (1977), 'Magical Rituals', in *Some Aspects of Hittite Religion*, Oxford (The Schweich Lectures for 1976)
Gutman, J. (1981), 'Synagogue origins: theories and facts', in Gutman, J. (ed.), *Ancient Synagogues. The State of Research*, Providence, RI
Haas, V. (1971), 'Ein hethitisches Beschwörungsmotiv aus Kizzuwatna; seine Herkunft und Wanderung', *Or.* n.s. 40, 410-30
Haas, V., Wilhelm, G. (1974), *Hurritische und luwische Riten aus Kizzuwatna*, Münster (AOATS 3)
Habicht, C. (1976), 'Eine hellenistische Urkunde aus Larisa', *Demetrias* 1, 157-68
Hallock, R.T. (1969), *Persepolis Fortification Tablets*, Chicago (OIP 92)
Handley, E. (1969), 'Notes on the *Theophoroumene* of Menander', *BICS* 16, 92-101
Harris, R. (1960), 'Old Babylonian temple loans', *JCS* 14, 126-37
— (1961a), 'On the process of secularization under Hammurapi', *JCS* 15, 117-20
— (1961b), 'The *Nadītu* laws of the Code of Hammurapi in praxis', *Or.* n.s. 30, 164-9
— (1962), 'Biographical notes on the *Nadītu* women of Sippar', *JCS* 16, 1-12
— (1963), 'The organization and administration of the cloister in ancient Babylonia', *JESHO* 6/2, 121-57
— (1964), 'The *Nadītu* woman', in Reiner, E. (ed.), *Studies presented to A. Leo Oppenheim*, Chicago, 106-35
— (1968), 'Some aspects of the centralization of the realm under Hammurapi and his successors', *JAOS* 88/4, 727-32
— (1969), 'Notes on the Babylonian cloister and hearth. A review article', *Or.* n.s. 38, 133-45
— (1972), 'Notes on the nomenclature of Old Babylonian Sippar', *JCS* 24, 102-4

— (1975), *Ancient Sippar. A Demographic Study of an Old Babylonian City (1894-1595 BC)*, Istanbul
— (1976a), 'On kinship and inheritance in Old Babylonian Sippar', *Iraq* 38, 129-32
— (1976b), 'On foreigners in Old Babylonian Sippar', *RA* 70, 145-52
Harris, W.V. (1982), 'The theoretical possibility of extensive infanticide in the Graeco-Roman world', *CQ* 32, 114-16
Hart, G.L. (1973), 'Women and the sacred in ancient Tamil-nad', *Journal of Asian Studies* 32, 233-50
Hartog, F. (1980), *Le miroir d'Hérodote*, Paris
Hastrup, I. (1978), 'The semantics of biology: virginity', in Ardener, S. (ed.), *Defining Females*, London, 49-65
Heckenbach, J. (1911), *De nuditate sacra sacrisque vinculis*, Giessen Religionsgeschichtliche Versuche und Vorarbeiten 9.3
Heinrichs, A. (1978), 'Greek maenadism from Olympias to Messalina', *HSCP* 82, 121-60
Henderson, I. (1967), *The Picts*, London
Hennecke, E., Schneemelcher, W. (eds.) (1973), *New Testament Apocrypha*, trans. R. Mcl. Wilson, London
Herrin, J. (1983), 'Women and the faith in icons in early Christianity', in Samuel, R., Stedman Jones, G. (eds.), *Culture, Ideology and Politics*, London, 56-83
Hill, B.H. (1965), 'Grain and spirit in medieval anatomy', *Speculum* 40, 63ff
Hoffner, H.A. (1968), 'Birth and namegiving in Hittite texts', *JNES* 27, 198-203
Hollis, F.J. (1934), *The Archaeology of Herod's Temple*, London
Hombert, M., Préaux, Cl. (1952), *Recherches sur le recensement dans l'Égypte romaine* (Pap. Lugd. Bat. V), Leiden
Hood, A.B.E. (ed. and trans.) (1978), *St. Patrick. His Writings and Muirchu's Life*, Chichester
Hooker, E.-M. (1963), 'The goddess of the golden image', *Parthenos and Parthenon*, *GR*, sp. 10, 17-22
Hopkins, Keith (1965), 'Contraception in the Roman Empire', *Comparative Studies in Society and History* 8, 124-51
— (1978), *Conquerors and Slaves*, Cambridge
Horton, R. (1960), 'The gods as guests: aspects of Kalebari religion', *Nigeria Magazine Publications* 3, Lagos
Hughes, K. (1966), *The Church in Early Irish Society*, London
— (1972), *Early Christian Ireland: Introduction to the sources*, London
Humphreys, S.C. (1978), 'Public and private interests in classical Athens', *CJ* 73, 97-104
— (1980), 'Family tombs and tomb cult in ancient Athens: tradition or traditionalism?', *JHS* 100, 96-126
Inan, J., Alföldy-Rosenbaum, E. (1979), *Römische und frühbyzantinische Porträtplastik aus der Türkei: neue Funde*, 2 vols., Mainz
India (1974), Government of India, Ministry of Education and Social Welfare, Department of Social Welfare, *Towards Equality: Report of the Committee on the Status of Women in India*, New Delhi
Jackson, A. (1971), 'Pictish social structure and symbol stones: an anthropological assessment', *Scottish Studies* 15, 121-40
Jackson, K.H. (1953), *Language and History in Early Britain*, Edinburgh
Jacob, H.E. (1963), *Felix Mendelssohn and His Times*, Englewood Cliffs, NJ
Jacobson, T. (1973), 'Notes on Nintur', *Or.* n.s. 42, 274-98
Jameson, S. (1965), 'Cornutus Tertullus and the Plancii of Perge', *JRS* 55, 54-8
— (1980), 'The Lycian League', *ANRW* II/7, 833-55
Jankovska, N.B. (1969a), 'Communal self-government and the king of the state

of Arrapha', *JESHO* 12
— (1969b), 'Extended family commune and civil self government in Arrapha in the 15.-14. century BC', in Diakonov, I. (ed.), *Ancient Mesopotamia*, Leningrad
Jebb, R. (ed.) (1900), *Sophocles, Antigone*[3], Cambridge
Jeffrey, P. (1979), *Frogs in a well: Indian Women in purdah*, London
Jenkins, D., Owen, M.E. (eds.) (1980), *The Welsh Law of Women*, Cardiff
Johansen, K.F. (1951), *Attic Grave-reliefs*, Copenhagen
Jones, A.H.M. (1940), *The Greek City from Alexander to Justinian*, Oxford
Jones, C.P. (1976), 'The Plancii of Perge', *HSCP* 80, 231-7
Jones, E. (1923), 'The Madonna's conception through the ear', *Essays in Applied Psychoanalysis*, London, vol. ii, ch. 13
Jones, G.R. (1972), 'Post-Roman Wales', in Finberg, H.P.R. (ed.), *The Agrarian History of England and Wales* 1/2, Cambridge, 283-382
Jones, J.E., Sackett, L.H., Graham, A.J. (1962), 'The Dema House in Attica', *BSA* 57, 75-114
Jones, J.E. (1963), 'A country house in Attica', *Archaeology* 16, 276-83
Jones, J.E. *et al.* (1973), 'An Attic country house below the cave of Pan at Vari', *BSA* 68, 355-452 (= 'An Attic Country House at Vari', undated reprint from *BSA* 68)
Jones, J.E. (1975), 'Town and country houses of Attica in classical times', *Thorikos and the Laurion in Archaic and Classical Times, Miscellanea Graeca* I, Ghent
Junge, P.J. (1944), *Dareios I König der Perser*, Leipzig
Kaibel, G. (ed.) (1878), *Epigrammata Graeca*, Berlin
Kammenhuber, A. (1977), *Hethitisches Wörterbuch: 2nd ed. = HW*$_2$, Heidelberg, Lieferung 2, 90
— (1980), *HW*$_2$, Lieferung 5, 323
Kavolis, V. (1964), 'Art style as projection of community structure', *Sociology and Sociological Research* 48, 165-78
Kay, M.A. (1982), *Anthropology of Human Birth*, Philadelphia, Penn.
Kent, R.G. (1953), *Old Persian. Grammar, Texts, Lexicon*, 2nd rev. ed., New Haven, Conn. (AOS 33)
Klibansky, R., Panofsky, E., Saxl, F. (1964), *Saturn and Melancholy*, London
Köcher, F. (1952), 'Ein akkadischer medizinischer Schülertext aus Boğazköy', *AfO* 16, 47-56
Kornemann, E. (1942), *Grosse Frauen des Altertums im Rahmen 2000-jährigen Weltgeschehens*, Leipzig
Körte, G. (1874), *Über Personifikationen psychologischer Affekte in der späteren Vasenmalerei*, Berlin
Koschaker, P. (1917), *Rechtsvergleichende Studien zur Gesetzgebung Hammurapis*, Leipzig
— (1928), *Neue keilschriftliche Rechtsurkunden aus der el-Amarna Zeit*, Leipzig (ASAW 39/V)
Kronasser, H. (1961), 'Fünf hethitische Rituale', *Die Sprache* 7, 140-67
Kurtz, E. (1899), 'Zwei griechische Texte über die Heilige Theophano . . .', *Mémoires de l'Académie impériale de S. Petersburg*, ser. VIII, 3/2
— (1902), 'Des Klerikers Gregorios Bericht über Leben, Wundertaten und Translation der Heiligen Theodora von Thessalonich', *Mémoires de l'Académie impériale de S. Petersburg*, ser. VIII, 6/1
La Borderie, A. le Moyne de (1896-1914), *Histoire de la Bretagne*, 6 vols., Rennes
Lacey, W.K. (1968 and 1980), *The Family in Classical Greece*, London, 2nd ed., Auckland
Lachemann, E. (1962), *Family Law Documents*, Cambridge, Mass. (HSS 19)

Laessøe, J. (1955), *Studies on the Assyrian Ritual and Series bit rimki*, Copenhagen

Lagrand, J. (1980), 'How was the Virgin Mary "like a man"?', *Novum Testamentum* 22, 97-107

Laín Entralgo, P. (1970), *The Therapy of the Word in Classical Antiquity*, New Haven

Laiou, Angeliki E. (1977), *Peasant Society in the Late Byzantine Empire. A Social and Demographic Study*, Princeton

— (1981), 'The role of women in Byzantine society', *16. Internationaler Byzantinisten Kongress*, Vienna, Akten I.1 (= *JOB* 31, 233-60)

Lambert, W.G. (1957-8), 'An Incantation of the *Maqlû* type', *AfO* 18, 288-99

— (1960), *Babylonian Wisdom Literature*, Oxford

— (1969), 'A Middle Assyrian medical text', *Iraq* 31, 28-39

Lanckoronski, K. Graf (1890-2), *Städte Pamphyliens und Pisidiens I-II*, Vienna

Laroche, E. (1947), *Recherches sur les noms des dieux hittites*, Paris

— (1955), 'Divinités lunaires d'Anatolie', *RHR* 148, 1-24

— (1956), Review of Otten, H., *Keilschrifturkunden aus Boghazköi, Heft 36*, *OLZ* 51, col. 421

— (1962), 'La Lune, chez les Hittites et les Hourrites', in *La Lune, Mythes et Rites*, Paris (Sources orientales, 5)

— (1965), 'Textes mythologiques hittites en transcription: 1. mythologie anatolienne', *RHA* XXIII/77, 62-176

— (1976-7), *Glossaire de la langue hourrite* (*RHA* 34-5)

Lattimore, R. (1942), *Themes in Greek and Latin Epitaphs*, Urbana, Ill.

Laum, B. (1914), *Stiftungen in der griechischen und römischen Antike*, Leipzig

Launey, M. (1949-50), *Recherches sur les armes hellénistiques*, 2 vols., Paris (Bibliothèque des Écoles françaises d'Athènes, 169)

Laurent, D. (1971), 'La déesse Brigitte et le culte de Saint Brigitte d'Irelande en Bretagne et dans les pays celtiques', *Bull. Soc. Arch. du Finistère*, 97, 102-7

Lawrence, A.W. (1967), *Greek Architecture*, Harmondsworth (Pelican History of Art)

Le Bas, Ph. and Waddington, W.H. (1870), *Voyage archéologique en Grèce et en Asie Mineure III. Inscriptions grecques et latines*, Paris

Lefkowitz, Mary R. (1981a), *The Lives of the Greek Poets*, London

— (1981b), 'Princess Ida, the Amazons and a Women's College Curriculum', *TLS* Nov. 27, 1399-401

— (1982), *Heroines and Hysterics*, London

— (1983), 'Wives and Husbands', *GR* 30 (forthcoming)

Lefkowitz, Mary R., Fant, M.B. (eds.) (1982), *Women's Life in Greece and Rome*, London

Lemerle, P., Guillou, A., Svoronos, N., Papachrysanthou, D. (eds.) (1970), *Actes de Lavra*, Paris

Levine, L.I. (ed.) (1981), *Ancient Synagogues Revealed*, Jerusalem

Lewis, A. Smith (ed. and trans.) (1902), *Apocrypha Syriaca*, London (Studia Sinaitica 11)

Lewis, H., Pedersen, H. (1974), *A Concise Comparative Celtic Grammer*, 3rd ed., Göttingen

Lewis, I.M. (1971), *Ecstatic Religion*, Harmondsworth

Lienhardt, G. (1961), *Divinity and Experience*, Oxford

Linton, R. (1942), 'Age and Sex Categories', *American Sociological Review*, 7, 589-602

Littré, E. (1839-61), *Oeuvres complètes d'Hippocrate*, Paris

Lloyd, G.E.R. (1975), 'The Hippocratic Question', *CQ* 25, 171-92

— (1979), *Magic, Reason and Experience*, Cambridge

Loeffler, I. (1963), *Die Melampodie*, Berlin
Loewe, R. (1966), *The Position of Women in Judaism*, London
Lord, A.B. (1970), 'Tradition and the Oral Poet: Homer, Huso and Aydo Medjedovíc', in *La Poesia epica e la sua formazione*, Rome, 13-28 (Atti del convegno internazionale; Accademia Nazionale dei Lincei, quad. 139)
Loth, J. (1890), *Chrestomathie Bretonne*, Paris
Luce, J.V. (1971), 'The large house at Dystos in Euboea', *GR* 17, 143-9
Lutz, C. (1957), *Musonius Rufus, 'The Roman Socrates'*, New Haven
MacCana, P. (1970), *Celtic Mythology*, London
MacCurtain, M., Ó Corráin, D. (eds.) (1978), *Women in Irish Society. The Historical Dimension*, Dublin
MacMullen, R. (1974), *Roman Social Relations 50BC to AD 284*, New Haven
— (1980), 'Women in public in the Roman Empire', *Historia* 29, 208-18
MacNiocaill, G. (1972), *Ireland Before the Vikings*, Dublin
Macurdy, G.H. (1932), *Hellenistic Queens*, Baltimore
Magie, D. (1950), *Roman Rule in Asia Minor*, 2 vols., Princeton
Maidman, M. (1976), *A Socio-Economic Analysis of a Nuzi Family Archive*, unpub. diss., Philadelphia
Mair, L. (1969), *Witchcraft*, London
Maloney, C. (ed.) (1976), *The Evil Eye*, New York
Mango, C. (1980), *Byzantium. The New Rome*, London
— (1981), 'Daily life in Byzantium', *16. Internationaler Byzantinisten Kongress* (see Laiou, 1981), 337-53
Marwick, M. (ed.) (1970), *Witchcraft and Sorcery*, Harmondsworth
Marshall, A.J. (1968), 'Pompey's organization of Bithynia Pontus: two neglected texts', *JRS* 58, 106-7
Maslev, S. (1966), 'Die staatsrechtliche Stellung der byzantinischen Kaiserinnen', *Byzantinoslavica* 27, 308-43
Mayer, P. (1954), 'Witches', in Marwick (1970)
Mayer, W. (1978), *Nuzi-Studien I. Die Archive des Palastes und die Prosopographie der Berufe*, Neukirchen, Kevelaer (AOAT 205/1)
McAll, C. (1980), 'The normal paradigms of a woman's life in the Irish and Welsh texts', in Jenkins, Owen (1980), 1-22
McCulloch, W.S. (1951), 'Why the mind is in the head', in Jeffreys, L.A. (ed.), *Cerebral Mechanism in Behaviour*, New York
McLaughlin, E. (1975), ' "Christ my mother": female naming and metaphor in medieval spirituality', *Nashotah Review* 15, 228-48
Meek, T.J. (1935), *Old Akkadian, Sumerian, and Cappadocian Texts from Nuzi*, Cambridge, Mass. (HSS 10)
Meier, G.R. (1937), *Die assyrische Beschwörungssammlung Maqlû*, Berlin (AfO Beiheft 2)
Meiggs, R. (1972), *The Athenian Empire*, Oxford
Merkelbach, R., West, M.L. (1967), *Fragmenta Hesiodea*, Oxford
Merskey, H. (1979), *The Analysis of Hysteria*, London
Meshel, Z. (1978), *Kuntillet 'Ajrud. A Religious Center from the time of the Judaean Monarchy on the Border of Sinai*, Jerusalem (Israel Museum Catalogue 175)
— (1979), 'Did Yahweh have a consort? The new religious inscriptions from the Sinai', *Biblical Archaeological Review* 5/2 (March), 24-35
Mettinger, T.N.D. (1982), *The Dethronement of Sabaoth. Studies in the Shem and Kabod Theologies*, Lund (Coniectanea Biblica, OT series 18)
Meuli, K. (1975), *Gesammelte Schriften* II, Basle
Milet 3 (1914), Kawerau, G., Rehm, A., *Das Delphinion im Milet*, Berlin (Wiegand, T. (ed.), *Milet. Ergebnisse der Ausgrabungen und Untersuchungen*

seit dem Jahre 1899, Band 3)
Millar, F.G.B. (1977), *The Emperor in the Roman World 31 BC-AD 337*, London
Miller, M. (1982), 'Matriliny by treaty: the Pictish foundation-legend', in Whitelock, D., McKitterick, R., Dunville, D. (eds.), *Ireland in Early Mediaeval Europe*, 133-61
Mitchell, S. (1974), 'The Plancii in Asia Minor', *JRS* 64, 27-39
Mitteis, L. (1891), *Reichsrecht und Volksrecht in den östlichen Provinzen des römischen Kaiserreichs*, Leipzig
Momigliano, A. (1977), 'Eastern elements in post-exilic Jewish and Greek historiography', in *Essays in Ancient and Modern Historiography*, Oxford, 25-35
— (1979), 'Persian Empire and Greek Freedom', in Ryan, A. (ed.), *The Idea of Freedom. Essays in Honour of Isaiah Berlin*, Oxford
Morey, C.R., Rand, E.K., Kraeling, C.H. (1931), *The Gospel-Book of Landevennec*, New York (repr. from *Art Studies*, 1930, 8, 225-86)
Morgenstern, J. (1956), 'The Origin of the Synagogue', *Studi orientalistic in onore di G. Levi della Vida* II, 192-201
Motte, A. (1973), *Prairies et jardins de la Grèce antique*, Brussels
Mulchrone, K. (ed.) (1936), 'The rights and duties of women with regard to the education of their children', in Binchy (1936b), 187-206
Mulder, J.J.B. (1920), *Quaestiones Nonnullae ad Atheniensium Matrimonium Vitamque Coniugalem Pertinentes*, Utrecht
Murphy, G. (ed.) (1956), *Early Irish Lyrics*, Oxford
Murray, R. (1971), 'Mary the second Eve in the early Syriac Fathers', *Eastern Churches Review* 3, 372-84
— (1975), *Symbols of Church and Kingdom. A Study in Early Syriac Tradition*, Cambridge
Neusner, J. (1973), *The Idea of Purity in Ancient Judaism*, with a critique and commentary by M. Douglas, Leiden
Nilsson, M.P. (1961-7), *Geschichte der griechischen Religion*, 2 vols., vol. 1 2nd ed., vol. 2 3rd ed., Munich (von Müller, I. ed. Handbuch der Altertumswissenschaft II, 1-2)
Nitti di Vito, F. (1900), *Codice diplomatico barese* IV, Bari
Nock, A.D. (1933), *Conversion*, London
Nyberg, H.S. (1954), 'Das Reich der Achämeniden', *Historia Mundi* 3, 56-115, Bern
O'Brien, J.V. (1977), *Bilingual Selections from Sophocles' Antigone: an Introduction to the Text for the Greekless Reader*, Carbondale
O'Brien, M.A. (ed.) (1962), *Corpus Genealogiarum Hiberniae*, Dublin
Ó Corráin, D. (1972), *Ireland before the Normans*, Dublin
— (1978a), 'Women in Early Irish Society', in MacCurtain, Ó Corráin (1978), 1-13
— (1978b), 'Nationality and kingship in pre-Norman Ireland', in Moody, T.M. (ed.), *Nationality and the Pursuit of National Independence*, Belfast, 1-35
Ó Cuív, B. (ed.) (1969), *A View of the Irish Language*, Dublin
Oden, R.A. (1979), 'The Persistence of Canaanite Religion', *BA* 39/1 (March), 31-6
Oesterley, W.V.E., Robinson, T.H. (1937), *Hebrew Religion. Its Origin and Development*, London
Oettinger, N. (1976), *Militärische Eide der Hethiter*, Wiesbaden (SBT 22)
Oikonomides, N. (1972), 'Quelques boutiques de Constantinople au Xe siècle: prix, loyers, impositions (Cod. Patmiacus 171)', *DOP* 26, 345-6
Onians, R.B. (1951), *The Origins of European Thought about the Body, the Mind, the Soul, Time and Fate*, Cambridge (2nd ed. 1954)

Otten, H. (1952), *Beiträge zum hethitischen Lexikon, ZA* n.f. 16, 230-6
— (1953), 'Pirwa – Der Gott auf dem Pferd', *JKF* 2, 62-73
— (1958), *Hethitische Totenrituale*, Berlin (Institut für Orientforschung Veröffentlichung 37)
— (1975), *Puduhepa: eine hethitische Königin in ihren Textzeugnissen*, Mainz
Owen, M.E. (1980), 'Shame and Reparation: women's place in the kin', in Jenkins, Owen (1980), 40-68
Özgüç, N. (1965), *The Anatolian Group of Cylinder Seal Impressions from Kültepe*, Ankara
Padel, R. (1974), 'Imagery of the elsewhere: two choral odes of Euripides', *CQ* 24, 227-41
— (1980), 'Saddled with ginger: women, men and horses', *Encounter* (November), 46-54
— (forthcoming), *In and Out of the Mind: Consciousness in Greek Tragedy*
Pagel, W. (1981), 'The Smiling Spleen', in Lloyd-Jones, H. (ed.), *History and Imagination*, London, 81-7
Panagopoulos, J. (1977), 'Vocabulaire et mentalité dans les *Moralia* de Plutarque', *DHA* 3, 197-235
Papadopoulos-Kerameus, A. (1909), *Varia Sacra Graeca*, S. Petersburg
Paris, P. (1891), *Quatenus Feminae Res Publicas in Asia Minore, Romanis imperantibus, attigerint*, diss. Paris
Parke, H.W. (1977), *Festivals of the Athenians*, London
Parke, H.W., Wormell, D. (1956), *The Delphic Oracle*, 2 vols., Oxford
Patai, R. (1967), *The Hebrew Goddess*, New York
Patlagean, E. (1969), 'Sur la limitation de la fécondité dans la haute époque byzantine', *Annales ESC* 24, 1353-1369 (= 'Birth Control in the Early Byzantine Empire', in Forster, R., Ranum, O. (eds.), *Biology of Man in History*, Baltimore, 1-22)
— (1976), 'L'histoire de la femme déguisée en moine et l'évolution de la sainteté feminine à Byzance', *Studi medievali* ser. 3/17, 597-623 (repr. in Patlagean (1981), *Structure sociale, famille, chrétienté à Byzance*, London
Pearce, S.M. (1978), *The Kingdom of Dumnonia*, Padstow
Pedersen, L.R. (1968), 'Woman's life in Thailand', *Folk* 10, 134-53
Peek, W. (1955), *Griechische Versinschriften* I, Berlin
Peeters, P. (1911), 'S. Romain le Néomartyr († 1 mai 780), d'après un document géorgien', *Analecta Bollandiana* 30,
Pekary, T. (1978), 'Statues in inscriptions from Asia Minor', *SRKK*, 724-44
Pembroke, S. (1965), 'The last of the matriarchs: a study in the inscriptions of Lycia', *JESHO* 8, 217-47
— (1967), 'Women in charge: the function of alternatives in early Greek tradition and the ancient idea of matriarchy', *JWI* 30, 1-35
Peritz, I.J. (1898), 'Women in the ancient Hebrew cult', *JBL* 17, 111-47
Petitmangin, P. *et al.* (eds.) (1981), *Pélagie la pénitente: métamorphoses d'une légende I. Les textes et leur histoire*, Paris (Études Augustiniennes)
Pfeiffer, R.H., Speiser, E.A. (1936), *One Hundred New Selected Nuzi Texts*, New Haven (AASOR 16)
Pickard-Cambridge, A. (1968), *The Dramatic Festivals of Athens*², Oxford
Planiol, M. (1953), *Histoire des Institutions de la Bretagne*, 3 vols., Rennes
Pleket, H.W. (1969), *Epigraphica II, Texts on the Social History of the Greek World*, Leiden
— (1974), 'Griekse Epigrammen op Steen en de "Histoire des Mentalités" ', *Handelingen 29e Vlaams Philologencongres 1973*, 145ff
Pomeroy, S.B. (1973), 'Selected Bibliography on Women in Antiquity', *Arethusa* 6, 125-57

— (1975), *Goddesses, Whores, Wives and Slaves. Women in Classical Antiquity*, New York
— (1977), 'Technikai kai mousikai', *AJAH* 2, 51-68
— (1982a), 'Charities for Greek Women', *Mnemosyne* (forthcoming)
— (1982b), 'Wives of Hellenistic Soldiers', *Paper delivered at the annual meeting of the Association of Ancient Historians, University Park, Pa., May 7*
Pope, M.H. (1977), *Song of Songs*, New York (Anchor Bible 7C)
Porten, N. (1968), *Archives from Elephantine. The Life of an Ancient Jewish Military Colony*, Berkeley, Los Angeles
Power, N. (1936), 'Classes of women described in Senchas Már', in Binchy (1936b), 81-108
Power, P.L. (1976), *Sex and Marriage in Ancient Ireland*, Dublin
Pucci, P. (1977), *Hesiod and the Language of Poetry*, Baltimore
Ramsey, G.W. (1981), *The Quest for the Historical Israel*, Atlanta, London
Rassam, H. (1897), *Asshur and the Land of Nimrod*, New York
Redfield, R. (1977), 'The Women of Sparta', *CJ* 73, 141-61
Reed, W.L. (1962), 'Asherah', *Interpreter's Dictionary of the Bible* I, 250-2, Nashville, New York
Renger, J. (1967), 'Untersuchungen zum Priestertum in der altbabylonischen Zeit', *ZA* 58, 110-88
Reinach, T. (1893), 'Inscriptions d'Iasos', *REG* 6, 153-203
— (1906), 'Inscriptions d'Aphrodisias', *REG* 19, 201-98
— (1924), 'Un contrat de mariage du temps de Basile le Bulgaroctone', *Mélanges offerts à G. Schlumberger* I, Paris, 118-32
Reiner, E. (1966), 'La magie babylonienne', in *Le Monde du Sorcier*, Paris (Sources Orientales 7)
Reinhardt, K. (1960), *Tradition und Geist: gesammelte Essays zur Dichtung*, Göttingen
Robert, L. (1937), *Études Anatoliennes*, Paris
— (1945), *Le Sanctuaire de Sinuri, près de Mylasa 1. Les inscriptions grecques*, Paris
— (1948), *Hellenica* 5, Paris
— (1965), *Hellenica* 13, Paris
— (1966), *Laodicée du Lycos. Le Nymphée: cinquième partie, les inscriptions*, Paris
— (1974), 'Les femmes théores à Ephèse', *CRAI*, 176-81
Robertson Smith, W. (1894), *Lectures on the Religion of the Semites*, London
Robinson, D.M., Graham, J.W. (1938), *Excavations at Olynthos VIII: the Hellenic House*, Baltimore
Robinson, G. (ed.) (1929), *The History and Cartulary of the Greek Monastery of S. Elias and S. Anastasius of Carbone* (Orientalia Christiana 53)
Rose, H.J. (1925), 'The Bride of Hades', *CP* 20, 238-42
Rostovtzeff, M.I. (1941), *The Social and Economic History of the Hellenistic World*, 3 vols., Oxford
—— (1959), *The Social and Economic History of the Roman Empire*, 2nd ed. by P.M. Fraser, Oxford
Rousselle, A. (1980), 'Observation féminine et idéologie masculine: le corps de la femme d'après les médécins grecs', *Annales ESC* 35, 1089-115
Rozaldo, M.Z. (1980), *Knowledge and Passion: Ilongot notions of self and social life*, Cambridge
Russell, D.A., Wilson, N.G. (1981), *Menander Rhetor*, ed. with trans. and commentary, Oxford
Saleh, Saneya (1972), 'Women in Islam', *International Journal of Sociology of the Family* 2/1, 1-8; reproduced in Ibrahim, S.E., Hopkins, N.S. (eds), *Arab*

Society in Transition (Cairo, 1977).
Samuel, A.E., Hastings, W.K., Bowman, A.K., Bagnall, R.S. (1971), *Death and Taxes*, Toronto (American Studies in Papyrology 10)
Sancisi-Weerdenburg, H.W.A.M. (1980), *Yauná en Persai. Grieken en Perzen in een ander perspectief*, diss. Leiden
Sansone, D. (1975), *Aeschylean Metaphors of Intellectual Activity*, Wiesbaden (Hermes Einzelschriften 35)
Schaps, D. (1975), 'Women in Greek inheritance law', *CQ* 25, 53-7
— (1977), 'The women least mentioned: etiquette and women's names', *CQ* 27, 323-30
— (1979), *Economic Rights of Women in Ancient Greece*, Edinburgh
Scheil, J.V. (1902), *Une saison de fouilles à Sippar*, Paris
Schmitt, P. (1977), 'Athene Apatouria et la ceinture', *Annales ESC* 32, 1059-73
Schorr, M. (1913), *Urkunden des Altbabylonischen Zivil- und Prozessrechts*, Leipzig (VAB 5)
Schroeder, O. (1917), 'Ein Amulett aus Assur', *OLZ* 20/1, 7
Seager, A. (1975), 'The Architecture of the Dura and Sardis Synagogue', in Orlinsky, H.M. (ed.), *The Synagogue: Studies in Origins, Archaeology and Architecture*, selected with a prolegomenon by J. Gutman
Segal, J.B. (1970), *Edessa: the Blessed City*, Oxford
— (1976), 'Popular religion in ancient Israel', *JJS* 27/1 (spring), 1-22
— (1979), 'The Jewish attitude toward women', *JJS* 30/2 (autumn), 121-37
Sellers, R.V. (1953), *The Council of Chalcedon. A Historical and Doctrinal Survey*, London
Shaw, M. (1975), 'The female intruder: women in fifth-century drama', *CP* 70, 255-66
Sideras, A. (1971), *Aeschylos Homericus* (Hypomnemata 31)
Simon, B. (1978), *Mind and Madness in Ancient Greece*, Ithaca, NY
Simons, K. (1978), 'Women in Norman Ireland', in MacCurtain, Ó'Corráin (1978), 14-25
Slater, P. (1971), *The Glory of Hera: Mythology and the Greek Family*, Boston
Smid, H.R. (1965), *Protevangelium Jacobi: a Commentary*, trans. van Baaren-Pape, G.E., Assen
Smith, Morton (1971), *Palestinian Parties and Politics that shaped the Old Testament*, New York, London
Smith, W.D. (1965), 'So-called possession in pre-Christian Greece', *TAPA* 96, 403-26
Snodgrass, A. (1977), *Archaeology and the Rise of the Greek State*, Inaugural Lecture, Cambridge
— (1980), *Archaic Greece, the age of experiment*, London
Soggin, A. (1981), 'Jezabel, oder die fremde Frau', in Caquot, A., Delcor, M. (eds.), *Mélanges bibliques et orientaux en l'honneur de M. Henry Cazelles*, Kevelaer, Neukirchen, 453-9 (AOAT 212)
Sollberger, E. (1967-8), 'The Cruciform Monument', *JEOL* 20, 50-70
Sorre, M. (1955), *Les migrations des peuples*, Paris
Sorum, C.E. (1982), 'The family in Sophocles' *Antigone* and *Electra*', *CW* 75/4, 201-11
Sourvinou-Inwood, C. (1978), 'Persephone and Aphrodite at Locri: a model for personality-definition in Greek religion', *JHS* 98, 191-221
— (1981), 'To die and enter the house of Hades', in Whaly, J. (ed.), *Mirrors of Mortality. Studies in the Social History of Death*, London, 15-39
Spooner, B. (1970), 'The evil eye in the Middle East', in Douglas, M. (ed.) (1970), 311-19
Spycket, A. (1980), 'Women in Persian Art', in Schmandt-Besserat, D. (ed.),

Ancient Persia. The Art of An Empire, Malibu, 43-5 (Invited Lectures on the Middle East at the University of Texas at Austin 4)

Stadter, P. (1965), *Plutarch's Historical Methods: an analysis of* de mulierum virtutibus, Cambridge, Mass.

Starke, F. (1980), 'Das luwische Wort für "Frau" ', *KZ* 94, 74-86

Starr, R.F.S. (1937-9), *Nuzi. Report on the Excavations at Yorgan Tepe near Kirkuk, Iraq, conducted by Harvard University in conjunction with the American Schools of Oriental Research and the University Museum 1927-31*, 2 vols., Cambridge, Mass.

Steele, F.R. (1943), *Nuzi Real Estate Transactions*, New Haven (AOS 25)

Stern, E. (1982), *The Material Culture of the land of the Bible in the Persian Period*, Warminster

Stokes, W., Strachan, J. (eds.) (1901-3), *Thesaurus Palaeohibernicus*, 2 vols., Cambridge

Stone, E.C. (1982), 'The social role of the *Naditu* woman in Old Babylonian Nippur', *JESHO* 25/1, 50-70

Strong, H.A., Garstang, J. (1913), *The Syrian Goddess*, London

Strycker, E. (1961), *La forme la plus ancienne du Protévangile de Jacques*, Brussels (Subsidia Hagiographica 33)

Suda, The = Adler, A. (ed.) (1928-38), *Suidae Lexikon*, Leipzig

Sukenik, E.L. (1932), *The Ancient Synagogue of Beth Alpha*, Jerusalem

— (1934), *Ancient Synagogues in Palestine and Greece*, London

— (1935), *The Ancient Synagogue of El-Hammeh (Hammath by Gadara)*, Jerusalem

Taillardat, J. (1965), *Les Images d'Aristophanes*, rev. ed., Paris

Tanner, T. (1979), *Adultery in the Novel*, Baltimore

Taplin, O. (1977), *The Stagecraft of Aeschylus: the dramatic use of exits and entrances in Greek tragedy*, Oxford

Taubenschlag, R. (1938), 'La compétence du *Kyrios* dans le droit gréco-égyptien', *Archives d'histoire du droit oriental*, 2, 293-314

Thesleff, H. (1965-8), *The Pythagorean Texts of the Hellenistic Period*, Abö

Thomas, K. (1971), *Religion and the Decline of Magic*, Harmondsworth

Thompson, H.A. (1959), 'Activities in the Athenian Agora, 1958', *Hesperia* 28, 98-103

Thompson, H.A., Wycherley, R.E. (1972), *The Athenian Agora XIV: the Agora of Athens*, Princeton

Thompson, W.E. (1972), 'Athenian marriage patterns: remarriage', *OSCA* 5, 211-25

Thurneysen, R. (1936a), 'Cáin Lánamna', in Binchy (1936b), 1-80

— (1936b), 'Heirat', in Binchy (1936b), 109-28

Trachtenberg, J. (1961), *Jewish Magic and Superstition*, Cleveland

Travlos, J. (1971), *Pictorial Dictionary of Ancient Athens*, London

Trevor-Roper, H. (1967), 'The European Witch-Craze', in Marwick (1970), 121-50

Trible, P. (1976), 'God, nature of, in the Old Testament', *Interpreter's Dictionary of the Bible*, Abingdon, Nashville, New York, suppl. 368f.

— (1978), *God and the Rhetoric of Sexuality*, Philadelphia (Overtures in Biblical Theology 1)

Trinchera, F. (1865), *Syllabus Graecarum Membranum*, Naples

Urbach, E.E. (1975), *The Sages. Their Concepts and Beliefs*, trans. I. Abrahams, 2 vols., Jerusalem

van Dijk, J. (1972), 'Une variante du thème de l'esclave de la lune', *Or.*, n.s. 41, 339-48

van Praag, A. (1945), *Droit matrimonial assyro-babylonien*, Amsterdam (Archaeologisch-historische bijdragen 12) van Straaten, F.T. (1981), 'Gifts for the gods', in Versnel, H.S., (ed.), *Faith, Hope and Worship*, Leiden, 65-151

Vatin, C. (1970), *Recherches sur le mariage et la condition de la femme mariée à l'époque hellénistique*, Paris

Vernant, J.-P. (1965), 'Hestia-Hermès: sur l'expression religieuse de l'espace et du mouvement chez les Grecs', *Mythe et pensée chez les Grecs*, 97-143, Paris

— (1968), Introduction to *Problèmes de la guerre en Grèce ancienne*, Paris

— (1974), 'Le mariage', *Mythe et société en Grèce ancienne*, Paris, 57-81 = *Myth and Society in Ancient Greece*, trans. J. Lloyd, Oxford, 1980

— (1979-80), Cours, *Annuaire du Collège de France*, 435-66

Veyne, P. (1976), *Le Pain et le Cirque: sociologie historique d'un pluralisme politique*, Paris

Vogt, J. (1972), 'Die Hellenisierung der Perser in der Tragödie des Aischylos', in *Antike und Universalgeschichte, Festschrift H.E. Stier*, Münster, 131-45

von Arnim, H. (1905), *Stoicorum Veterum Fragmenta*, Leipzig

von Falkenhausen, V. (1967), *Untersuchungen über die byzantinische Herrschaft in Süditalien vom 9. bis ins 11. Jahrhundert*, Wiesbaden

von Rad, G. (1972), *Wisdom in Israel*, trans. J.D. Martin, London

von Soden, W. (1957-8), 'Die Hebamme in Babylonien und Assyrien', *AfO* 18, 119-21

Vööbus, A. (1951), *Celibacy: a requirement for admission to baptism in the early Syrian church*, Stockholm

— (1958), *History of Asceticism in the Syrian Orient*, 2 vols., Louvain (CSCO 184, subs. 14, 197 subs. 17)

— (ed.) (1961), *Syriac and Arabic Documents regarding legislation relative of Syrian Asceticism*, Stockholm

Walker, G.S.M. (ed.) (1957), *Sancti Columbani Opera*, Dublin (Scriptores Latini Hiberniae 2)

Walser, G. (1980), *Persepolis: die Königspfalz des Darius*, Tübingen

Walters, S.D. (1970), 'The sorceress and her apprentice', *JCS* 23, 27-38

Warner, M. (1976), *Alone of all her Sex: the myth and cult of the Virgin Mary*, London

Webster, T.B.L. (1972), *Potter and Patron in Classical Athens*, London

Weidner, E.F. (1954-6), 'Hof- und Harems-Erlasse assyrischer Könige aus dem 2. Jahrtausend v. Chr.', *AfO* 17, 257-93

Wemple, S.-F. (1981), *Women in Frankish Society, Marriage and the Cloister 500-900*, Philadelphia

Wenger, A. (1955), *L'Assomption de la Très Sainte Vierge dans la tradition byzantine du VIe au Xe siècle*, Paris

Wiegand, T. (1899), 'Dystos', *Ath. Mitt.* 24, 465-6

Wiesen, D. (1976), 'The contribution of antiquity to American racial thought', in Eadie, J.W. (ed.), *Classical Tradition in Early America*, Ann Arbor, 191-212

Wiesner, J. (1976), 'Achaemeniden und Altai', *Antike Kunst* 19, 59-60

Wilhelm, A. (1934), 'Zwei griechische Epigramme', *Wiener Studien*, 342-3

Wilhelm, Gernot (1970), *Untersuchungen zum Hurro-akkadischen von Nuzi*, Kevelaer, Neukirchen (AOAT 9)

Wilken, R.L. (1972), *The Myth of Christian Beginnings*, Chicago, repr. London 1979

Will, E. (1975), *Le monde grec et l'orient: le IVe siècle et l'époque hellénistique*, Paris

Williams, D. (1982), 'An oinochoe in the British Museum and the Brygos Painter's work on a white ground', *Jahrbuch des Berliner Museums* 24, 17-40

Williams, G. (1962), *The Welsh Church from Conquest to Reformation*, Cardiff

Winnington-Ingram, R.P. (1980), *Sophocles: an Interpretation*, Cambridge

Wistrand, E. (1976), *The So-called Laudatio Turiae*, Göteburg
Wolff, E. (1964), 'Das Weib des Masistes', *Hermes*, 51-8 (repr. in Marg, W. (ed.), *Herodot*, 668-78, Darmstadt (WdF 29))
Wolff, H.J. (1975), 'Hellenistisches Privatrecht', *ZSS*, 63-87
Wycherley, R.E. (1957), *The Athenian Agora* iii, Princeton
Yalman, N. (1967), *Under the Bo Tree: Studies in Caste, Kinship and Marriage in the Interior of Ceylon*, Berkeley, Los Angeles
Zeitlin, S. (1931), 'The origin of the synagogue', *PAAJR* 2, 69-81
Zimmern, A. (1931), *The Greek Commonwealth*[5], Oxford (paperback repr. New York, 1961)

INDEX OF PROPER NAMES

SUBJECT INDEX

lygos (agnos castus) 122

Maqlû 35, 36, 37, 38, 39, 40
marriage 173, 199; age of girls at 213;
    age of men at 214; Celtic 153f;
    civil and religious 181; spiritual
    179, 181
matriarchal/matrilineal societies
    30, 49
mediators, women as 61f; menarche
    112, 117, 213; menstruation
    112, 115, 123, 275; mid-
    wife(wives) 132, 133, 140, 172,
    God as 289; moneylending,
    women and 229
misogyny: Greek 53, 54; Syrian 295f
monasteries 180f
mourners, women as 50f, 283, 296
muchos 8, 15, 16
myth 136

nadîtu(s) 38, 260f
nazirites 279
nothoi 212
nuns 157, 180f

oikonomoi 228
orphanos 216

parthenos 111, 112, 114, 119, 120,
    123, 124
Patili priest 137, 139, 140
patriarchy 30
pnix 116, 117
politics, women in 54f, 59f, 149
pollution 5, 9, 41
polygamy 156
possession 14, 18
possessions, women's 174, 175, 202,
    264
pragmateutai 228
pregnancy 40, 130, 207
priestesses 71, 266
priesthoods 236
property, women and 82, 149, 150f,
    201, 231f
prostitutes/prostitution 97, 170, 267;
    sent to convents 168, 182

qadištu 38, 39
queens: Hellenistic 57; Hittite 133;
    Persian 24; *see also* empresses

releasing, metaphor of 122, 123
remarriage 155

Sabbath, women's duties on 283
saints, women 158, 296f
sale adoption 194
seclusion of women 4, 81f, 169, 236
Seder 283
segregation of sexes in synagogues 282
sex: hostility to 156; ratio 211, 214
shinapshi 137, 138, 139
silence: perceived as normal state for
    women 54, 59; recommended for
    women 239
sinništum 42
slaves 171; adopted by *nadîtus* 270;
    women owning slaves 231
slave women 153
social class 183, 205; effects on women
    236, 263
social structure, Celtic 146
sorcery 43, 44, 284
source materials, problems of 66, 109f,
    129, 147, 160, 168, 194, 208, 261f
spindle 94
spinning 94, 271
splanchna 10, 11, 14, 17
synagogues, women in 280f

taboo 41, 138, 140, 275
temple, Sippar 268f
theoretron 174
tragedy 3; women in Greek tragedy
    50f
transvestism, religious 161, 179, 297

ugbabtum 266f
umbilical cord 133
uncleanness, connected with men-
    struation and birth 275, 278
urban women 168, 169

vases, Athenian 93f
virginity *see* celibacy
Virgin Mary 62, 159, 182f; cult of and
    reasons for 290f, 292f

water, collection of 102
wealth, women's 225, 226
widows: Christian treatment of 156;
    in Greece 217
wills 175f, 200f, 204, 271
witch 36, 37, 41
witchcraft 34f, 284
womb 11, 113; 'wandering' 116
work, women's 160, 170, 271

zōnē 120, 121